Teacher's Resource Book

Maria Karyda

A2+ >

Business
Partner

FT Publishing
FINANCIAL TIMES

GSE
Global Scale of English

Coursebook contents

Contents

Overview

Business Partner is a flexible course designed for a variety of learners. It is suitable for students with mixed abilities, requirements and interests and for varied class sizes where the common requirement is to learn professional English language and develop key skills for the workplace.

When talking to learners, their reasons for studying business English almost always relate to their employability. Many tertiary students want to maximise their chances of finding a job in an international environment, while in-work professionals want to communicate more effectively in their workplace and improve their future career prospects. Other learners may simply need to study and pass a business English exam in order to complete their overall degree.

In all three cases, teachers need to be able to engage and motivate by providing learning materials which:

- are interesting and relevant to their life experiences.
- match their learning needs and priorities.
- are appropriate for the amount of study time available.

Business Partner has been designed to enable teachers to meet these needs without spending many hours researching their own materials. The content and structure of the course is based on three key concepts: **employability**, **flexibility** and **learner engagement**.

Course aims and key concepts

Employability

Balance between language and business skills training

In order to achieve their employability goals, learners need to improve their knowledge of English language as it is used in the workplace and also develop key skills for the international workplace. *Business Partner* provides this balance.

In addition to building their vocabulary and grammar and developing their writing skills, *Business Partner* trains students in Communication and Business skills. Language being only one aspect of successful communication, students also require an understanding of different business situations and an awareness of different communication styles, especially when working across cultures.

- 'Communication skills' (Lesson 3) provides the soft skills needed in order to work effectively with people whose personality and culture may be different from your own. This includes teamwork, decision-making and influencing skills.
- 'Business skills' (Lesson 4) provides the practical skills needed in different business situations, such as taking part in meetings, presentations and negotiations.

Flexibility

The modular approach means that *Business Partner* can be adapted to suit a variety of teaching requirements from extensive lessons to intensive short courses. In addition to the Coursebook, a wide variety of additional optional activities and resources are provided which can be used to focus on and extend material which is most useful to learners' needs.

Extra activities and extra grammar points

You can extend your lessons or focus in more depth on certain areas by using the large bank of extra activities in MyEnglishLab (clearly signposted for you throughout the Coursebook). These include extra vocabulary and grammar practice exercises for use in class as well as activities which draw attention to useful language in reading texts.

 Teacher's resources: extra activities

These are PDFs in MyEnglishLab that you can download and print or display on-screen.

 Teacher's resources: alternative video and activities

Alternative videos with worksheets are available for lessons 3.1 and 8.1 and are clearly signposted. You can use them in the classroom as an alternative approach to the topic in Lesson 1, depending on your students' needs.

 The text messages and email contain examples of the Present Continuous. Go to MyEnglishLab for optional grammar work.

Business Partner offers a flexible approach to grammar depending on whether you want to devote a significant amount of time to a grammar topic, or focus on consolidation only when you need to. There is one main grammar point in each unit, presented and practised in Lesson 2.

In addition, the Writing section (Lesson 5) includes a link to an optional second grammar point in MyEnglishLab, where students can watch short video presentations of the grammar points and do interactive activities.

---

 page 112 See Pronunciation bank — Pronunciation activities are included at the back of the book. This allows teachers to focus on aspects of pronunciation which are most useful for their students.

Teacher's Resource Bank: Photocopiables, Writing bank, Reading bank and Functional language bank

You can use these resources as and when needed with your classes. The Photocopiables further activate and practise, vocabulary from Lesson 1 and grammar from Lesson 2 as and when needed.

The Reading bank for each unit gives students more reading practice and can be also used for self-study. The activity types reflect those found in a range of business English exams. The Writing bank provides supplementary models of professional communication and the Functional language bank extends useful phrases for a range of business situations.

Learner engagement

Video content: We all use video more and more to communicate and to find out about the world and we have put video at the heart of *Business Partner*. There are two videos in every unit with comprehension and language activities:

- an authentic video package in Lesson 1, based on real-life video clips and interviews suitable for your learners' level of English.
- a dramatised communication skills training video in Lesson 3 which follows characters in an international team as they deal with different professional challenges.

Authentic content: Working with authentic content really helps to engage learners, and teachers can spend many hours searching for suitable material online. *Business Partner* has therefore been built around authentic videos and articles from leading media organisations such as the *Financial Times* and news channels. These offer a wealth of international business information as well as real examples of British, U.S. and non-native-speaker English.

Relevance for learners without work experience: Using business English teaching materials with learners who have little or no work experience can be particularly challenging. *Business Partner* has been carefully designed to work with these students as well as with in-work professionals. In the case of collaborative speaking tasks and roleplays, the situation used will either be:

- one that we can all relate to as customers and consumers; OR
- a choice of situations will be offered including a mix of professional and everyday situations.

Both will allow learners to practise the skill and language presented in the lesson, but in a context that is most relevant to them.

Business workshops: Learners have the opportunity to consolidate and activate the language and skills from the units in 8 business workshops at the end of the book. These provide interesting and engaging scenarios where students simulate real-life professional situations such as roleplaying meetings, negotiations or presentations.

Approach to language and skills

Business Partner offers fully integrated skills, including the essential critical thinking and higher-order thinking skills, which are built into the activities.

Vocabulary and video The main topic vocabulary set is presented and practised in Lesson 1 of each unit, building on vocabulary from the authentic video. Teachers are given lots of opportunities to use the vocabulary in discussions and group tasks, and to tailor the tasks to their classroom situations.

Functional language (such as making small talk, solving problems, rescheduling appointments on the phone,) supports learners' capability to operate in real workplace situations in English. Three functional language sets are presented and practised in every unit: in Lessons 3, 4 and 5. You will be able to teach the language in group speaking and writing tasks. There is a Functional language bank at the back of this Teacher's Resource Book which students can also find in MyEnglishLab so that they can quickly refer to useful language support when preparing for a business situation, such as a meeting, presentation or interview.

Listening and video The course offers a wide variety of listening activities (based on both video and audio recordings) to help students develop their comprehension skills and to hear target language in context. All of the video and audio material is available in MyEnglishLab and includes a range of British, U.S. and non-native-speaker English. Lessons 1 and 3 are based on video (as described above). In four of the eight units, Lesson 2 is based on audio. In all units, you also work with a significant number of audio recordings in Lesson 4 and the Business workshop.

Grammar The approach to grammar is flexible depending on whether you want to devote a significant amount of time to grammar or to focus on the consolidation of grammar only when you need to. There is one main grammar point in each unit, presented and practised in Lesson 2. There is a link from Lesson 5 to an optional second grammar point in MyEnglishLab – with short video presentations and interactive practice. Both grammar points are supported by the Grammar reference section at the back of the Coursebook (p.118). This provides a summary of meaning and form, with notes on usage or exceptions, and business English examples.

Reading *Business Partner* offers a wealth of authentic texts and articles from a variety of sources, particularly the *Financial Times* and the Nikkei Asian Review. Every unit has a main reading text with comprehension tasks. This appears either in Lesson 2 or in the Business workshop. There is a Reading bank at the back of this Teacher's Resource Book which students can also find in MyEnglishLab and which has a longer reading text for every unit with comprehension activities.

Speaking Collaborative speaking tasks appear at the end of Lessons 1, 3, 4 and the Business workshop in every unit. These tasks encourage students to use the target language and, where relevant, the target skill of the lesson. There are lots of opportunities to personalise these tasks to suit your own classroom situation.

Writing *Business Partner* offers multiple opportunities to practise writing. Lesson 5 in every unit provides a model text and practice in a business writing skill. The course covers a wide range of genres such as slides, letters, intranet updates and emails, and for different purposes, including formal and informal communication, explaining, confirming arrangements, making updates. There are also short writing tasks in Lesson 2 which provide controlled practice of the target grammar. There is a Writing bank at the back of this Teacher's Resource Book which students can also find in MyEnglishLab and which provides models of different types of business writing and useful phrases appropriate to their level of English.

Pronunciation Two pronunciation points are presented and practised in every unit. Pronunciation points are linked to the content of the unit – usually to a video or audio presentation or to a grammar point. The pronunciation presentations and activities are at the back of the Coursebook (p.112), with signposts from the relevant lessons. This section also includes an introduction to pronunciation with British and U.S. phonetic charts.

Approach to Communication skills

A key aspect of *Business Partner* is the innovative video-based communication skills training programme.

The aims of the Communications skills lessons are to introduce students to the skills needed to interact successfully in international teams with people who may have different communication styles from them due to culture or personality. Those skills include dealing with a problem, negotiating roles, giving explanations.

These lessons are based on videos that provide realistic examples of work situations. This is particularly important for pre-service learners who may not have direct experience of the particular situations they are about to see. In each of these videos students watch two videos (Video A and Video B) in which a different communication style is used. These options give students the opportunity to engage in critical viewing of each option and gain awareness of the impact of different communication styles.

Approach to testing and assessment

Business Partner provides a balance of formative and summative assessment. Both types of assessment are important for teachers and learners and have different objectives. Regular review and on-going assessment allows students to evaluate their own progress and encourages them to persevere in their studies. Formal testing offers a more precise value on the progress made on their knowledge and proficiency.

Formative assessment: Each Coursebook lesson is framed by a clear lesson outcome which summarises the learning deliverable. The lesson ends with a self-assessment section which encourages students to reflect on their progress in relation to the lesson outcome and to think about future learning needs. More detailed self-assessment tasks and suggestions for further practice are available in MyEnglishLab. (See also section on the Global Scale of English and the Learning Objectives for Professional English.)

The Coursebook also contains one review page per unit at the back of the book to recycle and revise the key vocabulary, grammar and functional language presented in the unit; they are structured to reflect the modularity of the course.

Summative assessment: Unit tests are provided and activities are clearly labelled to show which section of the unit they are testing to reflect the modular structure of the course. The tests are available in PDF and Word formats so that you can adapt them to suit your purposes. They are also available as interactive tests that you can allocate to your students if you wish to do so.

These Unit tests are based on task types from the major business English exams. There is also an additional LCCI writing task for professional English for every unit. This approach familiarises learners with the format of the exams and gives them practice in the skills needed to pass the exams.

MyEnglishLab also contains extra professional English practice activities. The content and level of the tasks match the Coursebook so they can also be used as additional revision material.

The Global Scale of English

The Global Scale of English (GSE) is a standardised, granular scale from 10 to 90 which measures English language proficiency. The GSE Learning Objectives for Professional English are aligned with the Common European Framework of Reference (CEFR). Unlike the CEFR, which describes proficiency in terms of broad levels, the Global Scale of English identifies what a learner can do at each point on a more granular scale – and within a CEFR level. The scale is designed to motivate learners by demonstrating incremental progress in their language ability. The Global Scale of English forms the backbone for Pearson English course material and assessment.

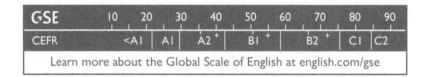

GSE	10	20	30	40	50	60	70	80	90
CEFR		<A1	A1	A2 +	B1 +		B2 +	C1	C2

Learn more about the Global Scale of English at english.com/gse

Business Partner has been written based on these Learning Objectives, which ensure appropriate scaffolding and measurable progress. Each Lesson outcome in each lesson in the Coursebook encapsulates a number of specific Learning Objectives which are listed in this Teacher's Resource Book in the Teaching notes. These Learning Objectives are also listed in the Self-assessment sheets available to students in MyEnglishLab. (See also Self-assessment above in Approach to testing and assessment.)

Course structure

Business Partner is an eight-level course based on the Global Scale of English (GSE) and representing the CEFR levels: A1, A2, A2+, B1, B1+, B2, B2+, C1.

	For the teacher	For the student
print	Teacher's Resource Book with MyEnglishLab	Coursebook with Digital Resources Workbook
blended	Pearson English Portal	Coursebook with MyEnglishLab

Business Partner is a fully hybrid course with two digital dimensions that students and teachers can choose from. MyEnglishLab is the digital component that is integrated with the book content.

Access to MyEnglishLab is given through a code printed on the inside front cover of this book. As a teacher, you have access to both versions of MyEnglishLab, and to additional content in the Teacher's Resource folder.

Depending on the version that students are using, they will have access to one of the following:

Digital Resources includes downloadable coursebook resources, all video clips, all audio files, Lesson 3 additional interactive video activities, Lesson 5 interactive grammar presentation and practice, Reading bank, Functional Language bank, Writing bank, and My Self-assessment.

MyEnglishLab includes all of the **Digital Resources** plus the full functionality and content of the self-study interactive workbook with automatic gradebook. Teachers can also create a group or class in their own MyEnglishLab and assign workbook activities as homework.

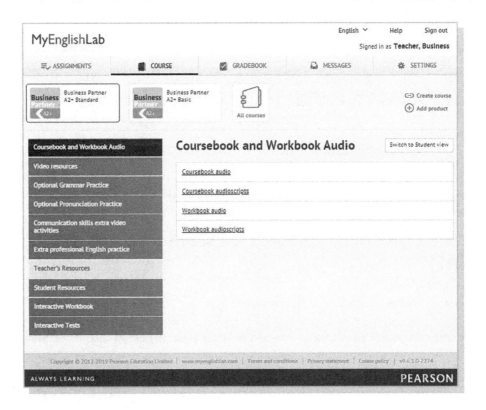

Coursebook
(with access code for MyEnglishLab)

- Eight units, each containing five lessons (see pages 2–3 for unit overview)
- Eight Business workshop lessons relating to each of the eight units
- A one-page Review per unit to revise key language and grammar
- A Pronunciation section which practises two points from each unit
- A Grammar reference with detailed explanations and examples
- Videoscripts and audioscripts
- A glossary of key business vocabulary from the book

Coursebook video and audio material is available on MyEnglishLab.

MyEnglishLab digital component

Accessed using the code printed on the inside cover of the Coursebook. Depending on the version of the course that you are using, learners will have access to one of the following options:

Digital resources powered by MyEnglishLab
- Video clips
- Audio files and scripts
- Extra Coursebook activities (PDFs)
- Lesson 3 extra interactive video activities
- Lesson 5 interactive grammar presentation and practice
- Reading bank
- Writing bank
- Functional language bank
- Extra professional English practice
- My Self-assessment
- Workbook audio files and scripts

Full content of MyEnglishLab
- All of the above
- Interactive self-study Workbook with automatic feedback and gradebook

Workbook

- Additional self-study practice activities, reflecting the structure of the Coursebook. Activities cover vocabulary, grammar, functional language, reading, listening and writing.
- Additional self-study practice activities for points presented in the Coursebook Pronunciation bank.
- Answer key
- Audioscripts

Workbook audio material is available on MyEnglishLab.

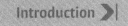

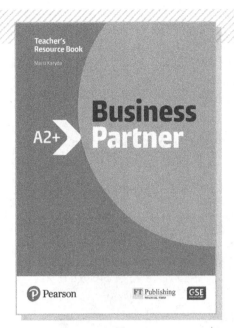

Teacher's Resource Book (with access code for MyEnglishLab)

- Teaching notes for every lesson including warm-ups, background /culture notes and answer keys
- Business brief for every unit with background information on the unit topic and explanations of key terminology; it gives teachers an insight into contemporary business practices even if they have not worked in these particular environments

- Photocopiable activities – two per unit with teaching notes and answer keys
- Reading bank – an extended reading text for every unit with comprehension activities (+ answer keys)
- Writing bank – models of different types of business writing with useful phrases
- Functional language bank – useful phrases for different business situations, e.g. meetings, interviews
- Videoscripts and audioscripts

MyEnglishLab digital component

Accessed using the code printed on the inside cover of the Teacher's Resource Book.

Coursebook resources

- Video clips and scripts
- Audio files and scripts
- Extra Coursebook activities (PDFs)
- Lesson 3 extra interactive video activities for self-study
- Lesson 5 interactive grammar presentation and practice for self-study
- Extra professional English practice
- My Self-assessment: a document that students can use to record their progress and keep in their portfolio

Workbook resources

- Self-study interactive version of the Workbook with automatic feedback and gradebook
- Teachers can assign Workbook activities as homework
- Workbook audio files and audioscripts

Teacher's Book resources

- Alternative video (Units 3 and 8) and extra activities
- Photocopiable activities + teaching notes and answer keys
- Reading bank + answer keys
- Writing bank
- Functional language bank

Tests

- Unit tests (PDFs and Word), including exam task types
- Interactive Unit tests, with automatic gradebook
- Tests audio files
- Tests answer keys

Pearson English Portal

- Digital version of the Teacher's Resource Book
- Digital version of the Coursebook with classroom tools for use on an interactive whiteboard
- Video clips and scripts
- Audio files and scripts
- Extra Coursebook activities (PDFs)

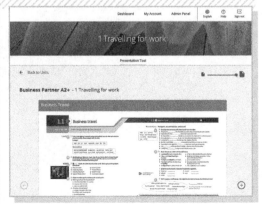

Unit overview page »

①➤ A well-known or provocative quote related to the unit topic is provided as a talking point. There are suggestions for how to use the quote in the Teacher's Resource Book notes for each unit.

②➤ The Unit overview summarises the contents of each lesson as well as the lesson outcomes.

③➤ Content at the back of the book which extends the unit is highlighted: the Business workshop, Review, Pronunciation bank and Grammar reference.

Business location 2»

> ① 'Be sure you put your feet in the right place, then stand firm.'
> Abraham Lincoln

② » Unit overview

2.1 »	**Dovetailed in Cambridge** **Lesson outcome:** Learners can use vocabulary related to places of work and business locations.	Video: Choosing a business location **Vocabulary:** Location **Project:** Researching the location of a company
2.2 »	**Visiting Singapore** **Lesson outcome:** Learners can use *enough* and *too* to express sufficiency and insufficiency.	**Reading:** Singapore creates a tropical wildlife paradise **Grammar:** *enough* and *too* **Speaking and writing:** Describing problematic situations
2.3 »	**Communication skills:** Checking and clarifying **Lesson outcome:** Learners can check, confirm and clarify information using a range of expressions.	Video: Clarifying information **Functional language:** Checking and clarifying **Task:** Checking and clarifying information in a meeting
2.4 »	**Business skills:** Starting a meeting **Lesson outcome:** Learners are able to use a variety of expressions to open meetings.	**Listening:** A meeting **Functional language:** Opening a meeting, referring to the agenda and stating purpose **Task:** Opening a meeting
2.5 »	**Writing:** Short communications **Lesson outcome:** Learners can communicate by text message, write short emails and use abbreviations and shortened forms appropriately.	**Model text:** Short messages **Functional language:** Abbreviations **Grammar:** Present Continuous **Task:** Informal and formal messages

③➤ Business workshop 2: p.90 | Review 2: p.105 | **Pronunciation:** 2.1 Syllables and stress 2.2 Stress in noun phrases p.114 | **Grammar reference:** p.119

» 17 «

Lesson 1 ❯

The aims of this lesson are:

- to engage students with the unit topic through a video based on authentic material.
- to present and practise topic business vocabulary, drawing on vocabulary from the video.
- to encourage students to activate the language they have practised in a group project.

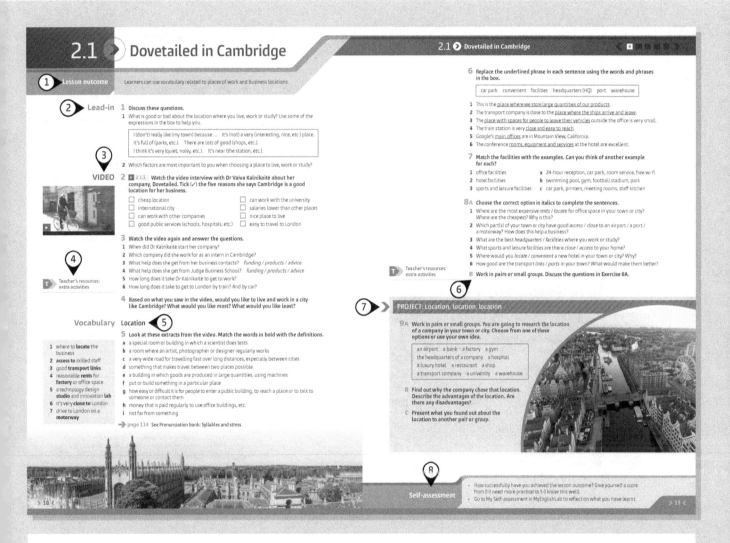

① The Lesson outcome defines a clear learning outcome for every lesson. Each Lesson outcome encapsulates a number of specific Learning Objectives for Professional English which are listed in this Teacher's Resource Book in the Teaching notes.

② Every lesson begins with a short Lead-in activity to engage learners with the lesson topic on a personal level.

③ Lesson 1 is based on an authentic video of about 4 minutes with comprehension activities.

④ **T Teacher's resources: extra activities** Extra activities are clearly signposted. These are PDFs in MyEnglishLab to display on-screen or print. They can be used to extend a lesson or to focus in more depth on a particular section.

T Teacher's resources: alternative video and activities Alternative videos with worksheets are available for some units and are clearly signposted.

⑤ The main unit vocabulary set is presented and practised in Lesson 1, building on vocabulary from the video. Extra activities are available in MyEnglishLab.

⑥ Follow-up questions provide an opportunity for personalisation.

⑦ The Project at the end of Lesson 1 is a collaborative group task with a strong emphasis on communication and fluency building. It can be done in class or in more depth over several weeks in and out of class.

⑧ Every lesson ends with a short Self-assessment section which encourages learners to think about the progress they have made in relation to the lesson outcomes. More detailed self-assessment tasks and suggestions for extra practice are available in MyEnglishLab.

Lesson 2 ≫ Reading or Listening

The aims of this lesson are:

- to provide students with meaningful reading or listening skills practice based on engaging, relevant and up-to-date content.
- to present and practise the unit grammar point, drawing on examples from the text.
- to encourage students to activate the grammar point they have practised through communicative speaking or writing activities.

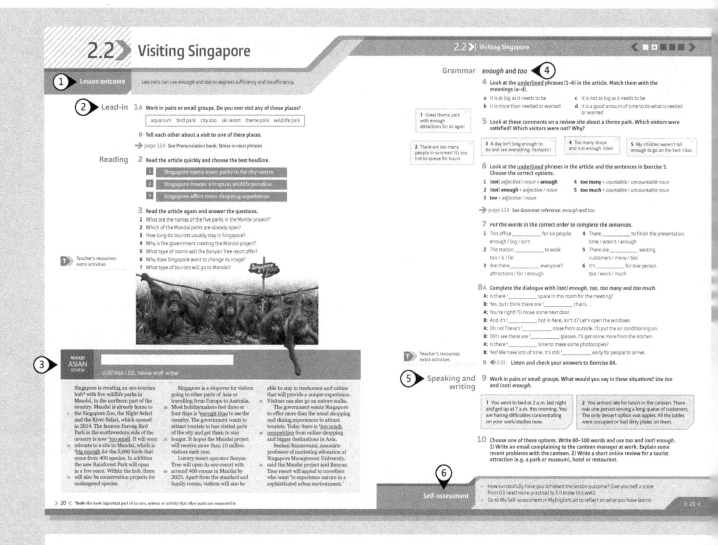

① The Lesson outcome defines a clear learning outcome for every lesson.

② Every lesson begins with a short Lead-in activity to engage learners with the lesson topic on a personal level. This section includes pre-teaching of vocabulary needed for the reading or listening to come.

③ The reading text is generally an article, often from the *Nikkei Asian Review* or *Financial Times*. The text focuses on a particular aspect of the unit topic which has an interesting angle, and it contains examples of the grammar point presented.

④ There is one grammar point in each unit, presented in Lesson 2. In general a guided discovery (inductive) approach has been taken to the presentation of grammar. The grammar is presented with reference to examples in the reading (or listening) text, followed by controlled practice.

⑤ Discussion questions and communicative practice of vocabulary and grammar is provided in the final Speaking or Writing section of this lesson.

⑥ Every lesson ends with a short Self-assessment section which encourages learners to think about the progress they have made in relation to the lesson outcomes.

Lesson 3 ➤ Communication skills

The aims of this lesson are:

- to introduce students to the skills needed to interact successfully in international teams.
- to encourage students to notice different communication styles and the misunderstandings that can arise as a result, by watching the scripted skills training video.
- to present and practise functional language associated with the communication skill in the lesson.

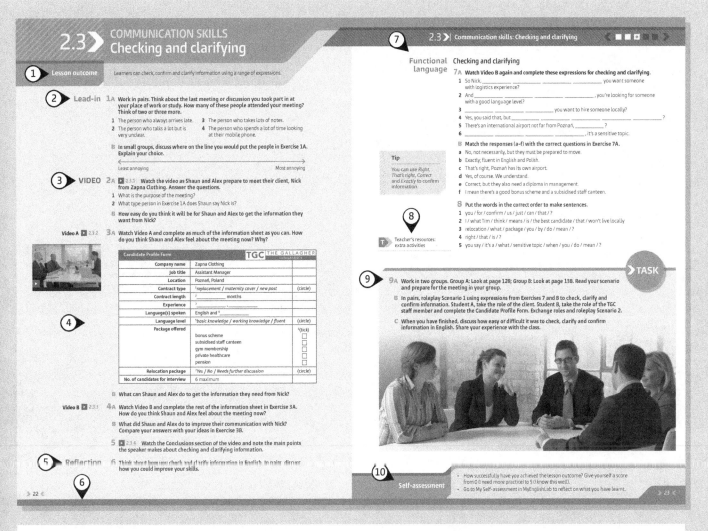

① The Lesson outcome defines a clear learning outcome for every lesson.

② Every Communication skills lesson begins with a short Lead-in activity to engage learners with the lesson topic on a personal level and to set-up the video which follows.

③ The Communication skills training video introduces learners to the skills needed to interact successfully in international teams, with people who may have different communication styles due to culture or personality. There is a storyline running through the eight units, with the main characters appearing in different situations. Note: Each clip, however, can be watched separately and each lesson done independently without the need to watch the preceding video clips.

④ In each Communication skills lesson, you will:
- **a** watch a set-up video which introduces the main characters and challenge of the lesson;
- **b** watch the main character approach the situation in two different ways (Options A and B);
- **c** answer questions about each approach (Option A and Option B) before watching the conclusion.

⑤ Students work alone on a short reflection activity. The approach to this reflection activity may change to suit each lesson. The idea is to encourage students to think about communication styles and their implications.

⑥ The lesson to this point works as a standalone lesson for teachers who have a limited amount of time to work on communication skills. In other teaching situations, the lesson can be extended using the activities on functional language.

⑦ This page presents and practises a set of useful functional language from the video in the Communication skills lesson.

⑧ **Ⓣ Teacher's resources: extra activities** The optional extension activities for this lesson provide controlled practice of the functional language.

⑨ The lesson ends with a collaborative group task designed to practise the functional language and the communication skill presented in the lesson. There is a scenario or scenario options which pre-work students can relate to, as well as an element of personalisation in the scenario to help with mixed-ability classes.

⑩ Every lesson ends with a short Self-assessment section which encourages learners to think about the progress they have made in relation to the lesson outcomes.

Lesson 4 ⟫ Business skills

The aims of this lesson are:

- to give students exposure to a functional business skill or sub-skill using a listening comprehension, encouraging them to notice successful and unsuccessful techniques.
- to present and practise relevant functional language drawing on examples from the listening.
- to encourage students to activate the skill and language they have practised by collaborating on a group task.

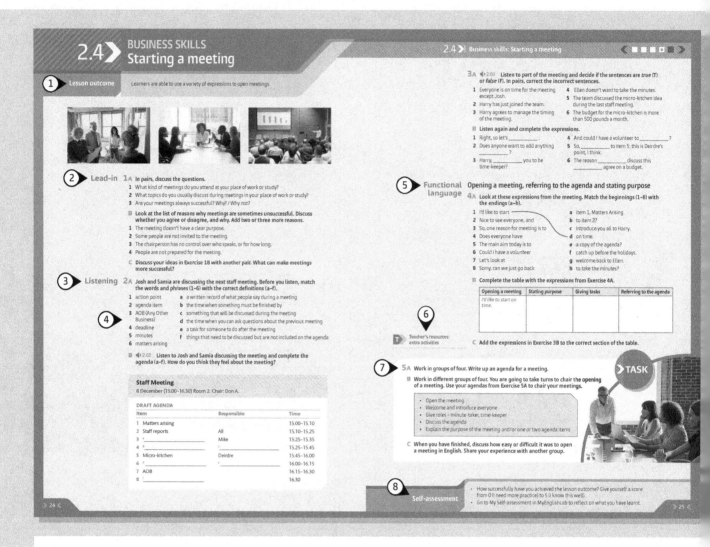

① The Lesson outcome defines a clear learning outcome for every lesson.

② Every Business skills lesson begins with a short Lead-in activity to engage learners with the lesson topic on a personal level.

③ An original listening comprehension introduces the business skill and related key techniques and key functional language.

④ Listening comprehension activities check that students have understood the meaning of key concepts or vocabulary, and move on to listening for detail.

⑤ The section on Functional language offers presentation and practice of a set of useful functional language related to the business skill of the lesson. The language exponents come from the audioscript, and common tasks include gap-fill activities.

⑥ **T** Teacher's resources: extra activities The optional extension activities for this lesson provide controlled practice of the functional language and additional listening practice using the lesson listening text.

⑦ The lesson ends with a significant collaborative group task to practise the target business skill and provide an opportunity to use the functional language presented. A scenario or several scenario options are provided to help with mixed classes, and often include an opportunity for personalisation.

⑧ Every lesson ends with a short Self-assessment section which encourages learners to think about the progress they have made in relation to the lesson outcomes.

Lesson 5 ➤ Writing

The aims of this lesson are:

- to present and practise a specific aspect of business writing, focusing on either genre, function or register.
- to present and practise relevant functional language, drawing on examples from the model text.

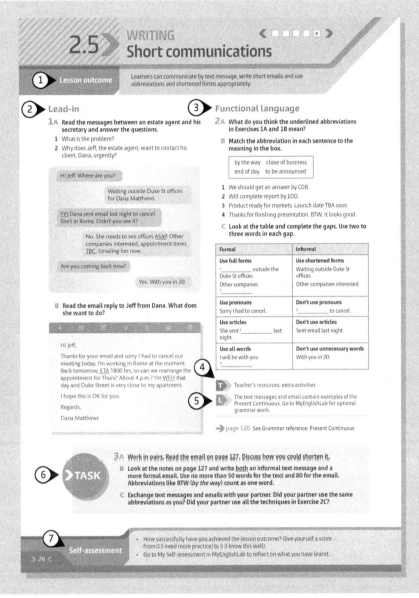

① The Lesson outcome defines a clear learning outcome for every lesson.

② Every Writing lesson starts with a writing model with an associated task. The task often requires students to notice or do something with the language within the model text.

③ The functional language is presented in a table summarising useful language associated with the target writing skill, and includes a related activity. The table is likely to be categorised according to the different sections of the writing model. Tasks include completing exponents in the table or identifying which ones are formal and informal.

④ **T** Teacher's resources: extra activities The optional extension activities for this lesson provide controlled practice of the functional language.

⑤ **L** The text messages and email contain examples of the Present Continuous. Go to MyEnglishLab for optional grammar work.

There is a signpost to the optional second grammar point. Some examples of the target language point are included in the writing model. The teacher's notes include instructions to focus students on the examples before directing them to the activities in MyEnglishLab if they choose to do so.

⑥ The lesson ends with at least two writing tasks, from controlled to freer practice.

⑦ Every lesson ends with a short Self-assessment section which encourages learners to think about the progress they have made in relation to the lesson outcomes.

Business workshops ❯

The aims of the Business workshops are:

- to simulate a real-life professional situation or challenge which is related to the theme of the unit.
- to provide multiple opportunities for free, communicative practice of the language presented in the unit.

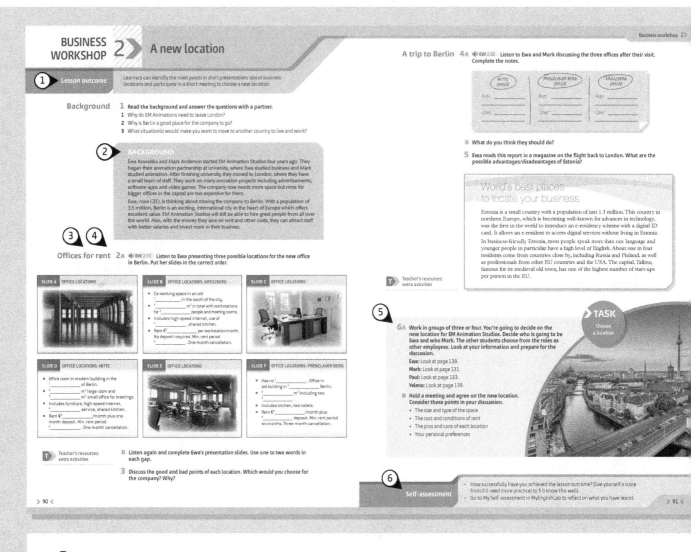

① The Lesson outcome defines a clear learning outcome for every lesson.

② The workshop begins by providing some background information on the company and the situation or challenge the scenario focuses on.

③ Business workshops always include a significant additional listening or reading practice. In many of the workshops, both skills are practised.

④ This section includes an activity to check understanding.

⑤ The task is a practical, collaborative task which addresses the challenge set out in the background section. It focuses on speaking, but usually also includes an element of writing. The Business workshops provide a good variety of output task types.

⑥ Every lesson ends with a short Self-assessment section which encourages learners to think about the progress they have made in relation to the lesson outcomes.

Extra material ▶

Extra coursebook activities (PDFs)
▶ go to MyEnglishLab, Teacher's Resources

Photocopiables (PDFs)
▶ at the back of this Teacher's Resource Book, and on MyEnglishLab, in the Teacher's Resources

Resource Bank: Reading bank, Writing bank, Functional language bank (PDFs)
▶ at the back of this Teacher's Resource Book, and on MyEnglishLab, in the Teacher's Resources

Unit tests, with audio files and answer keys (PDFs and Word documents)
▶ go to MyEnglishLab, Teacher's Resources; also available as Interactive tests.

1 ▶ Travelling for work

Unit overview

	CLASSWORK	FURTHER WORK
1.1 ▶ **Business travel**	**Lead-in** Students discuss different aspects of travel. **Video** Students watch a video about different aspects of business travel. **Vocabulary** Students look at vocabulary related to transport, accommodation and travel. **Project** Students roleplay a conference call giving advice to a colleague who is visiting from overseas.	**MyEnglishLab:** Teacher's resources: extra activities **Teacher's book:** Resource bank Photocopiable 1.1 p.134 **Workbook:** p.4 Exercises 1–3
1.2 ▶ **Events management**	**Lead-in** Students talk about planning different corporate and social events. **Listening** Students listen to an interview with an Events Manager. **Grammar** Students study and practise comparatives and superlatives. **Speaking** Students practise the grammar from the lesson by talking and writing about venues for a party.	**MyEnglishLab:** Teacher's resources: extra activities; Reading bank **Grammar reference:** p.119 Comparatives and superlatives **Pronunciation bank:** p.114 The letter 'r' **Teacher's book:** Resource bank Photocopiable 1.2 p.135 **Workbook:** p.5 Exercises 1–4, p.6 Exercises 1–3
1.3 ▶ **Communication skills:** Small talk	**Lead-in** Students discuss their views on making small talk. **Video** Students watch a video giving a model for making small talk in professionally related social contexts. **Reflection** Students reflect on the conclusions from the video and discuss their own small-talk skills. **Functional language** Students look at useful questions for making small talk. **Task** Students practise making small talk with colleagues in different situations.	**MyEnglishLab:** Teacher's resources: extra activities; Interactive video activities; Functional language bank **Pronunciation bank:** p.114 Showing interest in small talk **Workbook:** p.7 Exercises 1 and 2
1.4 ▶ **Business skills:** Dealing with problems	**Lead-in** Students talk about the first day at a new college/job. **Listening** Students listen to conversations between a new employee and some of his colleagues. **Functional language** Students look at useful language for explaining and solving IT problems. **Task** Students roleplay a telephone call where they explain and solve IT problems.	**MyEnglishLab:** Teacher's resources: extra activities; Functional language bank **Workbook:** p.7 Exercises 3A–B
1.5 ▶ **Writing:** Email – Asking for information	**Lead-in** Students read and complete an email asking for information. **Functional language** Students look at useful language for writing emails asking for information. **Task** Students write an email asking for information.	**MyEnglishLab:** Teacher's resources: extra activities; Interactive grammar practice; Writing bank **Grammar reference:** p.119 *can* and *could* to ask for information **Workbook:** p.8 Exercises 1–3
Business workshop 1 ▶ A business trip	**Reading** Students read about an Australian music talent agency. **Listening** Students listen to phone communications about the details of a business trip. **Task** Students write an email rearranging travel plans.	**MyEnglishLab:** Teacher's resources: extra activities

Business brief

The main aim of this unit is to introduce students to the concept of **travelling for work**. Many employees travel for work; this can be divided into **commuting**, travelling daily to get to and from their place of work, and **business travel**, where certain roles within a company require employees to travel outside the office for research, promotion, meetings, etc.

Recent surveys show that the countries where workers spend the longest time commuting are Kenya, Hong Kong, India and the United Arab Emirates. In these places people commute for around one and a half hours each day. In the UK there has been a significant rise in those who now spend more than two hours on their daily **commute** in the last decade. In contrast, employees in Japan are likely to have the shortest commute globally, with an average of less than forty minutes daily.

While the majority of **commuters** still rely on traditional means of transport like trains and buses to get to work, there has been a rise in the last fifteen years in the use of **car-pooling** and **ridesharing apps**. These apps allow people who are travelling in the same direction to travel in one car. In the case of car-pooling, they are usually work colleagues who live in the same area. Ridesharing apps, on the other hand, allow people who don't know each other to share a car. This is often quicker and less stressful than public transport and reduces the impact of traffic pollution as it means there are fewer cars overall on the road.

Mobile technology has also had an impact on travelling for work, making it possible for **commuters** to use some of their journey time to work. Employees can check and reply to emails, make calls to clients, and even write reports using their smart phones, tablets and laptops while on the move. Some companies also now allow their employees to **work remotely** part of the time, usually from home, in order to avoid travel delays due to long commutes. Effective working from home allows them to manage their time more efficiently.

Although the volume of business travel traffic continues to increase worldwide, recent technological advances mean that **video conferencing** is now frequently used to communicate instead, making it unnecessary for people to meet face-to-face. However, because human communication is both verbal and non-verbal, time invested in actually meeting people and getting to know them still plays a vital role in the success of negotiations. This is particularly true in cross-cultural business situations where nuances in communication can be difficult to pick up or via a computer screen. Furthermore, in some cultures the **small talk** which precedes a face-to-face business meeting is extremely important and this type of **networking** can build stronger **business relationships**.

Business travel can come at a high price for both companies and employees. For businesses, sending employees abroad to do business in person is an expensive part of their budget which they are sometimes forced to reduce to contain costs. Employees who travel a lot for work find that the experience is often far from glamorous. The reality can consist of frustrating delays, flight cancellations and sitting in long meetings while coping with **jetlag**!

Travelling for work and your students

Many students regard travel as an attractive part of a corporate role but they should also be aware of its wider implications. Pre-work students need to understand the effects of commuting and business travel on employees' lives, as well as their professional success, when applying for jobs. Students who are in work also need to be aware of the high costs of travel to their employer and the need to measure this against the desired business outcomes.

Unit lead-in

Elicit a brief description of the photo and draw students' attention to the unit title. Look at the quote with the class and check that they understand the meanings of *modest* and *occupy*. Briefly discuss the quote as a class: Can students explain it in simpler words? Do they agree with it? Why? / Why not?

1.1 > Business travel

GSE learning objectives

- Can understand simple informal advice on a work-related situation.
- Can identify key details in a simple recorded dialogue or narrative.
- Can identify simple information in a short video, provided that the visual supports this information and the delivery is slow and clear.
- Can give simple opinions using basic fixed expressions.
- Can make and respond to suggestions.
- Can ask for basic advice using simple language.

Warm-up

Put students in pairs or small groups and dictate or write the following questions on the board: *How often do you travel? Where to? What for? What do you like about travelling?* Give pairs/groups 3–5 minutes to discuss the questions, then invite brief feedback from the class.

Lead-in

Students discuss different aspects of travel.

1 Go through the words in the boxes with students and check understanding. Give them a minute to tick the items they have used, then get feedback from the class. If time allows, you could get students to discuss their answers in pairs or small groups first.

2 Go through the questions with students and teach or elicit the meanings of *comfort* and *location*. Then put them in groups and give them 2–3 minutes to discuss the questions. Invite a few students to share their answers with the class. If time allows, you could draw a table on the board with rows for the criteria (see example below) and invite volunteers to tick the criteria they each use to choose transport and accommodation. For the other items, get students to explain what each criterion is and why it is important for them.

Transport	
price	
speed	
comfort	
Accommodation	
price	
comfort	
location	
something else	

Video

Students watch a video about different aspects of business travel.

3 ▶ 1.1.1 Explain to students that they are going to watch a video where businesspeople talk about different aspects of travelling for work. Give them a minute to look at the list of topics, play the video then check answers with the class.

a, b, d, e, g

4 ▶ 1.1.1 Before you play the video again, give students two minutes to go through the questions and options and ask you about any words they do not understand. To check answers, you could play the video again and tell students to ask you to pause when an answer is heard.

1 b **2** c **3** a **4** c **5** b **6** a

Extra activities 1.1

A ▶ 1.1.1 Explain to students that the sentences in this exercise are from the video. Get them to match the sentence halves individually or, in weaker classes, in pairs, then play the video again to check answers. Get students to tell you which words in each half helped them match the two parts of each sentence: was it a grammatical or lexical clue? Do not focus on the meanings of the words in bold at this point as students will look at them in the next exercise.

1 c **2** d **3** a **4** f **5** e **6** b

B This activity practises useful vocabulary from the video. Students could do it individually or in pairs. Encourage them to read the sentences carefully, thinking about the meaning of the whole sentence each time. This will help them work out the meanings of the words in bold. Allow them to use their dictionaries to help them if necessary. Check answers with the class and clarify meanings as necessary.

i stay overnight **ii** the locals **iii** timings **iv** overseas **v** organisation **vi** workplace

5 Put students in pairs or small groups and give them 3–4 minutes to discuss the question. As feedback, invite students from different pairs/groups to share their ideas with the class, giving reasons.

Possible answers

Probably. They all speak about it with enthusiasm.

Vocabulary: Transport, accommodation and travel

Students look at vocabulary related to transport, accommodation and travel.

6 Go through the words in the box with students before they begin, or let them use their dictionaries to check any unknown vocabulary. Get them to complete the exercise individually and compare answers in pairs before checking with the class. During feedback, clarify any vocabulary items as necessary.

You could then ask students to categorise the sentences: write the headings *Air travel*, *Accommodation* and *Travelling around town* on the board and ask them to match each sentence with the correct heading (*Air travel*: 2, 5, 7; *Accommodation*: 1, 6, 8; *Travelling around town*: 3, 4, 9).

> **1** reservation **2** flight **3** vehicle **4** ridesharing app
> **5** gate **6** stay **7** lounge **8** location
> **9** public transportation

7A You could do this as a whole-class activity, checking answers and meanings as you go. Alternatively, get students to complete it individually or in pairs, then check answers with the class.

> **1** c **2** a **3** e **4** b **5** d

7B Students could do this individually or in pairs, using their dictionaries if necessary. Check answers with the class and encourage students to record the pairs of opposites in their vocabulary notebooks.

> **1** short-haul **2** landing **3** departure **4** delayed
> **5** abroad

Extra activities 1.1

C This activity practises key vocabulary from the lesson. It is a consolidation exercise, so you may prefer students to do it individually. Get students to compare answers in pairs before class feedback.

> **1** flight **2** delayed **3** reservation **4** gate
> **5** vehicle **6** departure lounge **7** location **8** local
> **9** arrival **10** on time

8 Put students in pairs or small groups, explain the activity and refer them to the example sentence. Check that they understand the meanings of the phrases on the left before they begin. You could also elicit a few opinion adjectives they could use in their sentences (*interesting*, *boring*, *easy*, *difficult*, *helpful*, *exciting*, etc.) and list them on the board for students to refer to during the activity. To help students, you could give them a couple more example sentences, using the adjectives on the board (e.g. *Using a ridesharing app is easy because you can book in advance. Driving when you're abroad is exciting because you get to see new places.*) Allow pairs/groups 3–5 minutes to make the sentences, then invite students from different pairs/groups to share their ideas with the class.

Project: Helping a business traveller

Students roleplay a conference call giving advice to a colleague who is visiting from overseas.

9A Put students in pairs or small groups and explain the task. Go through the list of categories with students, refer them to the example sentence and set a time limit. Encourage students to make notes and remind them that they can refer to Exercises 1, 6 and 7 for useful vocabulary to use in their advice. During the activity, monitor and help as necessary.

9B Students now roleplay their conference calls in pairs. Explain the task and read through the example exchange with students. Set a time limit and remind students to talk about all the categories in Exercise 9A and refer to their notes. During the activity, monitor and note down any points to highlight during feedback, but do not interrupt the conference calls. When students have finished, have a brief feedback session, highlighting any points you noted while monitoring.

MyEnglishLab: Teacher's resources: extra activities

Teacher's book: Resource bank Photocopiable 1.1 p.134
Workbook: p.4 Exercises 1–3

1.2 ❯ Events management

GSE learning objectives

- Can identify specific events from short spoken descriptions.
- Can identify key details in a simple recorded dialogue or narrative.
- Can form the superlative of longer regular adjectives with *most*.
- Can form the superlative of regular adjectives with *-est*.
- Can use all forms of comparatives and superlatives of adjectives.
- Can make simple, direct comparisons between two people or things using common adjectives.
- Can give an extended description of everyday topics (e.g. people, places, experiences).
- Can make simple comparisons between people, places or things.

Warm-up

Ask students to think about the last social or corporate event they went to and put them in pairs or small groups to discuss the following questions: *What was the event? Do you think it was well organised? Why? / Why not? What did you like/dislike about it?* Give pairs/groups 3–5 minutes to discuss, then get brief feedback from the class.

Lead-in

Students talk about planning different corporate and social events.

1 Put students in pairs or small groups for this activity. Check that they understand the meaning of the events in the box before they begin. You could get students who understand some of the more difficult terms (e.g. *anniversary celebration, grand opening of a new business, launch of a new product*) to explain them in their own words to the rest of the class. This activity can also be done with the whole class, asking for a show of hands for each event.

2A Do this as a whole-class discussion, inviting different students to share their views. Make sure they give reasons for their answers.

Suggested answers

organised, able to pay attention to details, good with budgets

2B If time allows, let students discuss the question in pairs or groups first, then broaden this into a class discussion. Again, remind them to give reasons for their answers. In weaker classes, before students discuss the question, you could help them by writing some prompts on the board, e.g. *I'm (not very) ... , I'm (not very) good at/with ... , I (don't) like ... , I can/can't ... , I enjoy ... .*

Possible answers

No. I'm not organised. I don't like budgets.
Yes. I enjoy paying attention to details.

Listening

Students listen to an interview with an Events Manager.

3 Explain the activity and give students 2–3 minutes to note down ideas for each category, individually or in pairs. Go over the answers with the class to get the biggest possible pool of ideas before students listen. List students' ideas on the board. If your students are not familiar with circuses, draw their attention to the photo and elicit what they know about them, so they have a general idea before they listen to the interview.

See answers to Exercise 4.

4 ◀)1.01 Explain the activity and remind students to refer to the list on the board and/or their notes as they listen. Play the recording, then check answers with the class.

The types of events she plans: parties, conferences, corporate hospitality events, not weddings, events for corporate clients, parties for individual people, grand openings, welcoming new employees

Important things to think about: type of event, schedule, budget, location, theme – an original idea, entertainment, food, tables and chairs, sound system for speeches and music

Important skills for an Events Manager: attention to detail, organisation, people skills

5 ◀)1.01 Allow students to read through the statements before they listen again, then play the recording. In weaker classes, students may need to listen twice for this activity: once to decide whether the statements are true or false and then a second time to correct the false statements. Get students to compare answers in pairs before checking with the class.

1 F – She doesn't help people plan weddings because they're usually done by people who only plan weddings. She helps people plan parties, conferences, corporate hospitality events, etc.
2 T
3 F – She talks about budget in the first meeting.
4 F – She once planned an event that had a circus theme.
5 T
6 T

Extra activities 1.2

A ◀)1.01 This activity practises key vocabulary from the listening. Explain to students that the sentences are things Alicia said in her interview, and give them 3–4 minutes to complete the exercise. Play the recording again for students to check their answers. Pause after each sentence is heard, eliciting the correct answer and clarifying meanings as necessary.

1 plan 2 client 3 venue 4 guests 5 arrange
6 organise 7 staff 8 manage

6 Depending on time available, you could let students discuss this in small groups first, then get brief feedback from the class.

Grammar: Comparatives and superlatives

Students study and practise comparatives and superlatives.

7A Before students do the exercise, write the following sentences on the board: *Planning a business lunch is easier than planning a wedding. Planning a small party is the easiest event.* Underline *easier than* and *the easiest*, explain or elicit that they are comparative/superlative adjectives and check students understand meaning. At this point, you may wish to refer students to the Grammar reference on page 119, go through the explanations and examples with them and answer any questions they may have. Alternatively, students can look at the Grammar reference after Exercise 7B. The exercise can be done individually or in pairs.

Sentences 1, 5, 7 and 8 are comparatives.
Sentences 2, 3, 4 and 6 are superlatives.

7B Do this as a quick whole-class activity.

1 superlative 2 comparative 3 irregular

8 Get students to do the exercise individually and then compare answers in pairs. Check answers with the class and go over any points that need clarification.

1 the most 2 less difficult 3 harder 4 the worst
5 more 6 easier than 7 The best 8 The least

9 Explain the activity and point out that students may need to add *than* or *the* in some items. Go over the answers with the class, checking that they have spelt the adjectives correctly. If there are any difficulties with spelling, refer students to the table on page 119 again.

1 the biggest 2 worse than 3 easier than
4 the least expensive 5 the cheapest 6 better than
7 smaller than 8 the best

Extra activities 1.2

B This activity gives further practice of comparatives and superlatives and can be done individually or in pairs. As an extension, after checking answers, you could ask students to underline the comparative/superlative adjectives in the sentences and use them to make their own sentences.

1 We want the cheapest option.
2 A party for 50 is cheaper than a party for 500.
3 We need the biggest dining room.
4 We want to hire the best staff.
5 An informal meal is easier than a formal meal.
6 Rain is the worst weather for an outdoor party.
7 Orange juice is more expensive than water.
8 Managing three people is less difficult than managing twenty people.

Speaking and writing

Students practise the grammar from the lesson by talking and writing about venues for a party.

10A Put students in pairs, explain the activity and go over the example sentences with them. With weaker classes, you may wish to do another example on the board or write some possible adjectives for students to use in their sentences (e.g. *large, expensive, good, bad*). During the activity, monitor and note down any errors students make with comparatives and superlatives, for some brief class feedback afterwards.

Possible answers

The ballroom is the most expensive.
The barbecue is the least expensive.
The ballroom is the biggest.
The barbecue is bigger than the restaurant.
The ballroom has the most staff.
The barbecue has the least staff.
The country band is more exciting than the jazz band.

10B Students should do this in the same pairs as Exercise 10A. To help them explain their reasons for choosing a venue, you could list some prompts on the board, e.g. *location, price, entertainment, size.* Give pairs 2–3 minutes to discuss the question, then invite different pairs to share their ideas with the class.

11 Depending on the level of your class, students could do this individually or in the same pairs as the previous two exercises. Before they begin, you could do an example on the board: write three different venues from the students' town on the board and some details about each one (e.g. capacity, location, price). Then write (or elicit from stronger students) one comparative sentence and one superlative sentence about each venue. During the activity, go round monitoring and correcting students' sentences as necessary.

Possible answers

Metropole Hotel, city park, community centre
The community centre is smaller than the park.
The Metropole Hotel is bigger than the community centre.
The city park is worse than the others in bad weather.
The Metropole is the most expensive hotel in town.
The city park is the least formal venue.
The community centre is the most boring option.

❯ Pronunciation bank
p. 114: The letter 'r'

Warm-up

🔊 P1.01　Refer students to the explanation in the box and go through it with them. Play the recording for students to just listen and compare the rhotic and non-rhotic pronunciation. Do not focus on students' own pronunciation at this point.

1 Get students to do this exercise individually. You may wish to copy or project the sentences onto the board, and record the answers there.

1 A party for 50 is cheaper than a party for 500.
2 The better option is a big tent in the park.
3 Some people think this is the worst hotel in town.
4 The barbecue is bigger than the restaurant.
5 A circus theme is more fun than just having a meal.
6 Are some venues better than others?

2A 🔊 P1.02　Play the recording, twice if necessary, and get students to compare their answers in pairs before checking with the class. If you have the sentences written or projected on the board, invite students to come to the board and circle the 'r's that are pronounced.

1 A party for 50 is cheaper than a party for 500.
2 The better option is a big tent in the park.
3 Some people think this is the worst hotel in town.
4 The barbecue is bigger than the restaurant.
5 A circus theme is more fun than just having a meal.
6 Are some venues better than others?

2B You may wish to play the recording again for this activity. Remind students of the explanation in the box: 'r' is usually pronounced by American, Irish and Scottish English speakers; British English speakers usually only pronounce 'r' after a vowel.

British: 1, 4, 5
American: 2, 3, 6

3 Put students in pairs. Before they begin, make sure they understand that pronouncing or not pronouncing the letter 'r' is something native speakers do, but that does not mean students, as non-native speakers, have to do it. Also point out that an advantage of rhotic pronunciation is that it makes it easier for listeners to identify words.

MyEnglishLab: Teacher's resources: extra activities; Reading bank
Grammar reference: p.119 Comparatives and superlatives
Pronunciation bank: p.114 The letter 'r'
Teacher's book: Resource bank Photocopiable 1.2 p.135
Workbook: p.5 Exercises 1–4, p.6 Exercises 1–3

1.3 > Communication skills
Small talk

GSE learning objectives

- Can follow a simple conversation or narrative about familiar, everyday activities.
- Can extract key details from conversations between colleagues about familiar topics.
- Can make basic inferences in simple conversations on familiar everyday topics.
- Can make and respond to suggestions.
- Can initiate, maintain and close simple, restricted face-to-face conversations.
- Can participate in short conversations in routine contexts on topics of interest.
- Can use fixed expressions to keep a conversation going (e.g. *I see., right*).
- Can show interest in conversation using fixed expressions.

Warm-up

Write the following questions on the board: *How do you feel about small talk? Do you think you're good at it?* Underline *small talk* and check that students know what it means. Then put them in pairs or small groups to discuss the questions. After 2–3 minutes, invite different students to share their answers with the class. If time allows, ask for a show of hands on who has had to make small talk in English. Invite students who raise their hand to share their experience with the class: What was the situation? How did they feel?

Lead-in

Students discuss their views on making small talk.

1A Put students in pairs and refer them to the comment on small talk. Give pairs 2–3 minutes to discuss whether they agree or disagree, then get brief feedback from the class. Encourage students to give reasons for their answers.

1B Depending on time available, students could discuss the questions in pairs or small groups first, then as a whole class. For questions 1 and 3, list students' ideas on the board.

Possible answers

1 in a lift, on a bus/train/plane, in the staff canteen, in a queue, by the coffee machine, before a meeting, at a conference
2 to be polite as they are waiting for a meeting, etc., to learn about the other person, to develop new contacts, i.e. for business
3 Students' own answers

1C Put students in small groups and give them 3–4 minutes to rank the topics on the line. Then invite a few students to share their answers with the class, giving reasons. Are there any other topics they definitely would or wouldn't talk about?

Notes

- Your home town, music, the place you are in, sports, travel and the weather are considered safe topics in most countries/cultures. The weather is a good starter as it is something that affects everyone and is an immediate context.
- Asking about someone's family often means you are making assumptions about the other person, e.g. 'Do you have children?' may be interpreted as discourteous in some cultures.
- Health, personal finances, politics and religion are generally considered as subjects too personal to discuss with someone you have just met.

Video

Students watch a video giving a model for making small talk in professionally related social contexts.

2 ▶ 1.3.1   Before students watch the video, briefly explain the context and characters' roles (or refer students to page 6 of the coursebook). The Gallagher Consultancy (TGC), an Irish HR consultancy firm, have recently hired four new people. Senior management have invited the new starters to a welcome dinner. Play the video and ask students to make notes in answer to the questions. Check answers with the class. In weaker classes, students may need to watch the video a second time to check/complete their answers.

1 trainee at TGC, an HR consultancy
2 It gives advice to companies about recruitment, company strategy, etc.
3 They are new recruits and their managers/bosses. It's a welcome dinner for the new recruits.
4 She is stuck in traffic.

3A ▶ 1.3.2   Explain that students are going to watch the next part of the welcome dinner. Give them a minute to read the questions and check that they understand the meaning of *typical*. Play the video and get students to compare answers in pairs before checking with the class.

1 home town, the place they are in (the restaurant)
2 Turkey, Dublin
3 **a** It sometimes takes him hours to get home because there is a lot of traffic.
   b Los Angeles: the traffic was bad and he missed the time to give his presentation. Bangkok: the airline lost his luggage.

3B Put students in pairs and give them time to discuss the question. Check the answer with the class.

b

4A ▶ 1.3.3   Explain that Video B will show the next part of the dinner and a different approach to making small talk. Explain the activity and encourage students to make notes about each character. Check answers with the class.

1 She's an American from Boston. She went to university in Boston. She met Orla at her interview. She thinks Orla is a nice person.

2 He's never been to Boston, but would like to go. His name is Brazilian, but he's from Italy. His father is Brazilian. He doesn't know much about working at TGC.

3 Azra is originally from Turkey. She was born in Istanbul, but moved to London when she was five. She returns regularly to Istanbul to see family. She loves London and Istanbul, and it is difficult to say which she prefers.

4 Alex knows Turkey a bit. He went to Turkey on holiday three years ago.

4B ▶ 1.3.3   Before students watch again, go through the table with them and check that they understand the meanings of *lean forward* and *eye contact*. Use this as an opportunity to teach *body language* (= changes in your body position and movements that show what you are feeling or thinking), which will come up in the Conclusions video in Exercise 5. Play the video and check answers with the class.

All four speakers do all the things in the table, so students should tick all the boxes.

5 ▶ 1.3.4   Explain that students are going to watch the last section of the video, with conclusions on the different approaches to small talk they looked at in Videos A and B. Play the video and elicit the answer. With stronger classes, you could ask students to watch the video a second time and note down the four tips the speaker gives for making small talk (*1 Choose your topic carefully and don't be too negative. 2 Listen and show interest in what the other person is saying. 3 Don't dominate the conversation and change the subject if the other person looks bored. 4 Follow the AAA model.*).

The AAA model is:
Answer the speaker's question,
Add new information and then
Ask him or her another question.

Reflection

Students reflect on the conclusions from the video and discuss their own small-talk skills.

6 Allow students to work individually on this so that they can reflect on what they do when they make small talk and whether they notice any difference in doing this in their native language and in English. Ask them to think about their answers and make notes. Then put them in pairs to discuss and compare their ideas. Get brief feedback from the class.

Possible answers

Don't talk about personal finances, politics or religion, and don't be too negative.
Show interest in the other person and their views.
Don't dominate the conversation and if the other person looks bored, change the subject.
Use the AAA model.

Functional language: Making small talk
Students look at useful questions for making small talk.

7A You could do this as a whole-class exercise, checking answers as you go. Alternatively, get students to do the matching individually, then check answers with the class.

1 g **2** a **3** d **4** b **5** f **6** h **7** c **8** e

7B Students could do this individually or in pairs. Encourage them to think about the type of information after each expression in bold to help them do the matching (e.g. Is it a place? A verb? A name?). Point out that more than one answer may be possible in some items.

1 live
2 David / the company / the food / the project / Angelina's Pizzeria / fashion / the town / Prague or Barcelona
3 flight
4 David / Angelina's Pizzeria / the company / the food / the project / the town / fashion / Prague or Barcelona
5 David / Angelina's Pizzeria / the company / the town / Prague or Barcelona
6 Prague or Barcelona
7 David / Angelina's Pizzeria / the company / the town / Prague or Barcelona / the project
8 in Boston

7C Give students time to write their questions individually, then get them to compare answers in pairs. Monitor and help as necessary. If time allows, you could put students in pairs to practise asking and answering their questions.

8A Students should do this individually. To check answers, you could play the extract from the video again.

1 you from   **2** That's right   **3** to university
4 you know it   **5** I'd like to

8B Elicit or remind students of the AAA model: when someone asks you a question, *answer*, *add* some new information and *ask* another question. If time allows, put students in pairs to discuss the questions and come up with suggestions for question 2. Then discuss the answers with the class.

1 Yes. She answers Thiago's question, adds some more information (*I'm from Boston.*) and then asks him a question (*Do you know it?*).
2 Yes. He could ask Jasmine another question after ... *but I'd like to*, e.g. *Have you ever been to Italy?*

8C Play Video B again and elicit the answers. Alternatively, you could refer students to the videoscript on page 142 and ask them to find the examples there – this option might be easier for weaker classes. There are three examples in the video; in stronger classes, you could ask students to find all three.

Possible answers

1 **Jasmine:** Thiago, that's a Brazilian name, isn't it?
Thiago: It is. My father's from Brazil, but I'm Italian. So …
Do you know Orla?
Jasmine: Yeah, I met her at the interview.
2 **Alex:** So, I heard you come from Turkey. Whereabouts?
Azra: Well, I was born in Istanbul, but my parents moved to London when I was five. We go back there quite often to see family. Do you know Turkey?
3 **Alex:** A little. I went there on holiday about three years ago. Which do you prefer, London or Istanbul?

9 Put students in pairs and explain the activity. Allow 3–4 minutes for pairs to ask and answer the questions, then invite different pairs to act out their AAA exchanges to the class. If your students need more practice, you could put them in new pairs and get them to repeat the activity with the questions from Exercise 7B and/or the ones they wrote in Exercise 7C.

❯ Pronunciation bank
p. 114: Showing interest in small talk

Warm-up
🔊 P1.03 Elicit or remind students that intonation is how we say things to create expression and variation in speech. Explain that intonation can convey our attitude and emotions. Refer students to the information in the box and go through it with them. Play the recording and ask: *In which version did the speaker sound more interested?* (the second one) *How do you know?* (The intonation was different – the speaker used falling intonation to sound interested.) Model the question again and drill it around the class.

1 🔊 P1.04 Play the recording, twice if necessary, and check answers with the class.

1 b 2 b 3 a 4 b 5 a

2 🔊 P1.05 Play the recording for students to listen and repeat. If time allows, put them in pairs to practise saying the questions while you monitor and correct their intonation as necessary.

3 Put students in pairs and set a time limit for the activity. Keep the focus on intonation rather than speaking and, again, monitor and correct students' intonation as necessary.

Extra activities 1.3

A This activity practises the functional language from the lesson. As it is a consolidation exercise, you may wish to ask students to work individually. Weaker classes could compare answers in pairs before class feedback. Depending on time available, students could also practise the conversation in pairs.

a 4 b 6 c 2 d 3 e 1 f 5

B Let students write their questions individually, then get them to compare them in pairs. Monitor while they are writing, correcting any errors as necessary. As feedback, elicit questions from different students for each answer.

1 Do you know (Zurich)?
2 Do you know (Carla)?
3 How long was your trip?
4 What are you doing in Paris?
5 Which do you prefer, Dublin or Belfast?
6 What do you know about Buenos Aires?
7 Where do you live?
8 What do you think about (this hotel)?

Task

Students practise making small talk with colleagues in different situations.

10A Put students in pairs and ask them to imagine they are colleagues. In weaker classes or if your students find roleplays challenging, you could tell them that they invent their own character for the roleplay. Explain the activity and go through the list of situations with them. You could also ask students to suggest more situations, list them on the board and let them choose from those. Give pairs a minute to choose the situation they want to roleplay.

10B Let pairs choose their topic and remind them of the AAA model again. Write *Answer, Add* and *Ask* on the board for students to refer to during the activity. Remind pairs to use phrases from Exercise 7A and to think about their body language, make eye contact and remember to smile. Set a time limit of 5–10 minutes for the activity. Monitor and check that students are using the functional language correctly, and make notes for any points to highlight during feedback.

10C Students repeat the steps in Exercises 10A and 10B in new pairs.

10D Invite different students to share with the class what they found out about their partners. Did anything surprise them? Was there anything they found particularly interesting? Finally, highlight any points you noted while monitoring.

MyEnglishLab: Teacher's resources: extra activities; Interactive video activities; Functional language bank
Pronunciation bank: p.114 Showing interest in small talk
Workbook: p.7 Exercises 1 and 2

1.4 ❯ Business skills
Dealing with problems

GSE learning objectives

- Can extract key details from conversations between colleagues about familiar topics.
- Can identify key details in a simple recorded dialogue or narrative.
- Can follow the sequence of events in a short, simple dialogue or narrative.
- Can suggest possible solutions to a problem using simple language.
- Can describe how often a work-related problem has occurred using simple language.
- Can make and respond to suggestions.

Warm-up

Write the following statement on the board: *Starting a new job is scary – it's like the first day of school.* Discuss the statement as a class. Do students agree? Why do many people feel scared in this situation?

Lead-in

Students talk about the first day at a new college/job.

1A If time is short, discuss this briefly with the whole class, nominating a few different students to answer. Alternatively, let students discuss in pairs or small groups first, then get feedback from the class.

1B Put students in pairs and give them 3–4 minutes to note down their advice. You could provide or elicit a few examples before they begin or, if students are struggling, you could go round and help them with prompts/ideas (see possible answers below). Then invite different pairs to share their advice with the class. Once students have shared their ideas, the class could draw up a list of 'Top tips for your first day at work'.

Possible answers

smile at everyone, ask questions, apologise if you forget someone's name, offer to make coffee, reflect on the day

Listening

Students listen to conversations between a new employee and some of his colleagues.

2 🔊 1.02 Go through the instructions and list of tasks with students and check that they understand the meaning of *induction briefing* – ask them what kind of information is shared at one (details about a new job or a new employee's role, values of the organisation, terms of employment, etc.). Play the recording, then check answers with the class.

1 Go to the induction briefing
2 Meet the team
3 Do the health and safety training
4 Set up his email account

3A 🔊 1.03 To help students, you could tell them that they need to listen for *three* things Jakob is having problems with. Play the recording, then check answers with the class.

5 connecting to the company intranet
2 his user name
3 his email address

3B 🔊 1.03 Give students a minute to read the questions and play the recording. To check answers, you could play the recording again, telling students to ask you to pause each time an answer is heard.

1 intern32
2 He couldn't read Sue's writing and thought his username was intern82.
3 DAVIS
4 5182

Extra activities 1.4

A 🔊 1.03 Play the recording, twice if necessary, then check answers with the class. Students could then work in pairs and practise the conversation.

1 having problems with   2 kind of
3 can't connect to   4 how to log on   5 need to use
6 Can you try   7 it's not working   8 just check your

Functional language: Explaining and solving IT problems

Students look at useful language for explaining and solving IT problems.

4A 🔊 1.03 This exercise can be done individually or, in weaker classes, in pairs. With stronger classes, you could ask students to try to do the exercise first, then listen again to check/complete their answers. During feedback, check that students understand the meaning of all the expressions and point out the verb + infinitive or *-ing* patterns in some of the items (e.g. *can't / know how to* + infinitive; *try / have trouble + -ing*).

1 the IT   2 connect to the intranet   3 log on
4 use your login details   5 logging on   6 'intern32'
7 a company email address   8 set up my email account
9 set that up   10 finding my extension number

4B Ask students to do this individually and compare answers in pairs before checking with the class. Then look at the tip on page 15 with students. Explain/Clarify as necessary and elicit examples for each pattern from different students.

Explaining a problem

I'm having problems with the IT.
I can't connect to the intranet.
I don't know how to log on.
I need to get a company email address.
How do I set up my email account?
I'm having trouble finding my extension number.

Solving a problem

You need to use your login details.
Can you try logging on again?
Try 'intern32'.
I'll set that up for you.

Extra activities 1.4

B Quickly go through the expressions in the box with students and check understanding. Point out that more than one answer may be possible in some items. Get them to compare answers in pairs, then check with the class.

Possible answers

1 a company email address / logging on / my password / the internet / the login details
2 connect to the intranet / log on / set that up / set up my email account / use your login details
3 connect to the intranet / log on / set up my email account / set that up
4 connect to the intranet / log on / set up my email account / use your login details
5 finding my extension number / 'intern32' / logging on
6 a company email address / finding my extension number / 'intern32' / logging on
7 connect to the intranet / log on / set up my email account
8 connect to the intranet / set that up
9 finding my extension number / logging on / with that

5A Do this as a whole-class activity, checking answers and clarifying meanings as you go. Note that more than one answer is possible in some cases.

1 b/c/d 2 a 3 b/c 4 b/c

5B Explain the activity and look at the example with students. While they are practising their conversations, monitor and make sure they are using the expressions from Exercise 4A correctly. If time allows, invite a few pairs to act out their conversations to the class and highlight any errors/difficulties during feedback.

Task

Students roleplay a telephone call where they explain and solve IT problems.

6A Put students in pairs and explain that they are going to roleplay a phone call where they explain and solve IT problems. Assign roles (or let students choose) and give students a minute to read their information. Answer any vocabulary questions they may have and make sure they are clear about what they have to do.

6B Set a time limit for the preparation stage. Remind students to refer to the table in Exercise 4B and the information in the Tip box, then set a time limit for the roleplay and ask them to begin. During the activity, monitor and check students' use of the functional language. Note down any errors to highlight during feedback but do not interrupt the phone calls. When students finish the first phone call, they should swap roles and roleplay a different situation. Again, allow some preparation time and set a time limit for both stages.

6C Do this as a whole-class discussion, inviting different students to share their experience with the class. Finally, highlight any points you noted during Exercise 6B.

MyEnglishLab: Teacher's resources: extra activities; Functional language bank
Workbook: p.7 Exercises 3A–B

1.5 > Writing

Email – Asking for information

GSE learning objectives

- Can understand standard emails on work-related topics.
- Can write a simple email requesting work-related information.

Warm-up

Ask students if they've ever written emails in English to ask for information. If so, what kind of information have they asked for? Who did they write to?

Lead-in

Students read and complete an email asking for information.

1 Ask students to read the email quickly and answer the following questions: *Who is it from/to?* (from a conference manager, to a hotel manager) *Why did the writer send the email?* (to ask for information about the hotel) *Is the style formal or informal?* (formal) Then ask them to read the email again and do the exercise individually. Get them to compare answers in pairs before class feedback.

1 conference facilities 2 two large rooms 3 50 people
4 city centre 5 walk 6 book 7 five nights 8 desk
9 lunch 10 price

Functional language

Students look at useful language for writing emails asking for information.

2 Before students complete the table, look at the structure of the email with them. Refer them to the headings in the table and then get them to match the headings with the different parts of the email in Exercise 1. Then ask students to complete the table individually. During feedback, check that students understand the meanings of all the expressions in the table.

> 1 Dear Sir/Madam, 2 I am writing to ask for
> 3 We are looking 4 We need 5 We would like to
> 6 would also like 7 Please can you confirm
> 8 Could you tell 9 I look forward to 10 Kind regards,

Extra activities 1.5

A This exercise provides students with a second model answer and practises useful language for emails asking for information. Before they begin, tell students that they should look carefully at the words around each gap – this will help them decide what type of word is missing.

> 1 writing 2 for 3 Please 4 know 5 would
> 6 Can/Could 7 confirm 8 long 9 hearing
> 10 best

Optional grammar work

The email in Exercise 1 contains examples of *can* and *could* to ask for information, so you could use it for some optional grammar work. Refer students to the Grammar reference on page 119 and use the exercises in MyEnglishLab for extra grammar practice.

Task

Students write an email asking for information.

3A Put students in pairs and refer them to the questions on page 127. Explain that for each question, they should write a sentence asking for the information, using the language in Exercise 2. Check that they understand the questions before they begin. Monitor, checking students are using the phrases correctly. Have a brief feedback session to highlight any errors.

> **Suggested answers**
> 1 Please can/could you confirm / Can/Could you tell me / Please can/could you let me know how big your main conference rooms are?
> We would also like more information about the size of your main conference room.
> 2 Can/Could you tell us / Please can you let me know which hotels you recommend?
> 3 Please can/could you tell us if you offer other facilities? We would also like more information about other facilities you have.
> 4 Please can/could you confirm / Can/Could you tell me if you are near the city centre?
> 5 Can/Could you please confirm / Can/Could you let me know how many parking spaces are available?

3B Go through the information on page 130 with students and, if time allows, put them in pairs to plan their email. If there is no time to do the writing task in class, it can be set for homework.

> **Model answer**
> Dear Sir/Madam,
> I am writing to ask for information about your hotel as I am staying there for three nights next month. Please could you confirm that my room is a double room? I also need to have a large desk in the room. I would also like to know if meals are included in the price. Can you also let me know how far the hotel is from the AXCentre? In addition, could you tell me if there is parking, because I am driving to the hotel? Finally, I would like more information about other facilities you have. Do you have a swimming pool and gym for your guests?
> I look forward to hearing from you.
> Kind regards,

3C If students write their emails for homework, this exercise can be done in the next lesson. Put students in pairs and ask them to read each other's emails, underline the functional language phrases from Exercise 2 their partner has used and give their partner feedback: How many / Which phrases did they use? Did they use them correctly? In addition, they could discuss what their partner did well and if there is anything in their email that could be improved.

MyEnglishLab: Teacher's resources: extra activities; Interactive grammar practice; Writing bank
Grammar reference: p.119 *can* and *could* to ask for information
Workbook: p.8 Exercises 1–3

Business workshop ❱1
A business trip

GSE learning objectives

- Can identify specific information in simple letters, brochures and short articles.
- Can understand the key details of hotel, restaurant, and transport reservations.
- Can understand simple work-related questions asked on phone calls.
- Can make basic inferences in simple conversations on familiar everyday topics.
- Can make simple future arrangements and plans with reference to a diary or schedule.
- Can describe plans and arrangements.
- Can discuss what to do next using simple phrases.
- Can write a simple email, giving details of work-related events or plans.

Background

Students read about JK Talent Spot, a talent management agency in Japan.

1 Go through the questions with the class. Then put students in pairs and ask them to read the background and answer the questions. Check answers with the class.

> **1** music/entertainment **2** Australia
> **3** Students' own answers

Making contacts

Students read about an Australian music talent agency.

2A Ask students to look at the title of the text and explain that *Oz* is a nickname for Australia. Pre-teach *Down Under*, another nickname for Australia, which is used in the text. Ask them how they think these names originated. (See Notes below.) Set a time limit for the reading task and get students to compare answers in pairs before class feedback.

> **a** 2 **b** 4 **c** 6 **d** 1 **e** 5 **f** 3

> ### Notes
>
> An informal reference to Australia is the first three letters of its name, *Aus*; and an informal reference to a resident of the country is *Aussie*. When Australians pronounce these words it sounds as though they are saying *Oz* and *Ozzie*, which has resulted in the country being nicknamed *Oz*.
>
> The nicknames *Down Under* or *the Land Down Under* derive from the country's position in the Southern Hemisphere: looking at a globe, Australia is below the equator and many other countries, which is how the nickname originated. The term is often also used to refer to New Zealand.

2B Do this as a whole-class activity.

> Yes, it's exactly what Junko needs.

Extra activities Business workshop 1

A This activity provides students with extra reading practice. Give them time to read the statements first. Ask students to underline the parts of the text that give them the answers.

1 F – Australia's biggest cities
2 F – Bands don't need to do their own marketing. OzMusicNow deals with the advertising and promotion.
3 T
4 T
5 F – OzMusicNow offers professional advice. They help entertainers learn to manage their time, money and image.
6 T

A business trip

Students listen to phone communications about the details of a business trip.

3A 🔊 BW 1.01 Explain the activity and ask students to look at the notes carefully and think about the type of information they need to listen for (a date, a number, a place, etc.). Play the recording, then check answers with the class.

> **1** 2 June **2** one **3** Brisbane **4** bed and breakfast / B&B (in Spring Hill) **5** 5 June

Extra activities Business workshop 1

B 🔊 BW 1.01 This activity looks at useful language for discussing travel plans. Check students understand the verbs in the box and ask them to complete the exercise individually. Play the recording for students to check their answers and clarify meanings as necessary.

> Answers in parentheses are possible because they are logical and grammatical, but they aren't the words that are used in the recording.
> **1** finalise **2** arrive **3** book (or arrange)
> **4** recommend (or book/arrange)
> **5** arrange (or book/recommend) **6** depart

3B 🔊 BW 1.01 Go through the instructions with students and check that they understand the meaning of *itinerary*. Give them time to read the email and correct the mistakes, then play the recording again. In weaker classes, you may need to play the recording twice and/or pause at short intervals for students to complete their answers.

> The dates are June 2–5.
> In Sydney, she needs one room, not two.
> In Brisbane, she wants a bed and breakfast, not a town-centre hotel.
> On June 5 she flies to Singapore, not back to Japan.

4 🔊 BW 1.02 Ask students to read the questions first so they know what they need to listen for. Play the recording, then check answers with the class.

> **1** Junko's flight is going to land at Canberra, not Sydney.
> **2** a computer problem
> **3** He is going to make new arrangements for Canberra.

Task: Rearrange plans

Students write an email amending travel plans.

5A Put students in pairs and give them time to read the scenario. Point out that Junko is trying to save money but also wants to use her time in Australia well. Ask them what they think the implications of this might be for her travel plans. Then refer students to 1–3. Point out that there are two choices for each item and explain that students should first compare the two choices and then decide on the best one. Draw their attention to the example exchange. Before they begin, give them time to read the options and check they understand them. If time allows, they could make notes for each option individually first, then discuss in their pairs. Finally, allow pairs 3–4 minutes to discuss the three items, while you monitor and help as necessary.

Students' own answer (but see Note, below)

Note

Although the company doesn't have a lot of money, Junko's priority is to use her time well. The taxi is more expensive, but it's quicker. Savings can be made on the hotel. Although the coach (3hr30m) is quicker and cheaper than the train (4–4hr30m), the train leaves earlier than the coach. Therefore, Junko would arrive in Sydney earlier if she took the train.

5B Students should do this in the same pairs as Exercise 5A. Give them plenty of time to write their emails and offer help where necessary.

Model answer

Dear Junko,

Thanks for your messages. I'm sorry your arrival airport has changed. I'm writing to confirm your new travel arrangements. Please don't worry – everything is going to go well on your trip. Here's the new itinerary:

2nd June
Evening: Take taxi to Canberra Lodge Hotel. It takes about 10 minutes and costs $30. The hotel is near the city centre and costs $150 per night.

3rd June
Morning: Take 7:00 train from Canberra to Sydney. I will meet you at the train station at 11:10. It costs $80 for a ticket.

I'll send you the train ticket and the hotel reservation in a separate email. Let me know if you have any questions. I'm looking forward to meeting you!

Best regards,

Sam

MyEnglishLab: Teacher's resources: extra activities

Review ❮1

1 1 reservation 2 public transportation 3 long-haul
   4 stay 5 abroad 6 ridesharing 7 vehicle
   8 delayed
2 1 more difficult than 2 happier than 3 The worst
   4 the best 5 the least expensive 6 less important
   than
3 1 That's right 2 you come from 3 How long was
   4 About six hours 5 do you live 6 Do you know
   7 Yes, a little 8 What are you 9 visiting
4 1 having 2 how 3 need/have 4 can't 5 Try
   6 Can 7 How 8 do
5 1 Dear 2 ask 3 looking 4 would 5 need
   6 confirm 7 look 8 Kind

2 Business location

Unit overview

	CLASSWORK	FURTHER WORK
2.1 **Dovetailed in Cambridge**	**Lead-in** Students discuss the importance of location. **Video** Students watch a video about how the owner of a company chose its location. **Vocabulary** Students look at vocabulary related to places of work and business locations. **Project** Students prepare and give a presentation about the location of a company in their area.	**MyEnglishLab:** Teacher's resources: extra activities **Pronunciation bank:** p.114 Syllables and stress **Teacher's book:** Resource bank Photocopiable 2.1 p.136 **Workbook:** p.9 Exercises 1–3, p.11 Exercises 1–3
2.2 **Visiting Singapore**	**Lead-in** Students talk about visiting places of interest. **Reading** Students read an article about Singapore. **Grammar** Students study and practise *enough* and *too*. **Speaking and writing** Students talk about how they would react in problematic situations and write an email or review.	**MyEnglishLab:** Teacher's resources: extra activities; Reading bank **Pronunciation bank:** p.114 Stress in noun phrases **Grammar reference:** p.119 *enough* and *too* **Teacher's book:** Resource bank Photocopiable 2.2 p.137 **Workbook:** p.10 Exercises 1–3
2.3 **Communication skills:** Checking and clarifying	**Lead-in** Students discuss meeting etiquette. **Video** Students watch a video about the importance of asking questions in order to check and clarify information. **Reflection** Students reflect on the conclusions from the video and discuss their own clarification skills. **Functional language** Students look at useful language for checking and clarifying information. **Task** Students roleplay a meeting where they check, clarify and confirm information.	**MyEnglishLab:** Teacher's resources: extra activities; Interactive video activities; Functional language bank **Workbook:** p.12 Exercises 1 and 2
2.4 **Business skills:** Starting a meeting	**Lead-in** Students discuss reasons why a meeting might be successful or unsuccessful. **Listening** Students listen to a conversation between colleagues preparing for a meeting and then to part of a staff meeting. **Functional language** Students look at useful language for opening a meeting, referring to an agenda and stating the purpose of a meeting. **Task** Students write the agenda for a meeting and then practise chairing a meeting.	**MyEnglishLab:** Teacher's resources: extra activities; Functional language bank **Workbook:** p.12 Exercise 3
2.5 **Writing:** Short communications	**Lead-in** Students read text messages and an email and answer comprehension questions. **Functional language** Students look at abbreviations and shortened forms often used in short communications. **Task** Students write an email and a text message using abbreviations and shortened forms.	**MyEnglishLab:** Teacher's resources: extra activities; Interactive grammar practice; Writing bank **Grammar reference:** p.120 Present Continuous **Workbook:** p.13 Exercises 1–4
Business workshop 2 A new location	**Listening** Students listen to people discussing possible new locations for a company. **Reading** Students read a report on good business locations. **Task** Students roleplay a meeting to choose a business location.	**MyEnglishLab:** Teacher's resources: extra activities

Business brief

The main aim of this unit is to introduce students to the concept of **location** in business. The decision about where to locate a business can have a marked impact on its success, so it is a very important consideration for any firm. The main factors influencing where to locate a business are **ease of access** (how convenient is it for customers, clients or employees to reach the **site**) and proximity to the **services** or **facilities** needed to support the organisation.

Costs are a big consideration when selecting a good site for a business. **Prime locations** in a town centre are considerably more expensive to buy or rent than sites on the outskirts of urban areas. However, the choice of location also depends on the type of business in question. For example, most retail outlets or restaurants need to be conveniently located in central areas to attract the passing customers who make up most of their business. In contrast, adequate space is likely to be the most important requirement for a **factory** or **warehouse**, so an out-of-town location where **rents** are lower and large units more affordable would be more suitable. Some areas might offer incentives such as lower rents in order to attract businesses to a particular region and boost local employment. Other areas might develop a reputation as a good location for a particular industry and therefore attract more businesses of the same type to set up there. When similar or complementary businesses group together they create a **hub**. Examples of this include Silicon Valley in California and Bangalore in India which are well known for the hi-tech organisations based there. Wall Street in New York and The City in London are famous for the number of financial services companies they are home to.

An organisation also needs to take into account its potential **workforce**. Staff need to be able to get to their place of work easily, so access to motorways and bus or rail **transport links** can be also an important factor in choosing where to locate a company. The number and type of roles that need to be filled can also be a factor in this. Some firms require a large pool of reliable workers to fill unskilled or low-skilled roles. In this case it would make sense to hire from the local area to keep salary costs stable and minimise commuting costs for lower-paid workers. Transport links would therefore be less of an issue as many of the workers would live nearby. Other companies may need to recruit **specially skilled staff** with particular experience or expertise. In this scenario good transport links to major centres are vital to allow the firm access to potential candidates living further away. Inter-city transport links are also very important for businesses that have to meet regularly with international clients and customers, or with colleagues from other domestic or overseas branches of the same organisation.

Depending on the type of company, **local infrastructure** may also be a key consideration. To allow goods to reach their markets quickly and economically, an effective transport network often needs to include airports and ports as well as road and rail links. An efficient infrastructure also refers to the **amenities** that support a business, such as electricity, gas or broadband, which can vary in cost and efficiency from one area to another. In a wider context, local infrastructure can have an impact on the employees a company can attract and keep: people are more likely to want to work in a location which is not only well connected but offers **affordable housing**, good schools, reliable medical services and good leisure facilities, than one which is remote and poorly served.

Larger organisations, such as a company's **headquarters**, or **industrial plants** and factories which are usually located at some distance from the nearest town, may decide to provide facilities for their staff on site, for example a **canteen** or restaurant, car parks and recreational facilities like a gym. Some companies also now provide crèches for staff with young children if adequate childcare facilities are not available locally.

Business location and your students

It is important that students are aware of the concept of work location and its effects. Both pre-work and in-work students need to appreciate the importance of a company's location when making their own employment choices. In addition, some students may eventually consider starting their own businesses and will need to give the concepts outlined in this unit serious consideration.

Unit lead-in

Elicit a brief description of the photo and a definition/translation of *location* in the unit title. Then look at the quote with the class. Teach or elicit the meaning of *stand firm*, and ask how the quote might be related to business location.

2.1 ❯ Dovetailed in Cambridge

GSE learning objectives

- Can follow the main points in a simple audio recording aimed at a general audience.
- Can identify key details in a simple recorded dialogue or narrative.
- Can identify simple information in a short video, provided that the visual supports this information and the delivery is slow and clear.
- Can give simple opinions using basic fixed expressions.
- Can use language related to location and position.
- Can use language related to places of work.
- Can use language related to public buildings and places.
- Can make and respond to suggestions.
- Can give an extended description of everyday topics (e.g. people, places, experiences).

Warm-up

Write the following statement on the board: *Location is the most important factor in buying a home.* Teach or elicit the meaning of *factor*. Ask students to think about their area. Do they agree with the statement? How important is location to them? Elicit ideas and reasons from different students.

Lead-in

Students discuss the importance of location.

1 Put students in pairs or groups and give them 2–3 minutes to discuss the questions. Get brief feedback from the class and ask students what sort of places or facilities the phrases in the box could refer to (e.g. *sports centres, shopping centres, green spaces*). Then do a quick class survey for question 2: What is the most important factor in the class when choosing a place to live, work or study?

Video

Students watch a video about how the owner of a company chose its location.

2 ▶ 2.1.1 Explain that students are going to watch a video about Dovetailed, a Cambridge-based company, and how its owner chose where to locate it. If desired, pre-teach the following vocabulary from the video: *brand, business network, collaborate, investment group, global recognition.* Play the video, then check answers.

> international city, can work with other companies, can work with the university, nice place to live, easy to travel to London

3 ▶ 2.1.1 Give students a minute to read the questions and check they understand *intern* and *funding*. Check answers with the class. If time allows, you could play the video again and ask students to tell you to pause when the answers are mentioned.

> **1** in 2010 **2** Microsoft **3** funding **4** advice
> **5** three minutes (by bike) **6** 50 minutes by train and just over an hour by car

Extra activities 1.1

A This activity practises useful vocabulary from the video. Play the video, then get students to compare answers in pairs before checking with the class. During feedback, clarify meanings as necessary and write (or invite students to write) the answers on the board, to make sure they have spelt them correctly.

> **1** get right **2** launched **3** human
> **4** design software **5** vibrant **6** start-ups
> **7** set up **8** attracted **9** support **10** journey
> **11** amazing **12** grow

4 Put students in pairs or groups and give them 2–3 minutes to discuss the questions. Make sure students give reasons for their answers. In stronger classes, you could also ask students to number their choices in order of preference; e.g. if they mention four things they would/wouldn't like about living and working in Cambridge, they could number them 1–4 (1 = what they would like least, 4 = what they would like most).

Vocabulary: Location

Students look at vocabulary related to places of work and business locations.

5 In stronger classes, you could ask students to complete the exercise individually or in pairs using their dictionaries to check any unknown words, clarifying meanings as necessary during feedback. In weaker classes, you could do this as a whole-class activity, checking answers and clarifying meanings as you go.

> **a** lab **b** studio **c** motorway **d** transport links
> **e** factory **f** locate **g** access to **h** rents **i** close to

❯ Pronunciation bank
p. 114: Syllables and stress

Warm-up

🔊 P2.01 Go through the explanation in the box with students and play the recording for them to listen to the examples. Get them to repeat the words, to make sure they can hear and imitate the stress patterns. Then check understanding by asking them to give you examples of words they know which are stressed on the first syllable (e.g. *popular, conference, travel, personal*), and words which are stressed on the second syllable (e.g. *expensive, location, machine, important*).

1 Put students in pairs to complete the exercise. Encourage them to say the words aloud to check which syllable is stressed each time. Do not confirm answers yet as students will check them in the next exercise.

2 🔊 P2.02 Play the recording for students to check their answers, then play it a second time for students to listen and repeat.

> **1** <u>ac</u>cess **2** con<u>ven</u>ient **3** fa<u>cil</u>ities **4** ho<u>tel</u>
> **5** <u>stu</u>dio **6** <u>trans</u>port

3 🔊 P2.03 Put students in pairs to practise saying the sentences. Monitor and check for any errors in word stress, then play the recording for them to check. As feedback, highlight any errors you noted while monitoring and, if necessary, get pairs to practise saying the sentences again.

6 Go through the words in the box with students and get them to complete the exercise individually. Check answers with the class, clarifying meanings as necessary.

> **1** warehouse **2** port **3** car park **4** convenient
> **5** headquarters (HQ) **6** facilities

7 This could be done as a whole-class activity, checking answers as you go.

> **1** c **2** a **3** b
>
> **Other items:**
> Office facilities: canteen, vending machines, staff gym, photocopy service, toilets
> Hotel facilities: restaurants, spa, sauna, bar, fitness room, business centre, rooftop terrace
> Sports and leisure facilities: tennis courts, golf club, sports arena/hall, hockey pitch, ice rink, skateboard park

8A This exercise looks at vocabulary covered in previous exercises, so students should be able to do it individually. Check answers with the class and ask students to explain why the incorrect option cannot be used each time.

> **1** rents **2** access **3** facilities **4** close **5** locate **6** links

8B Put students in pairs or small groups and give them 3–5 minutes to discuss the questions. Encourage them to use vocabulary from Exercises 4–7. Get brief feedback from the class.

Extra activities 2.1

B Get students to do this individually as a quick vocabulary quiz. You could get them to compare answers in pairs before checking answers with the class.

> **1** c **2** b **3** a **4** b **5** a **6** c **7** c **8** a

Project: Location, location, location

Students prepare and give a presentation about the location of a company in their area.

9A Put students in pairs or small groups, explain the task and give them a minute to decide on a company to research.

9B Pairs/Groups now carry out their research. Allow plenty of time for this stage and encourage students to make notes for their presentation. If there is no time to do this in class, or if your students do not have access to the internet, you could ask them to do their research at home and do Exercise 9C in the next lesson. As an alternative approach to the activity, instead of asking students to research a particular company's reasons for choosing a location, you could get them to say why *they* think the company they chose in Exercise 9A chose their location, and what are its advantages and disadvantages. You may also wish to do some research before the class, in order to be able to help students with ideas if they struggle. A web search for *why companies choose a location* or *business location strategy* should return some useful results.

9C If students did their research at home, give them a few minutes to discuss their notes, decide on information to include and plan their presentation. In either case, encourage them to use vocabulary from Exercises 5–7 (*is close to, is convenient for, has easy access to,* etc.). Point out that both/all students in each pair/group should speak, so they should decide between them who will give which part of their presentation.

MyEnglishLab: Teacher's resources: extra activities
Pronunciation bank: p.114 Syllables and stress
Teacher's book: Resource bank Photocopiable 2.1 p.136
Workbook: p.9 Exercises 1–3

2.2 ❯ Visiting Singapore

GSE learning objectives

- Can scan a simple text, identifying the main topic(s).
- Can identify specific information in a simple factual text.
- Can express sufficiency and insufficiency with *enough* and *too*.
- Can qualify adverbs with *enough* and *too*.
- Can make a complaint.
- Can make and respond to suggestions.
- Can write a letter or email of complaint with supporting details.
- Can write a short review of a restaurant, movie, etc. using simple language.

Warm-up

Put students in pairs and ask them to tell each other about the most interesting place they have ever visited. What was it like? What did they like about it? After 3–4 minutes, invite different students to share their experience with the class.

Lead-in

Students talk about visiting places of interest.

1A–B Put students in pairs or small groups and teach or elicit the meanings of the words in the box. Give them 3–4 minutes to discuss in their pairs/groups, then get brief feedback from the class. If time is short, do this as a whole-class activity, eliciting answers around the class.

> **Pronunciation bank**
> **p. 114: Stress in noun phrases**
>
> ### Warm-up
>
> ◀) P2.04   Write *city centre* on the board and elicit or explain that it is a noun phrase (two or more words which join together to make a single noun). Refer them to the information in the box and play the recording for them to listen to the examples. See if students can give you more examples of noun phrases, stressing the correct word each time. If your students are keeping vocabulary notebooks, tell them that when they learn new noun phrases, it may be useful to note which word is stressed each time.
>
> **1** ◀) P2.05   With stronger classes, you could ask students to try and complete the exercise before they listen, then play the recording for them to check. Go over the answers with the class.
>
> city zoo
>
> **2** ◀) P2.05   Students may need to listen twice for this activity: once to underline the stressed word in each noun phrase, then a second time to underline the stressed syllable in each stressed word. Check answers with the class.
>
> **1** <u>ski</u> resort   **2** <u>bird</u> park   **3** city <u>zoo</u>
> **5** <u>wild</u>life park   **5** <u>shopp</u>ing experience
>
> **3** ◀) P2.05   Play the recording for students to listen and repeat. Drill the words around the class.
>
> **4** Put students in pairs, explain the activity and do an example with a stronger student. Monitor and correct students' pronunciation as necessary.

Reading

Students read an article about Singapore.

2 Tell students they are going to read an article about Singapore. Before they read, you could show a map and elicit or give students some basic information about the island (see Notes below) to raise interest. Give students time to read the headlines and teach or elicit the meanings of *tropical* and *paradise*. Ask students to read the article quickly and choose the best headline, then check the answer with the class.

2

Notes

Singapore

Location: island city-state south of Malaysia, Southeast Asia

Size: 722 km² (main island and 62 other islands)

Population: 5.6 million, estimate in 2019

Languages: four official languages: English, Malay, Mandarin, Tamil; Singlish widely spoken (Singlish = an English-based language which incorporates elements of Chinese and Malay)

Cultures: major ethnic groups are Chinese, Malay and Tamil (the largest Indian ethnic group in Singapore)

Climate: tropical

Economy: global financial centre

3 Get students to read the questions first and teach or elicit the meaning of *image*. Ask them to complete the exercise individually, underlining the parts of the text where they find the answers. Get them to compare answers in pairs, then check answers with the class.

1 Singapore Zoo, the Night Safari, the River Safari, the Jurong Bird Park, the new Rainforest Park
2 Singapore Zoo, the Night Safari, the River Safari (the Jurong Bird Park is open, but in a different part of the country)
3 three or four days
4 to attract visitors to other parts of the city and to get tourists to spend more time in Singapore
5 standard rooms, family rooms, treehouses and cabins
6 because online shopping and other destinations compete on shopping and dining experiences
7 those who want to 'experience nature in a sophisticated urban environment' – i.e. people who want the comfort of hotels and shops as well as an opportunity to see wildlife and nature

Notes

The Mandai area is next to the large Central Catchment Nature Reserve on the main island of Singapore. An eco-bridge, for both humans and animals, links the two areas.

Extra activities 2.2

A This exercise practises useful vocabulary from the reading text. Students could do it individually or in pairs, using their dictionaries to help them if necessary. Check answers with the class, clarifying meanings as necessary.

1 relocate   2 conservation   3 stopover
4 holidaymakers   5 attract   6 cabins   7 appeal

B Students could do this individually or, if time is short, you could do it with the whole class, checking answers as you go.

1 attract   2 relocate   3 conservation   4 cabins
5 stopover   6 appeal   7 holidaymakers

Grammar: *enough* and *too*

Students study and practise *enough* and *too*.

4 Do this as a whole-class activity, checking answers as you go. Do not focus on the grammar details yet – students will look at the patterns for *enough* and *too* in Exercise 6. After checking answers, ask students which of the options express positive ideas (a and d) and which express negative ideas (b and c).

> **a** 2 (big enough) **b** 4 (too much competition)
> **c** 1 (too small) **d** 3 (enough time)

5 You may wish to let students work in pairs for this activity to discuss their answers. To check answers, write the headings *Satisfied* and *Not satisfied* on the board, eliciting answers from students and writing them under the correct heading.

> **1** satisfied – There was the right number of attractions.
> **2** not satisfied – There were more people than he/she wanted, the temperature was hotter and the queues were longer than he/she liked.
> **3** satisfied – He/She wanted more time to see everything because it was enjoyable.
> **4** not satisfied – There were more shops than he/she wanted and fewer rides.
> **5** not satisfied – His/Her children were not the right height to enjoy the best rides so they were probably unhappy about the experience.

6 Again, you could get students to work in pairs so that they can discuss and compare their answers. If you wrote the answers to Exercise 5 on the board, underline the *too/enough* phrases in them (or invite students to come to the board and underline them). After checking answers, refer students to the Grammar reference on page 119, go through the explanations and examples with them and clarify any points as necessary.

> **1** adjective **2** noun **3** adjective **4** countable
> **5** uncountable

7 Get students to complete the exercise individually, then check answers with the class. Word order with *enough* is often a problem area for students, so during feedback, highlight that it is used *after* adjectives but *before* nouns.

> **1** isn't big enough **2** is too far **3** enough attractions for
> **4** wasn't enough time **5** too many customers
> **6** too much work

8A–B ◀◗ 2.01 Give students 3–4 minutes to complete the exercise and refer them to the Grammar reference on page 119 if they need help. Play the recording for them to check their answers, then clarify any errors or queries as necessary.

> **1** enough **2** too many **3** too **4** too much
> **5** not enough **6** enough **7** too

Speaking and writing

Students talk about how they would react in problematic situations and write an email or review.

9 Put students in pairs or small groups. Explain the activity, give students time to read the scenarios and teach or elicit the meanings of *concentrate*, *queue* and *occupied*. Allow 2–3 minutes for pairs/groups to come up with one response for each scenario, then invite different students to share their answers with the class.

> **Possible answers**
> **1** I went to bed too late last night and got up too early this morning. I'm too tired to concentrate (on my work/ studies) today.
> **2** There weren't enough staff serving in the canteen, and there were too many people in the queue. There weren't enough dessert options, only apples. There were too many dirty plates on the tables and there weren't enough tables for everyone.

10 This writing task can be done in class or for homework. If there is enough time to do it in class, you could set the second option (the one students did not write in class) as homework.

> **Model answers**
> **1**
>
> Dear Mrs O'Donnell,
>
> I'm writing to you because I feel the canteen service is not good enough at the moment. Firstly, there aren't enough staff and the service isn't fast enough. Yesterday, only one person was serving food and the queue was too long. Secondly, on most days, there aren't enough clean tables for staff to have their lunch. Finally, there aren't enough dessert options. When clients come for lunch, they like to have a choice.
>
> I hope you can offer a quick solution to these problems.
>
> Best regards,
>
> Amal

2

I went to the national museum to see the new animal wildlife photography exhibition at the weekend. The exhibition is so large that there isn't enough time to see all the photos! There were also too many photos of birds so it felt too similar to the birdlife exhibition last year. I still enjoyed it, and I think it's interesting enough for everyone, not just animal lovers! However, there were too many people in the afternoon. The waiting time in the queue is too long if you're busy, so go early.

MyEnglishLab: Teacher's resources: extra activities; Reading bank
Pronunciation bank: p.114 Stress in noun phrases
Grammar reference: p.119 *enough* and *too*
Teacher's book: Resource bank Photocopiable 2.2 p.137
Workbook: p.10 Exercises 1–3, p.11 Exercises 1–3

2.3 ➤ Communication skills
Checking and clarifying

GSE learning objectives

- Can identify key details in a simple recorded dialogue or narrative.
- Can recognise when a speaker is checking that the listener has understood something in a conversation conducted slowly and clearly.
- Can make basic inferences in simple conversations on familiar everyday topics.
- Can make and respond to suggestions.
- Can use language related to agreement or disagreement.
- Can explain what they like or dislike about something.

Warm-up

Ask the following questions, eliciting answers from different students: How often do you take part in meetings in your place of work/study? When you don't understand information during a meeting, are you more likely to ask someone to explain it or try to figure it out yourself? When someone asks you to explain something, how easy is it for you to give a clear answer? Why?

Lead-in

Students discuss meeting etiquette.

1A Put students in pairs and give them 3–4 minutes to discuss the questions, then get feedback from the class. If time is short, do this as a whole-class activity: ask for a show of hands for each of the points 1–4, then elicit more ideas around the class.

Possible answers

The person who: asks lots of questions / hates meetings / thinks he/she is more important than everyone else / never takes meetings seriously / takes meetings too seriously.

1B Put students in small groups and explain the activity. Point out that they should give reasons for their opinions and try to reach agreement as a group. As feedback, invite students from different groups to share their decisions with the class, explaining their reasons.

Video

Students watch a video about the importance of asking questions in order to check and clarify information.

2A ▶ 2.3.1 If your students watched the Unit 1 video, ask them to give you a short summary of the situation and the main characters. If this is the first communication skills video for your class, briefly set up the context and/or refer students to page 6 of the Coursebook. Encourage students to make notes in answer to the questions while watching, and play the video. You could get students to compare answers in pairs before discussing them with the class. During feedback, check that students understand the meaning of *maternity leave*.

1 to help the client, Nick from Zapna Clothing, to find someone to cover maternity leave for an Assistant Manager in Poland
2 someone who talks too much and is unclear about what he wants

2B Discuss the question with the whole class. Make sure students give reasons for their answers.

Possible answer

They will have problems getting Nick to provide clear information about what he wants.

3A ▶ 2.3.2 Explain that students are going to watch the first part of Alex and Shaun's meeting with Nick. Give them time to read the candidate profile form and ask you about any terms they do not understand. Point out that they will only be able to complete some of the information in the form – the rest will come the next video. In weaker classes, you may wish to tell them which items they need to watch for now (1 and 2). Play the video and check answers with the class. To extend the activity, you could refer students back to their answer to question 2 in Exercise 2A and ask them what things Nick said / didn't say / did / didn't do which confirm that answer. Students may need to watch the video again for this.

1 maternity cover 2 15

3B If time allows, let students discuss their ideas in pairs/groups first, then invite different students to share them with the class. Alternatively, discuss the question as a class. Ask students to make notes so they can refer to them in Exercise 4B.

Ask questions to check/clarify what he says; Ask closed questions (where the answer is only one word or *Yes/No*) to clarify

4A ▶ 2.3.3 Explain that students are going to watch the next part of the meeting to complete the rest of the candidate profile form in Exercise 3A. Play the video and check answers with the class. Finally, discuss as a class how Shaun and Alex might feel about the meeting now.

3 experience of logistics, diploma in management
4 Polish
5 fluent
6 bonus scheme, subsidised staff canteen
7 Needs further discussion

4B Refer students to their notes from Exercise 3B. Let them discuss the question in pairs/group first, then broaden this into a class discussion.

They asked questions to check and clarify. They asked very specific questions to complete the candidate profile form.

5 ▶ 2.3.4 Explain that students are going to watch the last section of the video, with conclusions and learning points on the importance of checking and clarifying information in a business context. They should watch carefully and note the main points the speaker makes. If necessary, play the video a second time for students to check/complete their notes. Discuss the answers with the class.

Possible answer

It is important to check and ask for clarification in communication to understand each other.

Be careful how you ask for clarification. 'What?' may not give you the answer you want. Use expressions from the unit and rephrase questions to be more specific.

Closed questions are useful in getting the other person to confirm their needs. Or, you can repeat the other person's question and ask 'Is that right?'.

The listener's body language and facial expressions will show you if he/she understands. If not, give clarification.

Reflection

Students reflect on the conclusions from the video and discuss their own clarification skills

6 Allow students to work individually on this so that they can reflect on their own skills and ideas first. Ask them to make notes. Then put them in pairs to discuss and compare their answers. Get brief feedback from the class.

Functional language: Checking and clarifying

Students look at useful language for checking and clarifying information.

7A ▶ 2.3.3 Play Video B for students to complete the questions. Check answers with the class, clarifying meanings as necessary. Point out or elicit the function of the expressions: checking and clarifying.

1 what you're saying is **2** can I just check
3 Does that mean **4** could you be more specific
5 right **6** What I mean is

7B This activity can be done individually or, in weaker classes, in pairs. After checking answers with the class, refer students to the tip box. Explain that in addition to the two phrases they

saw in the responses (*That's right* in sentence c and *Correct* in sentence e), they can use *Right* and *Exactly* in the same way, to confirm information.

a 3 **b** 2 **c** 5 **d** 6 **e** 1 **f** 4

8 Get students to complete the exercise individually and then to compare answers in pairs. During feedback, check that they understand the meaning of each expression.

1 Can you just confirm that for us?
2 I think what Tim means is that the best candidate won't live locally.
3 What do you mean by relocation package?
4 Is that right?
5 What do you mean when you say it's a sensitive topic?

Extra activities 2.3

A–B Students can do both activities individually, as consolidation exercises. You could get them to compare answers in pairs before checking with the class.

A

1 saying **2** meant **3** check **4** right **5** specific
6 think **7** mean

B

1 Can I just check you have all the information you need?
2 I think what she means is, she wants someone with lots of experience.
3 I think what they meant is, a knowledge of logistics is important.
4 So what you're saying is, you need more staff to get the job done.
5 Does that mean you need to provide French lessons for staff?
6 Could you be more specific about the details of the role?
7 You're looking for someone with an MBA, is that right?

Task

Students roleplay a meeting where they check, clarify and confirm information.

9A Divide the class into two groups, A and B, and explain that they are going to hold a meeting where they will need to check, clarify and confirm information. This will be done in pairs in the next stage, and students in each pair will take turns being clients and TGC staff members. Refer groups to their respective information on pages 128 and 138 and explain that in Scenario 1, Group A will be the clients and Group B will be TGC staff members. They will then swap roles for Scenario 2. Ask groups to read the information and look at the forms for both scenarios. Check that both groups understand the categories on the forms. Allow plenty of time for students to prepare for both meetings while you monitor and help as necessary.

9B Students now hold their first meeting. Put them in A/B pairs, set a time limit and remind them to use phrases from Exercises 7 and 8. During the meetings, monitor, checking students are using the functional language correctly and noting any points to highlight during feedback. When students have finished, ask them to swap roles and do the same for the second meeting.

Scenario 1 Group B
1 temp
2 accountancy
3 Cardiff
4 12 months
5 experience of small or medium-sized companies
6 Welsh
7 basic knowledge
8 free tea/coffee and lunch vouchers (students can invent salary details)
9 No
10 3–5

Scenario 2 Group A
1 temp
2 Dublin
3 18 months to begin with
4 generate more business in Europe
5 graduate preferred / knowledge of html / number of years not specified
6 Spanish or French
7 fluent
8 18-month contract / lunch vouchers / cheaper Bike-co tours / free travel card
9 Yes – must be willing to travel in Europe at least once a month
10 5

9C In their pairs, students now discuss their meetings: Did they find checking and clarifying easy or difficult? Why? Did they use the functional language correctly? Did it help them get the clarification they needed? Get brief feedback from the class and highlight any points you noted while monitoring.

MyEnglishLab: Teacher's resources: extra activities; Interactive video activities; Functional language bank
Workbook: p.12 Exercises 1 and 2

2.4 > Business skills
Starting a meeting

GSE learning objectives

- Can follow the main points in a simple audio recording, if provided with written supporting material.
- Can identify the main points in a work-related meeting on a familiar topic.
- Can use language related to greeting, meeting, introducing, and leave-taking
- Can use language related to focusing.
- Can understand the main information in the agenda for a work-related meeting.
- Can write the agenda for a meeting on a work-related topic in a simple way.
- Can explain what they like or dislike about something.

Warm-up
Put students in pairs or groups and draw their attention to the photos. Ask them to say what kind of meetings they think they show, giving reasons. Give them 3–4 minutes to discuss their ideas, then elicit ideas from the class. Accept all answers, as long as students can justify them.

Lead-in
Students discuss reasons why a meeting might be successful or unsuccessful.

1A Put students in pairs and give them 3–4 minutes to discuss the questions. Invite different students to share their answers with the class.

1B Students should do this in the same pairs as Exercise 1A. Go through the instructions and list of reasons with them before they begin and remind them to give reasons for their answers.

Possible answers
There is no agenda.
The meeting is too long.
The meeting isn't necessary.
The meeting doesn't have a clear purpose.
Too many people have been invited.
No clear decisions.
Minutes are inaccurate.
Technical problems.
It's unclear who carries out the action points.
There is no time limit set for the meeting.
There is no consensus or conclusion to the meeting.
Action points for attendees for the next meeting are not set or are unclear.

1C Join pairs together into groups of four to discuss the question. If you did the Lead-in activity, remind them of the ideas mentioned there. Give students 3–4 minutes to discuss in their groups, then get brief feedback from the class.

Possible answers
Have a time-keeper.
Start and finish on time.
Set an agenda.
Invite only the people who need to be at the meeting.
Check all technical equipment before and at the beginning of the meeting.

Listening
Students listen to a conversation between colleagues preparing for a meeting and then to part of a staff meeting.

2A This activity pre-teaches some vocabulary from the listening Exercises 2B and 3A. Get students to complete it individually or in pairs, using their dictionaries if necessary, then check answers with the class.

1 e 2 c 3 f 4 b 5 a 6 d

2B ◢) 2.02 Explain that students are going to listen to Josh and Samia preparing the agenda for the meeting. Give them time to look at the agenda and check that they understand the meanings of *arise*, *staff report* and *AOB (Any Other Business)*. Play the recording, then check answers with the class. Then invite different students to say how they think Josh and Samia feel about the meeting, giving reasons for their answers.

> **a** Financial report **b** Results of market survey **c** Josh
> **d** Office party **e** Samia **f** Close
>
> **Possible answers**
> They are not very interested in the meeting. Samia says that item 6 is the only item she is interested in. Josh says he is looking forward to Close, which is the end of the meeting.

3A ◢) 2.03 Ask students to do this individually. Give them time to read through the statements before listening. Get them to compare answers in pairs before checking with the class. In weaker classes, students may need to listen twice for this activity: once to decide whether the statements are true or false and then a second time to correct the false statements.

> **1** F – Samia is late.
> **2** T
> **3** T
> **4** F – She agrees.
> **5** T
> **6** F – 500 pounds is suggested for the maximum budget.

3B Play the recording again for students to complete the expressions. Check answers with the class, clarifying meanings as necessary.

> **1** start **2** to the agenda **3** can I ask **4** take the minutes
> **5** moving on **6** I want to, is to

Functional language: Opening a meeting, referring to the agenda and stating purpose

Students look at useful language for opening a meeting, referring to an agenda and stating the purpose of a meeting.

4A Ask students to do this individually, then confirm the answers or play the recording again for students to check. Go over the expressions and check students understand them but do not focus on their functions yet as students will do this in the next exercise.

> **2** g **3** c **4** e **5** f **6** h **7** a **8** b

4B This exercise can be done individually or in pairs. Before students begin, check they understand the headings in the table. Check answers with the class.

> **Opening a meeting**
> I'd like to start on time.
> Nice to see everyone, and welcome back to Ellen.
> Does everyone have a copy of the agenda?
>
> **Stating purpose**
> So, one reason for the meeting is to introduce you all to Harry.
> The main aim today is to catch up before the holidays.

> **Giving tasks**
> Could I have a volunteer to take the minutes?
>
> **Referring to the agenda**
> (Does everyone have a copy of the agenda?)
> Let's look at item 1 – Matters Arising.
> Sorry, can we just go back to item 2?

4C Again, get students to complete the table individually or in pairs and check answers with the class. Encourage students to record the phrases in their notebooks.

> **Opening a meeting**
> Right, so let's start.
>
> **Stating purpose**
> The reason I want to discuss this is to agree on a budget.
>
> **Giving tasks**
> Harry, can I ask you to be time-keeper?
> And could I have a volunteer to take the minutes?
>
> **Referring to the agenda**
> Does anyone want to add anything to the agenda?
> So, moving on to item 5: this is Deirdre's point, I think.

> **Extra activities 2.4**
>
> **A** Get students to complete the exercise individually. Point out that the first letter of each word is given and do an example with the class if necessary. To extend the activity, you could ask students to write one example sentence for each word.
>
> > **1** minutes **2** chair/chairperson **3** action point
> > **4** agenda item **5** time-keeper **6** close
> > **7** deadline **8** matters arising
>
> **B** Again, as this is a consolidation exercise, students should work on it individually, referring back to the table in Exercise 4B if necessary. After checking answers, you could put students in pairs to practise the conversation.
>
> > **1** I'd like to start on time
> > **2** can I ask you to be
> > **3** Could I have a volunteer to take the
> > **4** want to add anything to the
> > **5** let's look at item 1

Task

Students write the agenda for a meeting and then practise chairing a meeting.

5A Put students in groups of four. Start by explaining the scenario and give them a couple of minutes to decide (a) what type of company they work for and (b) why they are having the meeting. Then ask them to think about their roles in the company: what does each group member do? When they have finished, give them time to write their agendas. Allow plenty of time for this stage and remind students that they can use the agenda in Exercise 2B as a model. Point out that they will all need a copy of their agenda in the next exercise, so they should all make notes. During the activity, monitor and help as necessary.

5B Put students in new groups of four. Make sure that each group does not have more than one student from the original groups of four (so that there are four different agendas per new group). Explain the activity: students are now going to take turns to chair the opening of a meeting, using their agendas from Exercise 5A. Refer them to the points in the box and explain that they only need to follow the steps in the box as they are only chairing the opening of their meeting. Before they begin, refer them to the table in Exercise 4B, and allow some time for them to prepare: they should think about what they are going to say, who the participants are, who they will assign the roles of minute-taker and time-keeper to, and which of the phrases in the table they could use for each step. Set a time limit and point out again that they will not be holding the full meeting each time – the aim of this activity is for them to practise using the functional language from Exercise 4.

5C Give groups 3–4 minutes to discuss the activity. What did they find easy about opening their meeting? What did they find difficult? Did they use the phrases from Exercise 4 correctly? What would they do differently next time? Join groups together into new groups of eight and give them 3–4 minutes to share their experiences. Finally, if time allows, get brief feedback from the class.

MyEnglishLab: Teacher's resources: extra activities; Functional language bank

Workbook: p.12 Exercise 3

2.5 **>** Writing
Short communications

GSE learning objectives

- Can understand short, simple emails on work-related topics.
- Can infer the meaning of abbreviations in emails from the context.
- Can write a simple email requesting work-related information.
- Can write short, simple notes, emails and messages relating to everyday matters.

Warm-up

Dictate or write the following questions on the board: *How often do you write short communications in English? How do you shorten information in messages when writing in your own language?* Put students in pairs or small groups to discuss the questions and invite different students to share their answers with the class.

Lead-in

Students read text messages and an email and answer comprehension questions.

1A–B Get students to read the messages and email quickly, then briefly discuss the answers with the whole class.

1A
1 The estate agent didn't get an email which said his client can't come because she's in Rome.
2 Because his client needs to see some offices as other companies are interested in renting them, too.

1B
She wants to make a new appointment for Thursday at 4 p.m.

Functional language

Students look at abbreviations and shortened forms often used in short communications.

2A If it did not come up in the Warm-up activity, explain or elicit the meaning of *abbreviation*. Ask students if they know any abbreviations in English like *LOL (laugh out loud)* or *ASAP (as soon as possible)*. Elicit a few examples and what they mean. Tell students that abbreviations are often used in business communications to keep them short. Refer them to the underlined abbreviations in Exercises 1A and 1B and elicit/confirm the answers.

FYI = for your information
ASAP = as soon as possible
TBC = to be confirmed
ETA = estimated time of arrival
WFH = working from home

2B Students could do this individually or in pairs. Encourage them to look at the first letter of each word in the box to help them match them with the abbreviations. Check answers with the class and clarify meanings as necessary.

1 close of business **2** end of day **3** to be announced
4 by the way

2C It may be better to do this exercise as a whole class, explaining and checking answers as you go. Try to elicit one or two more examples for each technique.

1 I am waiting **2** are interested **3** Sorry had
4 an email **5** in 20 minutes

Extra activities 2.5

A Explain the activity and get students to complete it individually. Remind them to refer to the table in Exercise 2C. During feedback, ask students to say which technique they used in each item.

1 FYI **2** appointment **3** TBC **4** Going to visit
5 email (me) plans **6** ASAP **7** WFH today **8** BTW
9 COB **10** check order **11** Have **12** in 10

Optional grammar work

The text messages and email in Exercises 1A and 1B contain examples of the Present Continuous, so you could use them for some optional grammar work. Refer students to the Grammar reference on page 120 and use the exercises in MyEnglishLab for extra grammar practice.

Task

Students write an email and a text message using abbreviations and shortened forms.

3A Put students in pairs and refer them to the email on page 127. Remind them to use abbreviations and the techniques in Exercise 2C. Monitor and help as necessary.

Model answer

Morning, Suki. How are you today?

Good news! Basixlife going to rent offices. Email them contract by COB.

BTW thanks for report. Very helpful. Also need sales figures by EOD.

John Welles to send payment but TBC when. Apologises for delay. Problem with his bank.

3B This writing task can be done in class or for homework. Refer students to the notes on page 127 and explain the activity. Make sure they understand that their email should be more formal and that they should not use abbreviations or shortened forms.

Model answers

Text message

Hi Jack. Meeting my office 2.30 today confirmed. Need short presentation on new office location, with reasons for moving. BTW don't forget appointment with building owner tomorrow AM. Time TBC. Call me if you need more information before meeting.

Email

Hi Susana,

How are you today?

This is to confirm our appointment for tomorrow morning. Could you tell me what time would be good for us to meet? I am out of the office today, so if you'd prefer to call me to make the arrangements, please call my mobile. I would also be grateful if you could send the contract details before the close of business today.

I'm looking forward to seeing you tomorrow and signing the contract.

Best wishes,

José

3C If students do the writing task for homework, you could do this exercise in the next lesson. Put them in pairs and ask them to read each other's text message and email and think about whether their partner has used (a) the same abbreviations and (b) all the techniques in Exercise 2C.

MyEnglishLab: Teacher's resources: extra activities; Interactive grammar practice; Writing bank

Grammar reference: p.120 Present Continuous

Workbook: p.13 Exercises 1–4

Business workshop ❯2
A new location

GSE learning objectives

- Can identify specific information in simple letters, brochures and short articles.
- Can make and respond to suggestions.
- Can follow the main points in a simple audio recording, if provided with written supporting material.
- Can explain what they like or dislike about something.
- Can explain what they like or dislike about their job or workplace.
- Can write short, simple notes, emails and messages relating to everyday matters.

Background

Students read about EM Animation Studios, a London-based company whose owners are considering relocating to Berlin.

1 Put students in pairs and ask them to read the background and discuss the questions. Check answers with the class.

1 Because they need more space, but rents in London are too high.
2 It's exciting, international, and offers excellent value. They will be able to hire people from all over the world. They can save money on rent and offer higher salaries and invest more in their business.
3 Students' own answers

Offices for rent

Students listen to a conversation about possible new locations for EM Animation Studios.

2A 🔊 BW 2.01 Draw students' attention to the slides and photos and elicit brief descriptions of the photos in slides A, C and E. Explain that Ewa and Mark are discussing possible locations for their Berlin office and that students should listen and number the slides in the order they talk about them. Tell them not to worry about the gaps for now. You may wish to pre-teach the following from the recording: *trendy, fashionable* (as in *trendy/fashionable neighbourhoods*), *workstation, multicultural, bohemian, buzz* (as in *a buzzing neighbourhood*). Play the recording, then check answers with the class.

1 A 2 F 3 E 4 B 5 C 6 D

2B 🔊 BW 2.01 Students now listen again and complete the gaps in the slides. Point out that they should not use more than two words in each gap.

Prenzlauer Berg office
1 furniture 2 northeast 3 120 4 meeting rooms
5 2,600 6 7,800
Kreuzberg office
1 factory/building 2 400 3 40 4 printer 5 300
6 two months
Mitte office
1 heart/centre/middle 2 25 3 15 4 cleaning
5 1,200 (one room), 1,800 (two rooms) 6 three months

Extra activities Business workshop 2

A ◀) BW 2.01 Refer students to the three office locations on page 90 and ask them to listen again and match statements 1–6 with the office locations. Check answers with the class. Additionally, you could refer students to the audio script and ask them to find the point that led them to the correct answer.

| 1 PB | 2 M | 3 PB | 4 K | 5 K | 6 M |

B ◀) BW 2.01 This activity practises useful vocabulary from the listening. You could go through the words in the boxes with students before they begin or let them use their dictionaries to look up unknown words and clarify meanings during feedback.

1 estate agents 2 wooden 3 fashionable
4 distance 5 reach 6 properties 7 bright
8 trendy 9 arts 10 bohemian 11 floor
12 sights 13 prestigious 14 lifts, views

3 If there is time, put students in pairs or small groups to discuss the question, then invite different students to share their ideas with the class. Alternatively, do this as a whole-class activity. Remind students to give reasons for their answers.

A trip to Berlin

Students listen to a conversation and read a magazine report on good business locations.

4A ◀) BW 2.02 Explain that Ewa and Mark have now visited three of the offices and are discussing their pros and cons. To help them, you could tell them that they need to listen for two or three pros and two or three cons for each office and think about the sort of language which would introduce these in the conversation. Play the recording, twice if necessary, then check answers with the class.

Mitte office
Pros: location/address, love the idea of working in the city centre
Cons: nothing in common with finance company, expensive flat rents in the area

Prenzlauer Berg office
Pros: great old building, room to grow, save money in future
Cons: expensive, darker than expected, three flights of stairs and no lift

Kreuzberg office
Pros: lot of fun people (make friends quickly), terrace, cheapest option
Cons: get distracted from work, no privacy, difficult to book the meeting room

4B Do this as a whole-class discussion. Encourage students to give reasons for their opinions.

5 Give students time to read the report and ask you about anything they do not understand. Put them in pairs or groups to discuss the question, then invite different students to share their answers with the class. Again, remind them to give reasons.

Possible answers
Advantages
advances in technology – might be good for an animation start-up; most people speak more than one language, including high levels of English; there are lots of professionals from other countries; Tallinn has the highest number of start-ups per person in the EU which their company might work with

The biggest advantage would be the e-residency, which allows businesses access to digital services without living in Estonia – this means they could potentially rent office space anywhere in the world.

Disadvantages
No disadvantages appear in the magazine report, but in the discussion we learn that Mark thinks he'll miss London and is a little unsure about going to Berlin.

Extra activities Business workshop 2

C ◀) BW 2.02 Students could do this individually or in pairs (the second option may be easier for weaker classes). Before they begin, teach or elicit the meanings of *three flights of stairs*, *distracted* and *terrace*. Play the recording for students to check their answers.

| 1 d | 2 e | 3 c | 4 h | 5 b | 6 a | 7 f | 8 g |

Task: Choose a location

Students roleplay a meeting to choose a business location.

6A Put students in groups of three or four, explain the activity and let them select their roles. Refer each student to their role card and give them time to read the information. Teach or elicit the meaning of *digital nomad* in the information for Yelena. Give students 2–3 minutes to think about their preferences and prepare for the meeting.

6B Students now hold their meetings. Before they begin, go through the list of points to consider with them and set a time limit. Remind students to cover all of the points in their discussion. After the meetings, invite students from different groups to tell the class which location they chose and why.

MyEnglishLab: Teacher's resources: extra activities

Review ◀ 2

1 1 studios 2 lab 3 leisure 4 close 5 links
    6 warehouse 7 port 8 convenient
2 1 not big enough 2 too many changes
    3 too much money 4 too small 5 too far
    6 enough space 7 enough parking spaces
3 1 check 2 Correct 3 right 4 Exactly 5 specific
    6 mean 7 saying
4 1 see 2 copy 3 agenda 4 start 5 reason
    6 volunteer 7 minutes 8 time-keeper 9 add 10 item
5 1 working from home 2 by the way
    3 as soon as possible 4 to be confirmed
    5 estimated time of arrival
6 1 I am very sorry I can't come to the meeting.
    2 I will be with you in 15 minutes.
    3 We know other suppliers are interested.
    4 John sent a message to the boss yesterday.
    5 I'm reading the document now.

Unit overview

	CLASSWORK		FURTHER WORK
3.1 › **The Ziferblat café**	**Lead-in**	Students talk about going to cafés.	**MyEnglishLab:** Teacher's resources: alternative video and extra activities **Teacher's book:** Resource bank Photocopiable 3.1 p.138 **Workbook:** p.14 Exercises 1–3
	Video	Students watch a video about a café with an unusual business model.	
	Vocabulary	Students look at vocabulary related to shops and shopping.	
	Project	Students carry out a class survey to find out each other's shopping habits.	
3.2 › **The retail experience**	**Lead-in**	Students talk about different types of shopping experience.	**MyEnglishLab:** Teacher's resources: extra activities; Reading bank **Grammar reference:** p.120 Past Simple and Past Continuous **Pronunciation bank:** p.115 Past Simple **Teacher's book:** Resource bank Photocopiable 3.2 p.139 **Workbook:** p.15 Exercises 1–4, p.16 Exercises 1–3
	Listening	Students listen to people talking about recent shopping experiences.	
	Grammar	Students study and practise the Past Simple and Past Continuous.	
	Writing	Students practise the Past Simple and Past Continuous by writing short tweets.	
3.3 › **Communication skills:** Solving workflow problems	**Lead-in**	Students discuss possible workflow problems and causes.	**MyEnglishLab:** Teacher's resources: extra activities; Interactive video activities; Functional language bank **Pronunciation bank:** p.115 Stress in short sentences **Workbook:** p.17 Exercise 1
	Video	Students watch a video about different approaches to solving workflow problems.	
	Reflection	Students reflect on the conclusions from the video and their own approach to problem-solving and decision-making.	
	Functional language	Students look at useful language for solving problems.	
	Task	Students roleplay resolving different workflow problems.	
3.4 › **Business skills:** Presenting results	**Lead-in**	Students read and discuss advice on structuring a presentation.	**MyEnglishLab:** Teacher's resources: extra activities; Functional language bank **Workbook:** p.17 Exercises 2–4
	Listening	Students listen to a presentation about the results of a customer service survey.	
	Functional language	Students look at useful language for signposting a presentation.	
	Task	Students give a presentation with a colleague.	
3.5 › **Writing:** An online review form	**Lead-in**	Students read and complete an online review form.	**MyEnglishLab:** Teacher's resources: extra activities; Interactive grammar practice; Writing bank **Grammar reference:** p.121 Types of adverbs **Workbook:** p.18 Exercises 1–3
	Functional language	Students look at useful phrases in online review forms.	
	Task	Students complete an online review form.	
Business workshop 3 › Pop-up stores	**Reading**	Students read articles about the benefits of pop-up retail.	**MyEnglishLab:** Teacher's resources: extra activities
	Listening	Students listen to extracts from market research interviews.	
	Task	Students design and present their own pop-up store and then create an advertisement for it.	

Business brief

The main aim of this unit is to introduce the concept of **retail** business and some issues affecting it. In recent years there have been many changes in **consumer** expectations and the way we buy goods, which have drastically changed the retail industry.

A few decades ago the **opening hours** of most retail businesses were similar to those of other types of business – 9 a.m. to 5 p.m., Monday to Friday. In many countries, shops also had shorter opening hours on Saturdays and were closed on Sundays and festivals. However, in the last twenty years, evolving working hours and changes in shopping habits have in turn led to changes in the legislation affecting **trading hours**. There has been a huge increase in the number of **retail outlets** like supermarkets which are open 24 hours a day, seven days a week (**24/7**), and a marked increase in shops which offer longer opening hours overall. Customers now expect trading hours to fit around their work and lifestyle, and the overall trend is towards trading that allows them to shop day or night.

Another major change is that many larger **retail chains** sell a wider range of goods than in the past, as customers' expectations about product choice have increased. For example, when food shopping forty years ago, people would buy fruit and vegetables that were largely local to their area and in season. In contrast, a supermarket today can offer its customers the same produce all year round, imported from many countries. Items which were once seen as luxury are now bought as part of the standard **weekly shop**. As a consequence of offering more products, retail chains need more space and there has been a rise in the number of large-scale outlets like **superstores** and **hypermarkets**. The large sites needed to build these mean that many businesses have relocated to out-of-town **shopping malls** and **retail parks** where land is cheap. These changes have had a big impact on traditional **high street shopping areas**.

Conditions for smaller retail businesses are becoming extremely challenging. In some areas independent shops are being forced off the High Street by **chain stores** due to high rents. They are also facing stiff competition from online retailers. Customers may visit a shop on the High Street to browse products, but often go online to buy them more cheaply. A decline in retail businesses on the High Street also impacts on other local businesses which provide facilities for shoppers, such as cafés, restaurants and hairdressers.

The USA, the UK, Sweden, France, Germany and Japan currently spend the most on online shopping among developed nations, with **e-commerce** in the USA now making up 10 percent of all retail sales. However, although e-commerce may be changing the retail landscape, it's not all bad news for smaller operations. For instance, new retailers can now start up online with much lower **overheads** than in the past since they no longer need to rent premises to display their goods. In the online marketplace all you need is a website to **showcase** your products and a contract with a reliable delivery company to ensure they get to your customer.

The rise of e-commerce has also led to changes in attitudes towards **customer service**. **Customer feedback** from surveys is now extensively used to inform retail business strategies such as which new products or services to offer and how to promote them. Businesses that wish to survive in a competitive marketplace have to find effective ways to respond to customer opinions and complaints in the very public forum created by social media. Technology means that the relationship between the retailer and the customer is more important than ever before.

Retail and your students

Pre-work students may have experience of retail business through part-time or holiday jobs they have had while studying. Some in-work students may be employed in the retail environment in customer-facing roles or administrative roles. All students will be familiar with some of the aspects of retail from the point of view of the customer. This unit will build on that experience and expand their understanding of the how the industry works and the challenges it faces in the modern world.

Unit lead-in

Refer students to the unit title and check they understand *retail* (the sale of goods to customers for their own use). Look at the quote and photo with the class and ask how they might be related (e.g. being able to buy certain things can make us feel happier). Discuss the quote with the class. Do they agree? Why? / Why not? Can shopping make us feel happier? Can money buy happiness? How?

3.1 ❯ The Ziferblat café

GSE learning objectives

- Can follow the main points in a simple audio recording aimed at a general audience.
- Can identify key details in a simple recorded dialogue or narrative.
- Can make and respond to suggestions.
- Can use language related to shops and the shopping experience.
- Can use language related to money.
- Can recognise phrases and content words related to familiar topics (e.g. shopping, local geography).
- Can describe habits and routines.
- Can ask and answer questions about habits and routines.
- Can explain what they like or dislike about something.
- Can identify specific information in a simple factual text.
- Can write simple lists as part of a work-related task.

Warm-up

Dictate or write the following questions on the board: *When was the last time you went out with a friend or colleague? Where did you go? What did you do there?* Get students to discuss the questions in pairs or small groups, then invite some to share their answers with the class.

Lead-in

Students talk about going to cafés.

1 Go through the questions with the class and check students understand the activities in question 2. If time allows, let them discuss the questions in pairs or small groups first, then elicit answers around the class. For question 2, you could ask for a quick show of hands to find the most popular activity.

Video

Students watch a video about a café with an unusual business model.

2 ▶ 3.1.1 Explain the activity and go through statements 1–3 with the class. Draw their attention to *retailer* and remind them of the word *retail* from the unit Lead-in. Check they understand the meaning of both. Play the video, then check answers with the class. Be prepared to check the meaning of the following phrasal verbs if students ask about them: *fit in* (manage to do something in a short period of time), *work out* (calculate), *dash in* (go in a place very quickly), *wolf down* (eat something very quickly), *mount up* (gradually increase in amount).

```
3
```

3 ▶ 3.1.1 Play the video again for students to complete the notes, then check answers with the class. You could ask students to complete as many of the gaps as they can before watching, then watch again to check/complete their answers.

```
1 free   2 hotel   3 minute   4 German   5 three
6 writing   7 month   8 expensive
```

Extra activities 3.1

A ▶ 3.1.1 This activity looks at useful vocabulary from the video. You could go through the words in the box with students before they begin, or let them use their dictionaries to look up unknown words. While checking answers, elicit what part of speech each gapped word is – this will help students with Activity B.

```
1 help yourself   2 unique   3 stopwatch   4 abuse
5 pocket   6 counts   7 atmosphere   8 uploading
9 loo   10 laptop
```

B Get students to match the words with the definitions individually, then check answers with the class and clarify meanings as necessary.

```
a laptop   b loo   c uploading   d atmosphere
e pocket   f help yourself   g unique   h stopwatch
i abuse   j counts
```

4 Put students in pairs or small groups and let them discuss the question for 2–3 minutes, then elicit answers around the class.

Alternative video worksheet: Pop-up shops

1 If time is short, discuss the questions with the whole class, nominating a few different students to answer. Alternatively, let students discuss in pairs or small groups first, then get feedback from the class. Teach or elicit the meanings of *bricks-and-mortar* store and *publicise* before students discuss the questions (refer them to the definition of *publicise* at the end of the activity).

```
Students' own answers
```

2 ▶ ALT 3.1.1 Tell students that they are going to watch a video about pop-up shops. Do not explain the term yet or how pop-up shops work – the video will explain this. Explain the activity and give students a minute to read the statements before they watch. Play the first part of the video (0:00–0:29), then check answers with the class.

```
1 long   2 days   3 customers   4 products
```

3 ▶ ALT 3.1.1 Explain that students are going to watch the next part of the video and decide if the statements are true or false. Give them time to read the statements and check that they understand *skincare* in question 2. Play the next part of the video (0:30–3:24), then check answers with the class. Students may need to watch the video twice for this activity: once to decide if the statements are true or false, then a second time to correct the false statements.

1 F – The Dirt Creative was a successful online business before its pop-up shop opened.
2 T
3 T
4 F – Customers cannot visit the shop on Monday.
5 F – The Dirt Creative did not pay a lot of rent to open the shop.
6 T

4 ▶ ALT 3.1.1 Tell students they are going to watch the whole video again, and give them time to read the questions and options before they watch. Make sure they understand that they need to choose two correct options in each question. Play the video and get students to compare answers in pairs before class feedback.

1 a, c 2 b, c 3 a, b

5 Put students in pairs or small groups to discuss the questions. After 3–4 minutes, invite some students to share their answers for question 1 with the class. For question 2, elicit ideas and list them on the board. Ask students which types of products are / would be popular in their country.

Students' own answers

6 ▶ ALT 3.1.1 Get students to do the matching activity individually or in pairs. Play the video and check answers with the class.

1 b 2 d 3 e 4 a 5 f 6 c

7 Ask students to do this individually and get them to compare answers in pairs before checking with the class.

1 attract customers 2 open a pop-up store
3 test the market 4 financial risk 5 target market
6 expand the business

8 Put students in pairs or small groups and give them a minute to read the questions. Remind them of the meanings of *target market* and *attract customers* if necessary. Give pairs/groups plenty of time to discuss their ideas and encourage them to make notes. Then get feedback from the class – make sure students give reasons for their answers.

Students' own answers

Vocabulary: Shops and the shopping experience

Students look at vocabulary related to shops and shopping.

5 Get students to do the matching exercise individually or in pairs. Encourage them to underline the key words in each definition before they do the matching. Check answers with the class, clarifying meanings as necessary. Explain what *VAT* stands for if students ask (*value-added tax*, a tax added to the price of certain goods and services in Britain and the EU).

1 customers 2 bill 3 branch 4 chain 5 serves
6 charge 7 VAT 8 profit

6 ◀⁾ 3.01 Check students understand the words before playing the recording. To check answers, you could play the recording again and pause after each extract, asking students which words helped them choose the correct answer.

1 butcher's 2 department store 3 bookshop 4 pharmacy
5 clothes shop 6 shopping centre 7 bakery

7 Before students do the matching exercise, check they understand the meaning of verbs 1–8. Give them a minute to look at the nouns/phrases in a–h and ask you about any they do not understand. Check they understand JP¥ (*Japanese yen*). Point out that in order to match a verb with a set of phrases, *all* the words in the set must be possible with the verb. Students may be tempted to choose h for 1, but it is not possible to *charge nothing* – you can only charge an amount, e.g. *He charged me £1.* However, it is possible not to charge someone at all: *They didn't charge me.* Check answers with the class, clarifying meanings as necessary.

1 c 2 d 3 b 4 a 5 h 6 e 7 g 8 f

Extra activities 3.1

C This activity looks at key vocabulary from the lesson. Students should be familiar with the words, so it might be better for them to work individually. Encourage them to look at the words around each gap to help them choose the correct word. Check answers with the class.

1 spend 2 chains 3 bakery 4 customers
5 order 6 serve 7 charge 8 cost 9 VAT 10 bill

8 This activity should be done in two stages. First, get students to choose the correct options individually and check answers with the class. Then put students in pairs or small groups to discuss the questions. Encourage them to give reasons for their opinions. Give them 3–5 minutes to discuss in their pairs/ groups, then elicit ideas around the class.

1 shop 2 chains 3 pay 4 charge 5 make
6 bookshops

Project: Shopping habits

Students carry out a class survey to find out each other's shopping habits.

9A Put students in pairs or small groups, explain the activity and go through the questions with them. Check they understand *discount card*. Refer them to the survey on page 129 and give them 3–4 minutes to choose the correct questions for the gaps. Check answers with the class.

> **1** b **2** g/j **3** i **4** j/g

9B Allow plenty of time for pairs/groups to decide on additional questions for their survey. Explain that they can choose from the questions in Exercise 9A or use their own ideas. Monitor and, if students are writing their own questions, help them with any vocabulary they may need.

9C Put students in new groups to conduct their surveys. Make sure that each new group does not have more than one student from the original pair/groups, so that each student answers a different set of questions. Allow plenty of time for them to ask and answer their questions, and encourage them to make notes of the other students' answers – they will need these for Exercise 9D. For a more extensive survey, you might like students to use an online survey tool. Students could then survey more people and present their findings in graphical form.

9D Put students back in the same pairs/groups as Exercise 9A. Explain that they will now discuss their findings and go through questions 1–3 with them. Allow plenty of time for students to discuss in their pairs/groups, then broaden this into a class discussion. Invite different students to share their findings with the class. What did they find out from their survey? Did any of the answers surprise them?

MyEnglishLab: Teacher's resources: extra activities
Teacher's book: Resource bank Photocopiable 3.1 p.138
Workbook: p.14 Exercises 1–3

3.2 ❯ The retail experience

> ### GSE learning objectives
>
> - Can follow the sequence of events in a short, simple dialogue or narrative.
> - Can identify key details in a simple recorded dialogue or narrative.
> - Can identify specific events from short spoken descriptions.
> - Can distinguish between the Past Simple and Past Continuous.
> - Can use *when* to link two clauses in the past simple.
> - Can ask and answer questions about past times and past activities.
> - Can write short basic descriptions of past events and activities.

Warm-up

Put students in pairs or small groups and ask them to tell each other about their favourite place to shop. What kind of shop is it? How often do they shop there? What do they like about shopping there? Allow them 3–4 minutes to discuss in their pairs/groups, then invite different students to share their answers with the class.

Lead-in

Students talk about different types of shopping experience.

1A Put students in pairs to match the photos with the words in the box, using their dictionaries if necessary. Explain that they need to match two words to each photo. Go over the answers with the class, checking that students understand the vocabulary in the box.

> Photo 1: bazaar, covered market
> Photo 2: magic mirror, try something on
> Photo 3: convenience store, self-service

1B Read out the question and check that students understand *augmented reality* (see Notes below). If time allows, let students discuss in the same pairs as Exercise 1A first, then invite them to share their shopping experiences with the class.

> ### Notes
>
> Students may have used augmented reality (AR) or virtual reality (VR) for gaming and/or on their phones.
>
> - **AR** overlays digital information on real-world elements like maps or photos. *Pokémon GO* is among the best-known examples.
> - **VR** is full immersion in a totally computer-generated environment, usually wearing a headset.
> - **MR** (mixed reality) allows you to interact with and manipulate both physical and virtual items and environments. It provides the ability to have one foot (or hand) in the real world and the other in an imaginary place.

Listening

Students listen to people talking about recent shopping experiences.

2 🔊 3.02 Explain the activity and pre-teach the following words: *QR code* (*Quick Response code* – a code with black and white square patterns that is machine-readable), *scan* (e.g. *scan the QR code*), *self-service*, *browse*, *carpet*. Play the recording, then invite different students to share their ideas with the class, giving reasons. Accept any reasonable answers as long as students can justify them.

> **Possible answers**
>
> The man who visited the Grand Bazaar in Istanbul seems to have had the most positive experience. The woman who visited the automated shop seems the most dissatisfied with her retail experience.

3 3.02 Give students a minute to read the questions. Let them answer as many of the questions as they can, then play the recording again for them to complete/check their answers.

> **1** b **2** a **3** a **4** c **5** c **6** b

Extra activities 3.2

A 3.02 This activity looks at useful vocabulary from the recording. It can be done individually or in pairs. To check answers, play the recording again, pausing at each answer, and clarifying meanings as necessary.

> **1** dinner, evenings **2** browsing **3** seller **4** bargain
> **5** putting on **6** queues, changing rooms **7** cashier
> **8** choose **9** ordering **10** QR **11** bar **12** complain

Grammar: Past Simple

Students study and practise the Past Simple.

4A 3.03 Before students do the exercise, write the following sentence from the recording on the board: *Yes, we had a great time.* Underline *had* and ask students what tense it is in (Past Simple). Refer students to the Grammar reference on page 120. Go over the section on the Past Simple (but not the Past Continuous) with them and make sure they understand why the tense is used and how it is formed. Give them a few minutes to do the exercise individually, then play the recording for them to check their answers.

> **1** Did, have **2** served, sat **3** could **4** left, sent
> **5** didn't speak, arrived **6** went, chose

4B–C Do these as quick whole-class activities. Remind students that there is a list of common irregular verbs on page 126 of the Student's Book. After Exercise 4C, you could refer them to audioscript 3.03 on page 149 to find more examples of regular and irregular verbs in the Past Simple.

> **4B** We use *didn't* + infinitive to make negative sentences in the Past Simple.
> We use *Did* + subject + infinitive … ? for questions in the Past Simple.
>
> **4C** Regular verbs: serve, arrive
> Irregular verbs: have, sit, can, leave, send, speak, go, choose

5 3.04 Get students to work individually for this exercise. Remind them that they can use the Grammar reference on page 120 and the list of irregular verbs on page 126 if they need help. Play the recording for them to check their answers.

> **1** were **2** got **3** Did , pay **4** wrote **5** rang **6** said
> **7** did, meet **8** didn't see **9** didn't come **10** thought

Extra activities 3.2

B This activity gives further practice of the Past Simple. Get students to complete it individually and then to compare answers in pairs before checking with the class.

> **1** bought **2** didn't go **3** Did you go **4** saw, visited
> **5** took, was **6** rang, heard **7** did you catch
> **8** couldn't, weren't

> ## Pronunciation bank
> ## p. 115: Past Simple
>
> ### Warm-up
>
> P3.01 Go through the information in the box with students. Before playing the recording, give an example for each of the vowel sounds mentioned in the box: /aɪ/: tr**ie**d; /eɪ/: m**a**de; /iː/: agr**ee**d; /ɜː/: h**ur**t; /ɔː/: t**au**ght. Play the recording for students to notice the differences between the spelling and the sound actually pronounced.
>
> **1** P3.02 Depending on the strength of your class, you could put them in pairs first and get them to choose their answers before listening. Encourage them to say the words aloud in order to decide, then play the recording for them to check. If time allows, play the recording again for students to listen and repeat.
>
> > **1** different **2** different **3** same **4** different
> > **5** same **6** same **7** same **8** different **9** same
> > **10** different
>
> **2** Do the first item as an example with the class. Then give students a few minutes to do the exercise individually, and get them to compare answers in pairs before checking with the class. During feedback, you could draw a table on the board with one column for each vowel sound and list the different spellings students identify for each one.
>
> > h**ear**d – s**er**ved
> > s**aw** – th**ou**ght
> > agr**ee**d – rec**ei**ved
> > c**a**me – pl**ay**ed
> > arr**i**ved – cr**ie**d
>
> **3** Put students in pairs and explain the activity. Do an example with a stronger student if necessary. While students are working, monitor and correct their pronunciation as necessary.

Past Continuous

Students study and practise the Past Continuous.

6 Do this as a whole-class activity. Look at the examples with students and elicit the form of the Past Continuous. You might like to write the patterns for the positive (subject + *was/were* + *-ing*), negative (subject + *wasn't/weren't* + *-ing*) and question (*was/were* + subject + *-ing*) forms on the board, for students to refer to during Exercise 7. Refer students to the Grammar reference on page 121 and go over the explanations and examples with them. Answer any questions they may have.

> We use *was/were* + verb + *-ing* to make the positive form of the Past Continuous.
> We use *wasn't / was not / weren't / were not* + verb + *-ing* to make the negative form.
> We use (question word) + *was/were* + subject + verb + *-ing* to make the question form.

7 Put students in pairs, explain the activity and do an example with a stronger student before they begin. While they are working, monitor and note down any errors students make with the Past Continuous. Highlight these during feedback. With a stronger class an alternative way to do this activity would be to get them to give unlikely-sounding answers (e.g. *A: What were you doing yesterday at 7 o'clock in the morning? B: I was doing karate in the garden.*), with their partner guessing whether these are true or false.

Extra activities 3.2

C This activity gives further practice of the Past Continuous. Get students to complete it individually, then check answers with the class.

> 1 were preparing   2 was raining   3 was writing
> 4 wasn't listening   5 Were you reading
> 6 weren't working, were chatting   7 was living
> 8 Was she listening

Writing

Students practise the Past Simple and Past Continuous by writing short tweets.

8 Explain the activity and give students a minute to look at the example tweets. Before they begin, teach or elicit the meaning of *tweet* (a short message on social media) and point out the character limit for each tweet. If time is short, students can write some or all of their tweets as homework. If they write them in class, monitor and help as necessary, checking students' use of the Past Simple and Continuous.

Model answers

2
(work)
Yesterday I was presenting product prototypes at the #VideoGames industry conference. We presented some incredible new features in our games and were very happy with the audience response! We met some interesting customers and got some great feedback. Thanks to all! @videogamesconference @Stargames

(college)
I was still writing my #economics essay last night when I heard that we got a deadline extension. Great news! We completed our case study project and gave our presentations in the morning so tonight I can focus on the essay. What time does the library close this evening? @collegelibrary @businessstudiesgroup

3
Last weekend I went to Madrid with friends. We visited the Prado Museum and Parque Retiro, ate tapas and went shopping in the #Salamanca neighbourhood. We also went to a football match at #Atletico_Madrid – but I missed the only goal because I was getting a drink! @placestovisit @longweekend

MyEnglishLab: Teacher's resources: extra activities; Reading bank
Grammar reference: p.120 Past Simple and Past Continuous
Pronunciation bank: p.115 Past Simple
Teacher's book: Resource bank Photocopiable 3.2 p.139
Workbook: p.15 Exercises 1–4, p.16 Exercises 1–3

3.3 ❯ Communication skills
Solving workflow problems

GSE learning objectives

- Can follow the sequence of events in a short, simple dialogue or narrative.
- Can identify key details in a simple recorded dialogue or narrative.
- Can identify specific events from short spoken descriptions.
- Can make and respond to suggestions.
- Can explain what they like or dislike about something.

Warm-up

Ask students to think about a time they worked in a team when not everything went well. What problems were there? What do they think caused these problems? How could these problems have been avoided? Put students in groups and give them a few minutes to discuss, then invite different students to share their experiences with the class. Ask the class if they like working in teams and why / why not.

Lead-in

Students discuss possible workflow problems and causes.

1A Put students in pairs and give them 2–3 minutes to discuss the question. Teach or elicit the meaning of *deadlines* in question 3. As feedback, invite different students to share their views with the class, giving reasons.

1B Students could do this in the same pairs as Exercise 1A or in new pairs. Go through the definition of *workflow* with them and also check they understand the phrases in the box. Once students have discussed in their pairs, broaden this into a class discussion. In stronger classes, you could also ask students to suggest possible solutions for the problems (see below).

Possible answer

A lot of time is wasted trying to contact people who don't return their phone calls or answer their emails and this negatively affects workflow. As working in project teams is so common these days, missing deadlines is even more serious. If others are waiting for you to complete your task before they can begin theirs, you may be holding up an entire project. When projects fall behind schedule, it can cost a company a large amount of money. People who don't work well in teams probably cause the biggest problems of all. With so much work now involving teams (and virtual teams), it is probably not a good idea to employ such people.

Video

Students watch a video about different approaches to solving workflow problems.

2A ▶ 3.3.1 If your students watched the Unit 2 video, ask them to give you a short summary of the situation and the main characters. If this is the first communication skills video your class have watched, briefly set up the context and/or refer students to page 6 of the Coursebook. Encourage students to make notes in answer to the questions while watching, and play the video. Check answers with the class.

1 Thiago is worried about a project he's doing for Shaun. He's nearly a week late with it.
2 Azra suggests he asks for an extension because a few days won't make much difference. But the report is already a week overdue, so this may not be a great idea.
3 Thiago jokes about it, but it seems Shaun was angry.

2B Check that students understand *avoid* and discuss the question as a class.

By avoiding Shaun, Thiago is probably making things worse. At some point, he will have to face him, so the sooner he does this, the better.

3A ▶ 3.3.2 Explain that students are going to watch Thiago's conversation with Shaun and give them time to read the questions. Check they understand *reject, excuse, blame, workflow problem* and *outcome*. Play the video, twice if necessary, then check answers with the class.

1 Shaun. By catching Thiago and making him discuss the problem, he is in a strong position to question Thiago's ability to complete the task and get him to him do things he doesn't want to do.
2 a) Shaun rejects Thiago's explanations as excuses. (He tells him that time management is part of the job, and criticizes Thiago for not asking him to help with getting the figures from Accounts.)
3 Yes (He blames Thiago for 1) not being able to manage his time, 2) holding up the whole project team, 3) being a week late with the report, 4) leaving him with nothing to show the directors at the meeting he has the next day, and 5) not asking for help to get the figures he needs for the report yet.)
4 Shaun suggests that Jasmine helps Thiago finish the report by tomorrow afternoon. Thiago doesn't like this, but has to accept it. (Thiago suggests that Shaun gives him an extension, but Shaun rejects this idea.)
5 Shaun

3B Elicit ideas around the class for this question.

Shaun should be less aggressive towards Thiago. Thiago also needs to be less defensive and try to make some suggestions of his own to complete his task.

3C ▶ 3.3.3 Explain that students are going to watch another version of Thiago's meeting with Shaun, where Shaun approaches the situation differently, and answer the same questions they answered for Video A. Play the video, then check answers with the class.

1 Thiago. By going to see Shaun in his office Thiago takes responsibility for his failure to meet the deadline. This puts him in a stronger position to explain why he has failed and what he needs to complete the report.
2 b) Shaun listens and tries to think of ways to help.
3 Shaun doesn't blame Thiago for anything directly, but he does make it clear that he urgently needs the report to be finished.
4 Shaun makes two suggestions: 1) that he talks to Accounts about getting the figures Thiago needs and 2) that he gets another trainee to share some of Thiago's workload for a few days. Later he also suggests that Jasmine helps, as well as giving Thiago a three-day extension to complete the report. Thiago suggests that he produces an executive summary of the main points in the report for Shaun to show at the directors' meeting. They both agree on these suggestions.
5 Thiago is very happy with the outcome of the meeting. Shaun is also satisfied that he will finally get the report he needs, but he realises that he needs to talk to Thiago about time management.

4A–B Discuss the questions as a class. Invite different students to share their views, giving reasons.

4A In most cases, the most important question to ask is 'How can we fix it?' Looking back at what went wrong is less useful than looking forward at what needs to go right.

4B It can be useful to ask 'What is going wrong?' if you are worried that the same problem may happen again or if the problem is a technical one (e.g. software that doesn't work properly). 'Whose fault is it?' is only useful if one person in a team is repeatedly causing workflow problems and holding up the others. This person may need to be retrained or replaced.

5 ▶ 3.3.4 Explain that students are going to watch the last section of the video, where the speaker talks about the advantages and disadvantages of the different approaches they watched in Videos A and B. They should watch and compare what is said with their answers to Exercise 4. Play the video and, if time allows, let students discuss briefly in pairs or small groups first. Round up ideas in a class discussion.

Reflection

Students reflect on the conclusions from the video and their own approach to problem-solving and decision-making.

6 Allow students to work individually on this so that they can reflect on their own preferred style and ideas. Ask them to think of their own answers to the questions and to make notes. Then put them in pairs to discuss and compare their answers. Get brief feedback from the class.

Functional language: Solving problems

Students look at useful language for solving problems.

7 Draw students' attention to the diagram and explain that it shows three steps for asking someone about their progress with a task, and that items 1–6 are useful questions/phrases they can use in each step. Let them complete the exercise individually or in pairs, then check answers with the class, clarifying meaning as necessary.

> 1 b 2 c 3 a 4 b 5 c 6 a

8A Explain that the phrases in the box are different ways to make suggestions. Let students try to complete the exercise individually, then get them to compare answers in pairs before checking with the class. During feedback, clarify meanings as necessary and point out the different patterns used with each of the phrases in the box (*let me* + infinitive, *how about* + *-ing*, etc.). This will help students select the correct phrases in Exercise 8B.

> 1 Let me   2 I'll see   3 What else   4 What if / How about
> 5 How about   6 Why don't I

8B Explain the activity and get students to complete it individually. Remind them to think about the pattern used with each phrase. Check answers with the class. You might also like to teach/check understanding of some useful vocabulary here: *increase the budget, rethink the schedule, flexibility, (give someone an) extension, assistant.*

> 1 Let me   2 I'll see   3 What else   4 What if / How about
> 5 How about   6 Why don't I

8C Tell students that 1–6 are all ways to respond to the suggestions they looked at in Exercises 8A and 8B. Point out that some responses may match more than one suggestion. Let them complete the exercise individually and allow them to compare answers in pairs before checking with the class. During feedback, check understanding of each response, focusing on the words in bold.

1 **Thanks, I'm not great with numbers!**
Let me deal with Accounts.
What if / How about I bring in [someone] to help you out?
How about asking [someone] to help you with some of the figures?
Why don't I get you some help? / give you an assistant?

2 **Someone to assist with the paperwork would be a big help.**
I'll see if I can get [someone] to share some of your workload.
What else can we do to get this report finished?
What if / How about I bring in [someone] to help you out?
What else can I do to help? / do we need to do?
How about adding more people to the project team?
Why don't I get you some help? / give you an assistant?

3 **Having a couple more people on the team would really speed things up.**
What else can we do to get this report finished?
What if / How about I bring in [someone] to help you out?
How about asking [someone] to help you with some of the figures?
What else can I do to help? / do we need to do?
How about adding more people to the project team?
Why don't I get you some help? / give you an assistant?

4 **Good, I'm having problems with some of the software.**
Let me try and get you some IT support.

5 **Great, another five days should be enough.**
What if / How about we make the deadline later?
What if / How about I give you an extension?
How about rethinking the schedule?

6 **An extra 10 percent would make a big difference.**
I'll see if we can increase the budget / if there's any flexibility in the budget.

Extra activities 3.3

A This activity practises the functional language from the lesson. Ask students to do it individually and get them to compare answers in pairs before class feedback. If time allows, you could put students in pairs to practise the conversations. In stronger classes, you could also ask them to choose one of the conversations and rewrite it using different phrases from Exercises 7 and 8. If time is short, divide the class into three groups, get each group to look at one conversation, then go over all of them during feedback.

> **Conversation 1:**
> a 1 b 6 c 9 d 2 e 8 f 7 g 5 h 4 i 3
> **Conversation 2:**
> a 1 b 6 c 5 d 8 e 9 f 3 g 7 h 4 i 2
> **Conversation 3:**
> a 1 b 9 c 3 d 5 e 8 f 7 g 6 h 2 i 4

Speaker 1 and page 131 for Speaker 2). If time allows, you could get a few pairs to act out their conversation for the class.

10 Do this activity as a whole class, inviting students to share their experiences. You could also ask them to rate themselves for each point (e.g. out of 5). In stronger classes, students could discuss what could be done to avoid a problem next time. Finally, discuss any points you noted while monitoring.

MyEnglishLab: Teacher's resources: extra activities; Interactive video activities; Functional language bank
Pronunciation bank: p.115 Stress in short sentences
Workbook: p.17, Exercise 1

> ## Pronunciation bank
> ### p. 115: Stress in short sentences
>
> ### Warm-up
> 🔊 P3.03 Write the following phrase from Exercise 7 on the board: *Any progress with that report?* Invite a different student to read out each of the words in isolation. Then say the sentence yourself, using the correct sentence stress (*Any progress with that report?*). Ask students if they notice anything about the way you said the sentence. Are any words stressed more than others? Refer students to the information in the box to explain the concept of sentence stress. Play the recording for them to hear the examples and drill them around the class.

1A–B Let students work individually, then compare answers in pairs. Encourage them to say the sentences aloud, tapping the desk or snapping their fingers on each stressed word. To help them, you could tell them that there are two stressed words in sentences 1–4 and three in sentences 5–8. Do not confirm answers yet, as students will check them in the next exercise.

> **1A**
> 1 <u>How's</u> it going?
> 2 You <u>look</u> a bit <u>worried</u>.
> 3 I'm <u>sure</u> he'll <u>understand</u>.
> 4 I'm <u>still</u> having <u>problems</u>.
>
> **1B**
> 5 I'm <u>going</u> as <u>fast</u> as I <u>can</u>.
> 6 <u>How</u> about <u>asking</u> someone to <u>help</u>?
> 7 I'll <u>see</u> if I can <u>get</u> you some <u>support</u>.
> 8 <u>How</u> are you <u>doing</u> with that <u>report</u>?

2 🔊 P3.04 Play the recording for students to check their answers.

3 Put students in pairs and demonstrate the activity with a stronger student. During the activity, monitor and check students are stressing the correct words.

Task

Students roleplay resolving different workflow problems.

9 Put students in pairs and ask them to read situation 1 and decide on their roles. Refer Speaker 1s to page 133 and Speaker 2s to page 139 to read the details of their roles. Monitor while students are reading and answer any questions. Tell students that they need to make sure they do all three things outlined for their role. Remind them of the three steps in Exercise 7 for asking someone about their progress with a task and tell them that they should use language from Exercises 7 and 8 in their roleplays. Allow students 4–5 minutes to prepare, while you monitor and help as necessary. Set a time limit for the meetings and ask students to begin. During the activity, monitor and note down any points to highlight during feedback. When pairs have finished the first meeting, they swap roles. Repeat the same steps for situation 2 (students should refer to page 129 for

3.4 ❯ Business skills
Presenting results

> ### GSE learning objectives
> * Can follow the main points in a simple audio recording aimed at a general audience.
> * Can identify key details in a simple recorded dialogue or narrative.
> * Can extract the key details from a presentation if delivered slowly and clearly.
> * Can use basic discourse markers to structure a short presentation.
> * Can make and respond to suggestions.

> ### Warm-up
> Discuss the following questions with the class: *Have you ever given a presentation? Have you ever been to a presentation? What was it like? What do you think went well? What do you think makes a presentation successful?*

Lead-in

Students read and discuss advice on structuring a presentation.

1 Put students in pairs and give them 1–2 minutes to read the text. Check they understand *audience, destination, move on, go back* and *change direction*. Once students have discussed their ideas, elicit answers as a class. Ask students what 'GPS for presenters' might mean. (It is what you need to do in order to make it clear to your audience where you are going in your presentation. The basic idea is: tell them what you're going to tell them, tell them, tell them what you told them!)

> 1 Like a journey, a presentation has a starting point and a destination. On the way to your destination you usually want to keep moving on, but sometimes you may want to change direction or go back. It's a good idea to indicate when you want to do this.
> 2 The text says you need to provide a clear map of your talk. What this means is that, at the start of your presentation, you explain the different stages that your presentation will go through and the order you will go through them.

Listening

Students listen to a presentation about the results of a customer service survey.

2A Put students in pairs and give them a minute to look at the slides and ask you about any vocabulary they do not know. Check they understand the following words: *customer satisfaction, ratings, in-store, focus group, data collection* and *people skills* and the adjectives in the word cloud. Let students discuss in their pairs for 1–2 minutes, then elicit ideas around the class. Do not confirm the answer yet as students will check their ideas in the next exercise.

2B 🔊 3.05   Give students a minute to read the questions, then play the recording and check answers with the class.

> 1 last month's customer service survey
> 2 **a** Carl **b** Carl **c** Inés
> 3 after the talk
> 4 from the in-store customer feedback stations (in megastores)

2C Put students in pairs and give them 2–3 minutes to discuss the question, then discuss as a class. Make sure students give reasons for their answers.

> Carl's overview is very clear. He tells listeners the subject of the presentation and why it's important. He then describes each stage of the presentation in advance and tells us who will speak about each stage.

3A 🔊 3.06   Check students understand *recommend*, then play the recording and check answers with the class.

> 1 Lots of customers don't use the customer feedback stations at all. And even customers who rate the service as 'great' don't say why, and don't say if they recommend the company to others.
> 2 On average, each happy customer recommends the store to five other people.
> 3 1 out of 12 unhappy customers leave feedback, so 11 out of 12 unhappy customers don't leave any feedback at all.

3B 🔊 3.06   Do this as a whole-class activity. Play the recording, then elicit ideas from different students.

> **Possible answer**
> Pauses give the audience (and Carl) more time to think before moving on.

4 🔊 3.07   Explain that students are going to hear the last part of the presentation and give them a minute to read the questions. Weaker students may need to listen a second time.

> 1 how the company's sales advisers can improve their service
> 2 Fifteen. The research team asked them to list ten adjectives to describe the ideal mobile phone Sales Adviser.
> 3 They were expecting more people to want a 'knowledgeable' and 'informative' sales consultant to help them with their purchase. But the focus groups were more interested in having 'helpful' and 'friendly' service.
> 4 The company's sales consultants have sufficient product knowledge, but insufficient people skills to deal with their customers, and Inés recommends training in this area.

Functional language: Signposting a presentation

Students look at useful language for signposting a presentation.

5 Draw students' attention to the heading and check understanding. Explain that they are going to look at useful phrases for presenting information in a clear, organised way. Do this activity with the whole class, clarifying meanings as necessary.

> 1 First of all, … 2 Secondly, … 3 Then … 4 Finally, …

6 For weaker classes, students could work in pairs for this activity. Let them try to work out the answers themselves, using dictionaries if necessary, clarifying answers during feedback.

> 1 start 2 move 3 brings 4 hand 5 sum 6 look
> 7 recap 8 jump 9 wrap 10 started

Extra activities 3.4

A This activity looks at the functional language from Exercise 6. Get students to complete it individually, then check answers with the class.

> 1 d 2 c 3 a 4 e 5 b 6 i 7 j 8 g 9 h 10 f

B This activity looks at useful vocabulary from the listening activities. Depending on the strength of your class, you could ask students to work individually or in pairs. Alternatively, you could do this as a whole-class activity, checking answers and clarifying meanings as you go. If this is done with students working individually / in pairs, check students' understanding of the words during feedback.

> 1 in-store interview 2 customer satisfaction ratings
> 3 focus group 4 research team 5 people skills
> 6 product knowledge 7 knowledgeable
> 8 Sales Adviser

Task

Students give a presentation with a colleague.

7A Put students in groups of four and divide each group into two pairs, A and B. Explain that each pair is going to give a presentation, and refer the pairs to their information for Presentation A or B (page 127).

7B Give pairs time to read their information while you monitor and help them with any questions they may have. Let students decide who will be Presenter 1 and Presenter 2 and make sure they are clear about what they have to do. Point out that they need to structure their presentations carefully, using the signposting phrases from Exercises 5 and 6. You might also like to refer them to the bullet points in Exercise 7D (or write these on the board) and tell them that they should do these things in their presentations. Set a time limit for the preparation stage and tell students that they can also prepare some simple slides if they like. Monitor and help as necessary.

7C In their groups, students take turns to give their presentations. Set a time limit for each presentation and ask students to begin. Monitor and note down any points to highlight during feedback.

7D Go through the bullet points and let students discuss in their groups. Again, monitor and note down any points to discuss during feedback. After 3–4 minutes, invite different students to share their experience with the class. Finally, discuss any points you noted while monitoring.

MyEnglishLab: Teacher's resources: extra activities; Functional language bank
Workbook: p.17 Exercises 2–4

3.5 ❯ Writing

An online review form

GSE learning objectives

- Can identify specific information in simple letters, brochures and short articles.
- Can use language related to reviews, success and awards.
- Can write a simple review of a film, book or TV programme using a limited range of language.

Warm-up

Dictate or write the following questions on the board: *Do you ever complete online review forms? If yes, what was the last one you completed for? Do you ever read online reviews? If yes, how useful do you think they are? Why do you think companies ask for them?* Put students in pairs or small groups and give them 3–4 minutes to discuss the questions, then get brief feedback from the class.

Lead-in

Students read and complete an online review form.

1 Ask students to read the review quickly before attempting the exercise. You might like to ask a few questions, e.g. *What is this a review of?* (a restaurant) *Is the writer a regular customer?*

(yes) *Are they generally happy with the food and service?* (yes, although the service is sometimes slow). Ask students to complete the review individually and get them to compare answers in pairs before class feedback.

> **1** eat   **2** ate   **3** brought   **4** were celebrating   **5** bring
> **6** changes   **7** didn't arrive   **8** have   **9** offers
> **10** recommend

Functional language

Students look at useful phrases in online review forms.

2A Go through the headings in the box with students and ask them to complete the exercise individually. Alternatively, if time is short, you could do this as a quick whole-class activity, checking answers as you go along.

> **1** Background   **2** Good points   **3** Bad points
> **4** Recommendation

2B Again, this can be done as a whole-class activity, nominating a different student to name the correct category for each phrase, and confirming answers as you go along.

> **Background**
> We sometimes have company lunches there.
> We had dinner there two days ago.
> **Good points**
> The view from the restaurant is wonderful.
> The food is always excellent.
> **Bad points**
> It is too expensive.
> The food was terrible.
> **Recommendation**
> I'm afraid I cannot recommend your restaurant to other people/businesses.

Extra activities 3.5

A–B These activities look at useful language for online review forms. First, ask students to match the sentence halves and check answers with the class. Then get them to match each sentence with the correct category. They could do this individually or in pairs. Weaker classes could refer to the table on page 36 if they need help.

> **A**
> **1** e   **2** g   **3** a   **4** f   **5** d   **6** h   **7** c   **8** b
>
> **B**
> **1** Background: 1, 2   **2** Good points: 3, 4
> **3** Bad points: 5, 6, 7   **4** Recommendation: 8

Optional grammar work

The review in Exercise 1 contains examples of adverbs, so you could use it for some optional grammar work. Refer students to the Grammar reference on page 121 and use the exercises in MyEnglishLab for extra grammar practice.

Task

Students complete an online review form.

3A Put students in pairs, refer them to the review form on page 130 and give them 3–4 minutes to complete the exercise. After checking answers, you could ask students to match the reviewer's comments with the categories in the table in Exercise 2A.

> **How often do you stay here?**
> Our company sometimes has conferences at the Flamingo Palace and has visitors staying there almost every week.
> **When did you last stay here?**
> Two of our clients stayed there a few days ago.
> **What was the purpose of your last visit?**
> They were visiting our new factory and attending meetings in our offices.
> **What do/did you like about the hotel?**
> Our clients are usually happy with the Flamingo. The location of the hotel is very convenient for our company. The food is always good in the restaurant and the price is reasonable.
> **Is/Was there anything you aren't/weren't happy with?**
> The rooms are a little small and sometimes they are not cleaned very well, so we think it is a little bit too expensive.
> **Would you recommend us?**
> We recommend the Flamingo Palace for low-cost business trips in the area, but unfortunately, we cannot recommend it to everyone.

3B Explain the writing task and remind students that they should use phrases from Exercises 2A and 2B. Tell them that they can use the reviews on pages 36 and 130 as models if they need help.

> **Model answer**
> **How often do you eat here?**
> I usually eat in the Flame once a week.
> **When did you last eat here?**
> I last ate there yesterday lunchtime.
> **What was the purpose of your last visit?**
> We often bring our clients to the restaurant and yesterday I had a meeting with one of our biggest clients.
> **What do/did you like about the restaurant?**
> The food is always excellent at the Flame and the location is perfect for us as it is close to our office. Also, our clients are always amazed because the view from the restaurant is wonderful.
> **Is/Was there anything you aren't/weren't happy with?**
> Sometimes the service can be quite slow and yesterday the restaurant was very busy and the food didn't arrive very quickly. Unfortunately, our client had to leave before dessert was served.
> **Would you recommend us?**
> I'm afraid I cannot recommend your restaurant to other businesses at this time.

3C If students do the writing task for homework, you could do this exercise in the next lesson. Put students in pairs and ask them to read their partner's review and think about the questions. You could also ask them to check if their partner

has used phrases from the table in Exercise 2 and if yes, if he/she has used them correctly. Students could then rewrite their reviews (or write a new review on the basis of their partner's feedback).

MyEnglishLab: Teacher's resources: extra activities; Interactive grammar practice; Writing bank
Grammar reference: p.121 Types of adverbs
Workbook: p.18 Exercises 1–3

Business workshop ❯ 3
Pop-up stores

> ### GSE learning objectives
> - Can identify specific information in simple letters, brochures and short articles.
> - Can identify specific information in a simple factual text.
> - Can communicate in routine tasks requiring simple, direct exchanges of information.
> - Can follow the main points in a simple audio recording aimed at a general audience.
> - Can follow the main points in a simple audio recording, if provided with written supporting material.
> - Can make and respond to suggestions.

Background

Students read about plans to open pop-up stores in an area of Vancouver, Canada.

1 Draw students' attention to the main title and teach or elicit the meaning of *pop-up stores* (temporary retail stores which open suddenly and usually exist for a short amount of time). Ask students if pop-up businesses are common in their country/city/area and if yes, what type of products they usually sell. You could mention that a a pop-up store may also be referred to as *pop-up shop* (usually in the UK or Australia), *pop-up retail* or *flash retail*. Ask students to read the background and discuss the questions in pairs. Check answers with the class. (Note that it is not necessary to spend long on question 4 as more answers are given in the next section.)

> 1 It was an old industrial part of the city with empty warehouses and factories. Today it is a popular area with new high-rise offices and apartments and some old buildings.
> 2 It is a temporary shop that can be open for a day or several months.
> 3 four types: people starting a new business, existing small businesses, online businesses and large retailers
> 4 Possible answers: It's cheaper than a long rental lease. It's a lower-risk way to see if a business idea will work.

Pop-up stories

Students read articles about the benefits of pop-up retail.

2A Check that students understand *experimenting* and give them time to read the article and discuss the question in pairs. Check the answer with the class.

They are opening pop-up stores and collection points in city centres and small stores in some areas. They are trying these types of store because their big warehouse stores outside of city centres are losing popularity.

Note

Students may be surprised to read that IKEA is based in the Netherlands. The company was founded in Sweden (in 1943) but its headquarters is actually in Leiden, Netherlands.

2B If there is time, let students discuss the question in pairs or groups first, then broaden this into a class discussion.

Possible answer

It seems likely that pop-up stores are a good way to create more interest in retailers' new products. However, it's more of a marketing strategy than a way to create huge sales.

3A Put students in groups of three and refer them to their articles on pages 93, 132 and 137. Explain that they are each going to read a different article but answer the same set of questions. Get them to read their article and make notes to answer the three questions. Monitor and help as necessary but do not discuss the answers with the class yet, as students will talk about their texts in the next exercise.

Richard's Pop-up Chocolates

1 He left his office job to start his business three years ago.
2 He sells artisan handmade chocolates which he makes at home. (He also sells online.)
3 He doesn't have to pay for a permanent store, he can plan his pop-up shops around major 'chocolate' holidays, he can have face time with customers, offer them samples to taste and get repeat customers. He can't do this when he sells online.

Angelica's Fashion Jewellery

1 She studied art and design at university.
2 She creates and sells her own jewellery and makes personalised jewellery. (She also sells online.)
3 She can sell her products at other people's stores, art galleries and temporary exhibitions, she doesn't have fixed retail opening hours and she likes the flexibility. People will come to her pop-up events to see her new designs. Retail habits are changing and younger customers want more urban boutique-style shopping experiences like pop-ups. Also there is a movement away from big stores towards shopping small and local.

Martine's Coffee Shop

1 She started her own business last week. Before that, she was a barista in a large coffee chain.
2 She sells top-quality coffee.
3 She can move around the city with the van. It's quick and easy to park and open for business. She often makes many stops in a day. Weekdays she focuses on the office workers and shoppers. Weekends she parks near big events. She's finding out the best places to be.

3B In their groups, students take turns to tell each other about their text. They can refer to their notes but they should use their own words and not read from the text. When they have finished, discuss the answers to Exercise 3A with the class.

3C If there is time, let students discuss the questions in their groups first, then elicit ideas around the class.

Suggested answers

Richard's Pop-up Chocolates

He mentions that the chocolates are expensive so people who are happy to pay for high-end handmade chocolates. This might be a good gift that people would buy for others.

Angelica's Fashion Jewellery

Again, these might make good gifts. Also people who are interested in art who go to the exhibitions where she has her pop-up events, and people who are looking for nice jewellery to buy in the clothes stores where she has her pop-ups, might be interested.

Martine's Coffee Shop

Office workers and shoppers who like good coffee and pass her van on the way to work or the shops during the day.

Yaletown is potentially a good place for all three pop-ups as there are a lot of office workers.

Extra activities Business workshop 3

A This activity looks at useful vocabulary from the reading texts. With stronger classes, you could let students use their dictionaries to complete the exercise, then clarify meanings during feedback. With weaker classes, you may prefer to do this as a whole-class activity, checking answers and clarifying meanings as you go along.

> **1** c **2** a **3** b **4** e **5** f **6** d **7** h **8** i **9** g **10** l **11** k **12** j

What people want

Students listen to extracts from market research interviews.

4 ◀BW 3.01   Explain that students are going to listen to extracts from market research interviews and correct the mistakes in the notes for each interview. Give them time to read the notes, then play the recording, twice if necessary. Check answers with the class.

One young person I interviewed said ~~all~~ *some of* the places to go in the evening were expensive. He said he and his co-workers liked to ~~have dinner~~ *socialise* together after work.

One office worker I spoke to said she likes to buy ~~natural health~~ *personal* care products. The price of the products was ~~more~~ *less* important to her than the quality.

Another shopper I interviewed told me she ~~likes~~ *doesn't like* to go to shopping malls. She ~~always wears~~ *doesn't want to wear* the ~~clothes~~ *fashions* and colours that are popular.

Extra activities Business workshop 3

B 🔊 BW 3.01 This activity provides students with extra listening practice. Give students a minute to read the statements and check they understand *personal care*, *fragrance* and *unique*. Play the recording, then check answers with the class. With stronger classes, you could ask students to correct the false statements – they may need to listen again for this.

1 True **2** False **3** False **4** True **5** False **6** True
7 True **8** False **9** True

Task: Design your own pop-up store

Students design and present their own pop-up store and then create an advertisement for it.

5A Put students in small groups and explain that they are going to design their own pop-up store. Go through the 'Remember to' points with them and check any unknown words. Then allow groups 3–5 minutes to discuss and decide on the type of pop-up store they are going to open. Ask students to make notes as they will need to present their ideas in the next activity.

5B Now put students in pairs with someone from a different group. They take it in turns to present their group's ideas to their partner, who then gives them feedback. To help them, you could list some points on the board to think about and comment on, e.g. *the suitability of the location for the types of good sold*; *the layout of the inside of the shop*; *the type of special offer chosen*. You could add *any other details* as a fourth point, so that students can be more creative. Remind them that they can refer to their notes from Exercise 5A.

5C Put students back into their original groups. They now take it in turns to report the other students' reactions to their group's special offer, and decide what changes/improvements they need to make to their original plan. Again, encourage them to make notes.

5D Students now design an ad for their pop-up store. Remind them to refer to the 'Remember to' points and the notes they made during the previous stages. Groups share their adverts and present their ideas, and the class can vote on the best ad / the best pop-up store.

Model answer

Angelica's Fashion Jewellery

Winter Pop-up Store

Hamilton Street, Yaletown

Come and shop in my new pop-up store.

Special new designs for the winter from an independent designer. You will not find these designs in any other stores. It's the perfect place to browse for an unusual item for yourself or an original gift for someone.

From 1 November to 21 December only.

For more information about my designs and the pop-up event visit: www.angelicasfashionjewellery.com.

MyEnglishLab: Teacher's resources: extra activities

Review ◀3

1 **1** pharmacy **2** bill **3** branch **4** charges **5** by
6 spend **7** stores **8** ordered
2 **1** decided **2** did not / didn't want **3** caught
4 arrived **5** went **6** rang **7** did not / didn't have
8 told
3 **1** were you doing **2** was having **3** were you talking
4 were discussing **5** Were you visiting
6 was not / wasn't **7** were sitting
4 **1** just **2** looking **3** moment **4** How are **5** with
6 about **7** Having **8** help
5 **1** Second = First **2** be = get **3** start = move
4 give = hand/pass **5** hand = recap **6** sum = wrap
6 **1** once a week **2** last **3** was visiting
4 always excellent **5** Unfortunately **6** highly

4 ⟩⟩ Work patterns

Unit overview

	CLASSWORK	FURTHER WORK
4.1 ⟩ **My working life**	**Lead-in** Students talk about their working week. **Video** Students watch a video of people talking about their working day and working lives. **Vocabulary** Students look at vocabulary to describe jobs and contracts. **Project** Students research work patterns in their country.	**MyEnglishLab:** Teacher's resources: extra activities **Pronunciation bank:** p.115 Vowel sounds: British English and American English **Teacher's book:** Resource bank Photocopiable 4.1 p.140 **Workbook:** p.19 Exercises 1–3
4.2 ⟩ **Executives at work**	**Lead-in** Students talk about an average day in their working week. **Reading** Students read two interviews with successful businesswomen. **Grammar** Students study and practise the Present Perfect Simple. **Speaking** Students practise the Present Perfect Simple by interviewing a partner.	**MyEnglishLab:** Teacher's resources: extra activities; Reading bank **Grammar reference:** p.122 Present Perfect Simple **Pronunciation bank:** p.116 Present Perfect Simple **Teacher's book:** Resource bank Photocopiable 4.2 p.141 **Workbook:** p.20 Exercises 1–4
4.3 ⟩ **Communication skills:** Making group decisions	**Lead-in** Students discuss different approaches to decision-making. **Video** Students watch a video about different approaches to decision-making. **Reflection** Students reflect on the conclusions from the video and discuss their own approaches to decision-making. **Functional language** Students look at useful language for decision-making meetings. **Task** Students roleplay discussing proposals in a meeting.	**MyEnglishLab:** Teacher's resources: extra activities; interactive video activities; Functional language bank **Workbook:** p.21 Exercises 1–4, p.22 Exercises 1 and 2
4.4 ⟩ **Business skills:** Phoning to change arrangements	**Lead-in** Students talk about making arrangements over the phone. **Listening** Students listen to phone calls where the speakers change arrangements. **Functional language** Students look at useful language for rescheduling appointments on the phone. **Task** Students roleplay a phone call to reschedule a meeting.	**MyEnglishLab:** Teacher's resources: extra activities; Functional language bank **Workbook:** p.22 Exercise 3
4.5 ⟩ **Writing:** Confirming arrangements	**Lead-in** Students read and complete two emails making and confirming arrangements. **Functional language** Students look at useful language for making and confirming arrangements in formal emails. **Task** Students write emails making and confirming arrangements.	**MyEnglishLab:** Teacher's resources: extra activities; Interactive grammar practice; Writing bank **Grammar reference:** p.122 Prepositions of time **Workbook:** p.23 Exercises 1–3
Business workshop 4 ⟩ The Holsted way	**Listening** Students listen to a presentation about company culture. Students listen to a meeting between senior managers about work patterns. **Task** Students roleplay a meeting negotiating new work patterns for Holsted. **Writing** Students write an email summarising decisions made at a meeting.	**MyEnglishLab:** Teacher's resources: extra activities

Business brief

The main aim of this unit is to introduce students to the concept of **work patterns** and different ways of working.

A work pattern describes the days, hours and regularity that a person works in their job. A typical pattern for a **full-time** position with a **fixed schedule** might be 9 a.m. to 5 p.m. (**nine-to-five**) from Monday to Friday. In contrast, someone working **part-time** would be employed for fewer hours or days, usually between 10 and 20 hours a week.

The consistency or security in work patterns varies from country to country. For example in the UK, for those on **zero-hours contracts**, an employer is not obliged to provide a minimum number of working hours at all. A employee simply signs a contract to say that they will be available for work when required. Around three percent of the population currently work on these controversial contracts, which are widely used in the hospitality and health sectors.

In **shift work** the work block is divided into set periods of time (**shifts**) during which employees carry out their **duties**. Shift workers usually work regular hours or days, but outside the nine-to-five work pattern. Shift work may include working during the night or early hours of the morning, the pattern **rotating** depending on requirements.

Whereas shift work allows an organisation to provide cover over a 24-hour period, **flexible hours** (or **flexitime**) allow employees to adapt their work hours to fit with their lifestyle. They need to be present in the workplace during **core hours** (usually 10 a.m.–3 p.m.) but outside of this can work longer or shorter days, depending on their commitments outside work as well as their workload. This popular work pattern can provide a better **work-life balance**. A variation of flexitime is **compressed hours**, where employees work the same number of weekly hours as their colleagues, but over fewer days.

Some countries have experimented with work patterns in recent decades. In France companies are encouraged to issue guidelines stating that staff should not read work communications in the evening or at weekends. In New Zealand and Sweden reduced working-hour trials have been conducted in order to improve working conditions and reduce stress – in New Zealand by switching to a four-day week and in Sweden by switching to a six-hour day. The results of both trials were positive, with increased employee productivity and improved well-being being reported. However, these strategies have not yet been adopted on a wider basis.

Work patterns often depend on the **mode** of employment. A person who is **self-employed** has greater flexibility regarding their working hours compared to a person who works in a company. However, a self-employed person's position might be less secure since regular hours are not guaranteed, contracts are often short-term, and they must make their own pension and healthcare contributions.

Another big change in recent years has been around people's **employment history**. In the past, an employee might join a company after school or university and then stay there for decades, or even until they **retired**. Now it is more usual for a person to have a number of jobs during their working life. There has also been a rise in the number of **temporary workers**, those working for a company on **fixed short-term contracts**. These are often used where a company has a project to complete within a specific time-frame and therefore requires more staff for a limited period.

In many countries, rising **unemployment** means that candidates need to show relevant work experience on their **CV**, as well as the right qualifications, in order to be considered for a full-time position. One result of this has been the increase in the number of **internships** being taken up in the workplace. An **intern** is usually a younger person who works unpaid for a limited time in order to gain work experience, which will eventually help them get started in their chosen career.

Work patterns and your students

It is important that students are aware of the concept of work patterns. It is helpful for pre-work students to begin thinking about what type of work pattern would suit them and for in-work students to describe their own work patterns. As work patterns differ from country to country, it may be useful for both pre-work and working students to be aware that what is normal in their country might not be the same elsewhere.

Unit lead-in

Draw students' attention to the unit title and elicit or give a brief explanation of the term *work patterns* (see Note below). Use this as an opportunity to pre-teach vocabulary for the video in Lesson 1, e.g. *part-time/full-time, temporary/freelance work, flexible working hours*. Refer students to the quote and discuss it briefly. What does it mean? Do students agree? Why? / Why not? How important is it to do a job you love? Can your feelings about a job change the way you do it?

Note

The term *work patterns* refers to the type of employment contracts people have and also how their contractual hours are split across the days of the working week (e.g. part-time work, temporary work – these and other related words are presented and practised in the unit). See the Business brief introduction for more information.

4.1 > My working life

GSE learning objectives

- Can follow the main points in a simple audio recording aimed at a general audience.
- Can identify key details in a simple recorded dialogue or narrative.
- Can use language related to the working day.
- Can use language related to work activities.
- Can use language related to places of work.
- Can identify key details in a simple recorded dialogue or narrative.
- Can take notes while researching a familiar topic.
- Can ask and answer questions about habits and routines.
- Can answer simple questions and respond to simple statements in an interview.
- Can ask what an employee likes or dislikes about their job.
- Can explain what they like or dislike about something.
- Can explain what they like or dislike about their job or workplace.
- Can ask what an employee likes or dislikes about their job or workplace.

Warm-up

Write the following questions on the board: *How do you feel at the start of your working/study week? Are there any days of the week you prefer at work / your place of study? Why?* Put students in pairs or groups to discuss the questions, then get brief feedback from the class. Encourage students to give reasons for their answers.

Lead-in

Students talk about their working week.

1 If time allows, let students discuss the questions in pairs/groups first, then invite different students to share their answers with the class. Ask some follow-up questions, e.g. *Who gets up earliest/latest? Who has the shortest journey to work/class? Who has the longest (working) day?*

Video

Students watch a video of people talking about their working day and working lives.

2 ▶ 4.1.1 Draw students' attention to the photos and explain that they are going to watch a video in which these people talk about their working lives. Play the video, then check answers with the class.

Sharni has one job. Lauren and Laurie both do various jobs. However, Lauren works in one job for a short time and then another in sequence, whereas Laurie has several jobs at the same time.

3 ▶ 4.1.1 Give students a minute to read the statements and teach or elicit the meaning of *security* in question 6. Play the video and get students to compare answers in pairs before checking with the class. In weaker classes, students may need to watch the video twice: once to decide whether the statements are true or false and then a second time to correct the false statements. Depending on time available, you could discuss the following questions with the class, as a follow-up: *Which person do you think enjoys their work most? Which job would you most/least like to do? Why?*

1 T
2 F – *Today's global economy needs more flexible work patterns, not nine-to-five jobs.*
3 F – Sharni works flexible hours. Some days she starts early and finishes early, and some days she starts later and finishes later.
4 T
5 T
6 F – Lauren doesn't have job security.
7 F – Laurie says he does lots of different jobs for different companies.
8 T

Extra activities 4.1

A ▶ 4.1.1 Ask students to complete the exercise individually and get them to compare answers in pairs before class feedback. Then play the video for them to check their answers. Do not focus on the meaning of the words in bold yet – students will do this in the next activity.

1 b 2 d 3 h 4 a 5 i 6 g 7 j 8 f 9 c 10 e

B Students now look at the meaning of the words in bold in Exercise A. They could do this individually or, in weaker classes, in pairs. To help them match the words with their definitions, encourage them to read the whole sentence carefully and think about a) the meaning of the whole sentence and b) the type of word: is it a noun, a verb, an adjective, etc.? Check answers with the class and clarify meanings as necessary.

1 e 2 d 3 b 4 g 5 c 6 a 7 f

Vocabulary: Describing jobs and contracts

Students look at vocabulary to describe jobs and contracts.

4A Students may already be familiar with some of these collocations from previous activities. Let them complete the exercise individually or in pairs, then check answers with the class, clarifying meanings as necessary.

> **1** patterns **2** employees **3** jobs **4** day **5** lives
> **6** hours **7** schedule **8** worker

4B This can be done individually or as a whole-class activity, checking answers as you go along.

> **a** working lives **b** working day **c** permanent employees
> **d** fixed schedule **e** full-time jobs **f** work patterns
> **g** flexible hours **h** temporary worker

> ⟫ **Pronunciation bank**
> **p. 115: Vowel sounds: British English and American English**
>
> **Warm-up**
>
> ◀) P4.01 Explain that there are differences between British and American pronunciation, and ask students if they have noticed any, (e.g. when watching films). Elicit any ideas, then refer students to the information in the box. Go through it with them and play the recording for them to listen to the examples.
>
> **1–3** ◀) P4.02, P4.03, P4.04 For each exercise, play the recording and check the answers with the class but do not focus on students' own pronunciation yet.
>
> > **1**
> > **1** A **2** A **3** B **4** A **5** B **6** A **7** A **8** B
> > **2**
> > **1** A–B **2** B–A **3** B–A **4** A–B **5** B–A **6** A–B
> > **7** B–A **8** A–B **9** A–B **10** B–A **11** A–B
> > **3**
> > **1** A **2** A **3** B **4** B **5** A **6** B **7** A **8** B **9** A
> > **10** B **11** A
>
> **4** Put students in pairs and let them practise saying the words. If time allows, you could put them in new pairs and get them to repeat the activity.

5 Depending on the strength of your class, you might like to go through the words in the box with students before they do the exercise or let them use their dictionaries to complete the sentences, then clarify meanings during feedback.

> **1** staff **2** employer **3** intern **4** unemployed
> **5** self-employed **6** retired **7** employee

6 Ask students to complete the exercise individually, then check answers with the class. During feedback, check students understand the meaning of the incorrect options. To do this,

you could give each student a number from 1 to 6 and ask them to write a sentence using the incorrect option corresponding to their number (so students numbered 1 would use *working lives*, students numbered 2 would use *part-time*, etc.).

> **1** working day **2** full-time **3** part-time **4** shifts
> **5** temporary **6** permanent

> **Extra activities 4.1**
>
> **C** This activity gives further practice of vocabulary from Exercises 4A, 5 and 6. Get students to complete it individually and then to compare answers in pairs before class feedback.
>
> > **1** c **2** a **3** a **4** b **5** b **6** a **7** c **8** c

7A ◀) 4.01 Explain that students need to make notes about each speaker's job and working hours. To help focus students' listening before playing the recording, ask them what type of information they expect to hear. Elicit a few ideas and list them on the board (e.g. *type of job, part-time/full-time work, shifts, hours, days per week*), then play the recording. Students, especially in weaker classes, may need to listen twice in order to check/complete their notes. Check answers with the class.

> **Speaker 1** is a nurse, she works part-time three days a week, her nine-hour shifts are often 11 or 12 hours, she often can't take her breaks.
> **Speaker 2** is a university student. She does temporary jobs for an agency in hotels, and for conferences and events. She starts work next week as an intern in a hotel and wants to get a permanent job there.
> **Speaker 3** works as a taxi driver through an app. He has a flexible schedule, decides his own working hours and likes to work five or six hours a day. He retired last year and the job supplements his pension.

7B Put students in pairs and explain the activity and give them 1–2 minutes to prepare. Encourage them to use vocabulary from Exercises 4A, 5 and 6. Monitor and help as necessary. As feedback, invite a few students to share their answers.

Project: Researching work patterns

Students research work patterns in their country.

8A–B This research project can be done in various ways. Students could go out to companies and interview people, send emails, or research the companies online. Pre-work students could investigate the work patterns of the staff in their institution as well as family members and friends. In-work students could talk about companies they, their family members or friends have worked for or have knowledge of. Students could research job adverts/job conditions on company recruitment pages and job sites. Some of these list benefits or conditions of employment such as hours, holiday leave or minimum commitment required. Whatever their choice, encourage students to interview at least 2–3 people from each company to make their research more meaningful. Point out the categories in the box and remind students to try to find out this information during their research. For the discussion in Exercise 8B, students could use notes they have made during their research, or you may wish to get them to prepare a more concrete record, e.g. flipchart notes, slides or a chart.

MyEnglishLab: Teacher's resources: extra activities
Pronunciation bank: p.115 Vowel sounds: British English and American English
Teacher's book: Resource bank Photocopiable 4.1 p.140
Workbook: p.19 Exercises 1–3

4.2 › Executives at work

GSE learning objectives

- Can identify specific information in a simple factual text.
- Can scan a simple text, identifying the main topic(s).
- Can identify the main topic and related ideas in a simple structured text.
- Can give a short, basic description of events and activities.
- Can make and respond to suggestions.
- Can use the Present Perfect to refer to personal experiences in the past.
- Can ask questions using the Present Perfect with *ever*.

Warm-up

Discuss the following questions with the class: *What is your busiest day of the week? Do you prefer to keep busy or do you like to have an easy schedule? Do you make a schedule for every week/day? Do you have enough time to do the things you like to do?* Elicit answers around the class, encouraging students to give reasons.

Lead-in

Students talk about an average day in their working week.

1A Go through the phrases in the box with students and check they understand *escape* and *heavy* in this context. Give them 2–3 minutes to make their lists. Monitor and help them with any vocabulary they may need.

1B Put students in pairs to compare and discuss their lists, and then to ask each other questions about their average day. Give them 2–3 minutes to discuss, then nominate a few students to tell the class about their partner's day: does their partner do anything unusual during their day?

Reading

Students read two interviews with successful businesswomen.

2 Put students in pairs and tell them that they will each read an interview with a successful businesswoman and complete it with the questions she was asked. Refer them to their text (Student A: page 132, Student B: page 40) and exercise and give them plenty of time to read it and complete the task. Confirm the answers but do not discuss either of the texts with the class yet. You might like to pre-teach the following words: *The*

Association of Business Schools (see Note below), *associate fellow, civilised, facilitate, ingredient, the tube, voluntary role.*

Student A text
Kathryn Bishop: **1** b **2** a **3** d
Student B text
Anne Kiem: **1** b **2** c **3** e

Note

The Chartered Association of Business Schools is an organisation that represents the interests of 120 business schools and higher education institutions in the UK, providing professional training and networking opportunities.

3 Give students a minute to read the questions and ask you about anything they do not understand before they read. During the activity, monitor and check students' answers, but do not discuss them with the class as students will tell each other about their interview in the next activity. You could ask the A students to sit on one side of the classroom, and the B students on the other, so you can feed back the correct answers to each group separately. Then students can return to their pairs for the next activity.

Student A text
Kathryn Bishop
1 She studied English and American Literature for a degree in the USA and English Studies for a Masters in Oxford, UK.
2 She has worked for financial services companies, universities and government.
3 She seems busiest on teaching days – she says 'I am on the go from breakfast until after dinner each night.'
4 She has three jobs and two voluntary roles.
5 Working in boardrooms (implying the members are mostly men) and in her marriage.
6 She tries to manage her energy and 'only do what only she can do', meaning that she tries to do the most important tasks that only she is capable of doing.

Student B text
Anne Kiem
1 She was a maths teacher.
2 The tube is less busy and she has 'quiet time' to work uninterrupted.
3 It is when managers leave their office door open to encourage the employees in that company to come and talk when they want.
4 By going outside at lunchtime.
5 The question 'Why?'
6 She got up at 3 a.m. and then couldn't concentrate in her maths classes at university.

4A In the same pairs, students tell each other about their text. Go through the ideas in the box before they begin and teach or elicit the meaning of *country of residence*. Point out that they should use their own words and not read from their text. After they have told each other about their texts, they should try to find some similarities and differences between the two women. Discuss the answers with the class.

Possible answers

Similarities

Both women went to university; have teaching experience; have worked in finance; live in the UK; spend a lot of time at work communicating with their staff, other people and departments.

Differences

Kathryn teaches now and Anne works in an office.
Kathryn has various jobs and Anne only mentions one current job.
Kathryn is probably from the USA and Anne is from Australia.
Kathryn works in Oxford and Anne works in London.

4B This question can be discussed with the whole class or, if time allows, students could discuss it in their pairs first. You could also ask students which woman they think has a busier working day and why. (Both women are clearly very busy, but Kathryn Bishop mentions three jobs and two voluntary roles, so that makes her seem even busier than Anne Kiem.)

Extra activities 4.2

A This activity looks at useful vocabulary from the reading texts. Get students to work in the same pairs as Exercises 2–4. They should each look for the words/phrases in the texts they read, then work together to match the words with their definitions. Check answers with the class, clarifying meanings as necessary.

1 chief executive 2 free time 3 afraid
4 successful 5 delivering 6 stay awake 7 degree
8 development 9 boardrooms 10 marriage
11 advice 12 manage

5 Keep students in the same pairs for this activity. Give them 3–5 minutes to interview their partner, then invite different students to share their answers with the class.

Grammar: Present Perfect Simple

Students study and practise the Present Perfect Simple.

6 Do this as a whole-class activity, checking and clarifying answers as you go along. When discussing question 2, tell students that these forms are called *past participles*. Elicit/Give students the form of the Present Perfect and write it on the board: *have/has + past participle*. Refer students to the Grammar reference on page 122 and go through it with them, clarifying any points as necessary. Also remind them that there is a list of common irregular verbs on page 126.

1 no
2 *Learn*, *have* and *teach* are all irregular verbs.
3 ever

7 Students complete the exercise individually, referring to page 126 if necessary. Alternatively, this can also be done as a whole-class activity, checking answers as you go along.

be – been; buy – bought; give - given; meet – met; read /riːd/ – read /red/; see – seen; sell - sold; speak – spoken; think – thought; take – taken; win – won; write – written

8A Get students to do the exercise individually. Ask them to use full forms. Do not confirm answers yet as students will check them in the next exercise.

1 Have you ever bought 2 have never bought
3 have read 4 have seen 5 has written 6 has won
7 have never seen 8 have started 9 have never finished

8B ◀ 4.02 Ask students to look at their answers in Exercise 8A again and change the full forms to short forms where possible. Play the recording for them to check their answers.

1 no contractions in questions 2 've never bought
3 've read 4 've seen 5 's written 6 's won
7 've never seen 8 've started 9 've never finished

Extra activities 4.2

B Students complete the activity individually. Do not confirm answers yet as they will check them in the next exercise.

1 They have won the contract.
2 I have been to the trade fair.
3 I have not seen the report.
4 He has worked in a bank.
5 He has never learnt to type.
6 She has not been to head office.
7 Has she ever met the Chief Executive?
8 Have you ever read a business book?
9 We have never been in the boardroom.
10 You have never worked in a big company.

C Again, ask students to work individually, then check answers with the class. You could get students to write the sentences out again or ask them to just note down the short forms next to the full forms in the sentences they have already written. Elicit both the full forms and the short forms when checking answers.

1 They've won the contract.
2 I've been to the trade fair.
3 I haven't seen the report.
4 He's worked in a bank.
5 He's never learnt to type.
6 She hasn't been to head office.
7 – (no contractions in questions)
8 – (no contractions in questions)
9 We've never been in the boardroom.
10 You've never worked in a big company.

> **Pronunciation bank**
p. 116: Present Perfect Simple

Warm-up

🔊 > P4.05, P4.06, P4.07 Refer students to the first sentence in the box and play recording P4.05 for them to hear the examples. Explain that auxiliary verbs like *have/has* in the Present Perfect have no stress and so are often 'weakened' in speech. These forms are called 'weak forms'. Model the example sentences again, then move on to the next sentence in the box. Explain that the weak form is used in questions because *have/has* have no stress, as mentioned above. However, when *have/has* are used in short answers, they are stressed and pronounced with the strong forms. Play recording P4.06 for students to hear the examples. Finally, look at the last sentence in the box and explain that strong forms are also used if we want to stress or emphasise something. Let them hear the examples in recording P4.07.

1 🔊 P4.08 Play the recording for students to complete the sentences. After checking answers, if time allows, play it a second time for them to listen and repeat before they practise on their own in the next exercise.

1 I've, I have **2** I've **3** I've, he's **4** he has, He's
5 Have you, I've **6** I've

2 Put students in pairs to practise saying the sentences. Monitor and correct students' pronunciation, modelling the strong/weak forms again if necessary.

Speaking

Students practise the Present Perfect Simple by interviewing a partner.

9A Get students to complete the exercise individually and remind them that they can refer to page 126 if they need help. Check answers with the class.

1 written **2** visited **3** spoken **4** been **5** sold/written
6 given **7** thought **8** wanted

9B Put students in pairs, explain the activity and draw their attention to the example dialogue. Remind students that when we give details about an experience, we use the Past Simple, not the Present Perfect. If necessary, refer them again to page 122 in the Grammar reference. You might also like to do an example with a stronger student before they begin. Fast-finishers or stronger students can ask their own *Have you ever … ?* questions.

MyEnglishLab: Teacher's resources: extra activities; Reading bank

Grammar reference: p.122 Present Perfect Simple

Pronunciation bank: p.116 Present Perfect Simple

Teacher's book: Resource bank Photocopiable 4.2 p.141

Workbook: p.20 Exercises 1–4

4.3 > Communication skills
Making group decisions

GSE learning objectives

- Can follow a simple conversation or narrative about familiar, everyday activities.
- Can extract key details from conversations between colleagues about familiar topics.
- Can make basic inferences in simple conversations on familiar everyday topics.
- Can make and respond to suggestions.
- Can use language related to decision or indecision.
- Can summarise the main ideas in a meeting using simple language.
- Can present a conclusion in a meeting using simple language.

Warm-up

Ask students to think about situations in their working or personal lives when they have had to make important decisions. Dictate or write the following questions on the board: *Do you think you make better decisions alone or in a team / with someone else? Why? When do you ask for help?* Put students in pairs / small groups to discuss the questions, then get brief feedback from the class.

Lead-in

Students discuss different approaches to decision-making.

1A Refer students to the diagram and go through it with them. Check they understand *hands-on, hands-off, consultative* and *democratic*. Before they discuss situations 1–6, ask them if they or anyone they work/study with has ever used any of these styles during a decision-making process. Invite students who answer 'yes' to share their experiences with the class: What was the situation? Which style did they use? Why did they choose to use this particular approach? Did it work? Then give them a minute to read the situations and check they understand *input, go ahead, full responsibility* and *relevant*. Put them in pairs and give them 3–4 minutes to discuss, then get feedback from the class.

1 approach 2 **2** approach 1 **3** approach 4
4 approach 3 **5** approach 2 **6** approach 1

1B Join pairs together into groups of four to discuss the advantages and disadvantages of each approach, then broaden this into a class discussion. As students provide their suggestions, you could get the rest of the class to vote on whether each one is a pro or a con, and write them in two columns on the board.

Possible answers

Approach 1 (Hands-on) – Pros: it's quicker and less complicated; you get the result you want. Cons: you may not get your team's support; they may feel undervalued; your team may not want to implement your decision.

Approach 2 (Consultative) – Pros: you get more commitment from your team; you create a better atmosphere as people feel more valued. Cons: it can take longer; your team may not have much to contribute; people may feel 'manipulated' because they are still not actually making decisions.

Approach 3 (Democratic) – Pros: you get even more commitment from your team than by using Approach 2; you become accepted more as one of the team. Cons: it may be difficult to get agreement; disagreements can hold up the decision.

Approach 4 (Hands-off) – Pros: it saves you time; it gives your team a sense of responsibility and helps train them in decision-making. Cons: you lose control of the decision to a great extent; your team may make a bad decision; some people don't like responsibility or delegation.

Video

Students watch a video about different approaches to decision-making.

2A ▶ 4.3.1   If your students watched the Unit 3 video, ask them to give you a short summary of the situation and the main characters. If this is the first communication skills video for your class, set up the context and/or refer students to page 6 of the Coursebook. Explain that in the video, Shaun is talking to Orla after a meeting he had with Léana, the Managing Director. Play the video, then check answers with the class.

1 The meeting went well. Léana liked Shaun's idea and she's already spoken to some of the other directors about his idea.
2 'Reverse coaching' involves getting younger members of staff who know a lot about technology to help older members of staff to use it.
3 Orla thinks it's a great idea.
4 The junior staff don't know about the idea yet – Shaun has a meeting with them later this afternoon.

2B Do this as a whole-class discussion, eliciting ideas from different students.

3A ▶ 4.3.2   Explain that students are now going to watch Shaun's meeting with the junior staff. Give them a minute to read the questions and check they understand the meanings of *sell* and *persuaded* in question 2. Refer them back to the diagram in Exercise 1 and remind them of the four approaches to decision-making. Then play the video, twice if necessary, and check answers with the class.

1 Hands-on. The junior staff are not there to give their views on the decision itself, just to discuss how the coaching can be done and who will work with whom.
2 He says it will be fun, they'll be working with the top people in the company and it will be good for their careers. They don't seem persuaded: the second two points, at least, may be true, but it may not be fun, and the junior staff may not like the responsibility.
3 a T b J c E d T
4 Shaun tells the junior staff that they have to go ahead with the coaching because Léana expects it now. Shaun has got the decision he wanted, but does not have the support of the group, and this may create problems when the coaching begins.

3B Discuss the question with the whole class. Invite different students to answer, giving reasons. As a follow-up, ask: Do you think a hands-on approach is always a bad idea? Would a different approach have worked better in this meeting? Why?

Possible answer

Shaun's main mistake was probably not mentioning his idea to the junior staff before taking it to Léana. But he doesn't listen enough to their concerns after he has told them either.

4 ▶ 4.3.3   Explain that students are going to watch another version of the meeting, where Shaun takes a different approach to decision-making. Encourage them to make notes in answer to the questions, and play the video. Check answers with the class.

1 Shaun's approach to decision-making in this version of the meeting is more consultative. The decision has been taken, but the details can be changed.
2 He listens to the group's concerns, makes a note of them and tries to think of possible solutions.
3 Thiago is concerned that the junior staff are too busy to fit the coaching into their usual work schedules. Shaun suggests that it should be programmed into their usual work schedules. Jasmine is concerned that the junior staff do not have any training as coaches. Shaun agrees that basic training could be arranged.
4 (1) Mike suggests that the scheme should simply be called 'tech assistance' rather than 'coaching'. The idea is that the junior staff will be less nervous about this. Jasmine agrees with him.
(2) Ethan suggests that the coaching could be two-way: the directors coaching the junior staff in the HR consultancy business and the junior staff coaching the directors in how to use everyday business technology.

5 If time allows, get students to discuss the question in small groups before discussing it as a class. Point out that they need to think about both similarities and differences in the group's response. You could provide points to consider based on the questions they discussed in Exercise 4, e.g. Shaun's response to the group's concerns, ways to deal with Thiago's and Jasmine's concerns, ideas that come out of the meeting, involvement of all the people at the meeting.

Possible answers

Shaun's approach in Video A is to simply tell the junior staff about the decision he and Léana have taken and ask them to decide who they would prefer to work with. As a result, they resist the proposal, and Shaun has to defend his idea. In Video B, Shaun is open to comments about the decision from the beginning and this creates a much more positive atmosphere. The junior staff even start to think of ways the idea could be improved. The decision itself (to do the coaching) is still fixed, but everything about the way it is put into action is open to discussion.

a) Both versions of the meeting end with the junior staff planning who they are going to coach, but in Video A nobody feels they have had any choice in the matter.

b) In Video B their concerns and suggestions have been listened and responded to.

6 ▶ 4.3.4 Explain that students are going to watch the last section of the video, where the speaker discusses the two approaches to decision-making they looked at in Videos A and B. Play the video and, if time allows, let students discuss the question in pairs or small groups before discussing it as a class.

Reflection

Students reflect on the conclusions from the video and discuss their own approaches to decision-making.

7 Allow students to work individually on this so that they can reflect on their own skills and preferred approach(es). Ask them to think about their answers to the questions and to make notes. Then put them in pairs to discuss and compare their answers. Get brief feedback from the class.

Functional language: Facilitating a decision-making meeting

Students look at useful language for decision-making meetings.

8A Explain that these are all expressions students can use when they want to encourage someone to speak during a decision-making meeting. Get them to complete the exercise individually or, in weaker classes, in pairs, then check answers with the class, clarifying meanings as necessary.

1 to get your input
2 what does everybody
3 are your thoughts on
4 you haven't said anything
5 to hear what you
6 do you think of
7 they'd like to add
8 thanks for your input

8B Do this as a whole-class activity, checking answers and clarifying meanings as you go.

to say (7)
do you think about (3, 6)
to hear your views (1)
to know what you (5)
we haven't heard much from you (4)

9 Give students time to attempt the exercise individually, then confirm the answer. Again, check students' understanding of each expression. You may also wish to point out that in English to just say *No, I don't agree* is considered rude. It is important to use expressions like the ones here, which are a more 'diplomatic' way of rejecting someone's point/idea.

point

10 Explain the activity and the meaning of *delay making a decision* (stop and take time to think before deciding). Let students complete the exercise individually, then check answers with the class.

1 b 2 c 3 a

11 Put students in small groups. Ask them to imagine that they all work for the same company and would like to introduce one of the ideas to their colleagues. They are now having a discussion with their colleagues and will take turns to lead it. Remind them to use expressions from Exercises 8–10, set a time limit for each discussion and ask them to swap roles when the time is up. During the activity, monitor and check students are using the expressions correctly. Highlight any errors during feedback.

Extra activities 4.3

A This activity gives further practice of the functional language from Exercises 8–10. Get students to complete it individually and compare answers in pairs before checking with the class. If time allows, after checking answers, students could practise the conversation in groups of four.

1 your input 2 everybody think 3 your thoughts
4 fair point 5 your point 6 said anything
7 hear what 8 a point 9 rush into 10 go away
11 immediate decision 12 anything else

Task

Students roleplay discussing proposals in a meeting.

12A Put students in groups of three. Explain the activity and draw their attention to the meeting plan. Make sure they understand that they can choose to make a final decision or defer it. Let groups choose their proposals (1–3) and allow plenty of time for them to read the details of each one. Monitor and help with any unknown vocabulary. In weaker classes, you might like to briefly discuss the details of each proposal with the class first. Another option for weaker classes would be to divide the class into three groups (1–3) first and allocate one proposal to each group. Students can prepare together for their meetings, and then be divided into groups of three, where each student has a different proposal, to hold their meetings.

12B Set a time limit for the preparation stage and for each meeting. Remind students to refer to the meeting plan and to use expressions from Exercises 8–10. You could also suggest that each group appoints a student as a time-keeper. During the activity, monitor and note down points to highlight during feedback, but do not interrupt the meetings.

12c Let students discuss in their groups first, then broaden this into a class discussion. Remember to highlight any points you noted while monitoring.

MyEnglishLab: Teacher's resources: extra activities; Interactive video activities; Functional language bank
Workbook: p.21 Exercises 1–4, p.22 Exercises 1 and 2

4.4 ❯ Business skills
Phoning to change arrangements

GSE learning objectives

- Can follow the main points in a simple audio recording aimed at a general audience.
- Can identify key details in a simple recorded dialogue or narrative.
- Can write short, simple notes, emails and messages relating to everyday matters.
- Can make an appointment on the phone.

Warm-up

Dictate or write the following questions on the board: *How often do you phone or email people to make arrangements? In what situations do you prefer to phone rather than send an email?* Put students in pairs or groups and ask them to discuss the questions, referring to their working (or study) life (rather than personal arrangements). After 3–4 minutes, invite a few students to share their answers with the class.

Lead-in

Students talk about making arrangements over the phone.

1a Explain the activity and check students understand *teleconference*, *reschedule* and *figures*. Put them in pairs and give them 3–4 minutes to complete the exercise, then check answers with the class.

Whether you prefer to phone or send an email is partly cultural. But in these situations, most people would probably choose:
1 email **2** phone **3** email **4** phone **5** phone

1b Let students think about the question in their pairs first, then invite different students to share their ideas with the class.

Possible answer

Situations 2, 4 and 5 seem more urgent, so it's probably better to communicate by phone in these cases.

Listening

Students listen to phone calls where the speakers change arrangements.

2a 🔊 4.03 Give students a minute to read the questions so they know what to listen for, then play the recording. To check answers, you could play the recording again, pausing after each answer is heard to elicit it from students.

1 on Wednesday the 17th
2 Sally can't make it. She's in Vienna all that week.
3 Sooner. She's going to the Berlin Expo the week after their original appointment.
4 a Ian **b** Lou **c** Lou **d** Ian
5 Ian offers to find out if he can move his training session on Wednesday afternoon.

2b 🔊 4.03 Explain the activity and make sure students understand *apologise*. Ask them to listen for phrases Lou uses which show she is apologising, and phrases Ian uses which show he is being helpful. You might like to elicit an example phrase for each attitude before students listen (e.g. *I'm very sorry. No problem.*). In weaker classes, students may need to listen twice in order to check/complete their answers.

Lou: Sorry to bother you; I'm afraid; It's my fault; I appreciate it; I know it's a bit short notice; Oh dear; I'm really sorry about this
Ian: Sure; No problem; Let me see if I can move the training session; Leave it with me

3a 🔊 4.04 Explain that Ian is now phoning his assistant to make changes to his schedule. To help students, you might like to tell them that they need to listen for four changes. Give students a minute to familiarise themselves with the schedule, then play the recording and check answers with the class.

Performance review
moves from Wednesday 10th morning to Friday 12th morning.
Meeting with IT team
moves from Friday 12th morning to Friday 12th afternoon.
Staff training
moves from Wednesday 10th afternoon to Wednesday 10th morning.
Meeting with Lou & Sally
moves from Wednesday 17th afternoon to Wednesday 10th afternoon.

3b Discuss the question with the whole class.

James is Ian's assistant. Lou is from head office. You can be a little more direct with people you know well and who work for you, as long as you're still polite. Ian makes sure to thank James at the end of their conversation.

4 🔊 4.05 Explain that Ian is calling back Lou to confirm the details of their meeting. Students should listen and complete Ian's Meeting planner. Again, you could tell them that they need to listen for four arrangements. Play the recording, then check answers with the class.

Date: Wednesday 10th **Time:** 3 p.m.
Location: my office **Attending:** Lou, Sally, Tom
Arrangements: set up presentation, book meeting room, reserve restaurant table for four

Functional language: Rescheduling appointments on the phone

Students look at useful language for rescheduling appointments on the phone.

5A Let students complete the exercise individually and get them to compare answers in pairs before checking with the class. During feedback, clarify meanings as necessary.

> 1 c 2 d 3 e 4 b 5 a 6 g 7 h 8 f 9 j 10 i

5B You could do this as a whole-class activity, checking answers as you go along. Encourage students to read the whole sentence carefully each time to help them match the words/phrases to their meanings. In weaker classes, you could write the sentences from Exercise 5A on the board, underlining key phrases which will help students with the matching task (see answers below).

> 1 (Friday's/It's) <u>out for me,</u> I'm afraid.
> 2 How does the afternoon <u>suit you</u>?
> 3 <u>I'm free</u> on Wednesday morning.
> 4 Let me just <u>check</u> my schedule.
> 5 <u>I'm busy</u> all day Thursday.
> 6 Let me just check <u>my schedule</u>.
> 7 Do you mind if we <u>fix</u> another time to meet?
> 8 I know it's a bit <u>short notice</u>.

6 Look at phrases 1–8 with the class and check students understand them. Then get them to complete the table, individually or in pairs, and check answers with the class. Alternatively, you could do this as a whole-class activity, checking answers and clarifying meanings as you go along.

> Making appointments: 2, 4
> Changing appointments: 6, 8
> Apologising: 1, 5
> Thanking: 3, 7

Extra activities 4.4

A Point out the first item in the activity and then get students to complete the exercise individually. Check answers with the class.

> 1 j 2 d 3 a 4 e 5 l 6 b 7 g 8 k 9 i 10 f
> 11 h 12 c

B Put students in pairs to practise the conversation in Exercise A. Encourage them to cover up the answers and try to remember the conversation by looking at the 'scrambled' version.

C 4.04 Get students to complete the exercise individually. Before they begin, make sure they understand that the pairs of words in the box are grouped together and that each pair completes one sentence. Play the recording for students to check their answers.

> 1 can + do 2 change + plan 3 time + free
> 4 day + thinking 5 scheduled + then
> 6 forgot + tell 7 that + wait 8 leaves + free

Task

Students roleplay a phone call to reschedule a meeting.

7A Put students in pairs, let them choose their roles and give them time to read the scenario and the information on pages 131 and 135. Help them with any unknown vocabulary and check they understand what they need to do by asking a few questions (e.g. (*Where do you work? Who is calling to confirm the appointment? Do you need to reschedule the meeting?*).

7B Allow time for students to prepare while you go round and provide help as necessary. In weaker classes, you may wish to group Student As and Student Bs together first, to briefly discuss their roles and prepare for their phone calls together before returning to their original pairs. Remind students to use phrases from Exercises 5 and 6 and set a time limit for the phone calls. During the activity, monitor and note down any points to highlight during feedback.

7C Let students discuss the questions in their pairs, then check answers as a class. Highlight any points you noted while monitoring.

MyEnglishLab: Teacher's resources: extra activities; Functional language bank
Workbook: p.22 Exercise 3

4.5 > Writing
Confirming arrangements

GSE learning objectives

- Can understand standard emails on work-related topics.
- Can understand short, simple emails on work-related topics.
- Can reply to a work-related email confirming arrangements.

Warm-up

Discuss the following questions with the class: *Have you ever had to write an email to make arrangements? What was it for? Why do you think emails confirming arrangements are important?*

Lead-in

Students read and complete two emails making and confirming arrangements.

1 Get students to complete the exercise individually, using their dictionaries if they need help. Get them to compare answers in pairs, then check with the class. Clarify any unknown words as necessary. After checking answers, highlight or elicit that both emails are written in a formal style.

> 1 confirm 2 discuss 3 place 4 invite 5 Feel 6 very
> 7 Thank 8 attend 9 am unable 10 meeting

Functional language

Students look at useful language for making and confirming arrangements in formal emails.

2 Explain the activity and check students understand the words in the box and the headings in the table. Get students to complete the exercise individually, then check answers with the class. Clarify meanings as necessary, highlighting the function of each phrase. Draw students' attention to the fact that *look forward to* in the *Concluding* section can be followed by both an *-ing* form (e.g. *seeing you*) and a noun (e.g. *our meeting*).

> **1** This **2** delighted **3** contact **4** free **5** Many
> **6** Unfortunately **7** meeting **8** seeing

Extra activities 4.5

A This activity practises the functional language from the lesson. It can also serve as a second model answer, which students can refer to when they complete the writing task in Exercise 3B. The exercise can be done individually or in pairs.

> **1** This **2** feel **3** questions **4** much **5** Thank
> **6** delighted **7** attend **8** Unfortunately **9** look

Optional grammar work

The emails in Exercise 1 contain examples of prepositions of time, so you could use them for some optional grammar work. Refer students to the Grammar reference on page 122 and use the exercises in MyEnglishLab for extra grammar practice.

Task

Students write emails making and confirming arrangements.

3A Refer students to the email on page 128 and explain the activity. Give them a minute to read the email and tell them they should use phrases from Exercise 2 in their email. Ask them which sections of the table the phrases will come from (*Confirming*, *Inviting questions* and *Concluding*). Set a time limit for the activity and remind them that they can also refer to the emails in Exercise 1 (and Extra activity A). While students are writing, monitor and help as necessary.

> **Model answer**
>
> Dear Mr Bankes,
>
> This is to confirm our meeting at 11 a.m. next Wednesday. It will take place at our factory in Milan. The meeting will last until 12.30 p.m. I would like to invite you to stay for lunch after the meeting. Please feel free to contact me if you have any questions.
>
> I very much look forward to meeting you on Wednesday.
>
> Kind regards,
>
> Marco Contini

3B Depending on the time available, students could plan their emails in class and write them for homework. Highlight the word limit and remind students to use the emails in Exercise 1 (and Extra activity A) to help them if necessary. Also remind them to include phrases from Exercise 2.

> **Model answer**
>
> Dear Mr Contini,
>
> Thank you for your email. I am delighted to confirm that I am able to attend the meeting with you at your factory in Milan. Unfortunately, I am unable to stay for lunch after the meeting because I have a flight to Australia in the afternoon. Could you book a taxi to take me from your factory to Milan Linate Airport, please?
>
> I look forward to our meeting on Wednesday.
>
> All the best,
>
> John Bankes

3C If students write their emails for homework, you could do this exercise in the next lesson. Put them in pairs and ask them to read each other's emails and answer the questions. You could also write the following questions on the board and get students to copy them: *Did your partner open and close his/her email appropriately? Did he/she use the right register? What did he/she do well? What could he/she improve?*

MyEnglishLab: Teacher's resources: extra activities; Interactive grammar practice; Writing bank
Grammar reference: p.122 Prepositions of time
Workbook: p.23 Exercises 1–3

Business workshop ❯4
The Holsted way

GSE learning objectives

- Can follow the main points in a simple audio recording, if provided with written supporting material.
- Can follow the main points in a simple audio recording aimed at a general audience.
- Can recognise when speakers agree in a conversation conducted slowly and clearly.
- Can recognise when speakers disagree in a conversation conducted slowly and clearly.
- Can describe habits and routines.
- Can explain what they like or dislike about something.
- Can write short, simple notes, emails and messages relating to everyday matters.
- Can write a simple email/letter in response to a request for information.
- Can write simple texts giving key information about their culture (e.g. food, national holidays, festivals).

Background

Students read about a Danish pharmaceutical company.

1 Put students in pairs and give them time to read the background and discuss the questions. Check answers with the class and clarify any unknown vocabulary.

1 It's an area with a lot of pharmaceutical and biotechnology companies and research institutions.
2 The company manufactures and markets pharmaceutical products and services.
3 Holsted recently bought a Spanish pharmaceutical laboratory based in Madrid and the Vice President plans to investigate the work culture and present Holsted's work culture to the managers in Madrid.
4 Students' own answer

The Holsted way

Students listen to a presentation about company culture.

2A 🔊 BW 4.01   Remind students of Clara Olsen's role at Holsted (Vice President for Europe) and explain the activity. Give them a minute to read the points, then play the recording, twice if necessary. Check answers with the class.

2 They are ~~often~~ *not* expected to work long hours.
3 The working hours are ~~fixed~~ *flexible* for most employees.
4 The work culture is very ~~strict~~ *relaxed* but effective.
5 Managers ~~are~~ *aren't* responsible for how employees organise their time and projects.
6 ~~Senior~~ *All* staff in the company can tell us their ideas and opinions.
7 It's important to arrive on time for ~~work~~ *meetings*; it shows you are professional.

2B Depending on time available, you could let students discuss the questions in pairs/groups first, then as a class.

Extra activities Business workshop 4

A 🔊 BW 4.01   Give students a minute to read the sentence halves and check the meanings of *adapt*, *openness* and *collect*. Get students to complete the exercise individually, then play the recording for them to check their answers.

1 e **2** c **3** g **4** f **5** a **6** h **7** d **8** b

Investigating work patterns

Students listen to a meeting between senior managers about work patterns.

3A 🔊 BW 4.02   Explain that Clara is now having a meeting with the company's senior managers to discuss work patterns. Students should listen and decide which questions in Clara's notes they are discussing. Get them to identify the key words in the list of questions first and then listen for these or words associated with them. Play the recording, then check answers with the class.

3 and 5

3B 🔊 BW 4.02   Play the part from the recording (0:00–0:36) again for students to complete the extract and check answers with the class. Then draw students' attention to the bar chart. Explain that they should complete it using information from the extract. To help them, you could tell them that they need to write times for the x (horizontal) axis and percentages for the y (vertical) axis. Get students to compare answers in pairs before class feedback.

1 half / 50% / fifty percent   **2** six/6   **3** seven/7
4 20/twenty   **5** 10/ten   **6** 8/eight (o'clock)

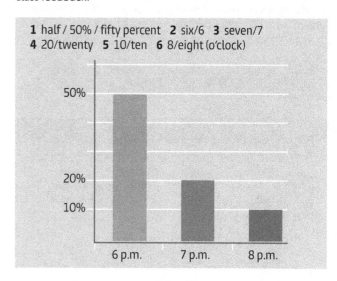

3C Put students in pairs and give them 2–3 minutes to brainstorm ideas, then elicit ideas around the class. For weaker classes, or if students struggle to come up with ideas, you could turn this into a multiple-choice exercise and give them three or four options to choose from (e.g. *A Percentage of staff arriving early; B Percentage of staff leaving early; C Percentage of staff working late; D Percentage of staff at work*).

Suggested answer
Percentage of staff at work (in the evening)

3D 🔊 BW 4.02   Ask students to make notes in answer to the questions and play the rest of the recording (0:37–2:24). In weaker classes, students may need to listen twice in order to complete their answers.

1 It's usual to have a two-hour lunch break from 2 p.m. to 4 p.m.
2 If staff like the long lunch break or not. Álvaro believes they like to have a good meal and socialise with colleagues, but Marina thinks most staff would prefer a shorter lunch break and the chance to go home earlier.
3 She thinks staff won't get so much work done later in the day, when they do a long working day, because they are tired.
4 She thinks there could be accidents at work and more sick leave because staff are tired (and probably stressed).

3E Explain the activity and remind students of the two issues being discussed (working hours, duration of lunch break). If there is time, let students discuss their answers in pairs or small groups first, and then as a class. Accept any reasonable answers as long as students can justify them. To help students, you could use the Note below to make some suggestions to start the discussion.

Note

Some of the more radical suggestions are switching off lights and blocking computers so people can't work late. Clearly, managers need to take the initiative and make changes. Often employees work late because they are worried that they will lose their jobs and they don't want to leave before the boss. 'Presenteeism' is a problem in some companies and cultures where unemployment is high and the best workers are seen as those who spend the longest time in the office.

Extra activities Business workshop 4

B This activity practises useful vocabulary from the listening. Ask students to do it individually, then get them to compare answers in pairs before checking with the class. During feedback, clarify meanings as necessary.

1 b **2** f **3** c **4** d **5** g **6** e **7** h **8** a

Task: Negotiate changes

Students roleplay a meeting negotiating new work patterns for Holsted.

4A Explain the activity, put students in groups of three and let them choose their roles.

4B Refer students to their role cards and give them time to read and check the information. Allow them to ask you about anything they are not clear about, and teach or elicit the meanings of *intensive* and *split working day* (working for one part of the day, then having a long break, then working again later in the day. Many workers have this working pattern in Spain, including shop workers, cleaners, restaurant staff and some office staff.). Draw their attention to the four negotiation points in the box and explain that students need to think about what they want to say about each one. Students could prepare for their meetings individually or you may prefer to group all the students with one role together, and then ask them to return to their original groups for their meetings.

4C Students hold their meetings. Remind them to discuss all the points on the agenda and try to reach agreement on them.

4D Put students in pairs with someone from a different group. Give them 3–5 minutes to discuss the questions, then get feedback from the class.

Writing

Students write an email summarising decisions made at a meeting.

5 Give students time to read the email and points they need to include. Teach or elicit the meaning of *official*. If time is short, students could plan their emails in class and then do the writing task for homework. For weaker classes, you may wish to let students plan their emails in pairs.

Model answer

Hello Carlos,

I'm writing to tell you about the new work patterns. Firstly, we decided to introduce an intensive working day from 7 a.m. to 3.30 p.m. every day from Monday to Friday.

We are introducing a more flexible timetable. Employees can decide what time they start work (from 7 a.m. to 8.30 a.m.) and finish (from 2 p.m. to 3.30 p.m.). Everyone must work 37 hours a week.

We also decided to make the lunch break flexible with a minimum break of 30 minutes and a maximum of two hours. Lunchtime can be any time between 1 p.m. and 3 p.m. We decided not to introduce working from home. Please don't tell anyone about these changes until it is official.

Let me know if you have any questions.

Best regards,

Clara

MyEnglishLab: Teacher's resources: extra activities

Review ❮4

1 1 intern **2** temporary **3** unemployed **4** retired
  5 self-employed **6** flexible
2 1 have/'ve spent **2** Have (you) worked **3** has taught
  4 has/'s gone **5** have/'ve been **6** has/'s visited
  7 has/'s won **8** have/'ve learnt
3 1 think **2** input **3** add **4** point **5** go **6** heard
  7 into **8** thoughts
4 1 calling about **2** if we fix **3** postpone **4** bring it
  5 check **6** free **7** suit **8** out for me **9** better for
  10 for being **11** set for
5 1 to confirm **2** contact me **3** to seeing
  4 am delighted **5** unable to **6** our meeting

5 > Money

Unit overview

	CLASSWORK	FURTHER WORK
5.1 > **Going cashless**	**Lead-in** Students discuss different types of cashless payment. **Video** Students watch a video about cashless payment systems in India. **Vocabulary** Students look at vocabulary related to money and the economy and collocations related to money, the economy and personal finance. **Project** Students create an advertisement to promote cashless payments.	**MyEnglishLab:** Teacher's resources: extra activities **Teacher's book:** Resource bank Photocopiable 5.1 p.142 **Workbook:** p.24 Exercises 1–3
5.2 > **Consumer spending**	**Lead-in** Students talk about their spending habits. **Listening** Students listen to a podcast about money. **Grammar** Students study and practise the first conditional. **Speaking** Students practise using the first conditional.	**MyEnglishLab:** Teacher's resources: extra activities; Reading bank **Grammar reference:** p.123 First conditional **Pronunciation bank:** p.116 Intonation in conditionals **Teacher's book:** Resource bank Photocopiable 5.2 p.143 **Workbook:** p.25 Exercises 1–3, p.26 Exercises 1–3
5.3 > **Communication skills:** Negotiating team roles	**Lead-in** Students talk about the skills needed in a good team. **Video** Students watch a video about negotiating roles in a team. **Reflection** Students reflect on the conclusions from the video and discuss their preferred approach to negotiating roles in a team. **Functional language** Students look at useful language for discussing team roles in meetings. **Task** Students practise the functional language from the lesson by playing a game.	**MyEnglishLab:** Teacher's resources: extra activities; Interactive video activities; Functional language bank **Workbook:** p.27 Exercises 1 and 2
5.4 > **Business skills:** Presenting facts and figures	**Lead-in** Students look at different ways of presenting facts and figures. **Listening** Students listen to a presentation about retail banking. **Functional language** Students look at useful language for quoting figures in presentations. **Task** Students give a presentation on equal pay.	**MyEnglishLab:** Teacher's resources: extra activities; Functional language bank **Pronunciation bank:** p.116 Numbers and figures **Workbook:** p.27 Exercise 3
5.5 > **Writing:** Letter about a price increase	**Lead-in** Students read and complete a formal letter explaining a price increase. **Functional language** Students look at useful language for a formal letter explaining a price increase. **Task** Students write a formal letter explaining a price increase.	**MyEnglishLab:** Teacher's resources: extra activities; Interactive grammar practice; Writing bank **Grammar reference:** p.123 *because, so, so that* **Workbook:** p.28 Exercises 1–3
Business workshop 5 > Local economy boost	**Reading** Students read about three community projects. **Listening** Students listen to a town council meeting and to local residents discussing different community projects. **Task** Students roleplay a meeting to discuss three community projects and decide on the best one. **Writing** Students write an announcement for the town council website.	**MyEnglishLab:** Teacher's resources: extra activities

Business brief

The main aim of this unit is to introduce students to various concepts related to money, including the **economy**, **methods of payment** and **personal finance**.

Global banks, which form part of the wider financial system, have experienced many challenges in the last decade. These started in 2007 with a crisis in the **mortgage** market in the USA, then developed into an international banking crisis after the collapse of the investment bank Lehman Brothers in 2008. Massive **bail-outs** for financial institutions and emergency **fiscal policies** were introduced by governments to try and prevent a possible collapse of the world financial system. The crisis was nonetheless followed by a **global economic downturn** now known as **The Great Recession**. The **European debt crisis**, a crisis in the banking system of the European countries who use the euro, followed soon after.

One result of the financial crisis of 2008 was a **credit crunch**, where banks and financial institutions became much less willing to lend money to individuals or corporations. In particular, the credit crunch created problems for smaller businesses which found it increasingly difficult to raise the **funds** they needed to operate in an adverse **economic climate** which was impacting their **revenues** and **cash flow**. The recovery since 2008 has been slow and the **International Monetary Fund (IMF)** reports that **global debt** is now worse than it was prior to the global financial crisis.

An important recent change in the banking industry is the move towards a **cashless economy** where **financial transactions** (buying goods and services, paying bills) are made digitally using **credit** or **debit cards**, **store cards** or **mobile wallets**. Other cashless methods used between businesses or individuals include **bank transfers**, **direct debits** and **online payment** methods like PayPal. One big advantage of cashless payments is that they make it easier to follow money; it is more difficult for people and companies to avoid paying taxes, or to use funds for criminal purposes, when all transactions are recorded online.

This move towards **online banking** and **mobile banking** means that although we might still see a queue at the **cash dispenser** (**ATM**), people rarely need to go into local **branches** to carry out financial transactions. As a result, many local bank branches have become under-used and some have closed. It also means that fewer businesses now use **petty cash** to pay for small expense items, or to pay casual workers **cash in hand**.

Another way of moving money without cash is by using a **crypto currency**. This is an **encrypted**, person-to-person system of making payments online that works outside a centralised banking system. Most digital payment systems use a central authority (such as a bank) to verify the payments, whereas crypto currencies use a peer-to-peer network. As a result, **international transaction fees** are much lower than those charged by banks. The first crypto currency is believed to have been **Bitcoin**, created in 2009, but there are now over 4,000 other crypto currencies. Although crypto currencies have gained in popularity, they are still not seen as stable or reliable enough for mass use.

The move towards a cashless economy has been enthusiastically adopted by some countries. Sweden is forecast to become completely cashless by 2030 and 900 of the country's 1600 banks no longer accept **cash deposits**. Canada is currently the country which uses credit cards most widely, with approximately two per person. China has experienced the highest growth in cashless payments over the last five years, while in the UK only 3.9 percent of payments are now made in cash.

Money and your students

It is important that students are aware of the concept of money in relation both to economics and personal finance. The financial world is changing rapidly and transaction methods are constantly evolving. However, both pre-work and in-work students should be able to talk about how they make personal payments. In-work students may also have experience of making financial transactions for their company. It's useful for students to be aware that the circulation of money will continue to change and that methods of payment already exist which may differ from those that are the norm in their environment.

Unit lead-in

Ask students to look at the photo and unit title, then draw their attention to the quote. Elicit or explain that it refers to the fact that a bank will only approve a loan after confirming a borrower will be able to repay it. Ask students what things a bank will usually check before approving a loan (e.g. financial status, annual income, type of employment, savings, assets, credit history). If your students are comfortable discussing the topic, you could ask them if they or someone they know have ever tried to take out a loan and how easy or difficult it was. Ask volunteers to share their experience with the class.

5.1 ❯ Going cashless

GSE learning objectives

- Can follow the main points in a simple audio recording aimed at a general audience.
- Can identify key details in a simple recorded dialogue or narrative.
- Can use language related to money.
- Can use language related to household finance.
- Can use language related to buying and selling.
- Can use language related to banking and insurance.
- Can write a short, simple marketing document, describing products or services.

Warm-up

Refer students to the lesson title and elicit or give a brief definition of the word *cashless* – help students understand by pointing out the suffix *-less* (= without). Introduce the concept of a *cashless economy* (an economy where all transactions are carried out through digital means rather than with money in the form of coins and notes). Ask what students know about cashless payments and whether they think moving away from *physical money* is a good idea. Keep the discussion brief at this point – students will discuss different aspects of the topic in more detail in the exercises that follow.

Lead-in

Students discuss different types of cashless payment.

1 Go through the words in the box with students and check that they understand them. Give them a minute to tick the methods they have used in the past month, then invite different students to share their answers with the class.

2 Get students to discuss the question in pairs or small groups first, then elicit answers around the class. Encourage students to give reasons.

Video

Students watch a video about cashless payment systems in India.

3 Explain to students that they are going to watch a video about cashless payments in India. Before they discuss the questions, you may wish to give them some background information (see Notes above). Some useful vocabulary from the video which could be pre-taught includes: *abolish,*

(payment) gateway (an e-commerce service which authorises the transfer of funds from the customer's credit card to the online retailer), *queue* and *buy something upfront*. Also check students understand *notes* and *track* in question 1.

> **1 Possible answer**
> All of the answers are reasonable except for b. Thieves can steal electronic money in various ways, including identity theft.
> **2** Students' own answers

> ### Notes
> In November 2016, India's Prime Minister Narendra Modi announced the demonetisation of all 500 and 1,000 rupee banknotes in one of a series of moves to make India a cashless society. The two notes accounted for approximately 85 percent of the currency in circulation, and their ban forced everyone to turn to alternative transaction methods, such as digital payments and credit and debit cards. Since the ban, the government has been promoting cashless transactions, offering consumers incentives for their use (e.g. discounts, free product insurance, service tax exemption).

4 ▶ 5.1.1 Play the video, then discuss the question as a class.

> **1** c and d **2** buy street food, buy vegetables, (you can't) pay for a taxi

5 ▶ 5.1.1 Go through the statements with students and check they understand the options in italics before they watch again. Then play the video and check answers with the class.

> **1** cash **2** at the time of delivery **3** credit card **4** a lot
> **5** in cash **6** cash

Extra activities

A ▶ 5.1.1 This activity practises useful collocations from the video. Get students to match the words individually, then play the video for them to check their answers. During feedback, teach or elicit the meaning of each collocation. If time allows, you could play the video again during feedback, pausing after each collocation, so students can hear it used in context again.

> **1** d **2** c **3** a **4** e **5** b

B Get students to complete the exercise individually and then compare answers in pairs before class feedback.

> **1** small business **2** everyday item
> **3** a common sight **4** difficult times **5** street corner

6 You may wish to get students to discuss the question in pairs or groups first, and then as a class. Remind students of their answers to question 2 in Exercise 3.

Vocabulary: Money

Students look at vocabulary related to money and the economy.

7 Students could do this exercise individually or in pairs. During feedback, clarify meanings as necessary. In weaker classes, this can also be done as a whole-class activity, checking answers and clarifying meanings as you go along.

> **1** b **2** a **3** f **4** d **5** c **6** e **7** g

Collocations

Students look at collocations related to money, the economy and personal finance.

8A Give students time to read the sentences, then elicit the answer. Do not focus on meanings yet as students will do this in the next exercise.

> cash

8B Put students in pairs and give them 4–5 minutes to complete the exercise, using their dictionaries if necessary. During feedback, point out that *pay in cash* in question 4 can also be used without the preposition *in* (*pay cash*).

> **cash crunch:** not having enough coins and paper notes in the economy; this is what happened in India in 2018
>
> **cash flow:** the movement of money coming into a business as income and going out as wages, materials, etc.
>
> **cash register:** a machine used in shops to keep the money in and record the amount of money received from each sale
>
> **pay (in) cash:** pay for something using paper notes and coins
>
> **withdraw cash:** take money out of a bank account
>
> **cash in hand:** pay someone directly and not into their bank account
>
> **petty cash:** a small amount of money that is kept in an office for making small payments
>
> **cash on delivery:** pay for something with paper notes and coins as soon as you receive it
>
> **cash dispenser:** another name for a 'cash machine' or 'ATM'; a machine from which customers can get money
>
> **short of cash:** not having enough cash

9A Teach or elicit the meaning of *small charge* and get students to complete the exercise individually. Remind them that they may need to change the form of some words.

> **1** mobile wallet **2** withdraw cash **3** short of cash
> **4** cash dispenser **5** currency

9B Put students in pairs or small groups and give them 3–5 minutes to discuss the questions. Then invite different students to share their answers with the class. Some students might be reluctant to talk about question 3, so you may prefer not to ask this question in open class.

> **Extra activities 5.1**
>
> **C** This activity gives further practice of vocabulary from Exercises 7 and 8. Get students to complete the activity individually and then compare answers in pairs before class feedback.
>
> > **1** petty cash **2** cash flow **3** cash dispenser
> > **4** cash register **5** cash in hand **6** cash crunch
> > **7** short of cash **8** withdraw **9** pay cash
> > **10** cash on delivery

Project: Let's go cashless!

Students create an advertisement to promote cashless payments.

10 Explain the activity and go through the expressions in the box with students. Check they understand *convenient*. Give them 2–3 minutes to complete the table individually, then briefly discuss the answers as a class.

> **Possible answers**
> **Cash**
> Advantages: *convenient*, you know how much you have
> Disadvantages: easy to lose, people can steal it
> **Cashless payments**
> Advantages: convenient, no need for correct change
> Disadvantages: not every seller accepts it, people can steal it

11A Put students in pairs, go through the instructions with them and get them to copy the table into their notebooks so that they can make notes. Before they begin, remind them of the vocabulary in Exercises 1 and 3. During the activity, monitor and help pairs with any vocabulary they may need. When they have finished, elicit ideas around the class and encourage students to add other pairs' ideas to their tables.

11B Pairs choose the type of advert they are going to create. List the types from the activity rubric on the board (*magazine, newspaper, television, radio*) and go through the list of points to think about. Give pairs 3–4 minutes to agree on how they want to present their information. Bear in mind that students will present their adverts to the class in Exercise 11D, so you might like to specify the format of the advert to avoid practical issues (e.g. avoid a TV/radio advert if students cannot access the equipment needed for one).

11C Students now create their adverts. Draw their attention to the list of points and remind them to use their ideas from Exercises 10 and 11A. Consider specifying the size of the advert (including the amount of text) if it's a poster, or, if in another format, stipulate a suitable length (i.e. for an interview, story, commercial) so that students know the level of detail (and language) required for the task. This will help to minimise variations in what is produced by each group.

11D Students present their adverts to the class. Ask them to divide up their presentation so that both students in each pair get a chance to speak. As a follow-up, you could do a class vote on which advert students think would be the most effective.

MyEnglishLab: Teacher's resources: extra activities
Teacher's book: Resource bank Photocopiable 5.1 p.142
Workbook: p.24 Exercises 1–3

5.2 ⟩ Consumer spending

GSE learning objectives

- Can follow the main points in a simple audio recording aimed at a general audience.
- Can identify key details in a simple recorded dialogue or narrative.
- Can describe possible future outcomes of a present action or situation using the first conditional.

Warm-up

Ask: *What sort of things do you like / not like to spend money on?* Put students in pairs or small groups to discuss the question. Then elicit answers around the class.

Lead-in

Students talk about their spending habits.

1A Look at the pie chart with students and check they understand the words for the different segments. Demonstrate or elicit the correct pronunciation of *debt*. Get students to discuss the question in pairs or small groups, then invite a few students to share their answers with the class.

1B Go through the words in the box and clarify any unknown vocabulary, then get students to complete the exercise individually or in pairs before checking with the class. Alternatively, this can be done as a quick whole-class activity.

Housing: mortgage payment, rent
Food, clothes, entertainment: business suit, cinema ticket, meals at work
Transport: bicycle, bus ticket
Debt repayment: mortgage payment, paying a car loan, paying interest on a credit card bill
Savings: pension payment, putting money in the bank for emergencies

2 Again, students could discuss the questions in pairs or small groups before sharing their answers with the class.

Listening

Students listen to a podcast about money.

3A ◀⟩ 5.01 Explain that students are going to listen to a podcast about money and go through the topics with them. Check they understand *emergency expenses*, *interest rates*, *currency exchange rates* and *changing money*. Do not focus on the meaning of *It all adds up!* yet as students will do this in the next exercise. Play the recording, then check answers with the class.

b, d, e

3B Give students time to read the information and check they understand the different uses of *add up*. Then discuss the answer with the class.

Because we literally add up when we look after our money, but also because the show gives advice about how to make small changes that will save lots of money over time.

4 ◀⟩ 5.01 Give students a minute to read the sentences, then play the recording and check answers with the class.

1 take your lunch   2 with your credit card
3 cinema tickets   4 borrowing   5 Mortgages
6 buy Chinese electronics

Extra activities

A ◀⟩ 5.01 This activity looks at useful vocabulary from the listening. Ask students to complete it individually, then play the recording for them to check their answers. Clarify meanings as necessary during feedback.

1 hundreds   2 thousands   3 borrowing   4 savers
5 imports

5 Get students to discuss the questions in pairs or small groups first, then elicit answers around the class. Encourage students to give reasons.

Grammar: First conditional

Students study and practise the first conditional.

6A–B Do these as whole-class activities. Refer students to the sentences in the table and draw their attention to a) the fact that each sentence has two parts and b) the verb forms in bold in each part. Check that they understand the meaning of *condition* (something that must exist or happen before something else can happen), then elicit the answers. Explain or elicit the main use of the first conditional: to talk about an action/a situation (= the condition) with a possible result in the future.

6A 1 a   2 b
6B 1 a possible result in the future   2 a condition

6C Let students think about the structures individually first, then check answers with the class. Explain or elicit that when a sentence starts with the condition (the *if* clause), we use a comma between the two clauses; when the result clause comes first, we do not use a comma.

1 *If*   2 *will*   3 infinitive   4 Present Simple

7 Before students do the exercise, refer them to the Grammar reference on page 123 and go through it with them, clarifying any points as necessary. Then get them to complete the sentences individually and compare answers in pairs before checking with the class.

1 will/'ll save   2 don't start   3 go down   4 sell   5 stops
6 will/'ll have

Extra activities 5.2

B This activity gives further practice of the first conditional. Do the first item as an example with the class, then get students to complete the exercise individually; remind them to use commas where necessary. Check answers with the class.

1 If you save money this year, you will be able to go on a nice holiday.
2 If he pays off his credit card bill next month, he won't have any more debt.
3 If she buys a new house, she will have more debt.
4 If I get a pay rise at work, I'll buy a new car.
5 If I don't prepare for the interview, I won't get the job.
6 If interest rates go up next month, savers will earn more money.

▶ Pronunciation bank
p. 116: Intonation in conditionals

Warm-up
🔊 P5.01 Write the first example sentence from the box on the board (*If I buy a car, I'll buy a second-hand one.*). Get students to read the sentence aloud and ask: *Which words are stressed?* (*car* and *hand*). Play the first sentence and ask students if they notice anything about the speaker's intonation. Elicit answers but do not confirm them yet; instead, refer students to the explanation in the box and go through it with them. Play the full recording and drill the sentences around the class. To help students, you could write the sentences on the board and mark the rising and falling intonation using arrows.

1 🔊 P5.02 Play the recording, twice if necessary, then check answers with the class.

1 money, English 2 cycle, thousands
3 money, bigger 4 car, bicycle
5 weather's, walk 6 lunch, hundreds
7 transport, money 8 deposit, house

2 Put students in pairs to practise saying the sentences. If necessary, play the recording again for them to listen and repeat before they practise on their own. During the activity, monitor and correct students' intonation as necessary.

Speaking
Students practise using the first conditional.

8A–B Get students to do the matching task individually and check answers with the class. Then put them in pairs to discuss the statements. After 3–4 minutes, invite different students to share their answers with the class.

1 c 2 a 3 e 4 b 5 f 6 d

8C–D Ask students to write their sentences individually. Monitor and make sure they are using the first conditional correctly. Then put them in small groups (in a different group to the students they worked with in Exercise 8A) to compare and discuss their sentences.

MyEnglishLab: Teacher's resources: extra activities; Reading bank
Grammar reference: p.123 First conditional
Pronunciation bank: p.116 Intonation in conditionals
Teacher's book: Resource bank Photocopiable 5.2 p.143
Workbook: p.25 Exercises 1–3, p.26 Exercises 1–3

5.3 ▶ Communication skills
Negotiating team roles

GSE learning objectives
- Can use language related to agreement or disagreement.
- Can make and respond to suggestions.
- Can give or seek personal views and opinions in discussing topics of interest.

Warm-up
Put students in pairs and ask them to tell each other about a good team they have been part of. What do they think made it a good team? What skills did the members of the team have? Give students 3–4 minutes to discuss in their pairs, then elicit answers around the class.

Lead-in
Students talk about the skills needed in a good team.

1A–B Draw students' attention to the chart and check they understand the words *challenge* and *comfort*. Then go through skills 1–9 with them and elicit or give an example for each: planning projects (e.g. a project for their place of study or work), working with figures (e.g. managing personal finance), personal communication (e.g. talking to / messaging friends), leading teams (e.g. at work or in sport), using technology (e.g. online shopping), public speaking (e.g. giving a presentation at work/college), doing research (e.g. for a project), managing your time (e.g. creating/keeping a deadline), making decisions (e.g. at work or in their personal life). Give students a minute to rate themselves, then put them in groups to compare and discuss their charts. Get brief feedback from each group: are they different enough to make a good team?

Video
Students watch a video about negotiating roles in a team.

2A ▶ 5.3.1 If your students watched the Unit 4 video, ask them to give you a short summary of the situation and the main characters. If this is the first communication skills video for your class, briefly set up the context and/or refer students to page 6 of the Coursebook. Pre-teach *client pitch*: refer students to the definition on the page. Give students time to read the questions, then play the video and discuss the answers with the class.

1 It's the first time all the members of the team have worked together.
2 The purpose of today's meeting is to allocate the team roles.
3 Orla is trying to decide whether to simply tell the team what their roles are or to get them to decide among themselves.
4 Shaun recommends the first option.

2B Discuss the questions as a class. Ask students who agree with Shaun's advice to say what advantages they think this approach may have (e.g. making sure that all roles are covered, avoiding people all opting for the interesting roles).

Possible answer

People generally prefer to be allowed to organise their workload according to their personal strengths. If Orla imposes roles on people without asking for their input, this may give rise to objections / a negative reaction.

3A ▶ 5.3.2 Explain that students are going to watch the meeting where Orla allocates roles to the team members and give them a minute to read the questions. Check they understand the different roles in question 2 and play the video. As a brief follow-up, you could ask students if they would react in the same way to Orla's approach.

1 Yes, she does. The reaction is mostly negative.
2 pitch leader: Alex; tech support: Thiago; lead presenter: Azra; learning designer: Jasmine
3 Alex has the most project management experience; Thiago is good with technology; Azra wants to develop her presentation skills; Jasmine is a learning and development specialist and a responsible person.
4 Azra doesn't think she's a good enough presenter for such an important pitch to a new client; Jasmine is anxious about the level of responsibility involved in being the learning designer; Thiago thinks he shouldn't have to always do the tech support.

3B Get students to discuss the questions in pairs or groups first, then elicit ideas around the class.

Suggested answer

Orla was too directive and not prepared to listen to the group's objections. The group were too direct in their objections.

4A ▶ 5.3.3 Explain that students are going to watch another version of the meeting, where Orla uses a different approach. Encourage students to make notes while watching, and play the video. Check answers with the class.

1 Because, although it's their first time together as a team, they already know each other quite well.
2 Azra thinks the situation is too important for her to be practising her presentation skills.
3 Because, although it's a new client and, therefore, especially important, Jasmine has the expertise and Orla will be there to support her.
4 He won two public speaking competitions at university.

5 Alex and Azra have swapped roles as pitch leader and lead presenter. Alex and Thiago are now sharing responsibility for both the presentation and the PowerPoint slides.

4B Discuss the questions with the whole class.

Possible answers

People are much more polite about their objections. They suggest roles rather than impose them. They say 'no' diplomatically and give reasons for saying 'no'.

5 ▶ 5.3.4 Explain that students are going to watch the Conclusions section of the video, which discusses the advantages and disadvantages of the two approaches in Videos A and B. Play the video and put students in pairs or small groups to compare the advice the speaker gives with their own reaction to each approach. Get brief feedback from the class.

Reflection

Students reflect on the conclusions from the video and discuss their preferred approach to negotiating roles in a team.

6 Allow students to work individually on this so that they can reflect on their own ideas. Ask them to answer the questions and to make notes. Then put them in pairs to discuss and compare their answers. Get brief feedback from the class.

Functional language: Agreeing on team roles in meetings

Students look at useful language for discussing team roles in meetings.

7A Ask students to do this exercise individually. Before they begin, check they understand *exchange/swap roles* and *head up (a project)*. Check answers with the class.

1 d **2** c **3** f **4** b **5** a **6** e **7** g **8** h

7B You could do this as a whole-class activity, checking answers as you go along.

Checking agreement

Is that OK with everyone?
How would you feel about that?
If you don't mind.
If you're both happy to exchange roles, then that's fine with me.

Making suggestions

I was thinking you could head up the project.
Perhaps Azra and I could swap roles.
I'd like you to be the learning designer.
How would you like to do the PowerPoint for us again?

8A Ask students to work individually. Explain that they have to use different pieces of the puzzle and that different combinations are possible. Give them 3–4 minutes to write their sentences and then put them in pairs to compare their answers. Elicit different combinations around the class.

Possible answers

I'd rather not be the lead presenter.
Sorry, but I'd rather not be the lead presenter.
Sorry, but I'd rather not be the lead presenter if that's OK.
Sorry, but I'd rather not be the lead presenter if that's OK with you.
I'd prefer not to do it again.
I don't mind, but I'd prefer not to do it again.
I don't mind, but I'd prefer not to do it again if I have a choice.

8B Go through the instructions with the class and draw their attention to the example sentences. Before students attempt the exercise, elicit the different ways to talk about strengths/weaknesses shown in the puzzle and list them on the board. Help students with the structures used:
Strengths: *I'm good / quite good with* + noun; *I'm good / quite good at + -ing*; *he/she is (much) better than me at/with … .*
Weaknesses: *I'm not very good with* + noun; *I'm not very good at + -ing*; *She's (much) better than me at/with … .*
Elicit or give examples of ways to end each sentence, e.g. different skills (*I'm good at solving problems on my own, I'm not very good with numbers*, etc.). Ensure students avoid boastful comparisons to others (e.g. *I'm much better at … than …*). Then ask students to work individually to write their sentences, while you monitor and help them as necessary. Finish by asking different students to share their sentences with the class.

Possible answers

I'm (quite) good at presenting.
I'm good with technology.
I'm not very good at presenting.
She's/He's (much) better than me at presenting / at presenting than me.
He/She is much better with technology than me.

Extra activities 5.3

A Put students in pairs and tell them that they are going to play a game. Go through the instructions with the class and elicit one or two example sentences from students. Give pairs two minutes to write their sentences, then invite them to read out their sentences in turn and give them one point for each correct sentence – you could note their scores on the board. In bigger classes, or if time is short, students could play in small groups so there are fewer lists to check during feedback.

Possible answers

I'd like you to give the presentation (if you don't mind).
How would you like to give the presentation?
I was thinking you could give the presentation (if you don't mind).
Perhaps you could give the presentation (if you don't mind).
Is that OK with you?
Is that OK with everyone?
How would you feel about that?
How would you feel about giving the presentation?
If you are happy to give the presentation, it's fine by me.
It's fine by me if you are happy to give the presentation.
If you don't mind (giving the presentation), it's fine by me.
It's fine by me if you don't mind (giving the presentation).

B Ask students to write the word *CHECKING* and the word *SUGGESTING* on two pieces of paper/card. Explain that you are going to read out possible sentences from activity A and students need to decide if each one is making a suggestion, checking agreement or both. They should hold up the correct card for each sentence (or both cards if they think the sentence is doing both). Do an example with the class, then read out the sentences below, pausing after each one.

I'd like you to give the presentation (suggestion) (if you don't mind). (both)
How would you like to give the presentation? (both)
I was thinking you could give the presentation (suggestion) (if you don't mind). (both)
Perhaps you could give the presentation (suggestion) (if you don't mind). (both)
Is that OK with you? (checking)
Is that OK with everyone? (checking)
How would you feel about that? (checking)
How would you feel about giving the presentation? (both)
If you are happy to give the presentation, it's fine by me. (checking)
It's fine by me if you're happy to give the presentation. (checking)
If you don't mind (giving the presentation), it's fine by me. (checking)
It's fine by me if you don't mind (giving the presentation). (checking)

Task

Students practise the functional language from the lesson by playing a game.

9A Put students in pairs and tell them that they are going to play a game. Refer them to the grid on page 132 and remind them of the three 'zones of ability' in Exercise 1A. Explain that in their pairs, they should each choose five 'comfort zone tasks' and five 'danger zone tasks'. The remaining six tasks on their grid will be their 'challenge zone tasks'. Go through the tasks on the grid and clarify meanings as necessary, then give them 1–2 minutes to select their tasks. Tell them not to show their grid to their partner. In weaker classes, or if time is short, you could ask students to choose fewer tasks for each category (e.g. three from each zone, finishing with three challenge zone tasks).

9B Go through the rules of the game with students. Make sure they understand what they need to do and how to keep score. You could note the following on the board for them to refer to:
- comfort zone: +2 points (agree to do task)
- danger zone: -1 point (say 'no' → explain why not → suggest someone else)
- challenge zone: +2 points (if you can say why it would be good to learn how to do task).

You may wish to do an example for each zone with a stronger student to demonstrate. Remind them to use language from Exercises 7 and 8. Stop the game after 10 minutes and ask students to count up their score.

9C Let students discuss this in their pairs first, then get feedback from the class. If time allows, they could play again in new pairs.

MyEnglishLab: Teacher's resources: extra activities; Interactive video activities; Functional language bank
Workbook: p.27 Exercises 1 and 2

5.4 ❯ Business skills
Presenting facts and figures

GSE learning objectives

- Can follow the main points in a simple audio recording aimed at a general audience.
- Can identify key details in a simple recorded dialogue or narrative.
- Can use basic discourse markers to structure a short presentation.
- Can make and respond to suggestions.

Warm-up

Keep this stage brief. Ask students to think about presentations they have attended at their place of work or study, or articles they have read which contained statistical information. Ask them if they find it hard to follow numbers in presentations/articles and if so, why. Use this as an opportunity to teach *exact figure* and *approximate figure* and ask students which they find easier to follow. Do not go into detail about the different ways to present figures yet – students will look at these in the exercises that follow.

Lead-in

Students look at different ways of presenting facts and figures.

1A Look at the three sentences with students and explain what is meant by *effective* in the instructions: if these were extracts from a presentation, which one would they find easier to remember? Why? Elicit answers around the class.

Possible answer

1 is a bit vague – how many is 'a lot'? 2 is the most accurate – some audiences (e.g. those whose jobs involve working with a lot of data) may prefer this. But 3 is generally the most effective because whole numbers are easier to remember than decimals.

1B Again, look at the statements with students and check they understand the phrases in bold. Put them in pairs to discuss the question, then invite different students to share their answers with the class. Encourage them to give reasons.

Possible answer

Both of these options are probably more effective than 1–3 in Exercise 1A because they don't just give the audience a figure – they also put that figure in context to show how significant it is. Twelve million sounds a lot, but is it? Statement 1 tells us how many American women out of the total female population of the USA are business owners. It would be easy to design a simple visual aid to show this. Statement 2 compares the number of women business owners in the USA with the entire populations of three economically developed countries and is perhaps an even more surprising statistic than 1.

2A It may be better to do this as a whole-class activity, clarifying meanings of the words in bold as you go along. Alternatively, in stronger classes, students could work individually or in pairs, using their dictionaries if necessary. Elicit or explain that all the words in bold except *under* and *over* mean 'about'. If you did not do the Warm-up activity, check that students understand the meanings of *exact figures* and *approximate figures*.

> **1** e **2** a **3** f **4** c **5** g **6** d **7** b

2B Get students to complete the exercise individually and compare answers in pairs before checking with the class.

> **a** ≈ (approximately) **b** < (less than) **c** ≈ (approximately)
> **d** < (less than) **e** < (less than) **f** > (more than)
> **g** ≈ (approximately)

2C Do this as a whole-class activity. Write *well over/under ...* and *just over/under ...* on the board and check the answers with the class. Elicit or give examples for each phrase (e.g. *just under/ over three percent, well under/over ten centimetres long*).

> **a** well (over/under) **b** just (over/under)

Listening

Students listen to a presentation about retail banking.

3A 🔊 5.02 Go through the instructions and questions with the class. Refer students to slide 1 for question 2 and check they understand the meaning of 'b.' (= *born*). With weaker classes, you may need to play the recording a second time or pause briefly after each answer is given, to allow students time to process the information and make notes.

> **1** She asks the audience a simple *yes/no* question, asks them to raise their hands if the answer is 'yes' and makes a little joke – all good ways of getting their attention.
> **2** Generation X (b. 1964–79), Generation Y (= Millennials) (b. 1980–1994), Generation Z (b. 1995–2012)
> **3** Generation Z because they are already over a quarter of the population and will soon be the bank's biggest customers.
> **4** Lifestyle – live for today (perhaps don't plan for the future); Technology – always online (perhaps not much face-to-face contact); Work – don't like to work (perhaps more interested in leisure activities); Money – no idea about money (perhaps spend more than they save).

3B Let students complete as much of the information as they can remember and if necessary, play the recording again for them to complete their answers. Check answers with the class.

> **2** early twenties **3** mid-nineteen-sixties **4** late seventies
> **5** early eighties **6** early twenty-tens

4A 🔊 5.03 Go through the instructions with students and refer them to slide 2. Check they understand the meanings of *savings account*, *account-holder*, *retirement* and *opposed to*. Point out that they need to listen for *approximate figures* in order to write the numbers as percentages in the slide. Refer them to the example and play the first part of the recording. Pause it after 'some kind of full- or part-time employment' and ask students which *approximate figure* Liz uses which translates to '76%' (*roughly three-quarters*). Explain that they will need to do the same for the other approximate figures Liz uses, i.e. match them with the exact figures given and write them in slide 2. Finally, pre-teach *a billion* and *a trillion* before playing the rest of the recording.

> own savings account 64%
> account-holders since age 10 21%
> already saving for retirement 12%
> opposed to all forms of debt 29%

4B 🔊 5.03 Give students time to read the questions before they listen. Again, you may need to play the recording a second time and/or pause after answers are given, to give students enough time to process the information and make notes.

> 1 The employment figures for Generation Z, which are almost the same as for the older Generation Y, prove that they are not afraid of work.
> 2 The most surprising figure is that 12% of Generation Z is already saving for their retirement, even though most of them will not retire for fifty years or more.
> 3 They are especially against college debt, which has been a major problem for Generations X and Y in the USA.
> 4 The good news for banks is that 16–21-year-olds like to save money. The bad news is that they don't like to borrow it.

5A 🔊 5.04 Tell students that they are going to listen to the last part of Liz's presentation, and explain the activity. Check they understand the abbreviation for *billion* (*bn*) in the slide, then play the recording. Check answers with the class.

> 1 10.6 = the average number of hours each member of Generation Z spends online per day
> 2 1 billion = the total number of hours Generation Z in the USA spends online per day
> 3 53% = the percentage of Generation Z who say they prefer face-to-face communication to online communication
> 4 42 million = the total number of members of Generation Z who say they prefer face-to-face communication to online communication

5B If students cannot remember the answer from the first listening, play the recording again. Discuss the answer as a class.

> Liz points out that, because more than half of Generation Z prefer face-to-face communication, the bank needs to connect with them on a personal level. This means doing more than just social media marketing.

6 Again, if students cannot remember the answer, play the recording again or refer them to the audio script on page 151.

Possible answer

Liz adds impact to the figure of 10.6 hours by putting it in context in two ways. First, she multiplies this figure by the number of Generation Z-ers in the USA to give the total number of hours this generation spends online – a billion. That's a surprising and easy-to-remember number. To give it even more meaning, Liz also tells her audience what they could do in that amount of time – watch every movie ever made (about 500,000 movies) one thousand times. This kind of information makes figures memorable and the presentation more interesting.

Functional language: Quoting figures in presentations

Students look at useful language for quoting figures in presentations.

7 Students complete the activity individually or in pairs, using their dictionaries if necessary. During feedback, clarify meanings and encourage students to highlight the completed expressions (or record them in their vocabulary notebooks).

> 1 look, shows 2 see 3 context, figure 4 idea 5 thing
> 6 takeaway 7 summary 8 terms, means

8 Explain the activity and refer students to the language they looked at in Exercises 2A and 2B. Give or elicit an example for the first figure, then ask students to write their sentences individually. Weaker students may need more than one minute for this. Then put students in pairs to compare their sentences. Monitor, checking answers and helping as necessary.

Possible answers

> 33.4% – more than / just over 33% / a third / one in three
> 27.8% – well over 25% / a quarter / one out of five
> 99.9 – nearly / almost / around / about / approximately 100
> €21m – over / above / around / about / roughly / approximately 20m euros
> 11% – just over / roughly / more than 10% / one in ten
> ¥497 – roughly / around / about / approximately / almost 500 yen
> 48.9% – nearly / almost / less than 50% / half
> £995bn – nearly / almost / around / about / approximately / roughly a trillion pounds

Extra activities 5.4

A Draw students' attention to the diagram and explain that it outlines three steps for quoting figures in presentations to make them easier for audiences to remember. Go through it with the class, then explain the activity and look at the examples with students. The exercise can be done individually or pairs.

> **a** 1 **b** 7 **c** 3 **d** 5 **e** 8 **f** 4 **g** 9 **h** 6 **i** 2 **j** 10

B Put students in groups of four and tell them that they are going to play a game using phrases for *exact* and *approximate* numbers. Let groups choose their cards and explain that each speaker reads out an *approximate* number. The rest of the group looks for the corresponding *exact* number on their cards. The student who has that number reads and crosses it out and then reads the next number on their card. The game continues until Speaker 1 reads out the last number on their card. If time allows, students can swap cards and play again.

> Speaker 1: 1 → Speaker 4: 1
> Speaker 4: 2 → Speaker 3: 1
> Speaker 3: 2 → Speaker 2: 1
> Speaker 2: 2 → Speaker 1: 2
> Speaker 1: 3 → Speaker 4: 3
> Speaker 4: 4 → Speaker 2: 3
> Speaker 2: 4 → Speaker 3: 3
> Speaker 3: 4 → Speaker 1: 4
> Speaker 1: 5 → Speaker 4: 5
> Speaker 4: 6 → Speaker 2: 5
> Speaker 2: 6 → Speaker 3: 5
> Speaker 3: 6 → Speaker 1: 6

⟩ Pronunciation bank
p. 116: Numbers and figures

Warm-up
◀) P5.03, P5.04, P5.05, P5.06, P5.07 Refer students to the information in the box and look at the points in turn, pausing after each one to drill the pronunciation. If students struggle with the pronunciation of *years* and the number *0*, do a few more examples on the board (e.g. *2003, 1908; room 103, 22.09*).

1–2 ◀) P5.08 Ask students to work individually first, then get them to compare answers in pairs. Play the recording for them to check.

> 1 room one oh one
> 2 forty-six point oh nine two / forty-six point nought nine two
> 3 the years sixteen oh five to sixteen fifteen
> 4 oh point five percent / nought point five percent
> 5 oh seven two, four six oh, seven oh five
> 6 ten-to-twelve-year-olds
> 7 eighteen point oh seven percent / eighteen point nought seven percent
> 8 below zero
> 9 twelve forty five to fourteen oh five
> 10 rooms four oh five to four oh nine
> 11 oh three seven one, oh five oh, three six eight, two eight oh
> 12 the years two thousand and six to twenty eighteen

3 Put students in pairs to practise saying the numbers and figures. If necessary, play the recording again before they practise on their own. During the activity, monitor and correct students' pronunciation as necessary.

Task

Students give a presentation on equal pay.

9A–B Put students in pairs or small groups and go through the instructions. Check they understand *equal pay* and *HR* (*Human Resources*) and refer them to the notes and slides on page 136. Give them time to read the information and ask any questions, and let them decide which slides each student will present. You could project the slides onto the board, copy the images onto a screen or save them onto a document and scale them up onto paper. Allow groups 4–5 minutes' preparation time, and set a time limit for each stage in Exercise 9B. Students should do stages 1 and 2 as group practice. For stage 1, they take turns to read the information directly from the notes. For stage 2, they should refer to the notes, but not read from them. Stage 3 is where groups give the presentation to the class, referring to their slides. During the activity, monitor and check students are using the functional language from the lesson correctly. Note down any errors to highlight during feedback.

9C Allow groups 4–5 minutes to discuss the points, then get feedback from the class. What do they think went well? What did they find difficult? Finally, discuss any errors you noted while monitoring.

MyEnglishLab: Teacher's resources: extra activities; Functional language bank
Pronunciation bank: p.116 Numbers and figures
Workbook: p.27 Exercise 3

5.5 ⟩ Writing
Letter about a price increase

GSE learning objectives
- Can identify specific information in simple letters, brochures and short articles.
- Can write a simple work-related email/letter to someone outside their company.
- Can write a basic formal email/letter requesting information.

Warm-up
Discuss the following questions with the class: *Have you ever received a letter informing you of a price increase? What was it for? How did you feel? How important is it for companies to explain why they are increasing prices?*

Lead-in

Students read and complete a formal letter explaining a price increase.

1 Before students complete the exercise, ask them to read the letter and answer the following questions: *What reason does the writer give for the price increase?* (rising costs) *What else is she sending with the letter?* (a new price list). Check students understand *remain competitive* and ask them to complete the exercise individually. Check answers with the class.

> 1 increase our prices by 5 percent from 1st October
> 2 if we do not raise prices 3 we will continue to use the best materials 4 our prices remain competitive

Functional language

Students look at useful language for a formal letter explaining a price increase.

2A Do this as a whole-class activity. After discussing the answers, you may wish to draw students' attention to the structure of a formal letter. Ask: *Where does the address go?* (top left) *Where does the date go?* (right-hand side of the page, before the greeting). Also point out the sender's name and title at the bottom.

> **1** b **2** a

2B Go through the headings in the table with students and check they understand each one. Then get them to complete the exercise individually or, for weaker classes, in pairs, and check answers with the class. During feedback, clarify meanings as necessary.

> **1** Unfortunately **2** rise **3** remain **4** Quality **5** enclose **6** with **7** for **8** supplying

Extra activities 5.5

A Get students to complete the activity individually and compare answers in pairs before class feedback.

> **1** Dear **2** prices **3** increase **4** keeping
> **5** remain **6** Enclosed **7** appreciate **8** supplying
> **9** in **10** sincerely

Optional grammar work

The letter in Exercise 1 contains examples of the linking words *because*, *so* and *so that*, so you could use it for some optional grammar work. Refer students to the Grammar reference on page 123 and use the exercises in MyEnglishLab for extra grammar practice.

Task

Students write a formal letter explaining a price increase.

3A Refer students to page 133 and get them to complete the exercise individually. After checking answers, you could also ask them to organise the letter into paragraphs, referring to the table in Exercise 2B (Para 1: e, g; Para 2: c, d, f; Para 3: h; Para 4: a).

> **1** e **2** g **3** c **4** d **5** f **6** h **7** a **8** b

3B Explain the task and refer students to the notes on page 135. Remind them to use phrases from Exercise 2B and organise the information in four paragraphs, referring to the model answer in Exercise 1 if necessary. If time is short, the writing task can be set as homework.

Model answer

Dear Sir/Madam,

As you know, we have not raised our prices for two years. Unfortunately, we now need to increase our prices by 7 percent from 9th September. This is because of the new design which improves our product line. However, the new design also uses more expensive materials.

We know that quality is very important to our customers so we need to use the best materials. We are keeping the price rise small so our prices still remain competitive.

Enclosed with this letter is the new price list. If you have any questions, please do not hesitate to contact us.

We thank you for your business and look forward to supplying you in the future.

Yours faithfully,

(name)

3C If students write their letters for homework, you could do this exercise in the next lesson. Put students in pairs and ask them to read their partner's letter and discuss the questions. You could then ask them to write a final, improved version of their letter in class or for homework.

MyEnglishLab: Teacher's resources: extra activities; Interactive grammar practice; Writing bank
Grammar reference: p.123 *because, so, so that*
Workbook: p.28 Exercises 1–3

Business workshop ❯5

Local economy boost

GSE learning objectives

- Can follow the main points in a simple audio recording, if provided with written supporting material.
- Can follow the main points in a simple audio recording aimed at a general audience.
- Can identify specific information in simple letters, brochures and short articles.
- Can identify specific information in a simple factual text.
- Can communicate in routine tasks requiring simple, direct exchanges of information.
- Can make simple, direct comparisons between two people or things using common adjectives.
- Can make and respond to suggestions.
- Can write short, simple notes, emails and messages relating to everyday matters.
- Can write a simple email/letter in response to a request for information.

Background

Students read about a community who want to improve the local economy and quality of life.

1 Go through the questions with students. Put them in pairs and give them time to read the background and answer the questions. Check answers with the class. During feedback, check they understand *town council* and pre-teach *town councillor*.

1 the local economy and quality of life
2 Some people want to encourage cash-only businesses and others want to avoid money in some situations.
3 other towns and cities around the world

Suggestions

Students listen to a town council meeting.

2A ◀» BW 5.01 Draw students' attention to the heading in the notes, check they understand it and elicit what ideas/solutions the people are looking for (*how to improve the local economy and quality of life in the community*). Play the recording, then check answers with the class.

1 (more) tourists 2 currency 3 time
4 exchange (marketplace) 5 market

2B ◀» BW 5.01 Give students time to read a–e and check they understand the word *trade*. Play the recording again, then check answers with the class.

1 d 2 a 3 e 4 b 5 c

3 ◀» BW 5.02 Explain to students that they are going to listen to the last part of the meeting and that they need to choose answers from the ideas in Exercise 2A. Play the recording, twice if necessary, then check answers with the class.

local currency, time bank, Saturday market

Looking more closely at options

Students read about three community projects and listen to local residents discussing them.

4A–B Explain to students that the town council have put information on their website about the three community projects they are considering more seriously. Explain the activity and go through the advantages and disadvantages in the boxes. Clarify any unknown vocabulary and give students time to read the information and complete the task. Do not confirm answers yet as students will check them in the next exercise. Put students in pairs and give them time to compare their notes from Exercise 4A. Then discuss the answers as a class.

Local currency
Advantages: increases the exchange of goods and services; helps small, cash-only businesses; keeps money in the local economy
Disadvantage: some businesses might not like the idea

Time bank
Advantages: makes all people's skills the same value; encourages people to get to know each other; gives unemployed people a work opportunity
Disadvantage: some people may think it isn't fair

Saturday market
Advantages: allows people to sell things they make; encourages people to make their own local products; encourages people to get to know each other
Disadvantage: might require expensive insurance

5A ◀» BW 5.03 Explain that two residents are now discussing the projects students read about in Exercise 4. Play the recording and check the answers with the class.

Ellen: Saturday market
David: local currency

5B ◀» BW 5.03 Explain the activity and give students time to read the statements before they listen. Point out that the speakers give a reason for their opinion in each statement. To check answers, you could play the recording again and pause after each speaker expresses each opinion to elicit the answer.

1 a D b E c N
2 a N b E c D
3 a E b D c N

Extra activities Business workshop 5

A Ask students to work individually, then to compare and discuss their answers in pairs before class feedback.

1 Saturday market 2 local currency
3 Saturday market 4 time bank 5 time bank
6 local currency

B ◀» BW 5.03 Play the recording for students to match the statements with the responses, then clarify meanings as necessary during feedback.

1 d 2 a 3 b 4 e 5 f 6 c

C You could do this as a quick whole-class activity, checking answers as you go along.

Agreeing: 2 a 4 e 5 f
Disagreeing: 1 d 3 b 6 c

Task: Choose a project

Students roleplay a meeting to discuss three community projects and decide on the best one.

6A Put students in groups of four. Explain that they are members of the community and are going to hold a meeting in order to decide which of the three projects is the best. As far as possible, try to give role A, the meeting leader, to a stronger student. If your class does not divide up into fours, role B (the shopkeeper) could be doubled (e.g. it could be a married couple or two business partners); they attend the meeting together but they only get one vote. Assign roles and refer students to their information. Give them time to think about their arguments and the advantages and disadvantages of the project they support, giving reasons for their opinions. Monitor and assist as necessary.

6B Students hold their meetings. Set a time limit, and remind them that their aim is to convince other community members to vote for the project they prefer, so they need to present their arguments clearly. If you did Extra activity B, you may wish to refer them to the language there, which they can use to respond to other members' arguments. Make sure the meeting leaders understand that they need to open the meeting, then move through each point on the agenda (so that the other participants can make the points given on their role cards). Remind leaders to keep the meeting on track and ensure each idea is discussed.

6C Invite students from different groups to say which project their group voted for. Encourage them to give reasons.

Writing

Students write an announcement for the town council website.

7 Explain the activity and if time allows, elicit phrases students could use in their announcement (e.g. *We would like to confirm the result of … , The people present at the meeting voted for … , They believe … , We hope that …*). List these on the board for students to refer to during the activity. In weaker classes, students could do the task in pairs. It can also be set for homework.

> **Model answer**
>
> We would like to confirm the result of the recent vote on which project our town will support. The people present at the meeting voted to support the local currency project. They believe this will encourage people to shop locally and will make people feel proud of our town. Local currencies have been very successful in other places. We hope everyone in town will support the project and benefit from it. If this project is successful, we may try one of the other two projects that we discussed.

MyEnglishLab: Teacher's resources: extra activities

Review ◀ 5

1 1 cashless **2** financial **3** mobile **4** currency **5** revenues **6** payment
2 1 hand **2** short **3** dispensers **4** delivery **5** petty **6** withdraw
3 1 will not / won't have, provides
2 don't pay, will / 'll need **3** walk, will / 'll save
4 will increase, get **5** eat, will not / won't feel
6 will stop, goes
4 1 with **2** mind **3** prefer **4** at **5** how **6** rather **7** feel **8** with
5 1 look **2** shows **3** see **4** quarter **5** context **6** third **7** thing
6 1 Sir **2** know **3** raised **4** Unfortunately **5** keeping **6** We enclose **7** list **8** appreciate **9** supplying **10** faithfully

6 Teamwork

Unit overview

	CLASSWORK	FURTHER WORK
6.1 **Working together**	**Lead-in** Students talk about activities they have done with other people. **Video** Students watch a video about a mountain rescue team. **Vocabulary** Students look at vocabulary related to teamwork and word building with verbs and nouns. **Project** Students plan and make a schedule for a meeting.	**MyEnglishLab:** Teacher's resources: extra activities **Pronunciation bank:** p.117 Vowel sounds: /ɪ/, /iː/, /aɪ/ and /ɪə/ **Teacher's book:** Resource bank Photocopiable 6.1 p.144 **Workbook:** p.29 Exercises 1–3
6.2 **Team building**	**Lead-in** Students look at parallels between sport and business. **Reading** Students read an article about the Importance of sport in the workplace. **Grammar** Students study and practise indefinite pronouns with *some-* and *every-*. **Speaking and writing** Students practise describing people, places, things and jobs and studies using indefinite pronouns.	**MyEnglishLab:** Teacher's resources: extra activities; Reading bank **Pronunciation bank:** p.117 Linking between words **Grammar reference:** p.123 Pronouns with *some-* and *every-* **Teacher's book:** Resource bank Photocopiable 6.2 p.145 **Workbook:** p.30 Exercises 1–3, p.31 Exercises 1–3
6.3 **Communication skills:** Supporting a colleague	**Lead-in** Students talk about ways of offering support. **Video** Students watch a video about different approaches to offering support to colleagues. **Reflection** Students think about their own approach to supporting a colleague. **Functional language** Students look at useful language for encouraging and motivating a colleague. **Task** Students roleplay conversations where they offer support to colleagues.	**MyEnglishLab:** Teacher's resources: extra activities; Interactive video activities; Functional language bank **Workbook:** p.32 Exercises 1 and 2
6.4 **Business skills:** Being positive in meetings	**Lead-in** Students discuss the importance of feeling safe in teams. **Listening** Students listen to a meeting about a recruitment problem. **Functional language** Students look at phrases for supporting, building on and questioning ideas in a team. **Task** Students hold a meeting where they support, build on or question each other's ideas.	**MyEnglishLab:** Teacher's resources: extra activities; Functional language bank **Workbook:** p.32 Exercises 3–5
6.5 **Writing:** Making requests	**Lead-in** Students read and complete an email making requests. **Functional language** Students look at useful phrases for making requests. **Task** Students write an email making requests.	**MyEnglishLab:** Teacher's resources: extra activities; Interactive grammar practice; Writing bank **Grammar reference:** p.123 Linking words for sequence **Workbook:** p.33 Exercises 1–3
Business workshop 6 The Amazing Chair Company	**Listening** Students listen to employees talking about their jobs. **Reading** Students read three business emails. **Task** Students have a group discussion about rearranging team roles and responsibilities.	**MyEnglishLab:** Teacher's resources: extra activities

Business brief

The main aim of this unit is to introduce students to the concept of **teamwork.** Job applications often ask candidates to demonstrate the ability to work well in a team, or **lead** a team, as a key requirement for a role, and interview questions often focus on this.

Some companies encourage activities which foster **collaboration** and teamwork and encourage good working relations. These can be in the form of social events such as company picnics, popular in the USA, which often include sporting competitions or teambuilding activities.

While it is true that many roles require employees to work independently, most employers want to be confident that a new employee has the right skills to work **effectively** with **colleagues** when necessary. The concept of teamwork can vary according to the degree of hierarchy in a particular work culture, or the communication style within a company. For example, in Scandinavia many companies have a **flat management structure** where it is common for everyone to contribute ideas and suggestions in a team environment, regardless of their status or position. In other cultures, respect for authority is key and the management structure is much more hierarchical. Team members may have more defined roles and important decisions might be made by the manager without much input from them.

Teamwork involves working collaboratively with others to complete a range of tasks and achieve a common goal. It is therefore important for each member to have some understanding of the roles and skills of the other people in the team. For effective working it is essential that team members meet regularly to communicate key information about what they are working on and to agree next steps towards their shared objectives. Colleagues might approach tasks in a variety of ways, so an important factor in successful teamwork is the ability to respect different perspectives and methods.

As individuals it is useful to be aware of differences in **communication styles** without making **assumptions** as to which ones are best. For example, some team members might be extroverted and keen to push their ideas forward, whereas more introverted people may need time and space to process theirs. A good leader will be able to bring together team members with different communication styles and foster a sense of **cooperation** in working towards common goals. It can, be useful to agree some **ground rules** early on in a shared project, for example, sending regular group emails to update everyone. A team leader who promotes a respectful interchange of ideas makes it easier for the team to work effectively.

Team management systems differ from business to business. In the linear approach or **Waterfall system**, each stage in a project is completed before the next begins. In contrast, the **Agile system** is based on an inter-departmental approach. Each project is divided into short blocks of time called **sprints**. After each of these, progress is evaluated by the whole team and the information is used to prioritise goals and tasks for the next sprint. Team members often have flexible roles and one person who has less to do during a particular sprint may pick up tasks for a colleague with a heavy workload to help achieve the team's common goals within the time frame.

Expectations of how a team operates may also depend on context. While some will emphasise the importance of **collaboration**, others, in areas such as sales, might encourage a sense of **competitiveness** between team members. When disagreements occur, it's useful to have **conflict management** strategies in place. Conflict can be a useful way of airing differences and allowing diverse opinions and approaches to be heard. Understanding different **viewpoints** can be a key factor in resolving issues within a team.

Teamwork and your students

It is important that students are aware of the concept of teamwork as it is an essential skill in most business environments. Pre-work students may be able to talk about teamwork in relation to their studies, playing sport or taking part in theatrical productions. Students who are in-work will probably have experience of working in a team. It's useful for students to understand various communication styles and learn to value the contribution of people with different approaches to their own.

Unit lead-in

Ask students what the photo shows (a school of fish) and how they think it relates to the unit title. (A possible answer might be that working in a team helps members face challenges more effectively – as swimming in schools helps fish to better protect themselves from predators.) Refer students to the quote and briefly discuss it as a class. Do they agree? Is 'staying together' important in the workplace? Does 'working together' always lead to success? Why? / Why not?

6.1 ❯ Working together

GSE learning objectives

- Can follow the main points in a simple audio recording, if provided with written supporting material.
- Can follow the main points in a simple audio recording aimed at a general audience.
- Can use language related to aptitude, ability, knowledge, and skills.
- Can describe skills and abilities using simple language.
- Can write simple sentences about personal skills.
- Can identify specific information in simple letters, brochures and short articles.

Warm-up

Discuss the following questions with the class: *Do you prefer to spend time alone or with friends/family? What sort of things do you prefer to do alone? What do you like to do with other people?*

Lead-in

Students talk about activities they have done with other people.

1 Ask students to do this task individually.

2 Put students in groups and ask them to tell each other about the things they ticked in Exercise 1 (e.g. if they've ticked *play music,* they should explain a little about it: *'When I was in high school, I played the trumpet in the school band.'*). Give them 3–4 minutes to discuss in their groups, then invite a few students to share their experiences with the class.

Video

Students watch a video about a mountain rescue team.

3 Draw students' attention to the photo and, if time allows, get them to discuss the questions in pairs first, then as a class. Do not refer to the topic of the video yet.

4 ▶ 6.1.1   Tell students that they are going to watch the first part of the video with the sound off and try to guess the answers to questions 1–4. Play the video (0:23–1:08), then check answers with the class.

> **1** b **2** b **3** a **4** b

5 ▶ 6.1.1   Ask students if they remember the name of the mountain in the video (Table Mountain – see Notes below).

Explain that they are now going to watch the whole video, which is about the mountain's rescue team. You may wish to pre-teach *rescue* (v, n,) *context, access* (n), *stretcher, reliable, conflict* (*management*) and *respect* (v, n).

> **1** dangerous **2** difficult **3** prepared to work **4** hurt
> **5** careful **6** communication skills **7** trust **8** relaxes

Notes

Table Mountain is a flat-topped mountain in South Africa, overlooking the port city of Cape Town. It is one of Cape Town's most famous landmarks and a very popular tourist attraction. Its highest point is Maclear's Beacon at 1,086 metres, named after Sir Thomas Maclear, an astronomer who built a stone cairn at the site in 1865. It got its distinctive shape as layers of sandstone were exposed through wind and water erosion.

Extra activities 6.1

A ▶ 6.1.1   This activity practises useful vocabulary from the video. Ask students to complete it individually or, in weaker classes, in pairs, using their dictionaries if necessary. Play the video for students to check their answers.

> **1** b **2** a **3** d **4** f **5** c **6** e

B You could do this as a whole-class activity, checking answers and clarifying meanings as you go along.

> **i** training **ii** to safety **iii** a solution **iv** hiker
> **v** patient **vi** at risk

6 Put students in pairs or small groups and give them 2–3 minutes to discuss the questions. Then invite different students to share their answers with the class, giving reasons.

Possible answer

They probably enjoy their work. They need a lot of special skills. These skills take a long time to learn, so they are probably very interested in the job and in using their skills. Helping people probably feels good.

> ❯ **Pronunciation bank**
> **p. 117: Vowel sounds:** /ɪ/, /iː/, /aɪ/ **and** /ɪə/
>
> ### Warm-up
>
> ◀》 P6.01   Refer students to the information in the box, play the recording for them to listen to the example words and drill the pronunciation. To check students recognise the phonetic symbol for each vowel sound, you could write the four example words on the board and with books closed, invite different students to come and write the correct symbol next to each one.

1 Put students in pairs to complete the table. Do not confirm answers yet as students will check them in the next exercise.

> /ɪ/   bu**s**y, **c**ity, **i**ssue, **s**imple
> /iː/   bel**ie**ve, compl**e**te, m**e**tres, p**eo**ple
> /aɪ/   cl**i**mbing, h**i**gh, h**i**ker, rel**i**able
> /ɪə/   cl**ea**rly, exper**ie**nced, r**ea**lise, z**e**ro

2 ◀ P6.02   Play the recording for students to check their answers. Then play it again for them to listen and repeat. As an optional extension for stronger classes, or for fast-finishers, you could ask students to add two or three more words to each group. They could then check their answers in a dictionary.

3 ◀ P6.03   Play the recording, then put students in pairs to practise saying the sentences. Monitor and check their pronunciation, modelling the vowel sounds if necessary.

Vocabulary: Teamwork

Students look at vocabulary related to teamwork.

7A   Explain the activity and do the first item as an example with the class. Draw students' attention to the grammatical clues in each sentence which can help them decide what part of speech is needed each time (e.g. *Can they find a main verb in the sentence? What type of word comes before/after the gap? What usually follows or precedes that word?*). Then get students to complete it individually or, in weaker classes, in pairs, and check answers with the class.

> **1** verb   **2** verb   **3** noun   **4** noun   **5** noun   **6** noun
> **7** verb   **8** adjective   **9** adjective   **10** verb

7B   Students could do this activity individually or in pairs. With stronger classes, ask students to use their dictionaries to check any unknown words. With weaker classes, go through the words in the box before students complete the text. Check answers with the class, clarifying meanings as necessary.

> **1** cooperate   **2** disagree   **3** conflict management
> **4** agreement   **5** respect   **6** argument   **7** trust
> **8** reliable   **9** experienced   **10** deal with

Word building – verbs and nouns

Students look at word building with verbs and nouns.

8   You could do this as a whole-class activity or ask students to complete the table individually and then check answers with the class, clarifying meanings as necessary. If appropriate, you could briefly focus on noun suffixes: ask students to look at nouns 1–6 and point out that they all end in *-ment* or *-tion*. Explain that these are called *suffixes* and are often used to form nouns from verbs. Ask students if they know more nouns which end in *-ment* or *-tion*, or provide examples yourself (e.g. *employment, improvement, development, presentation, information, organisation*).

> **1** agree   **2** argue   **3** communicate   **4** cooperation
> **5** disagreement   **6** manage   **7** respect   **8** trust

9A   Get students to complete the exercise individually. Encourage them to read the sentences first and think about what type of word is needed for each gap.

> **1** argue   **2** argument   **3** communication
> **4** communicate   **5** cooperate   **6** Cooperation

9B   Put students in pairs or groups and give them 3–4 minutes to discuss the statements. Invite students from different pairs/ groups to share their views with the class.

Extra activities 6.1

C This activity gives further practice of key vocabulary from the lesson. It is a consolidation exercise, so it would be better for students to do it individually. Check answers with the class.

> **1** c   **2** a   **3** b   **4** c   **5** a   **6** b

Project: Organising a team

Students plan and make a schedule for a meeting.

10A   Put students in pairs or small groups and explain that they are going to read an email from the CEO of ProgramsPro, a software development company, to all employees. Give them time to read the email and ask the following questions: *Who is tomorrow's surprise visit from?* (XYQ Global, an important client) *What does the CEO of ProgramsPro hope to do in tomorrow's meeting?* (improve their relationship with the client; give a formal presentation of their new products) Explain that students should make a list of everything that needs to be organised for the meeting. During the activity, monitor and help students as necessary.

Possible answers

decide who will attend the meeting; choose a location for the meeting; plan the material of the presentations and what will happen in the two hours – who will speak and when; plan lunch; set specific goals for the meeting

10B   Allow 5–7 minutes for this stage. During the activity, monitor and help as necessary. If students are struggling, help them with questions, e.g. *If ProgramsPro are unhappy, what will the people at the meeting need to find out? What will they need to explain? What skills will they need for this?* Once students have discussed their ideas, elicit answers around the class.

Possible answers

The people who attend the meeting will need to explain the new products, including a formal product presentation, and will need to help repair the relationship with XYQ Global. They will need to listen to XYQ Global to understand why they're unhappy with the product support. They will need to be good at communication and conflict management.

10C   Explain that the CEO has chosen five people to *plan* the meeting but only two will *attend* the meeting. Refer students to page 139 and give them time to read the information. Answer any vocabulary questions they may have. Then explain what they need to do: a) decide who will attend the meeting and b) refer to their lists from Exercise 10A and assign the tasks to the other three people. Draw students' attention to the example dialogue, set a time limit for their discussion and encourage them to make notes.

Possible answers
- A new Sales Manager – should attend the meeting to give the product presentation
- An Engineer – should explain the products to the new Sales Manager to prepare for the meeting
- A Vice President – should attend the meeting to listen to XYQ Global's complaints about product support
- A Sales Representative – should help the Engineer to explain the products to the new Sales Manager to prepare for the meeting
- A Project Manager – should organise the food, meeting room and all other logistical details of the meeting

10D Students now prepare a schedule for the meeting. Remind them to refer to their notes from the previous stages and, if you think it will help them, list the points they need to consider on the board, e.g.

2 hours
- *how many parts?*
- *how long is each part?*
- *person responsible for each part?*

When groups are ready, you could ask them to share their schedules with other groups.

Possible answer

11.30–11.40 – Introduction and welcome – CEO
11.40–12.10 – Discussion of problems that XYQ Global has with product support – Vice President
12.10–13.00 – Lunch, with formal product presentation – Sales Manager
13.00–13.30 – Questions and answers, planning for the future – CEO

MyEnglishLab: Teacher's resources: extra activities
Pronunciation bank: p.117 Vowel sounds: /ɪ/, /iː/, /aɪ/ and /ɪə/
Teacher's book: Resource bank Photocopiable 6.1 p.144
Workbook: p.29 Exercises 1–3

6.2 ❯ Team building

GSE learning objectives
- Can scan a simple text, identifying the main topic(s).
- Can identify specific information in simple letters, brochures and short articles.
- Can use a range of indefinite compound pronouns prefixed with *some-*.
- Can use a range of indefinite compound pronouns prefixed with *every-*.
- Can give an extended description of everyday topics (e.g. people, places, experiences).
- Can make simple comparisons between people, places or things.

Warm-up
Write *sport* and *business* on the board, then discuss the following with the class: *More and more companies are encouraging employees to take part in team sports. Why do you think this is? How could it help a company or its employees?* (Possible answers might include: improved communication and employee relationships, improved team spirit, lower stress levels, improved physical health, increased productivity.)

Lead-in

Students look at parallels between sport and business.

1A Start by teaching or eliciting the meanings of the words in the box. Put students in pairs, explain the activity and refer them to the example sentence. Give pairs 3–4 minutes to come up with their own examples, then elicit ideas around the class.

Possible answers

Teams and athletes compete against each other, for example in the Olympics. Companies compete against each other in the marketplace, like Apple competing against other computer makers.

A football team needs to cooperate to score a goal because several team members must move the ball nearer the net before the striker shoots. Businesspeople need to cooperate to win new business, salespeople need the support of product people to create good products and explain them.

Being good at football is a collection of skills. Players must learn about moving the ball well, strategy, teamwork and so on, and these skills can always improve. Being good at business means communicating well, understanding money, managing time and so on. But businesspeople can always improve on these things, too.

Athletes must train and practise to win. Successful companies train their employees in new skills – and allow them to practise and develop those skills so they can perform their jobs well.

1B Students should do this in the same pairs as Exercise 1A. Again, check they understand the meanings of the verbs in the box and draw their attention to the example sentence before they begin. Give them 3–4 minutes to share their sentences, then elicit a few examples around the class.

Possible answers

At work, I'm trying to develop my skills as a salesperson. I'm reading a lot of books about sales.
I've challenged myself to compete in a golf tournament next month, so I practise every weekend.
I want to reduce the amount of fast food I eat, so I'm taking a cooking course.

Reading

Students read an article about the importance of sport in the workplace.

2 Draw students' attention to the photos and title of the article and ask what they think it might be about. Before they read, pre-teach: *competitive*, *triathlon* (see Notes below) and *tonnes* (*of evidence*). Give students time to read the text and complete the exercise individually, then check the answer with the class.

2

Notes

Most triathlons are for individuals and involve swimming, cycling and running. In an Olympic triathlon, competitors swim 1.5 km, cycle 40 km and run 10 km, though shorter events are often put on at non-Olympic levels. A team triathlon is done as a relay, where each athlete does a segment of swimming, cycling and running.

3 Ask students to work individually and encourage them to underline the parts of the text that give them the answers. Get them to compare answers in pairs before checking with the class.

1 get fit **2** improve employees' fitness **3** talk to **4** became more competitive **5** some

Extra activities 6.2

A This activity practises useful vocabulary from the text. Students could do it individually or in pairs. Encourage them to read the sentences carefully, thinking about the meaning of the whole sentence each time. This will help them work out the meanings of the words in bold. Check answers with the class and clarify meanings as necessary.

1 b **2** d **3** e **4** a **5** c

4 Put students in pairs or small groups, give them 2–3 minutes to discuss the question, then invite a few students to share their answers. Encourage them to give reasons.

≫ Pronunciation bank
p. 117: Linking between words

Warm-up

◀) P6.04, P6.05 Check students understand the meaning of *consonant* and *vowel* by asking them to give you a few examples. Write *come in* on the board and ask them to say it quickly. Ask if they notice anything about the two words (they join together). Refer them to the information in the box, play recording P6.04 and drill the pronunciation of the example phrases. Then play recording P6.05 for them to compare the pronunciation in linked and unlinked words.

1 ◀) P6.06 Play the recording for students to listen and repeat. Point out that in Phrase 1, although the last letter in *you're* is a vowel, the sounds are linked because *you're* ends in a consonant sound.

2 Put students in pairs to complete the sentences. Do not confirm answers yet as students will check them in the next exercise.

1 Do you have_everything you need?
2 Print_out_an_extra copy.
3 I've looked_everywhere for_it.
4 A copy of the report_and_a pen_or pencil.
5 I'm glad you're_all here.
6 Just_ask_if you need help.

3 ◀) P6.07 Play the recording for students to check their answers. Then play it again for them to listen and repeat.

4 Put students in pairs to practise saying the sentences. Explain that they should listen to their partner, check they are linking consonant and vowel sounds correctly, and correct their pronunciation if necessary. Monitor and help/correct students, modelling the linked sounds again if necessary.

Grammar: Pronouns with *some-* and *every-*

Students study and practise indefinite pronouns with *some-* and *every-*.

5A Ask students to complete the exercise individually. During feedback, elicit the meaning of the indefinite pronoun in each sentence, but do not go into detail about the grammar of indefinite pronouns yet.

1 something **2** everyone **3** somewhere **4** everywhere
5 someone

5B Students could do this individually or in pairs. After checking answers, refer them to the Grammar reference on page 123, go through it and clarify any points as necessary.

a 1, 3, 5 **b** 2, 4

6 You could do this as a whole-class activity, checking answers as you go along.

1 b **2** d **3** a **4** c **5** g **6** e **7** h **8** f

7 Ask students to do this individually, then check answers with the class.

1 everyone/everybody **2** everything **3** something
4 somewhere **5** everywhere **6** someone/somebody

Extra activities 6.2

B This activity gives further practice of indefinite pronouns. Get students to do it individually and then to compare answers in pairs before checking with the class.

1 Did everyone get my email?
2 Someone is waiting for you.
3 Did somebody take my pen?
4 I've looked everywhere for my car keys.
5 I want to show you something.
6 They want to go somewhere that's quiet.
7 Everything is ready for the meeting.
8 Can everybody see the front of the room?

Speaking and writing

Students practise describing people, places, things and jobs using indefinite pronouns.

8A–B Explain the activity and refer students to the examples. Give them sufficient time to prepare their sentences while you monitor and help/correct them as necessary. Then put them in pairs or small groups and get them to say their sentences for their partner to guess each word.

9 This exercise could be assigned as homework if there is no time to do it in class.

MyEnglishLab: Teacher's resources: extra activities; Reading bank
Pronunciation bank: p.117 Linking between words
Grammar reference: p.123 Pronouns with *some-* and *every-*
Teacher's book: Resource bank Photocopiable 6.2 p.145
Workbook: p.30 Exercises 1–3, p.31 Exercises 1–3

6.3 > Communication skills
Supporting a colleague

GSE learning objectives

- Can follow a simple conversation or narrative about familiar, everyday activities.
- Can extract key details from conversations between colleagues about familiar topics.
- Can make and respond to suggestions.
- Can use language related to reassuring and encouraging.
- Can use some basic interjections to express understanding, surprise, disappointment, and excitement.
- Can initiate, maintain and close simple, restricted face-to-face conversations.
- Can give or seek personal views and opinions in discussing topics of interest.

Warm-up

Ask the following questions: *Who is the most supportive person you know? How do they show their support? How does it make you feel to be around this person? Why?* If time allows, get students to discuss the questions in pairs or small groups first, then invite a few students to share their answers with the class.

Lead-in

Students talk about ways of offering support.

1A–B Tell students that they are going to do a quiz to find out how good they are at understanding and sharing other people's feelings. Go through the quiz questions with them, check they understand *emotional* in question 2, and give them 3–4 minutes to answer the questions. Then refer them to page 129 and ask them to add up their score and read their results. Invite a few students to tell the class what they thought of their results: Did they surprise them? Is there anything they disagree with? Finally, check who has the highest score in the class and ask them the question on page 131.

Video

Students watch a video about different approaches to offering support to colleagues.

2A ▶ 6.3.1 If your students watched the Unit 5 video, ask them to give you a short summary of the situation and the main characters. If this is the first communication skills video for your class, briefly set up the context and/or refer students to page 6 of the Coursebook. Give students time to read the questions, then play the video and discuss the answers with the class.

1 Jasmine is on her phone and thinking about a proposal she submitted to give a talk at the Global HR Leadership conference in Miami.
2 The email is from the conference organisers. It's important to Jasmine because Orla encouraged her to send in a proposal, and it will look good on her résumé if she is a presenter.
3 Her proposal wasn't accepted. She is very upset about it.

2B Put students in pairs to discuss the questions. Ask them to think about what they would do in a similar situation. After 2–3 minutes, invite students from different pairs to share their answers with the class.

Possible answer

Thiago should show that he's sorry and listen as much as possible without trying too hard to make Jasmine feel better. He should *not* say that everything's OK or that she'll get over it.

3A ▶ 6.3.2 Explain that students are going to watch Thiago and Azra trying to support Jasmine and give them time to read the questions. Check they understand *positive side*, *pretend* and *change the subject*. You may also wish to pre-teach the following vocabulary from the video: *look on the bright side*, *it's no big deal*, *reject* and *cheer up*. Play the video and get students to compare answers in pairs before class feedback.

1 a 2 b 3 c 4 d 1 e 5
2 Thiago is not very successful at all, but saying something positive about Jasmine at the end of their conversation works best.
3 Azra is much more sympathetic than Thiago – perhaps too sympathetic. By telling Jasmine how sorry for Jasmine she is, she actually makes her feel worse rather than better. If anything, her approach is less successful than Thiago's, although she obviously cares more.

3B Put students in pairs and give them 2–3 minutes to discuss the questions, then get brief feedback from the class.

> **Possible answer**
> Thiago is probably trying too hard to pretend that Jasmine's bad news is not important and that she shouldn't be so upset. Trying to cheer her up by inviting her to go out with him and some friends for a drink seems a bit insensitive. He probably wants to help Jasmine forget about the Miami conference, but that's precisely what she can't do. Azra, on the other hand, is too sympathetic. She knows how much Jasmine wanted to give her presentation in Miami but two people being really sorry about something they can't change isn't very helpful.

4A ▶ 6.3.3 Explain that students are going to watch Jasmine sharing her news with Alex and give them time to read the questions. You may wish to pre-teach *work out* (develop in a successful way), *put something behind you* and *move on*. Play the video, then check answers with the class.

> 1 Alex is quite careful about how he introduces the subject of the Miami conference, which he has already heard about from Thiago. When Jasmine says that's it's no big deal, he is quick to tell her that her disappointment is totally understandable. This relaxes Jasmine who is still upset from receiving the news.
> 2 Alex says that Jasmine had the right topic (and therefore the organisers liked it), but the problem was that it didn't fit the conference theme for this year. It's a fairly obvious point, but one that Jasmine appreciates.
> 3 Alex mentions that he had to apply to engineering school three times before he finally got in. He does this to show Jasmine that he knows how she feels – and his situation was worse than hers.
> 4 Alex says everyone likes Jasmine, but suggests that she expects too much of herself, too soon. Compliments can be difficult – sometimes it's not a good idea to give them, but in this case Jasmine responds positively. In this case, compliments are a good way to balance the negative feelings of Jasmine's disappointment, so it was a good idea.
> 5 Alex's main advice is for Jasmine to put the Miami experience behind her and move on. He says this quite directly, but because he has already been supportive and understanding, Jasmine accepts it. He also suggests that she think about what she can learn from the situation.
> 6 The good news is that because Jasmine is not going to Miami later in the year she'll be able to work with him on the Ferguson pitch as his co-presenter. Because he told her after she explained her disappointment, it probably had a more positive impact – because the conversation ends with some positive news.

4B Put students in pairs to discuss the different approaches in Videos A and B, then broaden this into a class discussion.

> **Possible answer**
> At times Thiago seems not to care about Jasmine's situation, and Azra cares too much. Alex achieves a good balance. He is sympathetic but professional. He pays her a compliment, but is honest and is not afraid to talk about his own failures. Jasmine feels a lot better at the end of their conversation.

5 ▶ 6.3.4 Explain that students are going to watch the last section of the video, which discusses the advantages and disadvantages of the approaches in Videos A and B. They should watch and compare what is said with their answers to Exercises 3B and 4B. Play the video and, if time allows, let students discuss briefly in pairs or small groups first. Round up ideas in a class discussion.

Reflection

Students think about their own approach to supporting a colleague.

6 Allow students to work individually on this so that they can reflect on their own approach first. Ask them to think about the questions and make notes. Then put them in pairs to discuss and compare their answers. Get brief feedback from the class.

Functional language: Encouraging and motivating

Students look at useful language for encouraging and motivating a colleague.

7A Tell students that you are now going to look at useful expressions to encourage and support someone. Ask them to complete the exercise individually, then check answers with the class. Clarify meanings as necessary.

> 1 feel 2 big 3 bright 4 so 5 bad 6 up

7B Put students in pairs and give them 1–2 minutes to label each of the phrases, then invite students to share their answers with the class.

> 1 ☹ 2 ☺ 3 ☺ 4 ☹ 5 ☹ 6 ☺

8 Explain the activity and point out that the comments are grouped according to their meaning/function. Ask students to complete the exercise individually and get them to compare answers in pairs before checking with the class. During feedback, clarify meanings as necessary.

> 1 sorry, work 2 hope, disappointed 3 sounds, work
> 4 know, important 5 understand, feel 6 can, try
> 7 makes, better 8 behind, move 9 question, learn
> 10 Look, way

9 Put students in pairs, give them time to read the statements and check they understand *scholarship* and *back up*. In weaker classes, you could demonstrate the activity with a stronger student. Once they have practised in their pairs, invite a few pairs to act out their conversations to the class.

Extra activities 6.3

A This activity practises the language of offering support and encouragement. Ask students to complete it individually and get them to compare answers in pairs before class feedback. Point out that they should only refer to page 63 in their books if they need to.

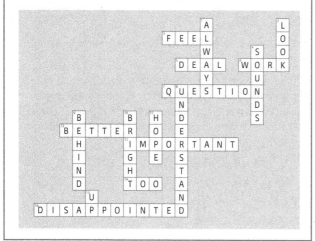

Task

Students roleplay conversations where they offer support to colleagues.

10A Put students in groups of three. Explain the task and the three different roles: the Speaker will describe a disappointment; the Helper will offer support and encouragement to the Speaker; the Observer will listen and take notes on the conversation. Allocate roles (or let students select them), refer students to their information and give them time to read it. Explain that Speakers may choose one of the scenarios on page 134 or talk about a real situation they are comfortable discussing. Remind Helpers that they need to use language from Exercises 7 and 8. Finally, make sure Observers understand that they need to take notes on each of the questions on their form. Note that there are two scenarios on page 134, so for the third conversation, the Speaker should either a) repeat one of the two options or b) talk about a real (or imaginary) situation.

Allow students plenty of time to prepare, while you monitor and help with any questions they may have. In weaker classes, you may wish to group all Speakers, Helpers and Observers together first to discuss their roles and prepare before returning to their original groups. Before students begin their conversations, make sure they understand that they will be rotating roles: there will be three different conversations, with students taking turns to be the Speaker, Helper and Observer. Set a time limit for each conversation.

10B Students now discuss the Observers' feedback. Make sure students do this after each conversation, before swapping roles for the next scenario. Allow plenty of time for this stage and class feedback at the end of the activity. Ask students what they found most challenging and how they think they could improve next time. Invite Observers to share any points they found interesting with the class.

MyEnglishLab: Teacher's resources: extra activities; Interactive video activities; Functional language bank

Workbook: p.32 Exercises 1 and 2

6.4 > Business skills

Being positive in meetings

GSE learning objectives

- Can follow the main points in a simple audio recording aimed at a general audience.
- Can identify key details in a simple recorded dialogue or narrative.
- Can make basic inferences from simple information in a short text.
- Can use language related to advising and suggesting.
- Can use language related to agreeing with a statement or opinion.
- Can understand standard emails on work-related topics.
- Can make and respond to suggestions.

Warm-up

Ask: *How comfortable are you sharing suggestions and ideas or expressing your opinion in a team? Why? What helps you to feel comfortable about sharing ideas / expressing your opinion?* Elicit answers around the class, making sure students give reasons.

Lead-in

Students discuss the importance of feeling safe in teams.

1 Put students in pairs and give them time to read the blog post. Before they discuss the questions, check they understand *a safe place to be great in* (a place (team) where people feel comfortable contributing without having to worry about negative reactions, conflict, etc.). Once students have discussed in their pairs, check answers with the class.

1 Possible answer
The feeling that it's safe to ask questions, share ideas and make mistakes without negative reactions.
Possible answer to 'Do you agree?'
It's also possible that a certain amount of conflict and risk in a team can sometimes make it perform better.

2 Students' own answers

3 Possible answer
The main thing a team leader can do to make a team feel a 'safe' place in which to share ideas and take risks, is to encourage team members to welcome and build on each other's ideas and not compete with each other to see whose idea is best.

Listening

Students listen to a meeting about a recruitment problem.

2 ◀) 6.01 Go through the instructions and questions with students and check they understand *recruitment/recruiter* and *work culture*. You may also wish to pre-teach *graduate application* and *management trainee*, which students will hear on the recording. Play the recording, twice if necessary, then check answers with the class.

1 The company is having problems recruiting recent graduates.

2 As a result, they are not recruiting the number of management trainees they need.

3 c, d, f

3A 🔊 6.02 Explain that students are going to hear the second part of the meeting and give them time to read the suggestions and responses. Pre-teach the following vocabulary: *careers fair*, *video promotion*, *sponsored diploma*, *MBA*, *internship*. After checking answers, ask students what all five responses have in common (they are *negative*).

1 d **2** a **3** e **4** c **5** b

3B Discuss the question as a class. Play the recording again if necessary.

Anatol suggests they stop the meeting and meet again in a couple of days when they've had time to think about the issue a bit more. He says there's too much negativity.

4 Get students to complete the exercise individually or, in weaker classes, in pairs. After checking answers, elicit or explain that in his text, Anatol is trying to be positive.

1 positive **2** possibilities **3** problem

5A 🔊 6.03 Pre-teach *mobile advertising* and *personal coaching* and play the recording. Check answers with the class.

a 3 **b** 5 **c** 6 **d** 1 **e** 2 **f** 4

5B Discuss the question as a class. Ask students to think about how the people at each meeting respond to each other's ideas.

Possible answer

In the first meeting, people are dismissing each other's ideas before there is a chance to discuss them. In the second meeting, a more positive atmosphere encourages people to build on other's ideas by thinking of further possibilities. Anatol and Michael both see possible problems with Erin's ideas, but they ask questions rather than criticising. In one case, a good idea comes from this. And in the other case, it becomes clear that this is a decision for the board of directors.

5C 🔊 6.03 You may wish to ask students to copy the suggestions from Exercise 5A into their notebooks and make notes there. With weaker classes, you may need to pause after each answer is heard to give students time to make notes, and/or play the recording a second time.

Possible answers

a Most young people use their mobiles to hunt for jobs these days.

b Young people prefer to work for smaller companies. By working in project teams, even in a large company, they get the feeling of being part of a smaller company.

c Erin pointed out that new graduates prefer a more informal, fun work culture.

d Insurance is not a popular career choice for new graduates. But getting paid internships is harder than getting a job, so by offering internships to students, the company can attract them before they graduate. Hopefully, some of them will then stay at the company.

e There are professional skills students need which they don't learn at university, which the company could coach them in.

f Currently, a quarter of the graduates they offer jobs to have taken another job by the time they make the offer. Mobile recruiting is a much faster way to stay in contact with job applicants.

5D Discuss the questions as a class.

Possible answer

Anatol sees a problem with the cost of offering student internships, but Erin suggests some of the money spent on graduate recruitment could be used for this instead. Michael wonders how the reorganisation of parts of the company into project teams can be managed, but Anatol says the board of directors can make a decision on that.

Functional language: Supporting, building on and questioning ideas

Students look at phrases for supporting, building on and questioning ideas in a team.

6A Get students to complete the exercise individually. Confirm the answers or play recording 6.03 again for students to check them, and clarify meanings as necessary.

1 like, idea **2** subject, don't **3** problem, about
4 might, idea **5** What, idea **6** doing, could
7 think, idea **8** do, can **9** wondering, manage

6B Put students in pairs and give them 1–2 minutes to label each of the phrases, then invite students to share their answers with the class.

1 ✔ **2** ↔ **3** ? **4** ✔ **5** ✔ **6** ↔ **7** ✔ **8** ↔
9 ?

Extra activities 6.4

A Explain to students that this is an extract from a meeting about making the workplace more fun. Get them to complete the exercise individually and then to compare answers in pairs before class feedback. After checking answers, you could put students in groups of three to practise the conversation.

> **a** 1 **b** 8 **c** 7 **d** 4 **e** 9 **f** 6 **g** 2 **h** 5 **i** 3 **j** 10

B Students could do this exercise individually or in pairs. You could also ask them to label the expressions according to their function (✔ = supporting an idea; ⟷ = building on an idea; ? = questioning an idea).

> Of course, there is the question of cost. **?**
> What can we do about that? **?**
> You know, that might not be such a bad idea. **✔**
> I really like that idea! **✔**
> I'm just wondering about … **?**
> How can we manage that? **?**
> Actually, I think that's a great idea! **✔**
> And while we're on the subject ⟷
> why don't we ⟷
> What a good idea! **✔**
> And socialising more means ⟷

C This activity looks at useful vocabulary from the lesson. Depending on the level of your class, it can be done individually or in pairs. During feedback, clarify meanings as necessary.

> **1** recruitment problem   **2** negative reactions
> **3** reputation   **4** salaries   **5** employee benefits
> **6** work culture   **7** career fairs   **8** sponsor
> **9** internships   **10** personal coaching

Task

Students hold a meeting where they support, build on or question each other's ideas.

7A Put students in groups of 3–6 and explain the scenario: they all work for an advertising agency in Los Angeles and are going to hold a meeting. Check that they understand *creative department* (the department of an advertising agency where advertisements are conceived, developed and produced). Give them time to read the email and then assign roles A–F in each group. Note that the meetings can be held in groups of 3–6; roles D–F are optional. Try to give roles A (the Chair) and B (the Note-taker) to stronger students. Refer each student to their information and give them time to read it, while you monitor and help with any unknown vocabulary or questions. Make sure that the students playing the Chairs are clear that they have to open the meeting, explain the rules, contribute ideas during the meeting and close the meeting. Also check that Note-takers understand they need to record everyone's ideas (on a flipchart or large piece of paper) *and* contribute ideas themselves. Remind everyone that they should use language from Exercise 6.

7B Allow students plenty of time to prepare for their meetings. Depending on the strength of your class, you might like to group all students with each role together for the preparation stage, to briefly discuss their roles and brainstorm ideas before returning to their original groups. Set a time limit and ask students to begin their meetings.

7C Allow groups 5–7 minutes to discuss the questions, then invite students from different groups to share their experience with the class. Encourage students to talk about what they found difficult and why.

MyEnglishLab: Teacher's resources: extra activities; Functional language bank
Workbook: p.32 Exercises 3–5

6.5 ❯ Writing
Making requests

GSE learning objectives

- Can write basic instructions with a simple list of points.
- Can write a simple email requesting work-related information.
- Can edit and improve a simple text.

Warm-up

Discuss the following questions with the class: Have you ever had to write an email making a request? If yes, what was it about? How important do you think it is to receive requests in writing?

Lead-in

Students read and complete an email making requests.

1 Before students complete the email, ask them to read it quickly and answer the following question: *What three things does the writer ask his team to do?* (visit new venue for product launch, check guest list and contact people who haven't replied, write a press release by the end of the week). Ask students to complete the email individually and then compare answers in pairs before class feedback. If you think your students need additional support, you could write the prepositions required (*for* (x2), *in, of* (x2), *on, to* (x3), *with*) on the board before they do the exercise.

> **1** to   **2** for/of   **3** in   **4** of   **5** to   **6** with/about   **7** to
> **8** for   **9** on   **10** of

Functional language

Students look at useful phrases for making requests.

2A Ask students to complete the exercise individually, then check answers with the class. Point out that *we* can be used in updates to help people feel part of a team, even though the team leader may not be doing any of the tasks themselves.

1 possible, I'd like **2** would you mind **3** Please
4 think I could

2B Explain to students that they are now going to look at different ways to say the things in the first column of the table in Exercise 2A. You could do this as a whole-class activity, checking answers as you go along, or get students to work individually and then check answers with the class.

5 Could **6** can you / would you **7** Would you / Can you
8 if I could have

Extra activities 6.5

A This activity gives further practice of the language of making requests. Ask students to complete it individually, then check answers with the class.

1 Can you / Could you / Would you
2 can you / could you
3 grateful if
4 can you / could you / would you
5 can you / could you / would you
6 Do you think

Optional grammar work

The email in Exercise 1 contains examples of linking words for sequence, so you could use it for some optional grammar work. Refer students to the Grammar reference on page 123 and use the exercises in MyEnglishLab for extra grammar practice.

Task

Students write an email making requests.

3A Put students in pairs to complete the email extract on page 139. Ask them to only refer to the phrases in the table in Exercise 2A if they need to.

Suggested answers

1 Alex and Miguel, would you mind doing
2 Please contact them
3 Do you think you could update me
4 Please send me a meeting invite.
5 Would anyone like to help with these two tasks?

3B Give students time to read the notes on page 129 and check they understand *international trade speaker* and *delegate*. Remind them to use phrases from Exercise 2A in their emails and point out the word limit before they begin. You may also wish to remind them to organise the information in paragraphs and make sure they open and close their email appropriately. If time is short, the writing task can be assigned as homework.

Model answer

Hi all,

I am writing to update you for the conference.

Unfortunately, the international trade speaker has cancelled, so we have to find out who else is available and book a new speaker. Please let me know if you have any ideas. We are already over budget, so if possible, I'd like Luis to try and make savings somewhere in the budget. Claire, would you find out how many people are coming? 40 percent of people have not replied to our invitations and we need to find out who's coming by the end of the week. After that, we need to look for 50 rooms in another hotel because the Blossom Hotel has closed. David, would you mind doing that? And finally, could you tell me what equipment we need in the venue?

Thank you for your hard work.

Regards,

(name)

3C If students do the writing task as homework, this exercise can be done in the next lesson. Put them in pairs and ask them to read each other's emails and think about the question. You could also ask them to answer the following questions: *Did your partner open and close their email appropriately? Did he/she organise the information in paragraphs? Did he/she make all requests using functional language phrases? Can any more be used?*

MyEnglishLab: Teacher's resources: extra activities; Interactive grammar practice; Writing bank
Grammar reference: p.123 Linking words for sequence
Workbook: p.33 Exercises 1–3

Business workshop ❯ 6
The Amazing Chair Company

GSE learning objectives

- Can identify specific information in simple letters, brochures and short articles.
- Can identify specific information in a simple factual text.
- Can understand standard speech on familiar matters, with some repetition or reformulation.
- Can identify key details in a simple recorded dialogue or narrative.
- Can ask and answer questions about basic plans and intentions.
- Can describe plans and arrangements.
- Can discuss what to do next using simple phrases.
- Can make and respond to suggestions.

Background

Students read about a furniture retailer in the USA.

1 Ask students to read the background and discuss the answers in pairs. Check answers with the class. Check students understand *accountant* and *bookkeeper*.

1 She made a chair as a hobby and her friends loved it and wanted to buy one.
2 designer, accountant/bookkeeper, director
3 **Possible answer:**
   As it's a busy, small business, they're probably all working very hard. Their jobs may feel insecure, as the business is just barely successful. They may not get along well on a personal level. João might wish for a full-time position.

Team roles

Students listen to employees talking about their jobs.

2A ◀ BW 6.01   Explain that students are going to listen to the three people who work for The Amazing Chair Company talking about their jobs. Ask them what João's role is in the company (part-time accountant and bookkeeper). Before students listen, you may wish to pre-teach or check understanding of *can afford*, *deal with* and *supplier*. Play the recording, then check answers with the class.

1 maths   2 not completely happy

2B ◀ BW 6.01   Check students understand *being creative* and play the recording. Check answers with the class.

Likes: solving problems, being creative
Isn't very interested in: numbers, accounting

3A ◀ BW 6.02   Ask students what Leila's role is in the company (furniture designer) and play the recording. Check answers with the class.

She liked working in a team.

3B ◀ BW 6.02   Go through the words in the box with students and check they understand *bother*, *concentrate* and *on time*. Play the recording, then check answers with the class.

1 bothers   2 talks to   3 concentrate   4 share ideas

4A ◀ BW 6.03   Ask students what Natalya's role is in the company (founder, director). Play the recording, then check answers with the class.

not completely

4B ◀ BW 6.03   Check students understand *challenge* and play the recording. Check answers with the class.

1 difficult   2 are not really happy
3 making a great product

Extra activities Business workshop 6

A ◀ BW6.01, BW6.02, BW6.03   Give students time to read the statements before they listen, then play all three recordings. Alternatively, if you think your students may remember some of the information from the first listening, you could ask them to answer as many of the questions as they can before listening again, then play the recordings for them to check/complete their answers. Check answers with the class.

1 F 2 T 3 T 4 F 5 F 6 T

Natalya's email inbox

Students read three emails to The Amazing Chair Company's director.

5A   Ask students to complete the exercise individually, then check answers with the class. Ask: *What do you think Natalya might do next?* Elicit answers from a few students and tell them that they will check their ideas in the next exercise.

A hotel group has placed an order for 20 chairs immediately, and 200 more in the next year.

5B ◀ BW 6.04   Ask students to listen to check their ideas from Exercise 5A. Play the recording, then elicit the answer.

She plans to hire a part-time employee to help manage the business.

5C   Explain that students are going to read two more of Natalya's emails and remind them of Leila's and João's roles (designer, part-time accountant and bookkeeper). Ask them to complete the exercise individually and then to compare answers in pairs. Check answers with the class.

1 She's having a few problems with the new designs.
2 She needs someone to talk to and she wants this person to be Natalya.
3 His other part-time job has ended.
4 He may look for a full-time job somewhere else.

Extra activities Business workshop 6

B   This activity looks at some useful phrases for informal emails. Ask students to do it individually. When they have finished, refer them to the emails on page 99 to check their answers, then confirm the answers.

1 touch   2 together   3 talk   4 free
5 conversation   6 call

Task: Rearrange team roles

Students have a group discussion about rearranging team roles and responsibilities.

6A Put students in small groups and explain the activity. Tell them that if they need help, they can refer to the emails on page 99 and audio scripts BW6.01, BW6.02 and BW6.03 on page 154. Give them 3–5 minutes to match the descriptions with the names, then check answers with the class.

> **1** J **2** L **3** J **4** N **5** N **6** J **7** L **8** N

6B Explain the activity and go through the list of tasks with students. Remind them that they should base their decisions on the information in the table in Exercise 6A, thinking about each person's skills, abilities and preferences. Give groups 3–5 minutes to discuss, then get brief feedback from the class. Ask students to explain their choices.

> **Possible answers**
> **1** J **2** N **3** J **4** J **5** L

6C Groups now make recommendations on how best to make use of each team member's skills and address their needs and preferences. Go through the list of points with students and remind them to think about the information for each team member from the previous exercises. Allow 3–5 minutes for the discussion. Again, ask students to explain their choices. When groups have finished, elicit ideas around the class.

> **Model answer**
> João wants a full-time job and Natalya can now offer another part-time job. So João could turn the two part-time jobs into one full-time job by taking over managing some of the business – solving problems with suppliers, for example – so Natalya can concentrate on selling. João could also work with Leila, listening to her and helping her develop her ideas. This makes sense because he has expressed an interest in being more creative and problem-solving, and because Natalya has said she really wants to focus on sales.

6D Explain to students that they will now make further suggestions for improving teamwork at The Amazing Chair Company. Go through the list of points with them and check they understand *shared social space*. During the activity, monitor and help students with any vocabulary they may need (you may need to provide words such as *open-plan office, seating arrangement*, etc.). Finally, invite students from different groups to share their ideas with the class.

> **Model answer**
> They could find an office where they can have an open-plan seating arrangement to make communication easier, or they could find an office with a shared social space if they want to keep their private rooms. However, this might be difficult because it might be more expensive. They could arrange to go out of the office at certain times, or for certain meetings – maybe for lunch – for more informal interaction. They could consider going out for a meal or a drink after work occasionally. As the Director, Natalya could arrange for occasional Friday afternoon trips to galleries or design companies, to inspire their work and help develop ideas. João has expressed an interest in being more creative; it might help the team if everyone discussed new chair designs together.

MyEnglishLab: Teacher's resources: extra activities

Review ◄ 6

> **1 1** cooperated **2** reliable **3** respect
> **4** arguments (disagreements) **5** Experienced
> **6** dealing **7** agree/communicate **8** disagree (argue)
> **2 1** everyone **2** everybody **3** everything **4** something
> **5** somewhere **6** everywhere **7** something
> **8** Someone **9** everyone
> **3 1** You must be so disappointed.
> **2** I know how important it was to you.
> **3** You can always try again.
> **4** I'm sorry it didn't work out for you.
> **4 1** really **2** wondering **3** subject **4** why don't
> **5** might **6** such **7** doing **8** could
> **5 1** If possible, I'd like **2** please **3** would you mind
> **4** could you let **5** can you **6** Do you think

7 › Research & development

Unit overview

	CLASSWORK	FURTHER WORK
7.1 › **A nimble company**	**Lead-in** Students talk about special products for elderly and disabled people. **Video** Students watch a video about a special product for elderly and disabled people. **Vocabulary** Students look at vocabulary related to the research and development of new products. **Project** Students plan the development, testing and launch of a new product.	**MyEnglishLab:** Teacher's resources: extra activities **Teacher's book:** Resource bank Photocopiable 7.1 p.146 **Workbook:** p.34 Exercises 1–3
7.2 › **Innovation**	**Lead-in** Students talk about innovation and technological advances in everyday life. **Reading** Students read an article about a hotel run by robots. **Grammar** Students study and practise modal verbs of obligation, necessity and possibility. **Speaking and writing** Students talk and then write about a process.	**MyEnglishLab:** Teacher's resources: extra activities, Reading bank **Grammar reference:** p.123 *can, have to, need to* **Pronunciation bank:** p.117 *can* and *can't* **Teacher's book:** Resource bank Photocopiable 7.2 p.147 **Workbook:** p.35 Exercises 1–4, p.36 Exercises 1–4
7.3 › **Communication skills:** Giving explanations	**Lead-in** Students talk about what makes a good presentation. **Video** Students watch a video about giving clear and effective explanations. **Reflection** Students reflect on the conclusions and learning points from the video. **Functional language** Students look at useful phrases for explaining things clearly and effectively. **Task** Students practise explaining how to use an app.	**MyEnglishLab:** Teacher's resources: extra activities; Interactive video activities; Functional language bank **Pronunciation bank:** p.118 Phrasing and pausing when giving instructions **Workbook:** p.37 Exercise 1
7.4 › **Business skills:** Dealing with technical problems	**Lead-in** Students talk about ground rules in meetings. **Listening** Students listen to part of a webinar where technical problems occur. **Functional language** Students look at useful expressions for signalling and dealing with technical problems. **Task** Students roleplay an online meeting where they have to deal with technical problems.	**MyEnglishLab:** Teacher's resources: extra activities; Functional language bank **Workbook:** p.37 Exercises 2 and 3
7.5 › **Writing:** Preparing slides	**Lead-in** Students complete slides for a presentation. **Functional language** Students look at tips for preparing effective presentation slides. **Task** Students prepare slides for a presentation.	**MyEnglishLab:** Teacher's resources: extra activities; Interactive grammar practice; Writing bank **Grammar reference:** p.124 *Wh-* questions **Workbook:** p.38 Exercises 1–4
Business workshop 7 › Zapatos Trujillo S.A.	**Listening** Students listen to conversations about shoe manufacturing. **Reading** Students read a progress report. **Task** Students discuss options for a production process and choose one to put in place. **Writing** Students write an email explaining a decision.	**MyEnglishLab:** Teacher's resources: extra activities

Business brief

The main aim of this unit is to introduce students to the concepts of **innovation** and **research and development**, and their roles in enabling a business to create successful products. Innovation is an important part of helping a company to grow and develop its business. Research and development (**R&D**) involves exploring ways in which new services or products could be created, or how existing services and products could be improved.

The first step in the R&D process is often noticing a problem or a lack in a business's products or services, and then examining different ideas to find the one with the most potential to provide an effective solution. The innovations resulting from R&D can have far-reaching consequences, benefitting not only the organisation carrying out the research, but also extending the knowledge (or **know-how**) in the industry as a whole. Sometimes innovations which arise as part of a company's specific research into a localised problem can develop to change the way people live, or improve the quality of their health. Examples of **game-changing** innovations resulting from initial research with more modest aims are the development of the driverless car and the smart technology that allows people to regulate the lighting and heating in their homes remotely.

Some influential innovations can be more controversial. The use of robots in factories, which increase production and profits but reduce the need for human workers, is a good example of this. Another is the use of artificial intelligence (**AI**) in education. This allows more personalised learning for the student and unbiased grading, but it also removes the valuable element of personal interaction from the learning experience.

Fields in which it is most common to have a dedicated company R&D department include the pharmaceutical industry, science, engineering and the design and technology sectors. Organisations which don't have dedicated R&D teams usually **outsource** this work to specialist companies or university departments which have particular expertise in the required area. Although scientists or engineers are likely to be involved in R&D research, it can involve experts, from software designers to dieticians, depending on the sector. Research can be of different types and have diverse aims. **Basic research** usually aims to build **general knowledge** while **applied research** usually has a specific **goal** in mind.

Note that there is a difference between research and development and **product development**. Whereas the focus of R&D is more **conceptual** and may only consist of gathering and processing information, product development has more practical outcomes. It is usually undertaken with the goal of developing or improving the features of an existing product. As well as an initial research phase, it includes successive phases of **product design, prototyping and testing**. The results of the initial research are used to develop trial versions of the product (**prototypes**) which are then tested and refined. During the testing phase feedback is given on the prototype by **focus groups** or **reviewers** who represent the target users/customers. Feedback is often guided by the design team though the use of **questionnaires** or interviews in which participants comment on the functions or aspects of the design which are of interest. During the testing phase developers identify the aspects of the proposed design which work well and those which require improvements or further research. The results are analysed and used to inform the final **product brief** which is the basis for the eventual new product/feature. After final adjustments have been made the product is then **launched** into the **market**.

Research & development and your students

Although students might not work in the field of research and development, it is important for them to be aware of how this process affects goods and services developed. Even pre-work students will have encountered a range of products which have been researched and developed. As consumers, all students will be able to discuss aspects of products which they think are well or badly-designed and to reflect on the processes which drove their development. Students who are in-work may not have direct experience of R&D, but the goods or services that they interact with are likely to have gone through the process of development, testing and refining outlined in this unit.

Unit lead-in

Elicit a brief description of the photo and refer students to the unit title. Check that they understand the meaning of *moving forward* and explain or elicit that *going forward* (which appears in the quote) has a similar meaning of progression. Draw students' attention to the quote and teach or elicit the meaning of *standing still* (in this context, the opposite of *going forward*). Discuss the quote with the class: what do they think it means? (One possible answer might be that, as long as you make an effort and work towards your goals, progress can come in many forms; if you don't, you will not develop, get better or achieve any of your goals.)

7.1 ❯ A nimble company

GSE learning objectives

- Can identify key details in a simple recorded dialogue or narrative.
- Can identify a simple chronological sequence in a recorded narrative or dialogue.
- Can make and respond to suggestions.
- Can communicate in routine tasks requiring simple, direct exchanges of information.
- Can describe what something is used for, using basic fixed expressions.

Warm-up

Ask students to think about the everyday tasks they do (e.g. making food, washing-up, house-cleaning, doing laundry, writing, typing, using a phone/computer). Ask: *What kind of clever products (gadgets) do you or would you like to have to help you with these tasks? What kind of products do you wish existed to help you with everyday tasks?* Elicit ideas around the class.

Lead-in

Students talk about special products for elderly and disabled people.

1 Draw students' attention to the picture and discuss the question with the whole class. Be prepared to explain *nimble* in the lesson title if students ask (a nimble company is one that can quickly and effectively respond to changes in the marketplace).

Possible answers

making food, eating and drinking, getting dressed, writing, typing, using a phone

2 Teach or elicit the meanings of the following words from the questions: *visual impairment, partially sighted, elderly* and *disabled.* You may also wish to pre-teach these words from the video: *research and development, trade show, 3D printing, prototype, user-testing, one-size-fits-all.*

Possible answers

1 cane / walking stick, glasses, special writing (Braille) that they can feel with their fingers
2 cane / walking stick, walking frames, stair lifts, wheelchairs, hearing aids
3 cane / walking stick, walking frames, stair lifts, wheelchairs

Video

Students watch a video about a special product for elderly and disabled people.

3 Draw students' attention to the photo and invite ideas for its use from around the class. It is OK if students cannot guess what the product is used for because it is not obvious. If you want to help students to guess the right answer, you could make some suggestions or ask related questions, e.g. *How big do you think it is? Do you think you can drink from it? Do you think it's a child's toy? What do you think it is made of?*

4A ▶ 7.1.1   Explain that students are going to watch a video about the product in the photo. Ask them to watch the first part of the video and answer the questions individually. Play the video (00:00–01:26), then check answers with the class.

> 1 It cuts things. (opens boxes and packages)
> 2 elderly and disabled people

4B ▶ 7.1.1   Get students to complete the exercise individually and then compare answers in pairs or small groups. Play the next part of the video (01:27–03.22) for students to check their answers.

> 1 c 2 a 3 d 4 b 5 f 6 e 7 h 8 g

4C ▶ 7.1.1   Ask students to watch the final part of the video and answer the question. Play the video (03:23–03:41), then check the answer with the class.

> a clip to help keep cables organised

5 Put students in pairs or small groups and give them 3–4 minutes to discuss the questions. Round up their ideas in a class discussion. They could also vote for the best suggestion.

Possible answers

2 cutting material from newspapers and magazines, cutting paper for wrapping presents, opening mail, for kids to use instead of scissors

Extra activities 7.1

A ▶ 7.1.1   This activity looks at vocabulary from the video. Get students to complete it individually, then play the video for them to check their answers. Do not focus on the meanings of the words in bold yet as students will check them in the next exercise.

> 1 c 2 b 3 a 4 e 5 f 6 i 7 d 8 h 9 g

B Get students to complete the exercise individually or in pairs. Encourage them to read the whole sentence carefully each time, as this will help them work out the meanings of the words in bold. You could also refer them to video script 7.1.1 on page 146 so they can read the sentences in context. Check answers with the class, clarifying meanings as necessary.

> i one-size-fits-all   ii tangling   iii blade   iv blind
> v arthritis   vi struggling   vii perspectives

Vocabulary: Research and development

Students look at vocabulary related to the research and development of new products.

6 Tell students that they are going to look at useful vocabulary related to research and development (R&D) and draw their attention to the diagram. Explain the activity and let students complete it individually or in pairs, using their dictionaries to help them if necessary. Go through the answers and clarify meanings as necessary. Alternatively, with weaker classes, you could go through the words in the box with students before they begin, then check answers with the class.

> **1** brief **2** solutions **3** sketches **4** prototype
> **5** challenges **6** improvements **7** feedback **8** Launch

7 You could do this as a whole-class activity, checking answers and clarifying meanings as you go.

> **1** b **2** c **3** a

8 This exercise practises vocabulary from Exercises 6 and 7, so you could ask students to complete it individually and get them to compare answers in pairs before checking with the class.

> **1** designer **2** create **3** function **4** brief **5** feedback
> **6** challenge

9 In this activity students choose which set of questions to discuss based on their previous experience in the R&D process. Put students in pairs to discuss the questions. As far as possible, try to get students with the same level of experience to work together. Give them 4–5 minutes to discuss in their pairs, then have a whole-class round-up.

Extra activities 7.1

C This activity gives further practice of key vocabulary from the lesson. Get students to complete the exercise individually and then check their answers in pairs before class feedback.

> **1** sketches **2** launch **3** usefulness
> **4** improvements **5** product testers **6** prototype
> **7** function **8** develop

Project: Planning product testing

Students plan the development, testing and launch of a new product.

10A Put students in pairs or small groups and explain that they are going to make a plan for developing, testing and launching a product. First, give them time to read the descriptions of the three products and check that they understand the meanings of *container* and *store*. Then explain that they need to answer questions 1–4 about each of the products. You could list the points they need to consider on the board as a reference:

1 What is the product used for? What problem does it solve?
2 Who will use it?
3 User testing: How? What does the company need to know?
4 Who should test the product?

Allow time for pairs/groups to discuss the questions and encourage them to make notes. During their discussions, monitor and help as necessary.

10B Students now choose a product and make their plan. Explain that it can be one of the products in Exercise 10A or their own idea, and remind them of the points they discussed in the previous stage. Refer them to the notes on the board and add: *5 Where and how should the product be launched?*

Point out that for this they need to think about the type of stores that will sell their product and how the product should be advertised. Tell them that they should discuss each of the points in detail and be prepared to present their ideas. Allow plenty of time for this stage and, again, monitor and provide help as necessary.

10C Students now present their plans to another pair/group or, if time allows, to the whole class.

MyEnglishLab: Teacher's resources: extra activities
Teacher's book: Resource bank Photocopiable 7.1 p.146
Workbook: p.34 Exercises 1–3

7.2 ➤ Innovation

GSE learning objectives

- Can identify specific information in simple letters, brochures and short articles.
- Can make basic inferences from simple information in a short text.
- Can identify specific information in a simple factual text.
- Can express obligation and necessity in the present and near future with *have to*.
- Can convey simple relevant information emphasising the most important point.
- Can make and respond to suggestions.
- Can describe the sequence in a process when writing a simple text, using common discourse markers.

Warm-up

Ask students to think about machines they use in their everyday lives (e.g. ATMs, snacks/drinks machines, ticket machines). Ask: *Do you ever have to use a machine when you'd rather communicate with a person? Do you ever have to deal with a person when you'd rather use a machine?*

Lead-in

Students talk about innovation and technological advances in everyday life.

1 Give students a minute to read the definitions and clarify meanings as necessary. Put them in pairs or small groups and give them 3–4 minutes to discuss the questions. Get feedback from the class.

Reading

Students read an article about a hotel run by robots.

2 Ask students to look at the title and the photo and tell you what they think the article might be about. Elicit ideas from a few students and check they understand the meaning of *run the show*. Pre-teach the following words from the article: *unique, check in* (v) / *check-in* (n), *innovation, lifestyle choice*. Get students to read the article quickly and answer the questions, then check answers with the class.

> 1 They are receptionists. / They check in guests.
> 2 Guests are attracted to the hotel because it is different – innovation attracts guests.

3 Give students time to read the statements and elicit or teach the meaning of *human contact* in question 6. Then ask students to read the article and complete the exercise, underlining the parts of the text that help them decide if a sentence is true or false. Check answers with the class.

> **1** F **2** F **3** T **4** T **5** T **6** T

4 If time allows, get students to discuss the questions in pairs or small groups first, then invite a few students to share their answers with the class.

Extra activities 7.2

A This activity practises opinion and commenting adverbs from the article. Start by getting students to complete it individually or in pairs, using their dictionaries to help them if necessary. Check answers with the class but do not focus on the function of the adverbs in bold yet.

> **1** a **2** c **3** b **4** a **5** b

B Give students enough time to find the adverbs in the article, then discuss the answer with the class. Depending on the level of your class, you could ask students to write their own example sentences using the adverbs.

> b

Grammar: *can, have to, need to*

Students study and practise modal verbs of obligation, necessity and possibility.

5 Get students to complete the exercise individually. During feedback, ask students which word(s) in each sentence show that something is 1) possible (*can*), 2) not possible (*can't*), 3) necessary (*have to* and *need to*) and 4) not necessary (*don't have to* and *don't need to*). Refer students to the Grammar reference on page 123, go through it with them and clarify any points as necessary.

> **1** d **2** f **3** a, c **4** b, e

6 Get students to complete the sentences individually, then check answers with the class. To extend the activity, you could ask them to match each sentence with the functions in Exercise 5 (see answers in brackets in the answer key below).

> **1** can (possible) **2** don't need to (not necessary)
> **3** don't have to (not necessary) **4** need to (necessary)
> **5** have to (necessary) **6** can't (not possible)

Extra activities 7.2

C This activity gives further practice of modal verbs of possibility, obligation and necessity. Get students to complete it individually, then check answers with the class.

> **1** b **2** e **3** a **4** d **5** f **6** c

7 Students can complete the exercise individually or, in weaker classes, in pairs. Check answers with the class.

> **1** don't have to **2** can **3** need to **4** can't **5** have to
> **6** can **7** can't **8** don't need to

❯ Pronunciation bank
p. 117: *can* and *can't*

Warm-up

◀ᐅ P7.01 Refer students to the explanation in the box and go through it with them. Model the strong and weak forms of *can/can't*, then play the recording. Drill the pronunciation of the example sentences.

1 ◀ᐅ P7.02 Play the recording for students to complete the sentences, then check answers with the class. Do not focus on students' pronunciation yet.

> **1** can't **2** can **3** can't **4** Can **5** can't, can
> **6** can

2 ◀ᐅ P7.03 Explain that students will hear the sentences with *can* from Exercise 1 and decide if they hear the weak form or the strong form. Remind them again of the pronunciation of each form, then play the recording and check answers with the class.

> Sentence 2: You <u>can</u> use the check-in kiosk. W
> Sentence 4: <u>Can</u> I check in without my ID? W
> Sentence 5: This robot can't talk, <u>can</u> it? S
> Sentence 6: Yes, it <u>can</u>! S

3 Put students in pairs to practise saying the sentences in Exercise 1. You might like to play recording P7.02 before they begin, so that they can hear the sentences once again before they practise on their own. During the activity, monitor and check/correct students' pronunciation as necessary.

Speaking and writing

Students talk and then write about a process.

8A Draw students' attention to the photo and elicit or explain what it shows (a *vending machine*). Put them in pairs, explain the activity and give them time to read the instructions and ask any questions before they begin. They should then take turns to tell their partner how to use the machine using the correct forms of *can*, *have to* or *need to*. Monitor and check that students are using the modal verbs correctly. In weaker classes, you could do an example with the class before students begin (see answer key below for model answers).

> ### Model answer
> You can't use a card with this machine – you have to use cash. If you want to pay by card, you can go to a shop. First, you have to put your money in the machine. You don't need to have the exact amount, because the machine can give change. You need to press the correct button to make your choice. You don't have to hold it or press it more than once. You have to wait for the product to come out, then you need to press the change button to get your change.

8B Join pairs together into groups of four and explain the activity. After groups have compared their answers, invite a few students to share their explanations with the class.

9 Explain the activity and point out that students should try to use each modal verb in the box at least once. Weaker students could plan their answers in pairs, then write their explanations individually. If there is no time to do the writing task in class, it can be assigned as homework.

> ### Model answer
> **Buying a train ticket at a self-service ticket machine**
> First, you need to choose your destination. Touch the screen to make your selection or you can find your destination by spelling it in the search area. Then, you have to choose the ticket type; for example, a day return ticket or a single journey. After that, you need to pay: insert your debit card and enter your PIN. You don't have to pay by card – you can also insert cash. Be aware that you can't get a refund after payment. Finally, wait for your ticket and receipt, and collect your change if necessary.

MyEnglishLab: Teacher's resources: extra activities; Reading bank

Grammar reference: p.123 *can, have to, need to*

Pronunciation bank: p.117 *can* and *can't*

Teacher's book: Resource bank Photocopiable 7.2 p.147

Workbook: p.35 Exercises 1–4, p.36 Exercises 1–4

7.3 ❯ Communication skills
Giving explanations

> ### GSE learning objectives
> - Can identify key details in a simple recorded dialogue or narrative.
> - Can identify a simple chronological sequence in a recorded narrative or dialogue.
> - Can make and respond to suggestions.

Warm-up
Ask students to think about a time when they've had to give instructions or explain a process to someone. Ask: *Do you think you are good at explaining things to others? What do you find easy or difficult? What do you think makes an explanation clear and easy to understand?* Discuss the questions with the class, eliciting ideas and reasons from different students.

Lead-in

Students talk about what makes a good presentation.

1 Put students in pairs and give them 2–3 minutes to discuss the question, then elicit ideas around the class. Alternatively, if you think your students will struggle, you could do this as a whole-class discussion, suggesting points to consider (e.g. the length of the presentation, engaging/addressing the audience, using visuals, structuring the presentation, the way the speaker uses their voice).

> ### Possible answer
> Use pictures, speak to the audience and ask them questions, speak slowly, vary your tone of voice to sound more interesting.

Video

Students watch a video about giving clear and effective explanations.

2 ▶ 7.3.1 If your students watched the Unit 6 video, ask them to give you a short summary of the situation and the main characters. If this is the first communication skills video for your class, briefly set up the context and/or refer students to page 6 of the Coursebook. Before students watch, refer them to the definition of *expenses claim* and pre-teach *expenses system* and *receipt*. Encourage them to make notes in answer to the questions while watching, and play the video. You could get them to compare answers in pairs before discussing them with the class.

> 1 It's complicated, and he doesn't like carrying receipts with him.
> 2 Something easy to use, like an app, would be an improvement.
> 3 He thinks it might be boring.
> 4 Possible answer: An interesting, interactive session.

3A ▶ 7.3.2 Explain that students are going to watch Thiago's training session with Shaun. At this point, you might like to pre-teach the following words from Videos A and B: *spreadsheet, expense item, currency, drop-down menu, manually, default setting, submit, enter* (*the date*). Again, encourage students to make notes while watching. Play the video, then check answers with the class.

> 1 It's an app, it's user-friendly, there's no need to fill in Excel spreadsheets or keep paper receipts.
> 2 Shaun's explanation is unclear, and she doesn't understand it.

3B You could play the video again before students discuss the questions. Put them in pairs and allow 3–4 minutes for their discussions, then have a whole-class round-up.

> 1 His description is unclear. His voice is monotonous, he just reads from his notes, he doesn't check to see that everyone understands, and the session is not interactive.
> 2 They find his explanation difficult to follow, become bored and frustrated, and start to switch off.
> 3 He should divide the explanation into steps or short sections, use sequencing expressions (*First, next,* etc.) to order the information, check the listeners understand, not assume everyone understands him, and make sure his tone of voice is lively and sounds interesting.

4A ▶ 7.3.3 Explain that students are now going to watch Azra's training session with Orla. Give them a minute to read the questions, then play the video. Check answers with the class.

> 1 **a** 5 **b** 6 **c** 7 **d** 3 **e** 1 **f** 4 **g** 2
> 2 Azra will explain it to him.

4B Students should do this in the same pairs as Exercise 3B. Give them 3–4 minutes to discuss the questions, then discuss the answers as a class.

> **Possible answers**
> 1 Very clear. The session is interactive and practical, she speaks clearly, checks the audience is following her explanation, uses sequencing expressions, gives information in short sections that are easy to follow, and invites questions from the audience.
> 2 They are able to understand immediately and enjoy the training session.

4C ▶ 7.3.3 Refer students to the tip box and go through it with them. Elicit or explain that these are techniques for giving clear explanations. Check that they understand the meaning of *sequencing words* by eliciting or giving a couple of examples (*First, then, next, after that,* etc.). Do not go into detail about each technique yet, as this would pre-empt the task as well as Exercise 8B. Play the video for students to identify each technique, then check answers with the class.

> Orla uses all of the techniques.

5 ▶ 7.3.4 Explain that students are going to watch the last section of the video, with conclusions and learning points from Videos A and B. They should watch and note the four main points the speaker makes about giving explanations. Play the video, then check the answers with the class. In weaker classes, you may need to play the video a second time or pause after each main point to give students time to make notes.

> 1 Speak clearly and make sure you sound interested in what you're saying.
> 2 Divide the procedure into smaller pieces of information to make it easier to understand.
> 3 Use sequencing words/expressions to order the explanation clearly (e.g. *First, next,* etc.).
> 4 Use examples and encourage listeners to ask questions to check they have understood.

Reflection

Students reflect on the conclusions and learning points from the video.

6 Allow students to work individually on this so that they can reflect on their own skills first. Draw their attention to the tip before they begin. Then put them in pairs to discuss their answers. Get brief feedback from the class.

Functional language: Explaining a procedure clearly and effectively

Students look at useful phrases for explaining things clearly and effectively.

7A Ask students to complete the activity individually, then check answers with the class, clarifying meanings as necessary. Draw their attention to the patterns used in 1 (*start by + -ing* form), 5 and 7 (*once/when + have* + past participle).

> **2** d **3** a **4** f **5** g **6** c **7** e

7B You could do this as a whole-class activity, eliciting the correct category for each expression as you go along.

> **Starting**
> You start by …
> **Ordering**
> Then, you … , After that, … , The next step is to … , Once you've done that, …
> **Finishing**
> The last step is to … , When you've completed all the steps, …

7C Ask students to complete the exercise individually and get them to compare answers before checking with the class.

> **Starting**
> The first thing you do is … , To begin, (you should) …
> **Ordering**
> When you finish that, then … , Next, … , Once you've finished …
> **Finishing**
> Finally, … The last thing you do is … ,

8A This can be done as a whole-class activity: read out each sentence (or invite a student to read it) and elicit the function of the underlined expression before moving on to the next one. Write the functions in four columns on the board and elicit the phrases to write in each column. Encourage students to record them in their notebooks.

> **1** like this   **2** Any questions so far?   **3** Do you see that?
> **4** because it's the easiest thing to do

8B Refer students to video script 7.3.3 on page 146 and ask them to find the examples, individually or in pairs. Check answers with the class and add them to the columns on the board.

> **Give an example:** So in this case, …
> **Give an opportunity to ask questions:** Any questions?
> **Check the listener has understood:** Does everybody understand?
> **Give a reason**: Accounts need the information for reporting reasons.

Extra activities 7.3

A–B These activities give further practice of the functional language from the lesson. Students should complete them individually and then compare answers in pairs before checking with the class. Exercise B could also be done as a whole-class activity.

> **A** **Possible answers**
> *(answers 2–5 in any order)*
> **1** You start by   **2** Then, you
> **3** After that,   **4** The next step is to
> **5** Once you've done that,   **6** The last step is to
> **7** When you've completed all the steps,
>
> **B** **1** e, g, k   **2** b, d, j   **3** f, h   **4** a, c, i

❯ **Pronunciation bank**
p. 118: Phrasing and pausing when giving instructions

Warm-up
◀ P7.04   Read out the following sentence fast and without pauses: *Start by selecting 'Create an expense report', then enter the expense item and after that select the calendar and enter the date.* Ask students if they notice anything about the way you read the instructions (too fast and without pauses). Ask: *Was this helpful? Was it easy for you to understand the instructions?* (They will probably say no.). Refer students to the explanation in the box and go through it with them. Play the recording and drill the example around the class.

1 ◀ P7.05   Before students listen, you could ask them to mark where they think the speaker will use pauses, then play the recording for them to check their answers.

> The first step / is to sign in to your account. / To do this / you'll need to enter your name / and ID number. / When you've done this, / go to the drop-down menu / in the top right-hand corner of the screen, / and select 'Create new report'. / Then / you can type your report / or paste it in.

2 Put students in pairs to practise the instructions in Exercise 1. You could let them listen once again before practising on their own. For further practice, you could also write the sentences from the Warm-up above on the board, model them for students using appropriate phrasing and pausing, then get them to practise the instructions in their pairs.

Task

Students practise explaining how to use an app.

9 Put students in pairs and explain the activity. Make it clear that they can use the app in their Student's Book or another app of their choice (e.g. one on their phone). For the app in the Student's Book, make sure they understand what type of information is needed for each box (a date, a place, a number, etc.). Refer them back to the tip box on page 72 and remind them of the four learning points from the video in Exercise 5. Also tell students that they should use phrases from Exercises 7 and 8 in their explanations. In weaker classes, you could demonstrate the activity using an app on your phone (or another procedure). Set a time limit and ask students to begin. When they have finished, give them another 3–4 minutes for the self-/peer-assessment stage: they should discuss how well they think they explained the procedure to their partner. You could do a whole-class round-up at the end if you feel that it would be useful *What did students find easy/difficult about explaining the procedure? Did they use the functional language? What can they do better next time?*

MyEnglishLab: Teacher's resources: extra activities; Interactive video activities; Functional language bank
Pronunciation bank: p.118 Phrasing and pausing when giving instructions
Workbook: p.37 Exercise 1

7.4 ❯ Business skills
Dealing with technical problems

GSE learning objectives

- Can understand standard speech on familiar matters, with some repetition or reformulation.
- Can identify key details in a simple recorded dialogue or narrative.
- Can make and respond to suggestions.

Warm-up

Put students in pairs and ask them to make a list of things that can go wrong during a meeting. Give or elicit a few examples before they begin (e.g. presentation tools not working, no internet access, problems with audio/video conferencing equipment, attendees arrive late, heating in meeting room not working). Allow 2–3 minutes for this, then elicit ideas around the class and write them on the board. Ask students if any of the things on the board have ever happened during a meeting they attended. Invite those who answer 'yes' to share their experience with the class. What happened? How was the problem managed/resolved? How could it have been avoided?

Lead-in

Students talk about ground rules in meetings.

1A Refer students to the definition of *ground rules*. Elicit or give a few examples of ground rules in your classroom (e.g. arrive on time, try to speak as much English as possible in class). Then put students in pairs and give them 3–4 minutes to discuss the questions. Elicit ideas around the class.

Possible answers

1 Ground rules help meetings run smoothly.
2 The group should agree on the ground rules together.
3 Students' own answers

1B Students could do this individually or in pairs, then share their ideas with another student/pair. Elicit ideas around the class and list them on the board. As a round-up, you could ask students if they agree with all the ideas on the board. Are some more important than others? Why?

Possible answers

Give everyone the chance to speak.
Announce your name and position / job title (especially if you are new or meeting people who don't know each other well).
Ask everyone to speak slowly.
Use people's names to indicate who you want to speak to.
Press 'mute' when you are not speaking to stop background noise.

Listening

Students listen to part of a webinar where technical problems occur.

2A This activity pre-teaches some useful vocabulary from the listening and also from the Functional language section that follows. Do it as a whole-class exercise, checking answers and clarifying meanings as you go along. Ask students what all these things have in common (they are all technical problems) and, if time allows, ask if any students have ever faced any of these problems during an online meeting/conversation.

1 echo **2** volume settings **3** mute button **4** cut out
5 blank (screen) **6** hang up

2B ◄)) 7.01 Go through the instructions with students and give them a minute to read the sentences. Teach or elicit the meanings of *webinar* and *division*. Play the recording, then check answers with the class.

1 name, before **2** brief, speak **3** slowly, clearly
4 button, noise

Extra activities 7.4

A ◄)) 7.01 This activity gives further practice of useful expressions for setting ground rules in meetings. It is a consolidation exercise, so it might be better to ask students to complete it individually. Give them 3–4 minutes to complete the expressions, then play the recording for them to check their answers. Go through the answers with the class and clarify any points as necessary.

1 We've got about **2** a few ground rules
3 name and division **4** keep your questions brief
5 slowly and clearly

3A ◄)) 7.02 Explain that students are now going to hear the beginning of the Q&A session, where the participants are having some technical problems. Play the recording for students to match the speakers with the problems – point out that they need to use one of the problems twice. Check answers with the class.

1 Donna c, b
2 Paul d, b
3 Karl f, e
4 Lena a

3B ◄)) 7.02 Put students in pairs and ask them to note down the solution to each of the problems in Exercise 3A. Explain that they should complete the information they remember from the first listening and will then have chance to check/complete their answers when they listen again. Play the recording, then check answers with the class.

1 Donna turns off her camera.
2 Paul hangs up and Sam calls him back.
3 Karl moves closer to the microphone / checks the volume settings / moves his mobile phone away from his computer.
4 Lena uses the mute button.

Functional language: Signalling and dealing with technical problems

Students look at useful expressions for signalling and dealing with technical problems.

4A Get students to complete the exercise individually and then to compare answers in pairs before checking with the class. To check answers, you could play recording 7.02 again or go through the sentences with the class. During feedback, clarify meanings as necessary.

See 4B below.

4B Students now look at the function of the sentences in Exercise 4A. You could let them complete the exercise individually and then check answers in pairs. Alternatively, you could do this as a whole-class activity, checking answers as you go along. You could draw two columns on the board, headed *Signalling a problem* and *Dealing with a problem*, and record the correct answers there. Students could then refer to the list on the board when they do Exercise 4C.

1 *Have you switched on your webcam? D*
2 *Your screen is blank. S*
3 You keep cutting out. S
4 The connection is bad. S
5 Would you mind hanging up and I'll call you back? D
6 I'm afraid we can't hear you very well, either. S
7 Could you move closer to the microphone? D
8 If you can just check your volume settings, please? D
9 There's a bit of an echo. S
10 Can you move your mobile phone away from your computer? D
11 I can hear a lot of background noise. S
12 Would you mind using the mute button? D

Extra activities 7.4

B This activity practises expressions to describe technical problems. Get students to match the sentence halves individually, then check answers with the class.

1 c 2 f 3 a 4 e 5 b 6 d

C ◀ 7.02 Students now match the problems in Activity B with possible solutions. Explain that some solutions may match more than one problem. Ask students to complete the exercise individually and compare answers in pairs before class feedback. If necessary, you could play recording 7.02 again for students to confirm their answers. Note that doing this activity at this point in the lesson will help students with Exercise 4C, below.

Possible answers

1 Could you use the mute button?
2 If you can just move your mobile phone away from your computer …
3 Could you just move closer to the microphone? / Would you mind checking your volume settings?
4 Why don't you switch on your webcam?
5 If you hang up, I'll call you back.
6 If you hang up, I'll call you back.

4C Put students in pairs and explain that they should take it in turns to signal a problem, using expressions from Exercise 4A. Their partner should respond with a suitable solution, again from Exercise 4A. Refer students to the example and point out that there may be more than one possible problem-solution combination each time. You may also wish to do an example with a stronger student. If you listed the answers to Exercise 4B on the board, encourage students to refer to it during the activity.

Possible answers

A: I can hear a lot of background noise.
B: Would you mind using the mute button? / Can you move your mobile phone away from your computer?

A: There's a bit of an echo.
B: Would you mind hanging up and I'll call you back? / Would you mind using the mute button?

A: I'm afraid we can't hear you very well.
B: If you can just check your volume settings, please? / Can you move closer to the microphone?

A: My screen is blank.
B: Have you switched on your webcam? / Would you mind hanging up and I'll call you back?

Task

Students roleplay an online meeting where they have to deal with technical problems.

5A Put students in groups of three. Explain that they are colleagues working for the same company, but they are not in the office today and so are going to hold an online meeting. First, they have to choose a topic for their meeting. Point out that they should also decide on other details, (e.g. what type of company they work for, their roles if appropriate, the reason they are holding a party (for topic 1), the topic of the next conference (for topic 2), the ideas for the team-building activity (for topic 3)). Make it clear that they can use one of the three topics given in their Student's Book or choose one of their own. Allow 3–5 minutes for this stage.

5B Allocate roles. Try to give role B to a stronger student. If your class does not divide into threes, roles A and C could be doubled. Give students time to read the information, think about their roles and decide on any further details that are specific to the scenario they chose in the previous stage. During the discussions, monitor and help students as necessary, and let them ask you any questions they may have.

5C Refer students to the Problem cards on page 138. Explain that during their meeting, a different technical problem will arise every 60 seconds. Students take it in turns to choose a Problem card and use the functional language from Exercise 4 to signal and deal with that problem before continuing with their meeting. During the meetings, monitor and check students' use of the functional language but do not interrupt – note down any errors to highlight during feedback.

5D When students have finished their meetings, they change roles, choose a different topic and hold a second meeting. Before they do, they should repeat the steps in stages 5A–5C to prepare for their meetings. Again, remind them to use phrases from Exercise 4 to signal and deal with the technical problems.

5E Students now assess their performance. Go through the instructions and give a few additional questions to help them: Did they use the functional language (correctly)? When signalling a problem, was it easy for the other participants to understand what was wrong? Did they manage to suggest appropriate solutions to each problem? What went well? What could they do better next time? Give students 3–5 minutes to discuss in their groups, then invite students from different groups to share their experience with the class. Finally, highlight any errors or difficulties you noted while monitoring.

MyEnglishLab: Teacher's resources: extra activities; Functional language bank
Workbook: p.37 Exercises 2 and 3

7.5 ❯ Writing
Preparing slides

GSE learning objectives

- Can understand standard speech on familiar matters, with some repetition or reformulation.
- Can identify key details in a simple recorded dialogue or narrative.
- Can write bullet points to summarise key points in a structured text.

Warm-up

Discuss the following questions with the class: *What types of visual aids can be used in presentations?* (possible answers: PowerPoint slides, flip charts, handouts, video) *What type of information do you think should be included on slides?* (possible answers: an agenda, key takeaways: summary of key points, charts/diagrams, infographics).

Lead-in

Students complete slides for a presentation.

1A 🔊 7.03   Draw students' attention to the slides. Tell them that they are going to hear the first part of a presentation and number the slides in the correct order (1–3). Tell them not to worry about the gaps at the moment. Play the recording, then check answers with the class.

> **1** C **2** B **3** A

1B 🔊 7.03   Give students time to look at the slides again and think about the type of word needed for each gap. Play the recording, then check answers with the class.

> **1** colours **2** production **3** line **4** yellow **5** colours
> **6** Why **7** What **8** When

Functional language

Students look at tips for preparing effective presentation slides.

2 Explain the activity. Before students find examples in the slides, go through the table with them. For the first tip, check that they remember the grammar forms listed by eliciting one example of each (e.g. infinitives: *work / to work*; *-ing* forms: *working*; nouns: *product*; Past Simple: *increased*; comparatives: *lower*). Allow plenty of time for students to complete the table, then check answers with the class. In weaker classes, students may find it easier to complete the activity in pairs.

> **1** decide, choose, start, send (out), launch
> **2** keeping, making, adding
> **3** (negative) customer feedback, falling sales, (eco-friendly) packaging, colour change, (use of) recycled materials, (three) months
> **4** decide on (the) colours, choose (the) material, start (the) production, launch (the) rebranded product line, keeping (the) yellow
> **5** choose (a) material, send out (a) press release

Extra activities 7.5

A In this activity, students practice the tips from Exercise 2. Before they complete the exercise, you could get them to match each slide with a tip from the table in Exercise 2. Ask: *How can slide 1 be improved?* (by using similar grammar forms for all the bullet points) *Slide 2?* (by cutting the articles) *Slide 3?* (by correcting the spelling mistakes) *Slide 4?* (by arranging the information with bullet points). Get students to complete the exercise individually and then compare answers in pairs before class feedback.

> **Slide 1**
> - do market research
> - get feedback from customers
> - give information to designers / inform designers
> - get schedule ready
>
> **Slide 2**
> - find a̶ new supplier
> - consult a̶n̶ international expert
> - update t̶h̶e̶ computer system
>
> **Slide 3**
> welcom = welcome
> contract = contact
> speek = speak
> langauge = language
> buy = by
>
> **Slide 4**
> - Why?
>   – sales increasing in USA and domestic market
> - What?
>   – buy, rent or build new factory
>   – move HQ to NY or London
> - When?
>   – by end of year

Optional grammar work

The presentation in Exercise 1 contains examples of *Wh-* questions, so you could use it for some optional grammar work. Refer students to the Grammar reference on page 124 and use the exercises in MyEnglishLab for extra grammar practice.

Task

Students prepare slides for a presentation.

3A Put students in pairs and refer them to the slides on page 140. Explain that they are examples of bad slides and that students should think about how they can be improved using the tips in Exercise 2. Point out that they should first identify *what* can be improved in each slide and then think about *how* to improve it. Give pairs 3–5 minutes for the activity and then discuss the answers with the class.

Possible answer

Slide 1 uses full sentences. It's what the presenter should be *saying*, not what they should be *showing* their audience. A bulleted approach like Slide C in Exercise 1 would be far more appropriate here.

Slide 2 has too much information on it. The font is too small and there is a spelling mistake (qwality = quality). The title is also something the presenter would say, not something they should show their audience.

Slide 3 mixes different sorts of grammar in the 'What?' list. Bullet points are used erratically and there are three spelling mistakes (bying = buying, enqueries = enquiries, mutlinational = multinational). The first and last points are expressed as full sentences.

The slides are also all different in terms of style, so would need unifying if they are to be used in sequence in a presentation.

3B 🔊 7.04 Explain that students are going to listen to a presentation about the redesign of a walking frame for elderly people and then create three slides for it. Teach or elicit the meaning of *walking frame*. You may also wish to pre-teach *mobility*, *slip* and *non-slip*, which students will hear on the recording. After listening, refer them to audio script 7.04 on page 151 and ask them to prepare their slides. Remind them to follow the tips in Exercise 2. During the writing task, monitor and help students as necessary.

Model answer

Slide 1

Reasons for redesign
- new technology available
- new competitors in the market

Slide 2

Key features
- lighter
- stronger
- more moveable
- better non-slip feet
- more stable

Slide 3

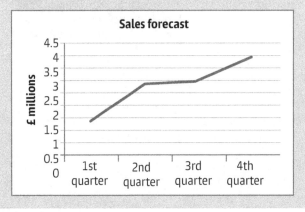

Sales forecast

3C Put students in pairs and explain the activity. Allow plenty of time for them to read and assess their partner's slides while you monitor and help as necessary. As a follow-up, you could ask students to rewrite their slides based on their partner's feedback; they could do this in class or for homework.

MyEnglishLab: Teacher's resources: extra activities; Interactive grammar practice; Writing bank

Grammar reference: p.124 *Wh-* questions

Workbook: p.38 Exercises 1–4

Business workshop ❯ 7

Zapatos Trujillo S.A.

GSE learning objectives

- Can identify specific information in simple letters, brochures and short articles.
- Can identify specific information in a simple factual text.
- Can identify key details in a simple recorded dialogue or narrative.
- Can recognise when speakers disagree in a conversation conducted slowly and clearly.
- Can recognise when speakers agree in a conversation conducted slowly and clearly.
- Can identify specific information in a simple factual text.
- Can identify key details in a simple recorded dialogue or narrative.
- Can ask and answer questions about basic plans and intentions.
- Can explain what they like or dislike about something.
- Can describe plans and arrangements.
- Can discuss what to do next using simple phrases.
- Can write a simple email, giving details of work-related events or plans.

Background

Students read about a shoe factory in Mexico.

1 Put students in pairs and get them to read the background and discuss the questions. Check answers with the class. Students may want to know the meanings of *product line* and *consultancy*.

1 producing shoes/footwear
2 well-known global shoe companies
3 producing their own line of shoes
4 shoe manufacturing consultancy
5 deciding what type of footwear to produce, and the best production processes to use

Discussing processes and products

Students listen to conversations about shoe manufacturing.

2A 🔊 BW 7.01 Remind students of Oscar and Sofia's roles (Oscar is the CEO of Zapato's Trujillo S.A., Sofia is the consultant from Due Scarpe). Explain that Oscar has just given Sofia a tour of the factory and they are now discussing the company's production process. Play the recording, then check answers with the class.

How long it takes to complete a shoe order; Making costs lower

2B ◆ BW 7.01 Give students time to look through the notes and think about the type of information needed for each gap. Teach or elicit the meaning of *automation* and *speed up*, then play the recording. Check answers with the class.

> **1** 3,000 **2** 12 **3** 20/twenty **4** 30/thirty **5** skill

3A ◆ BW 7.02 Explain to students that Sofia, Oscar and Mario are now talking about shoe designs. Ask what Mario's role is at Zapatos Trujillo S.A. (Head of Design) and give students time to read the sentence halves before they listen. Play the recording, then check answers with the class.

> Sofia: 1, 6 Oscar: 2, 4 Mario: 3, 5

3B ◆ BW 7.02 Play the recording again and quickly check the answer with the class.

> b

Extra activities Business workshop 7

A ◆ BW 7.01 ◆ BW 7.02 This activity looks at useful phrasal verbs and prepositional phrases from the recordings. Get students to complete it individually or in pairs, using their dictionaries if necessary. Point out that they should read the whole sentence each time to help them work out the meaning needed. Then play the recording for students to check their answers and hear the words in context. This will help them with the next exercise, where they have to think about meanings.

> **1** up, down **2** on **3** on **4** into **5** of

B This can be done as a whole-class activity, or with students working individually and then checking answers in pairs. Check answers with the class, clarifying meanings as necessary.

> **a** take on **b** speed up **c** work on
> **d** be proud of **e** cut down on **f** break into

C Get students to complete the exercise individually, then check answers with the class.

> **1** take on **2** speed up **3** be proud of **4** work on
> **5** break into **6** cut down on

Considering options

Students read a progress report.

4A Get students to read the report quickly and answer the questions. When checking answers, check that students understand the difference between *wholesale price* (the price at which Zapatos Trujillo S.A. sell the shoes to stores) and *recommended retail price* (the price at which stores sell the shoes to the public). Students may also ask about the meanings of *workforce* and *cut down*.

> Sofia wrote the report for her boss, John McDermott.

4B You could do this as a whole-class activity. Get students to read the report again, then discuss the answer with the class. Ask students to justify their answers.

> 2 (because the business would not make a profit)

5 ◆ BW 7.03 Play the recording, twice if necessary, then check answers with the class. Encourage students to make notes in answer to the questions while listening.

> Sofia's worried that Oscar won't accept the idea of automation. John recommends that she share some stories of other factories that have automated, but also points out that the decision is Oscar's. He recommends that Sofia give Oscar different options.

Extra activities Business workshop 7

D This activity looks at collocations with *production*. Get students to complete it individually, using their dictionaries if necessary, then check answers with the class. During feedback, clarify meanings as necessary.

> **1** time **2** rate **3** line **4** process **5** annual

Task: Manage production

Students discuss options for a production process and choose one to put in place.

6A Put students in pairs or small groups. Explain the activity and give them time to read the options and ask you about any unknown words. Remind or ask them what Mario's design is in Option 1 (he describes it as 'very high quality – with some really nice details that are finished by hand') and give them 3–4 minutes to discuss the questions. Encourage them to give reasons. You might like to discuss the answers with the class before the next stage or let students continue in their groups.

> **1** Option 1 (The other two simpler options, with cheaper materials, wouldn't result in a premium shoe.)
> **2** Option 3 (Oscar is against automation, prefers his staff to make shoes with their hands and doesn't want to lay off workers.)
> **3** Probably Option 1. In theory, the company would be proud of any shoe it decides to produce. However, Option 1 is the most complex design and probably the one Oscar would feel the most proud of. It could be argued that Option 2, also a handmade shoe, would make the company proud because producing it includes hiring ten additional workers, which is good for local people.

6B Put students in groups of 3–6 and explain that they are members of the board of Zapatos Trujillo S.A. and are each going to argue for one of the options in Exercise 6A. Depending on the size of your class, and of each group, assign each role to one or two students and give them time to think about their arguments. They should think of reasons why their option is better than the other two. You could group students who have the same role together for this stage – this would be particularly useful for weaker classes. Set a time limit and point out that students need to come up with convincing arguments and do not necessarily need to base them on how financially viable each option is; they can refer to other factors as well the profit (e.g. quality, automation, how many people will lose their jobs). While students are working, monitor and help as necessary. Encourage them to make notes.

Possible answers

Role A

This option will produce the highest quality shoe. Zapatos Trujillo S.A. will be proud to produce high-quality footwear. The workers will feel happy and comfortable because they will continue working in the same way. Options 2 and 3 aren't good because they produce a shoe of lower quality. Option 3 uses automation, which Oscar García wanted to avoid. Also, ten people will lose their jobs.

Role B

This is a good option because it is in the middle of the other two. The shoes will be handmade, but they will not be so expensive, so they will sell more easily. Also, it will give ten people a job. Option 1 isn't good because the expensive shoe may be difficult to sell. Sofia said it could be hard to enter the market at the high end. Option 3 uses automation, which Oscar García wanted to avoid. Also, ten people will lose their jobs.

Role C

This option creates the most profit. The company could use the extra money from this option to produce the Option 1 shoe in the future. It would be a good way to make the business grow. Option 1 isn't good because the expensive shoe may be difficult to sell. Sofia said it could be hard to enter the market at the high end. Option 2 isn't good because of the expense of hiring new workers. Both Option 1 and Option 2 are bad because they don't produce as much profit for the company.

Here are the calculations on overheads and profit:

Option 1 – Mario's design
Number of pairs: 12,000
Material: 50.00
Material total: 600,000.00
Workers: 50
Rate: 5,000
Total labour: 5,000
Mat + Lab: 850,000
Fixed overheads: 200,000
Cost per shoe: 87.50
Wholesale price: 131.25
Retail price: 236.25
Income: 1,575,000
Profit: 525,000

Option 2 – Simpler shoe and more workers
Number of pairs: 15,000
Material: 38.00
Material total: 570,000.00
Workers: 60
Rate: 5000
Total labour: 300,000
Mat + Lab: 870,000
Fixed overheads: 200,000
Cost per shoe: 71.33
Wholesale price: 107.00
Retail price: 192.60
Income: 1,605,000
Profit: 535,000

Option 3 – Automated simple
Number of pairs: 20,000
Material: 36.00
Material total: 720,000.00
Workers: 40
Rate: 5,000
Total labour: 200,000
Mat + Lab: 920,000
Fixed overheads: 300,000
Cost per shoe: 61.00
Wholesale price: 91.50
Retail price: 164.70
Income: 1,830,000
Profit: 610,000

6C In their groups, students now take it in turns to present their arguments, trying to convince the rest of the group that their option is the best choice. Remind them to refer to their notes from the previous stage. When everyone in the group has had a chance to present their arguments, they should choose one option to put in place. If time allows, do a whole-class round-up at the end: ask a few groups to tell the class which option they chose and why.

Writing

Students write an email explaining a decision.

7 If there is no time to do this in class, it can be assigned as homework. Explain to students that as board members, they are now going to write an email to Mario, informing him of their decision. Go through the list of points to remember with them and also point out the word limit. In weaker classes, you could let students plan their email in pairs, then complete the writing task individually, in class or for homework.

Model answer

I'm writing to let you know that we've discussed the options for producing a new line of shoes. We think Option 1 is the best option. Although it doesn't produce the most profit, it will allow Zapatos Trujillo S.A. to make a shoe that the company will be proud of, to continue making shoes by hand and to keep its full workforce. We hope that the new line of shoes will be a big success.

MyEnglishLab: Teacher's resources: extra activities

Review ◄7

1 1 product tester 2 feedback 3 launched
   4 usefulness 5 challenges 6 purchased
2 1 have to / need to 2 have to / need to
   3 can't / have to / need to 4 can 5 have to / need to
   6 have to / need to 7 can
3 1 start by 2 next step 3 Do you see 4 like this
   5 Any questions 6 Once you've 7 you've completed
   8 because
4 1 background 2 mute 3 connection 4 hanging up
   5 echo 6 switched on 7 volume 8 cutting out
5 1 report 2 new 3 recruited 4 very lightweight
   5 easy-to-use

8 ▶ Green solutions

Unit overview

	CLASSWORK	FURTHER WORK

8.1 ▶ Green business

Lead-in Students talk about places of natural beauty in their country.

Video Students watch a video about tourism in Punta de Lobos, Chile.

Vocabulary Students look at vocabulary related to environmental issues.

Project Students interview each other on their attitudes towards environmental issues.

FURTHER WORK

MyEnglishLab: Teacher's resources: extra activities

Pronunciation bank: p.118 Vowel sounds: /ɜː/, /ʊ/, /uː/ and /əʊ/

Teacher's book: Resource bank Photocopiable 8.1 p.148

Workbook: p.39 Exercises 1–3

8.2 ▶ Transport solutions

Lead-in Students talk about the transport system in their city/town.

Listening Students listen to an interview about public transport.

Grammar Students study and practise *should* and *could* for advice and suggestions.

Writing Students write an email giving advice and suggestions.

FURTHER WORK

MyEnglishLab: Teacher's resources: extra activities; Reading bank

Grammar reference: p.124 *should* and *could* for advice and suggestions

Pronunciation bank: p.118 *should* and *could*

Teacher's book: Resource bank Photocopiable 8.2 p.149

Workbook: p.40 Exercises 1–3, p.41 Exercises 1–3

8.3 ▶ Communication skills: Giving and receiving feedback

Lead-in Students talk about their own approach to giving and responding to feedback.

Video Students watch a video about feedback in a review meeting.

Reflection Students reflect on the conclusions from the video and think about their own approach to giving and receiving feedback.

Functional language Students look at useful phrases for giving and receiving feedback.

Task Students roleplay a review meeting.

FURTHER WORK

MyEnglishLab: Teacher's resources: extra activities; Interactive video activities; Functional language bank

Workbook: p.42 Exercises 1–3

8.4 ▶ Business skills: Managing questions

Lead-in Students look at tips for managing the Q&A session of a presentation.

Listening Students listen to the Q&A session of a presentation.

Functional language Students look at useful phrases for managing the Q&A session of a presentation.

Task Students roleplay the Q&A session of a presentation.

FURTHER WORK

MyEnglishLab: Teacher's resources: extra activities; Functional language bank

Workbook: p.42 Exercise 4

8.5 ▶ Writing: An intranet update

Lead-in Students read and complete an intranet update.

Functional language Students look at useful phrases for a short intranet update.

Task Students write a short intranet update.

FURTHER WORK

MyEnglishLab: Teacher's resources: extra activities; Interactive grammar practice; Writing bank

Grammar reference: p.125 Future forms

Workbook: p.43 Exercises 1–3

Business workshop 8 ▶ Walsh Ryan's green office

Reading Students read a report about office energy use.

Listening Students listen to a discussion about ways to reduce energy costs and waste.

Task Students give a presentation about waste and energy reduction in an office.

FURTHER WORK

MyEnglishLab: Teacher's resources: extra activities

Business brief

The main aim of this unit is to introduce students to the concept of **environmental issues** and the increasing drive in modern business to find **green solutions** to these.

Whether due to specific government legislation or consumer pressure, it is difficult for today's businesses not to engage with environmental issues. For some companies, 'going green' is good PR they can use as a visible part of their marketing strategy and corporate branding. Other businesses might have pressures (e.g., shareholders' expectations, or industry-specific legislation which limits the ways they can operate) to engage more fully with environmental issues. In these cases, an organisation may decide to draw up and publish **corporate policies** on issues such as recycling, CO_2 emissions or sustainability. Practical ways that organisations can improve their green credentials include promoting **paperless offices**, where employees are discouraged from printing documents and store everything online instead, opting to use energy from renewable sources, and using video conferencing instead of corporate travel in order to reduce their **carbon footprint**.

Research indicates that an organisation's commitment to sustainability can improve employee engagement and motivation. Consequently, some companies now encourage their employees to take part in green initiatives by offering them rewards such as extra days off work. Experts believe that introducing green practices which have obvious benefits for others can make workers feel more positively towards their company. Unilever and IBM are examples of companies successfully boosting employee engagement through an involvement in sustainability.

In some sectors, having green credentials is a crucial factor in attracting and retaining business. In the travel industry, a rising awareness of the impact that mass development can have on the environment has created the phenomenon of **green tourism** where hotels, travel companies and tourist attractions agree to adhere to environmentally friendly policies to protect the areas they operate in. These include trying to minimise the impact of visitors on indigenous cultures, creating jobs for local people, using local suppliers and produce, and supporting local **conservation projects**.

In other industries such as fashion, there is growing concern about production methods which cause environmental **pollution** or harm to communities involved in the manufacturing process. Consumers are increasingly aware that the ever-changing nature of the clothing industry, allied with an increase in cheap stores selling disposable items, leads to large increases in items which end up in landfill sites. Consumer groups are now putting pressure on big retail chains to account for the ecological damage that is done when manufacturing their goods. A direct result of this is that some clothing retailers now reward customers for recycling old clothes in the outlets where they buy new ones.

The technology industry is also being pressurised both by governments and consumers to find solutions to the pollution and toxic waste which often results from methods of production such as **built-in obsolescence** and using large amounts of non-recyclable materials in the production of goods.

Green solutions and your students

It is important that students are aware of the concept of environmental issues as they are becoming increasingly central to business policies. Pre-work students may be aware of green issues which have had an impact in their own country. Those who are in-work might already have seen changes in their company's attitude or policies regarding environmental issues in the workplace.

Unit lead-in

Elicit a brief description of the photo and draw students' attention to the unit title. Teach or elicit the meaning of *green* (environmentally friendly), then discuss the quote with the class. What do students think it means? How important do they think it is for companies to be environmentally responsible? Are companies more or less environmentally responsible today than they were in the past? Why?

8.1 ❯ Green business

GSE learning objectives

- Can follow the main points in a simple audio recording aimed at a general audience.
- Can make and respond to suggestions.
- Can use language related to environmental issues.
- Can answer simple questions and respond to simple statements in an interview.

Warm-up

Put students in pairs or small groups and ask them to tell each other about a natural place in the world they'd like to visit. Why do they want to go there? What do they know about the place? Give students 3–4 minutes to discuss in their pairs/groups, then elicit ideas around the class.

Lead-in

Students talk about places of natural beauty in their country.

1 Teach or elicit the meanings of the words in the box, then discuss both questions as a class. Ask students why they think these are some of the best places to visit and why they get/don't get many visitors. If all your students are from the same region or country, they could vote on the most beautiful natural place. If you have a multinational group, students could give mini-presentations about places in their countries, with internet images or videos.

Video

Students watch a video about tourism in Punta de Lobos, Chile.

2A ▶ 8.1.1 Tell students that they are going to watch the first part of a video about Punta de Lobos, a town in Chile which is a popular tourist destination, with the sound off. Go through the items and check that they understand the meanings of *cacti, fence, surfers* and *waves*. Play the video from 00:00 to 00:49, then check the answers with the class. After feedback, you could ask students about other things they spotted in the video (e.g. a family sitting on the other side of the fence, tourists on the cliffs, birds).

> cacti, cliffs, fence, rocks, surfers, waves

2B Discuss the questions as a class. Encourage students to give reasons why they would or wouldn't like to visit a place like Punta de Lobos.

3 ▶ 8.1.1 Explain the activity, give students time to read the information and teach or elicit the meaning of *construction projects* in item e. You might also like to pre-teach the following words from the video: *(huge) density, develop* (use land for construction), *developers, development, developing country, highway, resort, threatening*. Play the video, then check answers with the class.

> **1** d **2** e **3** a **4** c **5** b

4 ▶ 8.1.1 Give students a minute to read the statements before playing the video. In stronger classes, you could ask students to correct the false statements – they may need to watch the video again for this.

> **1** T
> **2** F – A 'huge density' of construction was planned, including a large resort.
> **3** T
> **4** F – It wants to keep the cliffs open to the public.
> **5** F – One problem was there were traffic jams on the road / too much traffic / there were no bathrooms.
> **6** T
> **7** F – 12 rooms
> **8** T

5 Put students in small groups, give them 4–5 minutes to discuss the questions, then have a whole-class round-up.

> **Pronunciation bank**
> **p. 118: Vowel sounds: /ɜː/, /ʊ/, /uː/ and /əʊ/**
>
> ◀ P8.01 Refer students to the box and play the recording for them to hear the examples. Drill the pronunciation of the example words.
>
> **1** ◀ P8.02 Explain that students are going to hear sentences which contain the vowel sounds in the box and that they should listen and identify the sound in each sentence. Point out that they should listen for the sound rather than similarities in the way the words are spelt – e.g., the sound /ɜː/ is not always spelt *-ir* as in the example word *bird*. Play the recording, then check answers with the class. Do not focus on students' pronunciation yet.
>
> > **1** s<u>ur</u>f **2** l<u>oo</u>king **3** impr<u>o</u>ved **4** c<u>oa</u>st
>
> **2** ◀ P8.02 Play the recording for students to listen and repeat.
>
> **3** Put students in pairs and explain the activity: they should take it in turns to say one of the words in brackets in Exercise 1, their partner saying the sentence next to it, paying attention to the pronunciation of the vowel sounds. During the activity, monitor and check/correct students' pronunciation of the vowel sounds as necessary.

Extra activities 8.1

A ▶ 8.1.1 Explain the activity and give students time to read the sentences. You could ask them to complete as much of the information as they can remember before watching again, then play the video for them to check/complete their answers. Check answers with the class.

1 P **2** P **3** M **4** M **5** P **6** M **7** P **8** P **9** J **10** M

Alternative video worksheet: Recycling

1 Discuss the questions as a whole class. Encourage students to give reasons for their answers to question 3.

Students' own answers

2 ▶ ALT 8.1.1 Tell students that they are going to watch a video about recycling *electronic waste*, or *e-waste*. Teach or elicit its meaning and ask for a few examples (phones, computers, appliances like refrigerators, smaller appliances like irons, etc.). Then explain the activity, refer them to the list and ask them which words they expect to hear in the video. Elicit ideas as a class and ask them to watch and check their predictions. Play the first part of the video (0:00–0:55), then check answers with the class.

1, 2, 6, 7, 8

3 ▶ ALT 8.1.1 Students complete the activity individually or in pairs, using a dictionary if necessary. Play the first part of the video again (0:00–0:55) for them to check their answers. Then go over the answers, checking that they understand the meanings of the words in italics.

1 opportunity **2** consumers **3** computer **4** away **5** electronic **6** pollution **7** Recycling **8** business

4 ▶ ALT 8.1.1 Students watch the second part of the video and choose the correct answers to questions 1–5. Give them time to read the questions and options before they watch, then play the video (0:56–2:58) and check answers with the class.

1 a **2** a **3** b **4** b **5** b

5 ▶ ALT 8.1.1 Go through the instructions and sentences with the students, then play the video (2:59–4:00) and check answers with the class.

1 d **2** a **3** c **4** b

6 ▶ ALT 8.1.1 Encourage students to make notes to answer the questions while watching. Play the whole video, twice if necessary, then check answers with the class.

1 plastic **2** Brazil, Peru, Chile
3 No. He thinks we need solutions from all types of businesses as well as governments.

7 Put students in pairs or small groups and give them 2–3 minutes to discuss the questions, then elicit answers around the class. For question 2, encourage students to give reasons for their answers.

Students' own answers

8 Students complete the activity individually or in pairs, using their dictionaries to help them if necessary. If time is short, you could do this as a whole-class activity, checking answers and clarifying meanings as you go along.

1 toxic **2** pollution **3** e-waste **4** environment
5 recycle **6** resources **7** rubbish dump

9 Get students to complete the sentences individually, then check answers with the class.

1 resources **2** rubbish dump **3** toxic

10 Students discuss the questions in pairs or small groups first, then as a class. Make sure students give reasons for their answers.

Students' own answers

Vocabulary: The environment

Students look at vocabulary related to environmental issues.

6 Get students to complete the exercise individually. Check that they understand the meaning of *harm* and *damage* in the definitions before they begin. Check answers with the class, clarifying the meanings of the words in bold as necessary.

1 b **2** d **3** c **4** a

7 You could go through the words in the box with students before they begin or let them use their dictionaries to look up unknown words and clarify meanings during feedback.

1 environment **2** pollution **3** damage **4** reduction
5 destruction

8 You might like to check the meanings of the nouns once again before students complete the table. You could also point out that for one of the items (*damage*), the verb and noun forms are the same. Ask them to work individually using their dictionaries if necessary, then check answers with the class. Alternatively, you could do this as a quick whole-class activity, checking answers and clarifying meanings as you go along.

conserve, damage, destroy, protect, pollute, recycle, reduce

9A This is a consolidation exercise, so students should do it individually. You could get them to compare answers in pairs before checking with the class.

> **1** recycle **2** pollution **3** reduce **4** protect **5** reduce

9B Put students in pairs or small groups to discuss the questions. After 4–5 minutes, invite students from different pairs/groups to share their answers with the class.

Extra activities 8.1

B This activity practises key vocabulary from the lesson. Get students to complete the exercise individually and compare answers in pairs before checking with the class.

> **1** a **2** c **3** b **4** c **5** a **6** b **7** c

Project: Protecting the environment

Students interview each other on their attitudes towards environmental issues.

10A Divide the class into A B and C groups. Explain that they are going to prepare a questionnaire and then interview other students to find out how much they do to protect the environment. Before they begin, ask everyone to read the questions on all three cards and ask about any unknown words. You might like to check the words *unplug, heating* and *towels*. Set a time limit and ask students to think of 2–3 more questions to add to their card. In weaker classes, you could circulate and help students with ideas, e.g.

- Habits at home (Group A): *Do you buy fresh or packaged food? How much meat do you eat? Do you buy organic food? Do you use plastic supermarket bags? How much food do you throw away? What do you recycle at home? Do you use a lot of cleaning products?*

- Habits where you work/study (Group B): *What do you recycle at work? How much paper do you use every day? How much do you travel for meetings? Do you drive an electric or hybrid car? Do you drink bottled water or tap water?*

- Habits on holiday (Group C): *How do you conserve water on holiday? What type of accommodation do you stay in? Do you buy a lot of souvenirs? What type of souvenirs do you buy? Do you do any activities on holiday which pollute the environment? Do you eat locally produced food?*

10B Put student in groups, with one student from each of the original groups (A, B and C). They take turns to interview each other using the questions on their cards. Encourage them to make notes of the other two students' answers as they will need to refer to them in the next stage.

10C Students return to their original groups and report back on what they found out about their classmates. As a group, they then decide which of the students they interviewed has the 'greenest' habits for each of the three categories. Remind them that they should give reasons for their answers. Set a time limit for students' discussions, then ask each group to tell the class what they decided.

MyEnglishLab: Teacher's resources: extra activities
Pronunciation bank: p.118 Vowel sounds: /ɜː/, /ʊ/, /uː/ and /əʊ/
Teacher's book: Resource bank Photocopiable 8.1 p.148
Workbook: p.39 Exercises 1–3

8.2 > Transport solutions

GSE learning objectives

- Can follow the main points in a simple audio recording, if provided with written supporting material.
- Can identify key details in a simple recorded dialogue or narrative.
- Can make and respond to suggestions.
- Can use *should(n't)* to offer or ask for advice or suggestions.
- Can make offers and suggestions using *could*.
- Can make basic informal suggestions in writing.

Warm-up

Write *public transport* on the board and ask students to give you examples (e.g. bus, train, taxi, tram, ferry, coach, underground). Discuss the following questions with the class: *How often do you use public transport? Do you only use it for travelling where you live or for going to other towns/cities? Do you use it on holiday? What is your least favourite form of public transport? Why?*

Lead-in

Students talk about the transport system in their city/town.

1A Discuss the question as a class, inviting different students to share their views. To help them, you could give them a few ideas to think about (e.g. cost, punctuality, cleanliness).

1B Teach or elicit the meanings of the words in the box (see Note below). You could ask students if they think a congestion charge would be a good idea in the major cities in their country/-ies.

Note

Congestion is the problem of too much traffic in a place. A *congestion charge* is a fee most motor vehicles have to pay to enter a central zone in a city. London introduced a congestion charge in 2003 in order to reduce high traffic flow and pollution in the central area and raise finance for the city's transport system.

Listening

Students listen to an interview about public transport.

2 ◀) 8.01 Explain that students are going to listen to an interview with an expert in public transport. You might like to pre-teach *urban areas* and *urban congestion* from the recording. Give them a minute to read the options, play the recording and check answers with the class.

> 2

3 ◀) 8.01 Go through the instructions with students and give them time to read the information. Encourage them to think about what type of word is needed for each gap so that they will know what to listen for. Play the recording, twice if necessary, then check answers with the class.

1 consultant 2 car 3 space 4 city streets 5 noise
6 technology 7 not enough 8 spend more
9 cleaner energy 10 quality of life

Extra activities 8.2

A 🔊 8.01 This activity practises useful vocabulary from the listening. In weaker classes, go through the words in the box with students before they begin. In stronger classes, ask them to work individually, using their dictionaries to check any unknown words. Play the recording for students to check their answers, then clarify meanings as necessary.

> 1 way to work 2 get around 3 convenient, efficient 4 driverless, software apps 5 satellite navigation 6 mass transit 7 promoting

4 Put students in pairs or small groups and give them 3–5 minutes to discuss the questions. Ask them to make notes in the table for question 1. Point out that for question 2, they should give their own opinions. Invite students from different pairs/groups to share their answers with the class. As an optional follow-up, you could ask students the following questions: *Do you think the government should promote walking and cycling more in your country/area? How? What do you think would encourage people to use public transport more?*

> **Suggested answers**
> **Private transport**
> Advantages: door-to-door, safer at night, faster, possible to stop whenever and wherever you like, can carry lots of things
> Disadvantages: cost of fuel, maintenance and insurance, time and stress of driving, problems finding parking spaces, dangerous drivers
> **Public transport**
> Advantages: time to relax during the journey, cheaper, gets you to the centre quicker than a car, no parking costs, saves money on fuel, maintenance and insurance
> Disadvantages: slower, not door-to-door, crowded, smelly, no privacy, no seats

Grammar: *should* and *could* for advice and suggestions

Students study and practise *should* and *could* for advice and suggestions.

5A Ask students to complete the exercise individually, then to compare answers in pairs before class feedback.

> 1 b 2 c 3 a 4 d

5B Do this as a whole-class activity. Elicit the answers and ask students what the verbs they underlined are called (modal verbs). Refer them to the Grammar reference on page 124 and go through it with them, answering any questions they may have and clarifying any points as necessary.

> 1 shouldn't 2 could 3 should 4 should
> An infinitive verb form comes after each.

> ## Pronunciation bank
> ### p. 118: *should* and *could*
>
> **Warm-up**
> 🔊 P8.03 Refer students to the explanation in the box and go through it with them. Model the strong and weak forms of *should* and *could* in isolation, and then the pronunciation of *shouldn't*. Play the recording for students to hear the examples, then drill the pronunciation of the example sentences.
>
> **1** 🔊 P8.04 Play the recording for students to complete the sentences, then check answers with the class. Do not focus on students' pronunciation yet.
>
> > 1 could 2 shouldn't 3 should 4 could
> > 5 should 6 should
>
> **2** 🔊 P8.05 Explain that students will hear the sentences with *should* and *could* from Exercise 1 and need to decide if they hear the weak or the strong form. Remind them of the pronunciation of each form, then play the recording and check answers with the class. Note that as sentence 2 contains *shouldn't* students should ignore this.
>
> > 1 We could catch a bus or get a taxi. (W)
> > 2 N/A – contains 'shouldn't'
> > 3 Do you think I should walk more? (W)
> > 4 Yes, and you could, easily. (S)
> > 5 They should spend more on public transport. (W)
> > 6 Yes, they definitely should. (S)
>
> **3** Put students in pairs to practise saying the sentences in Exercise 1. You might like to play recording P8.05 before they begin, so that they can hear the sentences once again before they practise on their own. During the activity, monitor and check/correct students' pronunciation as necessary.

6A–B Ask students to work individually for both exercises. For Exercise 6B, point out that there may be more than one possible answer for some questions.

6A
1 b **2** e **3** d **4** c **5** a

6B
Possible answers

1 You could/should take your CV to shops and restaurants in town. (Situation 2)
2 You could/should think about the job you want to do in the future. (Situation 1)
3 You shouldn't lie when they ask you questions. (Situation 5)
4 You could/should ask if you can work from home some days. (Situation 3)
5 You shouldn't work so hard. It's bad for your health. (Situation 4)

6C Students could do this individually or in pairs. In weaker classes, monitor and if students are struggling, help them with ideas (e.g. 1 *You should think about what you enjoy doing / what you're good at.* 2 *You could look online.* 3 *You should check if taking the train can save you time.* 4 *You should join a gym.* 5 *You could talk about your previous experience.*). Do not conduct class feedback at this stage – students will discuss their answers in the next exercise.

6D Put students in groups and ask them to compare and discuss their ideas and vote on the best ones. After 4–5 minutes, invite students from different groups to tell the class which ideas they thought were the best and why.

7A–B Put students in pairs and explain that they are going to ask for and give advice and suggestions to each other. First, they have to write three questions for another pair. Give them 3–4 minutes to do this, while you monitor and help/correct them as necessary. Then join pairs together into groups of four and ask students to swap questions and answer the ones they are given. Again, monitor and check that students are using the target language correctly.

7C Students now read each other's answers and decide on the best suggestions. In smaller classes, this can also be done as a whole-class activity, with the class voting on the best advice and suggestions.

Extra activities 8.2

B This activity gives further practice of *could* and *should* for advice and suggestions. Ask students to complete the exercise individually and, if there is time, get them to compare answers in pairs before checking with the class.

1 We shouldn't arrive late for the meeting.
2 … you could/should speak English with your colleagues.
3 I shouldn't eat all this chocolate.
4 You should go to bed early tonight.
5 Should I ask for a higher salary?
6 How many people should we invite to the conference?
7 We could/should open a window …
8 When should we have the next meeting?

Writing

Students write an email giving advice and suggestions.

8 Go through the instructions with students and give them time to read the email. Check that they understand the meanings of *capital* and *hire*. Point out the word limit and remind students to use *could* and *should* to give advice and make suggestions. Allow time for students to plan their answer and set a time limit for the writing task. Monitor and help as necessary. If time is short, students can write their emails for homework.

Model answer

Hello Jenny,

It's a great idea to visit Spain in spring because it's not too hot or crowded with tourists. After the conference you should spend a few days sightseeing in Madrid. The museums and restaurants are great.

After that you could take the high-speed train to Valencia or Barcelona, spend some time in the city and go to the beach to relax. Then you could fly to Seville. If you want to explore Andalusia and other cities in the south, you could hire a car. There are so many beautiful places to see. Enjoy!

Best wishes,

Sandra

MyEnglishLab: Teacher's resources: extra activities; Reading bank
Grammar reference: p.124 *should* and *could* for advice and suggestions
Pronunciation bank: p.118 *should* and *could*
Teacher's book: Resource bank Photocopiable 8.2 p.149
Workbook: p.40 Exercises 1–3, p.41 Exercises 1–3

8.3 ❯ Communication skills
Giving and receiving feedback

GSE learning objectives

- Can identify key details in a simple recorded dialogue or narrative.
- Can identify a simple chronological sequence in a recorded narrative or dialogue.
- Can make and respond to suggestions.
- Can use language related to reassuring and encouraging.

Warm-up

Refer students to the lesson title and start by teaching or eliciting the meaning of *feedback* – you could refer students to the definition next to Exercise 1A. Then briefly discuss the importance of feedback with them: *Is feedback a powerful influence on learning? Why? / Why not? What are the benefits or problems with feedback?*

Lead-in

Students talk about their own approach to giving and responding to feedback.

1A Discuss the questions as a class. Invite different students to share their views with the class. Encourage them to give reasons for their answers to questions 2 and 3.

1B Put students in pairs and before they begin, go through the points in the diagram with them. Check that they understand the meanings of *praise*, *compliment* and *on a positive note,* but do not explain *corrective feedback* yet as students will discuss this in question 1. Give pairs 3–4 minutes to discuss the questions, then broaden this into a class discussion.

> 1 feedback that gives examples of areas where the employee needs to improve
> 2 **Possible answers:**
>   a) to feel secure in your job, to understand your strengths and weaknesses, to understand when you are doing something well, to understand how you can improve, it can be rewarding
>   b) it reduces turnover of employees, it helps increase productivity, it indicates training needs for employees
> 3 **Possible answer:**
>   It shows a balanced approach for giving feedback. It encourages a positive experience.

Video

Students watch a video about feedback in a review meeting.

2A ▶ 8.3.1 If your students watched the Unit 7 video, ask them to give you a short summary of the situation and the main characters. If this is the first communication skills video for your class, briefly set up the context and/or refer students to page 6 of the Coursebook. Explain that Thiago is about to have a review meeting with Orla. Ask students to watch carefully and pay attention to the flashback scenes in the video. Give them time to read the questions, then play the video and discuss the answers with the class.

> 1 As shown in the flashbacks, he knows his performance over the past six months has not been perfect.
> 2 He feels pressured after receiving emails from Della.
> 3 She was concerned, and only following the usual procedure.

2B Put students in pairs and give them 2–3 minutes to discuss the question. If necessary, play the flashback scenes again. Invite different students to share their ideas with the class.

> **Possible answers**
> He doesn't have good time-management skills, he can seem disorganised, he can seem rude and disrespectful and he doesn't have good admin skills.

3A ▶ 8.3.2 Explain that students are going to watch Thiago's review meeting with Orla and give them time to read the questions. Play the video, then discuss the answers with the class. In weaker classes, you may need to play the video a second time or pause briefly after answers are given, to allow students enough time to make notes.

> 1 He believes he is doing well.
> 2 He's enthusiastic and works hard; he's great with technology; he is warm and has good interpersonal skills; he's supportive of colleagues; he has an excellent sense of humour.
> 3 When he tried to help Jasmine after her application for the Miami conference was turned down.

3B Put students in pairs to discuss their answers, then check with the class. Students may need to watch the video again in order to check/complete their answers.

> 1 positive feedback
> 2 She explains what will happen during the feedback session.
> 3 parts 1, 2 and 3

4A ▶ 8.3.3 Explain that students are going to watch Orla give Thiago some corrective feedback. Play the video, then check the answers with the class.

> 1, 3, 5

4B Students should do this in the same pairs as Exercise 3B. Again, give them time to discuss their answers in their pairs, then check them with the class. During feedback, you may wish to play the video again, pausing after each answer is given to confirm and discuss it with the class.

> 1 She gives an example.
> 2 pay more attention to how he speaks to colleagues in the future
> 3 positively

5 ▶ 8.3.4 Explain that students are going to watch the last section of the video, which discusses the advantages and disadvantages of the approaches in Videos A and B. They should watch and compare what is said with their answers to Exercises 3B and 4B. Play the video and, if time allows, let students discuss briefly in pairs or small groups first. Round up ideas in a class discussion.

> 1 Prepare the person for the feedback and ask for their agreement.
> 2 Provide clarification or examples if necessary.
> 3 Then invite the person to assess their own performance.
> 4 Try to stay positive and diplomatic when receiving corrective feedback. Always thank the other person for their feedback, positive or corrective.

Reflection

Students reflect on the conclusions from the video and think about their own approach to giving and receiving feedback.

6 Allow students to work individually on this so that they can reflect on their own skills first. Ask them to think about the question and make notes. Then put them in pairs to discuss and compare their answers. Get brief feedback from the class.

Functional language: Giving and receiving feedback

Students look at useful phrases for giving and receiving feedback.

7 Ask students to complete the exercise individually or in pairs, using their dictionaries to help them if necessary. Check answers with the class, clarifying meanings as necessary. After feedback, you could ask students to mark each sentence *P* if it gives positive feedback or *C* if it gives corrective feedback.

> **1** pleased with (P) **2** great with (P) **3** were (P)
> **4** have (P) **5** for improvement (C) **6** could improve (C)

8A You could do this as a whole-class activity, checking that students understand each heading and expression as you go along. You could also write the expressions in four columns on the board, under the correct heading, and encourage students to record them in their notebooks.

> **1** b **2** c **3** a **4** d

8B Again, this can be done as a whole-class activity. Alternatively, ask students to work individually and then check answers with the class, clarifying meanings as necessary. Add the expressions to the four columns on the board and, again, encourage students to record them in their notebooks.

> **Suggested answers**
> **Preparing someone for the feedback**
> Let me explain the process.
> We'll start with the positive feedback, then we'll move on to areas for improvement.
> **Asking for consent (agreement)**
> How about that?
> **Giving clarification**
> A good example of that was …
> Let me explain why we're concerned.
> One example of this is …
> We're worried because …
> **Encouraging self-assessment**
> How did you feel it went?
> What are your thoughts?
> What do you think about … ?

8C This activity is best done in two stages. Start by asking students to form the sentences individually and check the answers with the class. Then, once students have the complete sentences, they can classify them individually or in pairs.

> **2** I mostly agree with your assessment. (C)
> **3** That's an interesting idea, but … (C)
> **4** I'd like to try and do that in the future. (C)
> **5** I accept that this is a problem for me sometimes. (C)
> **6** I'm glad to hear that. (P)
> **7** Your feedback is very helpful, thank you. (B)
> **8** That's good to know. (P)

Extra activities 8.3

A This activity gives further practice of the expressions for giving feedback. Ask students to complete the exercise individually, then check answers with the class.

> **1** pleased **2** interpersonal **3** great
> **4** enthusiastic/positive/supportive **5** supportive, great/important **6** enthusiastic/positive

B This activity practises the key expressions for responding to feedback. It is a consolidation activity so, again, it would be better for students to do it individually. Check answers with the class.

> **1** d **2** a **3** e **4** b **5** g **6** f **7** h **8** c

Task

Students roleplay a review meeting.

9A Put students in A–B pairs and explain that they are going to hold review meetings, where they will give feedback to their partner. Refer students to their information, give them time to read it and answer any vocabulary questions. Point out that there are two gaps in each student's table, which they will have to fill in with positive qualities for their partner. Make sure students understand that there will be two meetings, and that they will take turns giving and receiving feedback. Help them prepare for the meeting by referring them back to the diagram in Exercise 1B again. Then remind them of the main points from the Conclusions section of the video in Exercise 5. Finally, tell students to use expressions from Exercises 7 and 8 to give and respond to feedback. Allow plenty of time for this preparation stage, monitoring and helping them as necessary.

9B Students now hold their meetings. Go through the steps with them and check they understand the meanings of *consent* and *carry out a self-assessment*. Set a time limit for each meeting and remind students again to use appropriate expressions to give and respond to feedback.

9C Students now assess their performance. Did they follow the steps in Exercise 9B? Was their feedback clear, but also tactful and balanced? How easy was it to do this in English? Allow some time for them to discuss in their pairs and then, as a round-up, ask students from different pairs to share their experience with the class.

MyEnglishLab: Teacher's resources: extra activities; Interactive video activities; Functional language bank
Workbook: p.42 Exercises 1–3

8.4 ❯ Business skills
Managing questions

Warm-up

Teach or elicit the meaning of *Q&A session* (*question and answer session* – the part of a presentation where a speaker answers questions from the audience). Refer students to the photo on page 84 and say: *Many people find the Q&A session the most difficult part of a presentation. Imagine you are the presenter in the photograph. How do you feel? Why?* Put students in pairs and give them 2–3 minutes to discuss the questions, then elicit answers around the class.

Lead-in

Students look at tips for managing the Q&A session of a presentation.

1 Put students in small groups and go through the advice with them. Give them 3–4 minutes to discuss in their groups, then get feedback from the class. Encourage students to give reasons.

Listening

Students listen to the Q&A session of a presentation.

2A Put students in small groups and explain the activity. Teach or elicit the meaning of *open-plan office* and *closed office*. Give them a few minutes to brainstorm ideas, then invite different students to share them with the class. You could give them some prompts to think about (e.g. privacy, communication, noise levels). To extend the activity, you could ask the following question around the class: *Would you prefer to work in an open plan office or a closed office? Why?*

Possible answers

Open-plan office: encourages collaboration between colleagues; stops colleagues feeling isolated; companies can save space and reduce costs; companies can be more eco-friendly – staff share printers, etc.; space can be used in a more creative way – e.g. for communal activities

Closed office: easier to concentrate; staff can design their own work space; staff don't have to keep their desks tidy; people can hold confidential meetings in their office; people can play music, etc. without disturbing colleagues

2B ◀) 8.02 Go through the instructions and topics with the class and check they understand the meanings of *timing* and *temporary*. You may also wish to pre-teach the following words from the recordings: *reserve, be scheduled for, branch, shuttle bus, allocate* (*space*), *hot-desking, policy, storage space.* Tell the students that one person mentions two topics. Play the recording, then check answers with the class.

> **1** b **2** c, d **3** a

2C ◀) 8.02 Ask students to work individually first. Give them time to read the statements, and play the recording for them to listen and decide if they are true or false. Check answers with the class. Put students in pairs to correct the false statements and let them listen again if necessary.

> **1** T
> **2** F (five rooms on each floor)
> **3** T
> **4** F (It's a 20-minute ride.)
> **5** T

3A ◀) 8.03 Explain that students are going to listen to the next part of the Q&A session. Give them time to read the questions and ask them to make notes as they listen. Play the recording, then check answers with the class.

> **1** She doesn't like it / thinks it will create lots of problems.
> **2** working in an open-plan office / who will sit where
> **3** She checks she has understood the question by asking for clarification, explains she can't answer it, thanks Jen for the question and asks Ted to respond.
> **4** to keep the office tidy / for their files
> **5** She wants to talk to someone and complain about the procedure for allocating desks.

3B Put students in pairs and give them 2–3 minutes to discuss the questions, then discuss the answers as a class.

> **1** wait a few seconds before you answer a question; repeat the question to check you have understood and make sure the audience have heard it
> **2** Students' own answer

Functional language: Managing a Q&A session

Students look at useful phrases for managing the Q&A session of a presentation.

4A Get students to complete the sentences individually and then to compare answers in pairs before checking with the class. During feedback, clarify meanings as necessary. Do not focus on the functions of the phrases yet as students will look at these in the next exercise.

> **1** have a question **2** is about **3** good question
> **4** answer your question **5** you're asking, that right
> **6** not sure

4B Go through the headings and examples in the table with students and check that they understand them. Then get them to complete the exercise individually. Alternatively, do this as a whole-class activity, eliciting the correct category for each phrase as you go along.

1 Does anyone have a question?
2 So the question is about meeting rooms.
3 It's a good question, thanks.
4 Sorry, you're asking how we allocate space. Is that right?
5 Does that answer your question?
6 I'm not sure I can answer that.

5 Put students in pairs and explain the activity. Reassure them that more than one answer is possible each time – they can choose expressions from different categories and then answer the questions using their own ideas. You could demonstrate the activity with a stronger student. During the activity, monitor and check that students are using the functional language correctly. Go over any errors during feedback.

Extra activities 8.4

A–B These activities gives further practice of the functional language from the lesson. Ask students to complete both exercises individually, then check answers with the class.

A
1 d **2** f **3** e **4** a **5** b **6** c
B
1 We just have time for one more question.
2 So Sara asked when the move will happen.
3 Thank you, that's an interesting question.
4 Sorry, you're asking about the deadline. Is that right?
5 I hope that answers your question?
6 Can I get back to you about that?

Task

Students roleplay the Q&A session of a presentation.

6A Put students in groups of three and explain that they are going to take part in a Q&A session of a presentation. One of them will manage the session. The other two students in each group will be asking the questions. At this point, you may wish to tell them that they will all get the chance to be the Presenter as each group will hold three different Q&A sessions. Give students time to read the scenario and ask you any questions they may have. Check that they understand the meanings of *improved communication*, *savings on equipment costs*, *heating bills*, *creativity*, *reserve* and *relaxation area*. Before they select their roles, you may wish to give them some time to add a couple of ideas of their own to the two boxes. Let students select their roles.

6B Divide the class into two groups: Presenters and Questioners 1 and 2. Refer all the Presenters to their information on page 136 and all the Questioners to the information for Q&A session 1 on page 137. Give them time to read their information. Point out to the Presenters that their role is to make sure that the session runs smoothly. Explain or elicit that in order to do this, they need to use strategies from Exercise 1, follow some of the steps (1–6) on their role card and use expressions from Exercise 4. Give students plenty of time to prepare for their sessions: the Presenters should try to anticipate some of the questions they will be asked and prepare their answers; the Questioners should prepare the questions they are going to ask. During this stage, monitor and provide help as necessary.

6C Students now return to their original groups of three and roleplay Q&A session 1. Set a time limit before they begin. When they have finished, ask them to swap roles and repeat the steps in Exercise 6B for Q&A session 2. When they are ready, set a time limit again and let them begin their roleplays. Repeat the process one final time for Q&A session 3.

6D Students should do this final stage in their original groups of three. Ask them to talk about how easy or difficult it was for them to manage the Q&A session. Did they use the functional language phrases? What would they change next time? After students have discussed in their groups, you could broaden this into a class discussion.

MyEnglishLab: Teacher's resources: extra activities; Functional language bank
Workbook: p.42 Exercise 4

8.5 ➤ Writing
An intranet update

GSE learning objectives

- Can make basic inferences from simple information in a short text.
- Can write a simple email, giving details of work-related events or plans.
- Can write a description of a future event or activity.
- Can write a simple email, giving details of work-related events or plans.

Warm-up

Discuss the following questions with the class: *What is a company's intranet? What is it used for?* (a private network for exchanging information within an organisation, accessible only to the organisation's staff). Ask if any students have ever used an intranet. Ask those who have if they have ever read (or written) an intranet update and if yes, what it was about.

Lead-in

Students read and complete an intranet update.

1 If you did not do the Warm-up activity, refer students to the lesson title and teach or elicit the meaning of *intranet*. Then refer them to the text in Exercise 1 and get them to complete the exercise individually and compare answers in pairs. Go over the answers with the class, clarifying the meanings of the words in italics as necessary.

1 know 2 more 3 suggestions 4 propose 5 result
6 Firstly 7 introduce 8 holding 9 put 10 questions

Functional language

Students look at useful phrases for a short intranet update.

2 Before students look at the table, point out that the information in the update in Exercise 1 is organised in three paragraphs and ask them if they can work out what each paragraph is about. Elicit ideas, then refer them to the headings in the table to confirm answers. Finally, get students to complete the table individually or in pairs, and check answers with the class. During feedback, clarify meanings as necessary. Tell students that when writing intranet updates, they should try to follow the structure given in the table and also include a title where possible.

> **1** As you know   **2** ready   **3** has decided
> **4** are going to   **5** This will reduce   **6** also plan
> **7** is planning to   **8** Finally   **9** therefore   **10** is arranging
> **11** will answer   **12** can explain

Optional grammar work

The intranet update in Exercise 1 contains examples of future forms, so you could use it for some optional grammar work. Refer students to the Grammar reference on page 125 and use the exercises in MyEnglishLab for extra grammar practice.

Extra activities 8.5

A This activity gives further practice of useful expressions for the different parts of an intranet update. Ask students to complete it individually, then check answers with the class.

> **1** g   **2** f   **3** a   **4** i   **5** e   **6** h   **7** c   **8** d   **9** b

Task

Students write a short intranet update.

3A Refer students to the intranet update on page 140 and point out the types of mistakes they need to look for. If you think it will help them, give them an example of each (e.g. grammar: *We have deciding **decided** to set up*; spelling: *We will discus **discuss** all ideas during …*; missing words: *We also plan **to** introduce a new system …*; unnecessary words: *We have made a number of ~~the~~ changes to …*). In weaker classes, you may wish to do the first item as an example. Get students to complete the exercise individually and then to compare answers in pairs before checking with the class.

> we trying = we are trying
> are we = we are
> Fristly = Firstly
> changing = change
> planning us to = planning to
> theirfore = therefore
> answered = answer

3B Refer students to the notes on page 140 and explain the writing task. Remind them to use a title, organise the information into paragraphs and use the functional language from the table in Exercise 2. If there is no time to do the writing task in class, it can be assigned as homework.

Model answer
Update on proposed changes

As you know, we are trying to provide a more eco-friendly environment by moving to smaller offices outside the city centre. The company has found offices and we are now ready to give you details.

Firstly, we are going to provide a free company bus service from the city centre to the new offices. This will mean that staff can leave their cars at home and arrive at work more relaxed. It will also reduce the amount of pollution in the city. We also plan to allow people to work from home, which also means that there will be fewer cars on the road. You can find out more about the new scheme soon.

We are holding a meeting next Friday to discuss the changes and answer any questions you have.

3C If students write their intranet updates for homework, this exercise can be done in the next class. Get students to do the exercise in pairs. Encourage them to suggest corrections if they think there is an error in their partner's text. During the activity, monitor and help as necessary.

MyEnglishLab: Teacher's resources: extra activities; Interactive grammar practice; Writing bank
Grammar reference: p.125 Future forms
Workbook: p.43 Exercises 1–3

Business workshop > 8
Walsh Ryan's green office

GSE learning objectives

- Can identify specific information in simple letters, brochures and short articles.
- Can identify specific information in a simple factual text.
- Can follow the main points in a simple audio recording aimed at a general audience.
- Can follow the main points in a simple audio recording, if provided with written supporting material.
- Can communicate in routine tasks requiring simple, direct exchanges of information.
- Can make and respond to suggestions.
- Can use basic discourse markers to structure a short presentation.

Background

Students read about Walsh Ryan, an insurance company in Dublin, Ireland.

1 Put students in pairs and ask them to read the background and discuss the questions. Check answers with the class.

> **1** It's an insurance company.
> **2** It's six kilometres from the city centre. It's on four floors and is designed to save energy.
> **3** It's responsible for day-to-day operations such as energy use, security, cleaning and maintenance.
> **4** to reduce costs and help protect the environment (and to give the company a better reputation)

The green office report

Students read a report about office energy use.

2A Ask students to work individually. Explain the activity and tell them to focus on understanding the general idea of each section rather than any words they don't know. After checking answers with the class, you could refer them to the pie chart and ask them to think about possible items in the *Other office & kitchen equipment* and *Other* categories. (Possible answers include: Other office & kitchen equipment: printers, photocopiers, meeting room equipment such as projectors; a kitchen and canteen equipment such as coffee makers, fridges, cookers, dishwashers and microwaves; Other: vending machines, lifts, external lighting.)

> **1** Energy use **2** Paper use **3** Waste

2B If there is time, put students in pairs or small groups to brainstorm ideas, then get feedback from the class. Alternatively, do this as a quick whole-class activity, eliciting a few ideas around the class.

Extra activities Business workshop 8

A This activity provides students with extra reading practice. It can be done individually or, in weaker classes, in pairs. Encourage students to underline the parts of the text that gave them the answers each time, and elicit these during class feedback.

> **1** c **2** c **3** a **4** c **5** a

B This activity looks at useful vocabulary from the report in Exercise 2. Students could do it individually or, in weaker classes, in pairs. Encourage them to find the words in the report before matching them with their definitions, so that they can see them used in context – this will help them work out their meanings. Check answers with the class.

> **1** budget **2** savings **3** waste **4** bill **5** utilities
> **6** disposal

The Facilities Department meeting

Students listen to a discussion about ways to reduce energy costs and waste.

3A 🔊 BW 8.01 Draw students' attention to the pictures and elicit what they show (from left to right: printer, cloud computing, recycling bins, motion sensor). You may wish to pre-teach the following words from the recording: *corridor, detect, equipment, install, look into (the options), motion sensor, multifunctional, run (machines), storeroom, toner.* Play the recording, then check answers with the class.

> **1** motion sensors **2** cloud computing **3** printers
> **4** recycling scheme

3B Do this as a quick whole-class activity.

> cloud computing, multifunctional printers, recycling scheme

3C Give students time to read the notes and point out the word limit before they listen. Play the recording, twice if necessary, then check answers with the class.

> **1** lights **2** toilets **3** car park **4** servers/machines
> **5** right temperature **6** (print) quality **7** image
> **8** reputation (as a green company)

Task: Present ideas on waste and energy reduction

Students give a presentation about waste and energy reduction in an office.

4A Put students in groups of six and divide the students in each group into, A, B and C pairs. Explain that they all work in the Facilities Department of Walsh Ryan and are going to present ideas for the G.O project. Refer them to their information on pages 130, 134 and 128 and give them time to read it. Monitor and help with unknown vocabulary or any questions, then set a time limit and ask students to begin the preparation; tell them that they can prepare slides or use flipcharts if they wish. Allow plenty of time for this stage and, again, monitor and provide help as necessary. If your class does not divide into groups of six, allow stronger students to work individually or less confident students to work in groups of three rather than pairs. In smaller groups students can work in groups of three and prepare their presentations individually.

4B In their groups, students now take turns to present their ideas. Refer them to the points in the box before they begin and set a time limit for the presentations.

4C When everyone has presented their ideas, groups should decide on the best option for the G.O project, giving reasons for their opinions. As a follow-up, invite students from different groups to tell the class which option they chose and why.

MyEnglishLab: Teacher's resources: extra activities

Review ◀8

> **1 1** pollutes **2** recycled **3** impact **4** destruction
> **5** protect **6** damage
> **2 1** should **2** shouldn't **3** could/should **4** could
> **5** shouldn't **6** should/could
> **3 1** e **2** g **3** a **4** d **5** f **6** b **7** h **8** c
> **4 1** anyone have **2** good question **3** you're asking
> **4** Does that **5** question, about **6** the answer
> **5 1** you know **2** now ready **3** are going to
> **4** will reduce **5** also plan to **6** therefore
> **7** are holding

Resource bank

Photocopiables

Reading bank

Writing bank

Functional language bank

1.1 ❭ Vocabulary

1 Brainstorm words and phrases connected to business travel.

public transport

business travel

accommodation

airports and flights

2 Match the questions (1–6) with the answers (a–f).

1 Shall we eat at the airport?
2 Is the public transport from the airport good?
3 Do you know when the departure time is?
4 How are we getting to the hotel?
5 Which gate number do we go to?
6 Where are we staying?

a It's not great, I think we should take a taxi.
b In a small hotel in the city centre.
c Yes, the airport lounge has some good restaurants.
d I'll check, but I think it's gate five.
e The plane leaves at 13.45.
f I think we should use a ridesharing app.

Student A

3 You are arranging a business trip to Stockholm with your partner. Write the questions you will need to find out the missing information on your card.

Place to eat	excellent restaurants / airport lounge
Departure and arrival time Question: _____ ?	
Terminal	2? 3? / not sure / will email
Travel to accommodation Question: _____ ?	
Accommodation	business hotel / reservation / two nights
Travel to client's office Question: _____ ?	

4 Call your partner. Find out the missing information in the table and give him/her the information you know.

Student B

3 You are arranging a business trip to Stockholm with your partner. Write the questions you will need to find out the missing information on your card.

Place to eat Question: _____ ?	
Departure and arrival time	departure 13.20 / arrival 16.50
Terminal Question: _____ ?	
Travel to accommodation	taxi or ridesharing app
Accommodation Question: _____ ?	
Travel to client's office	30 km / train or taxi / traffic bad in city centre

4 Call your partner. Find out the missing information in the table and give him/her the information you know.

1.2 ❯ Grammar

1 Are the sentences correct or incorrect? Correct the incorrect sentences.

1 The wi-fi in that hotel is the worst I've experienced.
2 Public transport in Europe is more better than in the USA.
3 Videoconferencing is easiest than teleconferencing.
4 I thought the conference was more interesting than last year.
5 Hotels in that city are a lot better they were in the past.
6 The venue's further from the airport than we'd like.
7 The facilities are the best I've ever seen.
8 What is the more expensive hotel you've stayed in?
9 This is most exciting conference I've been to.
10 What is the best thing about attending conferences?

2 Work in pairs. You are planning a conference for your company and must choose a venue. First, read about three venues and complete the sentences with the correct venue.

1 _____ is the closest to the city centre.
2 Marrakesh Conference Centre is closer to the city centre than _____ but further away than _____ .
3 _____ has the most conference rooms.
4 _____ is closer to the airport than the other two.
5 _____ has the most bedrooms.

Paradise Hotel & Conference Centre

Location: 2 hours outside London, UK

Nearest Airport: Gatwick, 30-minute taxi ride. No public transport available. Airport pickup available on request.

This luxury hotel and conference centre offers everything you need for your business conference.

Facilities:
- 200 bedrooms
- 25 conference rooms with full IT equipment
- Free tea and coffee
- 2 restaurants
- Pool, sauna and gym

Marrakesh Conference Centre

Location: 20 minutes from the centre of Marrakesh, Morocco

Nearest Airport: Marrakesh International, 45-minute taxi ride. No public transport available.

This modern conference centre in the heart of Marrakesh provides facilities for small- and large-scale conferences. Deals available with local hotels.

Facilities:
- 20 large conference rooms
- 15 small conference rooms
- Air conditioning in all conference rooms
- 5G wi-fi in all areas
- Five-star restaurant

Sydney House Hotel and Conference Centre

Location: Central Sydney, Australia

Nearest Airport: Sydney, 45-minute taxi ride. Train and bus transfer available.

This luxury hotel and conference centre offers everything you need for your business conference.

Facilities:
- 400 budget bedrooms; 50 luxury bedrooms
- 15 conference rooms with full IT equipment
- 3 restaurants
- Pool and gym
- Walking distance to all Sydney attractions

3 Make three more comparisons about the venues.

4 Look at your company's conference information. In pairs, discuss which venue to choose. Give reasons for your choice.

> **Jackie Jackson Fashion Corporation**
> **Conference dates:** January 14–16
> **Attendees:** 200 Sales Managers (from Europe, North America and Asia)
> **Conference purpose:** to share sales information and improve staff relationships

2.1 > Vocabulary

1 Complete the article with the words in the box.

| access   close   facilities   headquarters   labs   locate   rents   transport |

Do you want your city to be the next Silicon Valley?

Think carefully about where to [1]_____ your tech centre. Start-ups generally have weak finances, so an area with reasonable [2]_____ for office space is a good choice. However, if you manage to attract a lot of start-ups, big tech players may want to have their regional [3]_____ in your city, so make sure the area has enough space.

Tech companies require two key things: ideas and money. Try to create links with universities and innovation [4]_____ , and make sure banking [5]_____ are available. Good university links will also make sure there is [6]_____ to skilled staff.

Finally, tech is an international business, so make sure your new tech centre is [7]_____ to good [8]_____ links.

---

2 Match 1–5 with a–e to make sentences.

1 This is why you should locate
2 We can offer office space
3 We have lots of finance companies
4 We have six universities
5 Our airports provide

a offering excellent banking facilities.
b offering access to very skilled staff.
c your tech centre in our city.
d global transport links.
e for reasonable rent.

3 Work in groups. You are representatives of a city and are attending an event to attract tech start-ups to your city. Read the information about your city and prepare a short presentation.

Bangalore, India	Paris, France	Hanoi, Vietnam
Transport	**Transport**	**Transport**
• International airport	• 2 international airports	• International airport
• Trains, metro (41 stations), taxis and auto rickshaws	• Fast train network across Europe	• Trains, buses and (motorbike) taxis
• Over 30 bus stations, cheap fares	• Metro (245 stations), buses and taxis	• Metro system (not finished; 229 stations planned)
Business and innovation	**Business and innovation**	**Business and innovation**
• Many technology companies	• Global business centre	• Important business centre
• Indian banks	• All major international banks	• Vietnamese and Japanese banks
• Many science research institutes	• Famous and historic universities	• Over 20 universities (10 of them science universities)
Infrastructure	**Infrastructure**	**Infrastructure**
• Good internet	• Fast internet	• Good internet
• Electricity supply not good	• Good electricity supply	• Electricity supply OK
• Good roads in some places	• Great transport	• Busy roads
• Office rent OK	• Expensive office rent	• Cheap office rent

4 Present your city to the class.

5 Work in different groups of three. Discuss which city you think is the best choice for tech start-ups and why.

2.2 ❯ Grammar

1 Complete the sentences with *too* or *enough*.

1 There are _____ many problems with this place.

2 There's _____ much traffic in the city centre.

3 It's _____ hot in summer. We need air conditioning.

4 It's not big _____ . We need more space.

5 The rent's _____ expensive.

6 It's _____ big. Can we look for somewhere smaller?

7 The area's _____ busy in rush hour.

8 There are _____ transport links.

9 There aren't _____ parking spaces.

10 Are there _____ meeting rooms?

2 Your company is moving offices. The management board has found two possible locations and has asked you to make the final choice. Read the information about the company's needs and the two options. Then think of one positive and one negative opinion about each option using *too* or *(not) enough*. Make some notes.

The new office must:
- be close to the city centre but not in it.
- have air conditioning.
- have space for 1,500 employees.
- have good transport links.
- have car parking spaces for at least 700 cars.

Option A	Option B
• 50 minutes from city centre	• 20 minutes from the city centre
• 3 bus stops and a train station within walking distance	• No public transport
• Air conditioning on some floors	• Air conditioning on all floors
• Accommodates 1,450 employees	• Accommodates 1,700 employees
• 1,000 car parking spaces	• 450 car parking spaces

3 Work in small groups. Discuss the advantages and disadvantages of Options A and B. Then choose the best option.

It has …
It doesn't have …

It is …
There are …

4 Present your choice to the rest of the class.

3.1 > Vocabulary

1 Complete the sentences with the words in the box.

| bill   branches   chain   charges   cost   offer   order   pay   serve   shop |

1 We have 300 _____ across the country.
2 Customers can _____ in cash or by card.
3 You can _____ online and collect in store.
4 We _____ a 5 percent discount when you spend over €50.
5 Many customers prefer to _____ online.
6 Our branches _____ over 3,000 customers a day.
7 The _____ of food shopping is increasing every year.
8 Our town has lots of big _____ stores, and I don't like them.
9 The total _____ is $56.30.
10 My phone company _____ 6 cents a minute for calls to outside Europe.

2 Work in small groups. Place your counter on *Start*. Take turns to roll the dice and move your counter. When you land on a square, use the prompts to say a sentence about your own shopping experience or about a company you know well.

Rules:

- You must use all the words in your square.
- Your sentence must use four words or more.
- Your sentence cannot be a question.
- If you cannot make a sentence, you miss your next turn.

Start	**1** pay / cash	**2** offer / discount	**3** 100 / branches / country	**4** serve / customers
9 shop / online	**8** charge / fee	**7** High Street / chain	**6** cost / supplies	**5** bill / cash / card
10 pay / card / online	**11** make / profit	**12** shop / clothes	**13** charge / wi-fi	**14** cost / too much
19 branch / small towns	**18** pay / bill	**17** spend / money	**16** make / mistake / bill	**15** order / (type of tea or coffee)
20 offer / good service	**21** serve / slowly	**22** spend / $10	**23** popular / chain	*Finish*

3.2 ❯ Grammar

1 Choose the correct option in italics to complete the email.

> Dear Sir/Madam,
>
> I'm writing to complain about the bike I bought from your shop.
>
> I ¹*rode / was riding* my new bike home when a car ²*came / was coming* towards me. I ³*tried / was trying* to stop, but when I ⁴*pulled / was pulling* on the brake, I ⁵*heard / was hearing* a strange noise. The brake cable ⁶*snapped / was snapping*, and I had to jump off the bike. I ⁷*phoned / was phoning* your company, but I ⁸*waited / was waiting* for hours until someone ⁹*answered / was answering*.
>
> I would like my money back or a new bike.
>
> Regards,
>
> Michael Jones

2 Complete the reply email. Use the Past Simple or Past Continuous form of the verbs in brackets.

> Dear Mr Jones,
>
> I'm sorry you ¹_____ (have) problems with your new bike.
>
> I ²_____ (check) our records, and we ³_____ (ask) you to give us your bank details for the refund when you called us. But you didn't give us that information. We ⁴_____ (wait) for that information.
>
> Please give me a call.
>
> Best regards,
>
> Rachel Watson
> Customer Services Manager

Student A

3A You recently paid for an internet service for your home from Nyssan Net, but the internet connection is bad. You will phone customer service (Student B) to complain and negotiate a solution. Use the information below to help you. Don't forget to use both the Past Simple and the Past Continuous.

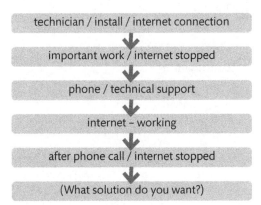

technician / install / internet connection
↓
important work / internet stopped
↓
phone / technical support
↓
internet – working
↓
after phone call / internet stopped
↓
(What solution do you want?)

B Make your call.

C You are a Sales Assistant at Caroo, a large car dealership. Student B will call to make a complaint. Listen to the complaint carefully and make notes. Then repeat the information to check you understand and suggest a solution.

Student B

3A You are a Customer Service Assistant at Nyssan Net, an internet service provider. A customer (Student A) will call to make a complaint. Listen to the complaint carefully and make notes. Then repeat the information to check you understand and suggest a solution.

B You recently bought a used car from Caroo, a large car dealership. However, the passenger door mirror is not working. Phone customer service (Student A) to complain and negotiate a solution. Use the information below to help you. Don't forget to use both the Past Simple and the Past Continuous.

used car – bought – good condition
↓
moved mirror / mirror stopped working
↓
phoned dealer / wait – long time
↓
serviced car / mirror – working
↓
moved mirror (yesterday) / stopped working
↓
(What solution do you want?)

C Make your call.

4.1 ❯ Vocabulary

1 Complete the questions with the words in the box.

| day   flexible   interns   patterns   permanent   retired   self |
| shifts   time   unemployed |

1 Are most people _____-employed, or do they work for a company?

2 Do most people prefer having _____ hours or a fixed schedule?

3 How many hours do full-_____ employees work?

4 Do _____ get paid, or do they work for free to get experience?

5 Do most people have a _____ or a temporary job?

6 Is the normal working _____ 9 a.m.–5 p.m.?

7 Do people work night _____ in factories, or is it common in other industries?

8 How are working _____ changing?

9 What do _____ people do in the later part of their lives?

10 How many _____ people are there in your country?

2 Work in small groups. Ask six questions from Exercise 1 and ask four questions of your own. Write your own questions in the boxes for each topic.

| Pay |
| |

| Hours |
| |

| Retirement |
| |

| (Another topic) |
| |

3 Give a short presentation on the differences in work between the people in your group. Use these three stages for your presentation.

Introduction
What is your presentation about?

Main points
Three pieces of information you learnt from your group.

Conclusion
What does the information mean?
Is it surprising?
Is it different from your experience/country?

4.2 > Grammar

1 Write sentences using the Present Perfect Simple. Use the phrases to help you.

1 They both / work / in sales. _____

2 He / manage / a small team. _____

3 She / manage / a big team. _____

4 He / not work / in finance. _____

5 She / work / in finance. _____

6 She / not set / sales targets. _____

7 They both / do / sales negotiations. _____

8 He / set / sales targets. _____

9 She / manage / sales budgets. _____

10 He / not give / presentations. _____

2 Work with a partner. Your company wants to hire a new Sales Manager. Read the job description and tell your partner what you think are the two most important qualities for this job.

Sales Manager

Full-time, permanent

Responsible for managing the sales team, the Sales Manager will have experience of leading sales teams, setting targets and preparing sales forecasts.

The successful candidate must have sales experience, negotiation skills and leadership ability.

Financial knowledge and presentation skills are desirable but not essential.

Student A

3 Read the achievements section of your candidate's CV and explain his experience to your partner (Student B).

John James

Key achievements

- led a four-person sales team

- created forecasts

- set targets

- negotiated with clients (5 yrs+)

- met sales targets ($2 million+)

- presented to clients

Main qualifications

- Business degree

---

4 Make some comparisons between the candidates with your partner. Ask the questions in the Present Perfect Simple and think about the answers.

1 Who / manage / a bigger team?

2 Who / set / sales targets?

3 Who / have / negotiation experience?

5 Look at the job description in Exercise 2 again. Decide who should get the Sales Manager job. Give reasons for your answer.

Student B

3 Read the achievements section of your candidate's CV and explain her experience to your partner (Student A).

Maria Delvechi

Key achievements

- led a 40-person sales team

- created forecasts

- managed the sales budget

- negotiated with clients (3 yrs+)

- met sales targets ($1 million+)

- prepared financial statements

Main qualifications

- Tourism and hospitality degree

- Accounting certificate

---

4 Make some comparisons between the candidates with your partner. Ask the questions in the Present Perfect Simple and think about the answers.

1 Who / have / presentation experience?

2 Who / study / finance?

3 Who / meet / sales targets?

5 Look at the job description in Exercise 2 again. Decide who should get the Sales Manager job. Give reasons for your answer.

5.1 > Vocabulary

1 Choose the correct word to complete the sentences.

1 I normally pay by _____ on the internet.
a cash card **b** credit card **c** bank card

2 The U.S. dollar is the world's most important _____ .
a currency **b** cash **c** money

3 I need to _____ some cash from the ATM.
a pull out **b** remove **c** withdraw

4 Taxi companies in India have introduced a cashless _____ system.
a pay **b** paying **c** payment

5 Restaurant staff like to be paid cash in _____ .
a pocket **b** hand **c** bank

6 Do you accept payment by _____ card?
a debit **b** direct **c** balance

7 Pay for your purchases at the cash _____ .
a machine **b** register **c** box

8 Banking provides a lot of tax _____ for the government.
a profit **b** turnover **c** revenue

9 I need to get some money out of the cash _____ .
a service **b** dispenser **c** device

10 Online payments are an important part of the _____ system.
a financial **b** money **c** business

2 Reorder the phrases to make questions.

1 do people use / in your country? / what currency

2 accept / does public transport / credit cards?

3 pay for / taxis? / how can you

4 by credit card / in restaurants? / can you pay

5 you tip / how should / waiters?

6 withdraw cash? / easy to / is it

Student A

3A Work in pairs. You are visiting Buenos Aires. Use the questions in Exercise 2 to ask your partner how to pay.

BUENOS AIRES
Currency:
Public transport:
Taxis:
Restaurants:
Tipping:
Cash dispensers:
Other information:

B You work in Melbourne, Australia. Your partner is visiting you on business. Use the information to answer his/her questions.

Currency: Australian dollar
Trains: cash and cashless payments
Taxis: cashless payments (some)
Restaurants: all restaurants = cashless payments
Tipping: waiters = cash (but cashless tipping also possible)
Cash dispensers: ✔ (many)
Other information: (*give some extra information*)

Student B

3A You work in Buenos Aires. Your partner is visiting on business. Use the information to answer his/her questions.

Currency: Argentine peso
Trains: cash only
Taxis: most = pesos; some = U.S. dollars
Restaurants: luxury restaurants = cashless payments
Tipping: waiters = cash (but cashless tipping also possible)
Cash dispensers: ✔ (city centre); ✘ (outside centre)
Other information: (*give some extra information*)

B Work in pairs. You are visiting Melbourne. Use the questions in Exercise 2 to ask your partner how to pa▸

MELBOURNE
Currency:
Public transport:
Taxis:
Restaurants:
Tipping:
Cash dispensers:
Other information:

5.2 > Grammar

Student A

1 Read each phrase aloud. Your partner (Student B) will tell you the matching phrase.

use less water
buy new equipment
get company car
offer higher salary
spend more on advertising
hire a new accountant

Student B

1 Read each phrase aloud. Your partner (Student A) will tell you the matching phrase.

make staff happy
can travel quickly to clients
find ways to save money
help the environment
get more customers
need new software

2 Use the phrases to make suggestions using the first conditional.

1 We can change electricity supplier. (save $300+)
If _____

2 Let's reduce the number of employees. (cut costs)
If _____

3 We reduce the amount of materials. (reduce the quality)
If _____

4 Change supplier (be cheaper)
If _____

5 We can buy cheaper paper. (save money)
If _____

3 You run a small coffee shop with your partner. You need to make your business more successful. Look at the proposals in the table. Using the first conditional, say how each proposal will have a positive or negative effect on the business. Then add three proposals of your own.

Proposal	Effect
move: beach → railway station	*get more customers*
coffee in each cup – reduce %	
cleaning staff – ~~two cleaners~~ one cleaner	
cheaper cake supplier	
hire a new accountant	

4 Work with another pair. Discuss the effect of each proposal on your coffee shop and try to agree on the two best ways to make more money.

> If we move from the beach to railway station, …

6.1 › Vocabulary

1 Which of the words in the box are the three most important things for building a great team?

> argument   cooperation   communication   disagreement
> experience   reliability   respect   trust

2 Rewrite the phrases in bold using the correct form of the words in Exercise 1. Some words are <u>not</u> used.

1 I have to **work together** with the IT team, but they don't answer our phone calls. _____

2 I don't **think very highly of** my colleagues. They leave the office early when we are very busy. _____

3 I don't **believe** her when she promises to meet deadlines. She's always late. _____

4 My boss doesn't really **say much** when he is busy. _____

5 He is often late with his work – I can't **depend** on him. _____

Student A

3A Work in groups of three. Read your information.

B Before you have the meeting, work with other Student As to

> You work in the finance department. You need to process invoices to pay suppliers every Friday.
>
> You are having problems getting information about the invoices from your colleague (Student B). You have experienced the following problems with your colleague.
>
> **PROBLEM 1** is about communication – information often late and missing
>
> **PROBLEM 2** is about cooperation – (*give example*)
>
> **PROBLEM 3** is about trust – (*give example*)
>
> **PROBLEM 4** is about reliability – (*give example*)
>
> You are going to meet your colleague and the Finance Manager (Student C) to discuss the problems.

prepare what you are going to say.

C Have the meeting.

Student B

3A Work in groups of three. Read your information.

> You work in the finance department. You manage orders from the purchasing department.
>
> You need to give information to your colleague (Student A) every week so that he/she can pay the supplier invoices. You often can't give him/her the information on time because purchasing are slow to send you the information.
>
> You know your colleague is unhappy about the situation. You have experienced the following problems with your colleague.
>
> **PROBLEM 1** is about arguments – doesn't communicate in a friendly way
>
> **PROBLEM 2** is about disagreements – (*give example*)
>
> **PROBLEM 3** is about respect – (*give example*)
>
> **PROBLEM 4** is about experience – (*give example*)
>
> You are going to meet your colleague (Student A) and the Finance Manager (Student C) to discuss the problems.

B Before you have the meeting, work with other Student Bs to prepare what you are going to say.

C Have the meeting.

Student C

3A Work in groups of three. Read your information.

> You manage the finance department. You know that two of your employees don't work very well together. You have asked to meet them to help with conflict management.
>
> You need to start the meeting.
>
> Then, listen to each person explain their problems. Give two solutions for Student A and two solutions for Student B.
>
> Think about these questions when giving solutions.
>
> - How can they communicate in a friendlier way?
> - How can they solve disagreements?
> - How can they cooperate better?

B Before you have the meeting, work with other Student Cs to prepare some phrases that you can use for managing a meeting and for giving advice.

C Have the meeting.

6.2 〉 Grammar

1 Choose the correct word to complete the sentences.

1 _____ likes finishing work early on Friday.

   a Everyone   **b** Someone

2 Can you tell me _____ about the clients?

   a someone   **b** something

3 I've looked _____ for my phone. Have you seen it?

   a somewhere   **b** everywhere

4 Do you know _____ with sales experience?

   a someone   **b** everyone

5 The CEO has told _____ the company is moving.

   a someone   **b** everyone

6 I'm looking for _____ to have a video call. Is there a room free?

   a somewhere   **b** everywhere

2 Work in pairs or small groups and use the clues on your cards for a quiz.

Clues:	Clues:	Clues:	Clues:
1 Everyone has probably tried it. **2** People can find advertisements for this drink everywhere around the world. **3** Someone invented it in the 19th century in the USA. **Answer:** Coca-Cola	**1** It's somewhere you can buy shares in a company. **2** Everyone talks about it in the news. **3** It's something companies use to raise money. **Answer:** the stock market	**1** This person usually sits somewhere away from other workers. **2** He/She is someone who talks to the board of directors. **3** He/She might be responsible for everything in a company. **Answer:** a CEO	**1** It's a good way to give everyone information at the same time. **2** It's something you see a lot of at conferences. **3** Nearly everyone uses PowerPoint to make them. **Answer:** a presentation
Clues: **1** It's something in a company that organises contracts and helps employees. **2** It's involved everywhere in the company. **3** Everyone in the UK and USA used to call this department 'personnel'. **Answer:** HR	**Clues:** **1** Someone started this company with a drawing of an animal around 100 years ago. **2** Everyone has probably watched one of its cartoons. **3** There are shops everywhere around the world that sell its characters, including a famous bear. **Answer:** (The Walt) Disney (Company)	**Clues:** **1** Someone with a computer or smartphone might use it. **2** You can use it to look up something you want to know. **3** Nearly everything on the internet can be found here. **Answer:** Google (search engine)	**Clues:** **1** It's somewhere that is not a city or a town, but a region. **2** Nearly everyone who works there thinks about the future of the world. **3** It's somewhere with a lot of tech companies. **Answer:** Silicon Valley
Clues: **1** It's something you use to sell products. **2** It's everywhere on TV, the internet and in magazines. **3** It's somewhere you can explain your products to customers. **Answer:** advert(s)/ advertisement(s)/advertising	**Clues:** **1** You can speak with and see someone far away with this technology. **2** Everyone can meet together online with this. **3** It's something you need a microphone and a webcam for. **Answer:** video conference(s) (brand names such as Skype and Google Hangouts acceptable)	**Clues:** **1** It's something that helps a company grow. **2** Everyone wants this number to be high. **3** If someone doesn't help make this, that person might lose their job. **Answer:** profit	**Clues:** **1** It's something no one wants to pay. **2** You have to pay it everywhere in the world, but you don't have to pay so much in some countries. **3** The government uses this to pay for everything. **Answer:** tax
Clues: **1** _____ **2** _____ **3** _____ **Answer:** _____	**Clues:** **1** _____ **2** _____ **3** _____ **Answer:** _____	**Clues:** **1** _____ **2** _____ **3** _____ **Answer:** _____	**Clues:** **1** _____ **2** _____ **3** _____ **Answer:** _____

7.1 ❯ Vocabulary

1 **Put the R&D stages in a suitable order.**

a   Think about possible solutions. ____
b   Develop a **prototype**. ____
c   Identify a problem.. __1__
d   Make simple sketches. ____
e   Get **feedback**. ____

f   **Test** the product. ____
g   Make improvements to the design. ____
h   Deal with design **challenges**. ____
i   Create a **design** brief. ____
j   **Launch** the product. ____

2 **Complete the sentences with the words in bold in Exercise 1.**

1   We would like to _____ the product with some small groups to check the functions work well.

2   The development of the _____ is exciting – it's the first opportunity to see what it might look like.

3   One of the design _____ will be to ensure all of the product functions are accessible.

4   The plan is to _____ the product in the shops in six months.

5   We received the _____ brief for the new phone, and we have made some sketches.

6   It's important to get customer _____ so that we can make improvements to the next model.

✂ -

Student A   **3**   **Work in pairs. You are developing a new app for your company. Discuss progress with a Salesperson (Student B). Update him/her on stages 1–3 and make notes on stages 4–6. Try to agree new dates if necessary.**

progress update meeting with Sales – 22 November

Stage and task(s)	Due date	Problems	New due date
1 Write product information - design brief	14th Nov	*(done)*	_____
2 Develop first product design - prototype - sketches	27th Nov	*design problems – delayed by 2 weeks*	_____
3 Develop second product design - make improvements	16th Dec	*if first product delayed → this stage = delay*	_____
4 _____	_____	_____	_____
5 _____	_____	_____	_____
6 _____	_____	_____	_____

✂ -

Student B   **3**   **Work in pairs. You are a Salesperson for your company. Discuss the progress of a new app with a Product Developer (Student A). Make notes on progress in stages 1–3 and explain the deadlines in stages 4–6. Try to agree new dates if necessary. If there are any delays, negotiate new due dates with your partner.**

progress update with Developer – 22 November

Stage and task(s)	Due date	Problems	New due date
1 _____	_____	_____	_____
2 _____	_____	_____	_____
3 _____	_____	_____	_____
4 Check if product works - test	17th Dec	*development delayed / delay task?* *2 weeks maximum*	_____
5 See what customers think of product - feedback	8th Jan	*date fixed*	_____
6 Start selling product - launch	1st Feb	*maximum delay – end March*	_____

7.2 ❯ Grammar

Student A

1 Write questions to ask your partner about where he/she works or a company he/she knows using the information and *can, have to* or *need to*.

	Questions	Notes
1	wear formal clothes: _____	
2	work from home: _____	
3	use your own phone: _____	
4	check social media: _____	
5	give presentations: _____	
6	meet clients: _____	
7	work late: _____	
8	start late on Mondays: _____	

2 Ask your partner your questions and make notes about his/her answers. Ask follow-up questions. Use your current company or a company you know to answer your partner's questions. Use *can, can't, (don't) have to* or *(don't) need to*.

3 Work with a different partner. Tell your new partner three pieces of information about your previous partner, such as something interesting, something funny and something unusual.

- -

Student B

1 Write questions to ask your partner about where he/she works or a company he/she knows using the information and *can, have to* or *need to*.

	Questions	Notes
1	wear jeans: _____	
2	work flexible hours: _____	
3	bring/use your own computer: _____	
4	use special equipment: _____	
5	write emails: _____	
6	work with other departments: _____	
7	work weekends: _____	
8	leave early on Fridays: _____	

2 Ask your partner your questions and make notes about his/her answers. Ask follow-up questions. Use your current company or a company you know to answer your partner's questions. Use *can, can't, (don't) have to* or *(don't) need to*.

3 Work with a different partner. Tell your new partner three pieces of information about your previous partner, such as something interesting, something funny and something unusual.

8.1 ❯ Vocabulary

1 Complete the solutions with the words in the box. Some words may be used more than once. Then match each solution to an environmental issue.

collect	create	conserve	damage	destroy	develop
impact	increase	pollute	protect	recycle	reduce

Environmental issue   **Solution**

a air pollution   **1** _____ the number of cars in the city.

b plants and animals   **2** _____ spaces for wildlife.

c recycling   **3** _____ rubbish and process it into new materials.

    4 _____ solar and wind power.

    5 _____ old and rare trees.

    6 _____ greenhouse gases.

2 Work in groups. You have entered a competition to develop ideas to improve the environment of your city. The prize is $100,000. Read the information on your card. Underline words and phrases in Exercise 1 that are connected to your idea. Then prepare answers to the questions on your card. Prepare to give your presentation or to listen and choose ideas.

Idea A: Marketing campaign to encourage bicycle use in the city

How will it help the environment? _____

What will it change about the city? _____

How will it improve peoples' lives? _____

(your own idea) _____

Idea B: Making city parks friendlier for wildlife

How will it help the environment? _____

What will it change about the city? _____

How will it improve peoples' lives? _____

(your own idea) _____

Idea C: Pay people to recycle more

How will it help the environment? _____

What will it change about the city? _____

How will it improve peoples' lives? _____

(your own idea) _____

Idea D: Free solar panels for every house in the city

How will it help the environment? _____

What will it change about the city? _____

How will it improve peoples' lives? _____

(your own idea) _____

Notes for judging

Idea A: Marketing campaign to encourage bicycle use in the city

How will it help the environment? _____

What will it change about the city? _____

How will it improve peoples' lives? _____

(other idea) _____

Notes for judging

Idea B: Making city parks friendlier for wildlife

How will it help the environment? _____

What will it change about the city? _____

How will it improve peoples' lives? _____

(other idea) _____

Notes for judging

Idea C: Pay people to recycle more

How will it help the environment? _____

What will it change about the city? _____

How will it improve peoples' lives? _____

(other idea) _____

Notes for judging

Idea D: Free solar panels for every house in the city

How will it help the environment? _____

What will it change about the city? _____

How will it improve peoples' lives? _____

(other idea) _____

---

3 Give your presentation or listen to the ideas and select a winner.

8.2 ❯ Grammar

1 Complete the sentences with *should(n't)* or *could*. There may be more than one possible answer.

1 We _____ use energy-saving light bulbs to help the environment.

2 In my opinion, we _____ leave computers on overnight because it wastes energy.

3 I guess we _____ stop using air conditioning so much, but it does get hot in here.

4 We _____ make sure the lights in the meeting room are turned off when we finish.

5 Well, we _____ put solar panels on the roof to reduce electricity costs.

6 We _____ use the heating in the summer, it's not necessary.

2 Play the board game in small groups. Take turns to throw a dice and move your counter. You can start from any square you like.

lights – on/off (2 green points)	**solar power** (3 green points)	**roof garden** (5 green points)	**MISS 2 TURNS**
heating (1 green point)			**bicycles** (2 green points)
computers (2 green points)			**organic lunch menu** (3 green points)
recycle paper (1 green point)			**electric cars** (2 green points)
energy-saving light bulbs (2 green points)			**coffee machine** (1 green point)
car-sharing (4 green points)	**recycled paper** (1 green point)	**air conditioning** (2 green points)	**printers and photocopiers** (3 green points)

Can you help
Green Solutions, Inc.
to save the environment?

Rules:

When you land on a square, make a sentence about how the company, Green Solutions, Inc., can help the environment.

Use the words in the square, and if your dice number is even (= 2, 4, 6), use *should* or *shouldn't*. If your dice number is odd (= 1, 3, 5) use *could*.

If you make a correct sentence, you can collect the green points for that square.

Your sentence must have more than seven words in it.

You must not repeat another player's sentence.

Continue playing for _____ minutes. The player with the most green points is the winner.

Start in any square.

Move this way

1.1 ❯ Vocabulary

- Tell students that they are going to practise using vocabulary related to business travel.
- Give everyone a copy of Exercises 1 and 2.
- Explain that students will review travel vocabulary and then look at some questions and answers related to travelling in the first two activities.
- Ask students to work in pairs or small groups and look at Exercise 1. Ask them to take turns to choose a category and say as many words for that category as they can think of within one minute.
- Move on to Exercise 2. Ask students to work individually and match the questions to the correct answers.
- Check answers as a class.
- Introduce Exercise 3. Divide the class into two halves and give half of the class the information for Student A and half of the class the information for Student B.
- Tell students they are going to discuss arrangements for a business trip with a partner. They have to ask their partner questions to find out missing information.
- Ask students to work individually, look at the information in the table and write questions to find out the missing information. They can use the language in Exercise 2 to help them.
- Ask students to think about what questions their partner will ask them and how they can respond.
- Get students to check their questions with someone from the *same* group (A or B).
- Walk around and help individual pairs if necessary.
- Put the class into new pairs of Student A and Student B.
- Ask students to ask and answer the questions and complete the table.
- If some students had difficulties sharing information, review possible questions and answers.

1 Possible answers
Public transport: train, bus, boat, car hire
Airports and flights: gate, arrival, departure, take off, landing, lounge, short-haul, connection
Accommodation: (five-star) hotel, room service, budget hotel, self-catering apartment, reservation
2
1 c 2 a 3 e 4 f 5 d 6 b
3 Possible answers
Student A
When does the flight take off and land?
How do we travel to our accommodation?
How do we get to the client's office?
Student B
Where can we eat?
What terminal do we (need to) go to?
Where are we staying?

1.2 ❯ Grammar

- Tell students that they are going to practise using comparatives and superlatives related to the topic of company conferences.
- Ask the class to think of some reasons why companies hold conferences. Write some of their ideas on the board.
- Ask students which cities in the world they think are good places to hold a conference and why. Add these ideas to the board.
- Give everyone their own copy of the worksheet.
- Ask students to read the instruction for Exercise 1. Tell them that the errors involve comparative and superlative grammar structures. Get them to complete the exercise individually.
- Check the answers as a class.
- Explain that students are going to read about some conference venues in Exercise 2 and that they will then choose a suitable venue for their company conference.
- Ask students to read the information in Exercise 2 about the three venues and complete the sentences.
- Ask students to check their answers in pairs and then check the answers as a class.
- For Exercise 3, ask students to make three more comparisons with their partner. Monitor that they use comparative and superlative structures.
- In Exercise 4, ask students to work with a different partner and look at the conference information at the bottom of the page. Tell them to discuss the suitability of each venue for the conference.
- Walk around and prompt students to give reasons for their answers if they are not already doing so.
- Ask each pair to present which venue they chose and why to the class.
- As an extra activity, ask students if they can remember three comparisons of the venues on the worksheet without looking.

1
1 correct
2 ~~more~~ better than
3 easier than
4 correct
5 a lot better than
6 correct
7 correct
8 the most expensive
9 the most exciting
10 correct

2
1 Sydney House Hotel
2 Paradise Hotel & Conference Centre, Sydney House Hotel
3 Marrakesh Conference Centre
4 Paradise Hotel & Conference Centre
5 Sydney House Hotel

2.1 ❯ Vocabulary

- Tell students that they are going to practise using vocabulary on the topic of location in the context of locations for technology (tech) start-up companies.
- Put students into small groups and ask them to make a list of things a city needs in order to attract technology start-ups. Do not spend too long on this.
- Give everyone their own copy of the worksheet.
- Ask students to read the article in Exercise 1 and complete it with the words in the box. Get them to work individually.
- Check the answers as a class.
- Ask students if any of the ideas in the list they made before Exercise 1 were the same as in the article.
- Ask students to match the two parts of each sentence in Exercise 2 individually.
- Students should check their answers in pairs. Then check the answers as a class.
- Explain that students will work in groups to prepare a short oral presentation about a city. After giving the presentations, they will decide which city is the best choice to locate technology start-ups.
- Divide the class into small groups (there can be three groups for a small class or six groups in the case of a larger class) and give each group information about one of the cities from Exercise 3.
- Tell students they can use the information on their paper, or if they have internet access, they can research extra facts about the cities.
- Give each group time to prepare their presentation and offer support if necessary.
- For Exercise 4, ask each group to give their presentation to the class.
- Finally, in Exercise 5, students should change groups and discuss which city they think is the best choice for tech start-ups. Walk around and encourage students to give reasons for their choices.
- As a class, elicit the preferred city.

1
1 locate **2** rents **3** headquarters **4** labs **5** facilities **6** access **7** close **8** transport
2
1 c **2** e **3** a **4** b **5** d

2.2 ❯ Grammar

- Tell students that they are going to practise using *enough* and *too* to make decisions about a suitable place for a new office building.
- Write the words *too* and *enough* on the board. Ask the class what makes an office building a good place to work. Elicit phrases that use *too* or *enough*, for example, *too much noise*.
- Give everyone their own copy of the worksheet.
- Ask students to work individually and complete the sentences in Exercise 1.
- Check answers as a class. If students are getting the answers wrong, review the grammar rules from Lesson 2.
- Move on to Exercise 2. Explain to students that their company is moving offices and the management board has selected two options.
- Ask students to read the information from the board and the two options individually.
- Then, ask students to make notes about one positive and one negative point about each option. They can use the sentence starter prompts on the page as well as the sentences from Exercise 1 to help them. Remind the students to use *too* and *enough*.
- For Exercise 3, divide the class into small groups and ask each group to discuss the advantages and disadvantages of each option together. Allow enough time for all group members to contribute ideas.
- Monitor and offer support if necessary.
- Once the groups have made a decision, explain that for the next exercise, they must present their decision to the rest of the class. Give them a couple of minutes to prepare.
- Ask each group to present their decision and note examples of good language and errors. As a class, agree on which option is the best one.
- Lead a feedback session highlighting good language usage and clarifying any errors.

1
1 too **2** too **3** too **4** enough **5** too **6** too **7** too **8** enough **9** enough **10** enough

2 Possible answers
Option A
It has enough car parking spaces.
It doesn't have enough air conditioning.
It's too far from the city centre / not big enough.
There are enough car parking spaces / transport links.

Option B
It has enough space / air conditioning.
It doesn't have enough transport links / car parking spaces.
It's close enough to the city centre.
The car park is too small / not big enough.

3.1 ❯ Vocabulary

- Tell students that they are going to practise language to talk about retailing.

- Give everyone their own copy of the worksheet.

- Ask students to complete the sentences in Exercise 1 individually.

- Ask students to check their answers in pairs.

- Introduce the board game in Exercise 2. Divide the class into groups of three to four. Give each group a dice and one counter for each player.

- Read the instructions and rules together with the class. As an example, write *charge / delivery* on the board. Elicit a sentence that uses those words, such as *Amazon doesn't* **charge** for **delivery** *on orders over 29 euros*.

- If you have a confident class, you could ask the group members who are listening to the player whose turn it is to judge if each sentence is correct and follows the rules. If the sentence is incorrect, the student who is speaking misses his/her next turn.

- Once students understand the rules, ask them to play it in groups. Help individual groups where necessary.

- During the activity, monitor and note down good language and errors.

- Lead a feedback session with the whole class at the end of the game.

- As an extension, you could use the sentences in the *Possible answers* section of the key and turn them into a quiz. Divide the class into two halves. Read a sentence from the *Possible answers*, but don't read the words in bold. Students need to say what the missing words are.

1
1 branches **2** pay **3** order **4** offer **5** shop **6** serve
7 cost **8** chain **9** bill **10** charges
2 **Possible answers**
1 I **pay** in **cash** at the supermarket.
2 Costco often **offers** big **discounts** on products.
3 Starbucks has over 100 **branches** in my **country**.
4 My company always **serves customers** quickly.
5 Utility companies usually allow you to pay a **bill** by **cash** or **card**.
6 The **cost** of basic **supplies** is rising.
7 On every **High Street**, you can find the same **chains**.
8 My phone company **charges** a large **fee** when I use my phone overseas.
9 I don't **shop online** very much.
10 I **pay** by **card** when I shop online.
11 My company **made** a **profit** last year.
12 I normally **shop** for **clothes** on Amazon.
13 Many coffee shops don't **charge** customers for **wi-fi**.
14 Shopping at the airport **costs too much**.
15 When I stay in a hotel, I always **order a cappuccino** after my meal.
16 I know a restaurant that often **makes mistakes** with the **bill**, and charge customers twice.
17 I like to **spend money** on designer brands.
18 One time, I had lunch at the Ritz, and I didn't have enough money to **pay** the **bill**.
19 Many bank **branches** have closed in **small towns**.

20 Some telecoms companies don't **offer** a **good service** when you contact them about a problem.
21 My garage always **serves** its customers so **slowly** – last time I waited several hours to get my car fixed.
22 You can get free delivery if you **spend** over **$10** on an online purchase.
23 MOS Burger is a very **popular** Japanese fast-food **chain**.

3.2 ❯ Grammar

- Tell students that they are going to practise using the Past Simple and Past Continuous in the context of making complaints to a company.

- Ask students if they often make complaints about products and services they buy.

- Give everyone a copy of Exercises 1 and 2.

- Tell students that they are going to review the two different tenses presented in Lesson 2. As a class, elicit the correct options for the first sentence in the email in Exercise 1. Elicit why the first answer uses the Past Continuous (it describes a longer action), and why the second answer uses the Past Simple (it describes a shorter action).

- Ask students to complete Exercise 1 in pairs.

- Check the answers as a class.

- Explain that Exercise 2 is an email reply to the complaint in Exercise 1. Ask students to complete the email in pairs.

- Check the answers as a class.

- Move on to Exercise 3. Divide the class into two halves, with half of the class being Student A and the other half of the class being Student B. Give students their respective information cards and tell them to read their information.

- Explain that Student A will call Student B and make a complaint about his/her internet service. Then Student B will call Student A and make a complaint about his/her car. The student who is listening to the complaint should make notes and offer a solution as part of his/her response. Remind students to consider using the Past Simple or Past Continuous.

- Before students start their roleplay, they should work with other students with the same role (i.e. all Student As work together, etc.) to prepare what they are going to say.

- Put students into A–B pairs and ask each pair to roleplay the phone calls.

- At the end, invite one or two pairs to perform their roleplays for the class. Other students should listen for examples of the Past Simple and Past Continuous and report them back to you.

1
1 was riding **2** came **3** tried **4** pulled ('was pulling' also possible if we consider it a longer action against 'heard a strange noise') **5** heard **6** snapped **7** phoned **8** was waiting ('waited' also possible because 'for hours' already implies a longer action) **9** answered
2
1 had **2** checked **3** asked **4** were waiting

4.1 ⟩ Vocabulary

- Tell students that they are going to practise talking about jobs and contracts.
- Ask the class if they can remember any of the key words from Lesson 1. Write them on the board.
- Give each student a copy of the worksheet and compare how many words they remembered with the words in the box in Exercise 1.
- Ask students to work in pairs to complete the questions.
- Check answers as a class.
- Explain that in Exercise 2, students will practise using the key words and the questions from Exercise 1 by asking other students the questions. Students can answer the questions either with information about their own company, or if they are not currently working, they can imagine a suitable response.
- Divide the class into groups of three or four. If you have a mixed-nationality class, try to have mixed nationalities in each group.
- Ask students to read the instructions for Exercise 2, and highlight that they need to create four questions of their own. They should look at the topics in the boxes and write one question in each box connected to those topics.
- Give students enough time to write the questions. Monitor and give individual support where necessary.
- When groups are ready, ask students to interview their group members and make notes about the replies.
- Walk around and encourage students to give details in their responses.
- When groups have finished, move on to Exercise 3. Tell students to prepare a short presentation about the information they found out. They can use the guidelines on the worksheet to help them. They should not spend too much time preparing.
- When students are ready, they should give a short presentation, either to their groups, or to the whole class.

1
1 self **2** flexible **3** time **4** interns **5** permanent
6 day **7** shifts **8** patterns **9** retired **10** unemployed
2
Possible questions
Pay: What is the average salary for Sales Managers?
Hours: How many hours a week do interns normally work?
Retirement: When do you receive a pension?
Training (Another topic): Do employers usually pay for training in your company?

4.2 ⟩ Grammar

- Tell students that they are going to practise using the Present Perfect Simple by talking about people's work experience.
- Give everyone a copy of Exercises 1 and 2.
- Ask students *Have you worked in sales?* Elicit *Yes, I have* or *No, I haven't*. Elicit what tense the questions and answers use (*Present Perfect Simple*). Remind students that the Present Perfect Simple can be used to talk about experiences.
- Ask students to complete Exercise 1 individually.
- Check answers as a class.
- Explain that the students will read a job description and later they will choose a suitable person for that job.
- Ask students to read the job description in Exercise 2, and then ask them to work in pairs to discuss what two qualities they think are the most important for this job.
- Split the class into two halves, A and B.
- Hand all the Student As and Student Bs their respective information card for Exercises 3–5.
- Explain that for Exercise 3, each student has information about a job candidate. They need to tell their partner about the information on their card.
- In Exercise 4, students should make some comparisons about the candidates using the prompts. Monitor and check that students are including examples of the Present Perfect Simple in some of their responses.
- For Exercise 5, students should discuss who they think should get the job.
- Ask each pair to present which candidate they would choose and why.

1
1 They've (They have) both worked in sales.
2 He's (He has) managed a small team.
3 She's (She has) managed a big team.
4 He hasn't (has not) worked in finance.
5 She's (She has) worked in finance.
6 She hasn't (has not) set sales targets.
7 They've (They have) both done sales negotiations.
8 He's (He has) set sales targets.
9 She's (She has) managed sales budgets.
10 He hasn't (has not) given presentations.
2
Students' own answers
4
Student A
1 Who has managed a bigger team?
2 Who has set sales targets?
3 Who has (had) negotiation experience?
Student B
1 Who has (had) presentation experience?
2 Who has studied finance?
3 Who has met sales targets?

5.1 ❯ Vocabulary

- Tell students that they are going to practise language around the topic of money.
- To review some key vocabulary, ask the class how they pay for things such as restaurant meals, books, bus/taxi fares. Write some of their ideas on the board.
- Give everyone a copy of Exercises 1 and 2.
- Tell students to look at Exercise 1. Tell them that they need to fill in the missing word in each sentence from the list of options. To make the exercise more interactive, students could work in pairs and take turns to ask each other what the gaps in the sentences are in the form of a quiz. You could ask students to cover up either sentences 1–5 or sentences 6–10 depending on which sentences their partner is asking them to complete.
- Check the answers as a class.
- Tell students that the next exercises will involve discussing payment systems in different countries. To prepare for this, Exercise 2 will provide some examples of questions that can be used to discuss this topic.
- Ask students to look at Exercise 2 and reorder the phrases to make questions. Decide whether students should make the questions orally or if they should write them down.
- Check the questions as a class.
- Introduce Exercise 3. Divide students into A and B pairs and give each student their respective information card. Ask students to read their information.
- Explain that they are visiting the other city for the first time and need to ask their partner questions to complete the information card. Ask students to think about the questions they need to ask and how they will reply. Remind them that they can look at Exercise 2 for ideas. For the 'Other information' line on their information cards, you could tell students to research some extra information, or they could imagine some extra information. You could give them the following categories to help them if they find it difficult to think of ideas: shopping, accommodation, wi-fi, transport from airport.
- Students ask and answer the questions.
- As an extra activity, you could ask students to share information about how they pay for things in their town/city.

1
1 b **2** a **3** c **4** c **5** b **6** a **7** b **8** c **9** b **10** a

2
1 What currency do people use in your country?
2 Does public transport accept credit cards?
3 How can you pay for taxis?
4 Can you pay by credit card in restaurants?
5 How should you tip waiters?
6 Is it easy to withdraw cash?

5.2 ❯ Grammar

- Tell students that they are going to practise using the first conditional.
- Write the clause *If we work hard …* on the board and ask the class for ideas to complete this sentence using the first conditional structure. (For example, *If we work hard, we will get more rewards*.) Ask the class what verbs and tenses are used in each clause (*work* – Present Simple, *will*).
- Divide students into A and B pairs and give each student their respective information card for Exercise 1. Ask students to take turns to read out a phrase from their paper. Their partner will then find and say a suitable matching phrase.
- Check answers as a class. Ask students which student had phrases that were *causes* (Student A), and which student had phrases that were *effects* (Student B).
- Give everyone a copy of Exercises 2 and 3.
- Ask students to read the instruction for Exercise 2 and write their answers individually. Monitor and check that students are using the first conditional correctly.
- Students check their answers in pairs.
- For Exercise 3, ask students to work in pairs. They need to imagine they are running a coffee shop, and they need to have ideas about how to improve their business and make more money. They should use the phrases in the table and use the first conditional to discuss their ideas. Then they need to think of three ideas of their own.
- After students have finished discussing their ideas in Exercise 3, tell them to join with another pair and do Exercise 4. Read the instruction for Exercise 4 with the class and highlight that they need to agree on *two* ideas.
- When the groups have finished discussing, ask each group to explain their decision to the rest of the class.

1
use less water – help the environment
buy new equipment – need new software
get company car – can travel quickly to clients
offer higher salary – make staff happy
spend more on advertising – get more customers
hire a new accountant – find ways to save money

2
Possible answers
1 If we (can) change electricity supplier, we'll save over $300.
2 If we reduce the number of employees, it'll/we'll cut costs.
3 If we reduce the amount of materials, it'll reduce the quality.
4 If we change supplier, it'll be cheaper.
5 If we buy cheaper paper, it'll/we'll save money.

3
Possible answers
If we change to a different location, we will get more customers.
If we reduce the amount of coffee in each cup, customers won't like it.
If we cut the number of cleaning staff, for example from two cleaners to one cleaner, the coffee shop will not be so clean.
If we use a cheaper cake supplier, we will save at least $100 every month.
If we hire a new accountant, we'll find ways to save money.

6.1 ❯ Vocabulary

- Tell students that they are going to practise using the verbs and nouns from Lesson 1.
- Give everyone their own copy of the worksheet.
- To prepare for Exercises 1 and 2, ask the class if the words in the box in Exercise 1 are nouns or verbs (*nouns*). Then write the word *disagreement* on the board and ask students what the verb form of this word is (*disagree*).
- Ask students to work in pairs and choose the three attributes from the box in Exercise 1 that they think are the most important for building a great team.
- Lead a short feedback session asking a few students which ideas they chose and why.
- Ask students to look at Exercise 2 and read the instruction. Point out that they need to decide if they need to use a word in noun form or if they need to change a word into a verb.
- Ask students to complete Exercise 2 individually and then check their answers in pairs.
- Check answers as a class.
- For Exercise 3, tell students that they are going to roleplay a situation which is connected to the topic of teamwork.
- Divide students into groups of three and give each student the role of Student A, B or C. Explain that students A and B are having problems working together. Student C is their manager and needs to manage the meeting and suggest solutions.
- Before the groups start their discussion, students should first work together with students who have the same role (i.e. all Student As should work together, etc.) to complete Exercise 3B.
- Give students some time to prepare individually and offer help if necessary.
- When the groups are ready, ask them to conduct their meeting.
- When the groups have finished, lead a feedback session eliciting solutions that were discussed.

> **1**
> Students' own answers
> **2**
> 1 cooperate 2 respect 3 trust 4 communicate 5 rely

6.2 ❯ Grammar

- Tell students that they are going to practise using pronouns beginning with *some-* and *every-*.
- Give everyone a copy of Exercise 1.
- Ask students to complete Exercise 1 by choosing the correct word to complete each sentence.
- When students have finished, ask them to check their answers in pairs and then check the answers as a class.
- Divide the class into teams of pairs or small groups. Tell them that they are going to do a quiz.
- Give each team eight cards from Exercise 2. The eight cards should include two 'empty' cards. Tell the teams not to show their cards to other teams.
- Ask each team to look at their questions. Tell them that

every question contains a pronoun beginning with *some-* or *every-*, and that every answer is connected to business. The first team should choose one of the squares and give the first clue in that square. Tell the teams that if they get the correct answer after the first clue, they get three points. If they get the correct answer after the second clue, they get two points, and if they get the correct answer after the third clue, they get one point. The team with the most points wins.

- Before they start asking the quiz questions, ask each team to create two questions of their own in the empty cards.
- When teams are ready, they can play together.
- Teams conduct the quiz and keep track of the points. At the end, they declare the winner.

> **1**
> **1** a **2** b **3** b **4** a **5** b **6** a

7.1 ❯ Vocabulary

- Tell students that they are going to practise language on the topic of research and development.
- Ask the class if they can remember any stages of the R&D process. Elicit some ideas and write these on the board.
- Give everyone their own copy of Exercises 1 and 2.
- Ask students to work in pairs. Tell them to read the stages in Exercise 1 and put the stages in a suitable order.
- Check answers as a class. Note that there could be more than one correct order.
- Ask students to complete Exercise 2 using the words in bold in Exercise 1.
- Ask students to check their answers in pairs, and then check answers as a class by selecting students to read out their answers.
- Divide the class into A and B pairs and give each student a copy of their respective role for Exercise 3.
- Explain that the students work for a company developing a new app and they are going to have a meeting to discuss development of the product. Their partner has the information they need to complete the table. Tell the students that they need to ask and answer questions to get the missing information and agree deadlines for stages 4–6.
- Before students start their 'meetings', give them some time to work individually and to read the information on their card and to make some notes about questions they might want to ask. When students feel ready, they can start their discussion with their partner.
- Monitor and help individual pairs and record examples of good language and errors.
- Lead a short feedback session highlighting good language and correcting errors.

> **1 Possible answers**
> **1** c **2** i **3** a **4** d **5** b **6** h **7** g **8** f **9** e **10** j
> **2**
> **1** test **2** prototype **3** challenges **4** launch **5** design
> **6** feedback

7.2 ❯ Grammar

- Tell students that they are going to practise using *can, have to* and *need to* in a discussion about working practices in their company or (if students are not working at the moment) in a company they know.

- Write *can, have to* and *need to* on the board. Ask students what the negative forms of these phrases are (*can't/cannot, don't have to, don't need to*). Elicit a sentence with *can*, such as *I can wear informal clothes at work*. Remind the students that the use of *can* in this sentence means it's possible (so that it is not confused with *can* for ability).

- Divide the class into A and B groups and give a copy of the Student A questionnaire to half the class and the Student B questionnaire to the other half. Tell the class that A and B have different questions to ask each other.

- Ask students to read the instructions for Exercise 1.

- Tell students that they will first need to make their questions. They should write these on their paper next to each prompt. Each question must include *can, have to* or *need to*. To help them, work through the first question on each card as a class. Write *wear formal clothes* on the board, and ask the class what question they can make using this phrase. Elicit an answer such as *Do you need to wear formal clothes (at work)?* Elicit another question for the phrase *wear jeans,* for example, *Can you wear jeans?*

- Ask students to work with other students who have the same questions and to prepare the questions together. Walk around and check that students are using *can, have to* and *need to*.

- When students have prepared their questions, they should work in a Student A–B pair for Exercise 2. Tell them to take turns to ask and answer each others' questions. They should make notes about the answers they hear. They should be encouraged to make notes rather than write down complete answers. Tell the students that the answers can use negative forms (*can't, don't have to* or *don't need to*).

- When students have finished Exercise 2, ask them to work with a different partner for Exercise 3 and report three things they found out about another company.

- As an extra activity, you could ask the class who found out the most interesting information, the funniest information and the most unusual information, and choose one piece of information from each category to write on the board.

Possible questions
Student A
1 Do you have to / need to wear formal clothes?
2 Can you work from home?
3 Do you have to / Do you need to / Can you use your own phone?
4 Can you check social media?
5 Do you have to / need to give presentations?
6 Do you need to / have to meet clients?
7 Do you have to work late?
8 Can you start late on Mondays?

Student B
1 Can you wear jeans?
2 Can you work flexible hours?
3 Do you have to / need to/Can you bring / use your own computer?
4 Do you have to use special equipment?
5 Do you have to / need to write emails?
6 Do you have to / need to work with other departments?
7 Do you have to / need to work weekends?
8 Can you leave early on Fridays?

8.1 ❯ Vocabulary

- Tell students that they are going to practise using words and phrases from Lesson 1 to talk about the environment.

- Give everyone their own copy of the worksheet. You will need to cut up the cards in Exercise 2 in advance.

- Ask students to look at Exercise 1 and complete the solutions with a suitable verb in the box.

- Then ask students to match each solution to an issue.

- Check answers as a class.

- Explain that for Exercises 2 and 3, there will be a competition to win money for an idea to improve the environment. Tell students that they will either need to prepare a short presentation or they will judge the presentations. Ask students to read the instructions for Exercise 2.

- Divide the class into five groups. There should be four presentation groups (A–D) and one group who will play the role of judges. Depending on your class size, you might need to configure the groups differently. For example, you might have fewer than four presentations (you could just use two or three of the presentation roles) and/or you might have a whole-class presentation or small group presentations with one or more judges.

- Give a role card from Exercise 2 to each student in each group.

- Ask students to read their role and identify sentences from Exercise 1 that might help them with their presentation. If students have the 'judge' role, ask them to match the environmental issues to each of the presentation topic ideas A–D.

- Ask students to make notes about the answers to the questions on their role card individually or in a group. The judges can work together to discuss how they are going to judge the presentations.

- Ask each group to give a short presentation of their idea. The judges should take notes while they listen.

- For Exercise 3, ask the judges to vote for the best idea(s).

1 Possible answers
1 Reduce, a   2 Create/Conserve/Increase/Protect, b
3 Collect, c
4 Develop, a   5 Protect/Conserve, b   6 Reduce, a

8.2 ❯ Grammar

- Tell students that they are going to practise using *should* and *could* in a board game about how companies can help the environment.

- Elicit some of the ways a company can help the environment (e.g. *Companies should turn off heating systems when the weather is not very cold.*). Write some of the ideas on the board.

- Give everyone their own copy of the worksheet.

- Ask students to work in pairs to complete the sentences in Exercise 1 using *should(n't)* or *could*. Point out that both *should* or *could* is possible for some of the sentences.

- Check the answers as a class. Elicit that sentences with *should* sound stronger and more certain than sentences with *could*.

- Move on to Exercise 2. Explain that students are going to play the board game in small groups. Divide the class into small groups and give each group a dice and one counter per player.

- Tell students that they can start on any square, and they must follow the rules of the game. Give students a few moments to look at the rules in Exercise 2.

- When students have read and understood the rules, tell them how much time they have to play the game. They should note this on their worksheet. The students can keep moving around the board and making sentences until the time is up.

- Tell the students who are listening to the person making a sentence to ensure that the sentence is correct. If a sentence is not correct, the person making the sentence cannot collect the points for that sentence. Also remind students that they need to keep track of the points that they collect.

- Allow students to start playing.

- Walk around and check that students are making suitable sentences and are following the rules of the game. Record examples of good language use.

- When time is up, tell the students to stop playing. The player with the most points is the winner.

- Lead a short feedback session highlighting examples of good language that was used during the game.

1 Possible answers
1 could/should 2 shouldn't 3 could/should
4 could/should 5 could/should 6 shouldn't

2 Possible answers
The company should turn lights off when no one is in the building.
If the company installed solar power, they could save electricity costs.
A roof garden could be a nice place to relax and could provide a space for wildlife.
Employees should come to work on their bicycles to reduce air pollution.
An organic lunch menu could encourage employees to eat more healthily.
Electric cars should be given to employees for short journeys to cut petrol use.
Staff shouldn't use the coffee machine frequently because it uses a lot of energy.
Printers and photocopiers should be turned off when nobody is using them.
Green Solutions should install more modern air conditioning that uses less electricity.
The company could use more recycled paper to help conserve forests.
The company should encourage car-sharing because this helps to reduce the number of cars on the road.
If the company uses more energy-saving light bulbs, it could save more energy and more money.
In my opinion, employees should recycle paper because they throw away too much good paper.
Computers shouldn't be left on during the night because this wastes energy.
The company could have a smart heating system so that the temperature indoors changes with the temperature outdoors.

Unit 1 ❯

1 Match the words in the box with their definitions.

capacity   demand   efficient   expansion   fuel   hub   merger

1 when two companies join to form one larger one: _____

2 an increase in size: _____

3 the amount that can fit inside a building, space or container: _____

4 something such as oil that produces power when it is burnt: _____

5 the central and most important part of a system or activity: _____

6 the amount of a product that people want: _____

7 working well, without wasting time, money or energy _____

2 Read the article quickly and find and underline the following information.

1 The percentage increase in air travel in July.

2 One type of airline cost that is rising.

3 The name of a new industrial area outside of Beijing.

4 The amount of money that LATAM will spend on its aircraft.

5 The two airlines that merged to form LATAM.

3 Read the article carefully. Which statement is the best summary of the article?

1 Air travel is increasing at the moment, but will decrease later in the year because of rising costs. China Southern Airlines is building a new departure lounge at Baiyun International Airport. Meanwhile, LATAM Airlines is buying new planes and will soon become the world's largest airline.

2 Air travel is increasing, and airlines are getting more efficient in filling seats on planes. At Baiyun International Airport, China Southern Airlines is making life easier for people who have connecting flights. Meanwhile, LATAM Airlines is improving the passenger experience on all its flights.

3 Air travel is increasing, and airlines are buying more planes to meet the growing demand. China Southern Airlines has had problems moving its hub airport from Guangzhou to Beijing. Meanwhile, LATAM Airlines has changed the interiors of its aircraft to provide extra legroom for all its passengers.

4 Complete the table with words from the article.

Noun	Verb
1 _____	expand
2 _____	grow
3 _____	increase
4 _____	develop
strength	5 _____
6 _____	connect

5 Complete the sentences with the words in the box. Check your answers in the article.

at	between	for	from	in (x2)	of	to

1 According _____ the IATA, there was a 6.2 percent growth in air travel this summer.

2 Airlines are getting better _____ filling the seats on each flight.

3 The growth _____ air travel is reflected in the expansion plans of two leading airlines.

4 Passengers who connect _____ international to domestic flights no longer need to collect their baggage and check it in again.

5 The Xiong'an New Area is about 50 miles southwest _____ Beijing.

6 LATAM Airlines will invest $400 million _____ improving the interiors of its aircraft.

7 LATAM Plus passengers will be able to pay more _____ extra legroom.

8 LATAM Airlines was formed from a merger _____ Chile's LAN Airlines and Brazil's TAM Airlines.

6 Choose the correct option in italics to complete the sentences about the text.

1 Airline fuel costs are becoming *higher / highest*.

2 Airlines are becoming *less efficient / more efficient* at using their capacity to meet demand.

3 The main reason for the growth in travel was *lower / lowest* ticket prices.

4 China Southern is one of the world's *largest / more large* airlines.

Leading airlines planning to expand

According to the IATA (International Air Transport Association), there was a 6.2 percent growth in air travel this summer. As well as air travel growing overall, airlines are also getting better at filling the seats on each flight. "The industry posted another month of solid traffic growth, and airlines are becoming more efficient in terms of using their capacity to meet
5 demand," said IATA Director General Alexandre de Juniac. Lower ticket prices were the main reason for the growth in travel, but de Juniac added a warning for the rest of the year: "Rising costs, particularly fuel, will likely limit the increase in travel we expect from lower airfares."

The growth in air travel is reflected in the expansion plans of two leading airlines, one Chinese and one Latin American. China Southern Airlines has moved to Terminal 2 of Guangzhou's
10 Baiyun International Airport and offers an improved system. Passengers who connect from international to domestic flights no longer need to collect their baggage and check it in again. China Southern will also use Beijing's new international airport as its second hub. This new airport services the Xiong'an New Area, which is about 50 miles southwest of Beijing. In the future, this area will be the location of several big businesses. These developments will help
15 strengthen the position of China Southern as one of the world's largest airlines.

Meanwhile, LATAM Airlines – Latin America's leading airline – is investing $400 million in improving the interiors of its aircraft. For long-haul routes there will be fully flat seats in Business class, and in Economy class there will be fast-charging USB ports and large touchscreens on the seat backs. All flights will have a strong wi-fi connection, and LATAM Plus
20 passengers will be able to pay more for priority check-in and extra legroom. LATAM Airlines has gone from strength to strength since it was formed from a merger between Chile's LAN Airlines and Brazil's TAM Airlines in 2012.

Unit 2 ❯

1 Match the phrases (1–6) with their definitions (a–f).

1 Global Competitiveness Index	**a** a place where there are lots of new businesses
2 renewable energy	**b** a measure of how successfully a country can offer a good business and living environment
3 logistics	**c** the practical arrangements to move goods from one place to another
4 artificial intelligence	**d** the level of health, comfort and happiness of a person or group
5 quality of life	**e** power from natural processes, such as solar power and wind power
6 start-up location	**f** computer systems that do tasks that people normally do (and usually do them faster and better than people)

2 Guess which location is number one in the world for phrases 1–6. Then read the article to find out if your guesses were correct.

1 top of the Global Competitiveness Index	*Dubai / Switzerland / Canada*
2 renewable energy	*Germany / India / China*
3 logistics	*Hong Kong / Rotterdam / Seoul*
4 artificial intelligence	*Japan / Singapore / USA*
5 quality of life	*Vienna / New York / Sydney*
6 start-up location	*California / London / Singapore*

3 Read the article again and decide if these statements are *true* (T) or *false* (F).

1 The World Economic Forum produces a report every year about business sectors such as renewable energy and logistics.

2 The Asia-Pacific region is good for start-ups because of its educated workforce and access to ports and shipping.

3 Professor Wong believes that innovation is closely connected to the number of new businesses in a region.

4 Professor Wong believes that Hong Kong will be less successful in the future. This is because in the old days manufacturing and trading were easy, but now innovation is more difficult.

4 Match the sentence halves.

1 The magazine produces a report about various	**a** pool of skilled young people.
2 Artificial intelligence and robotics are key industries	**b** business sectors.
3 Asia has a talent	**c** manufacturing and trading.
4 The Asia-Pacific region also has a business-	**d** friendly culture.
5 Start-ups are part of the	**e** of the future.
6 Hong Kong has always been good at	**f** process of innovation.

5 Put the words in the correct order to make sentences. Use correct punctuation.

1 such as banking, logistics and retail / different areas of business / are called industry sectors

_____

2 compared to something else / a ranking is a position on a list / to show how good something is

_____

3 workers in a country or city / can be called a talent pool / a large group of skilled

_____

4 of business in a country or region, / when there is a positive view / we can say there is a business-friendly culture

_____

6 Choose the correct answer, a, b or c, to complete the sentences. Then check your answers in the article.

1 The Asia-Pacific region has closed the gap on the USA and Europe in terms of business __ .

    a markets   **b** industries   **c** opportunities

2 The Global Competitiveness Index __ how successful a country is at doing business.

    a measures   **b** provides   **c** leads

3 China, the USA and Brazil lead the world in __ in renewable energy.

    a reports   **b** logistics   **c** investments

4 The Asia-Pacific has access to major sea __ .

    a manufacturers   **b** routes   **c** applications

5 Professor Wong said that start-ups are important in the __ of innovation.

    a trading   **b** process   **c** rankings

Asia-Pacific closes gap as best location to do business

A series of reports over recent months have shown that the Asia-Pacific region has closed the gap on the USA and Europe in terms of business opportunities.

Every year, the World Economic Forum produces the Global Competitiveness Index. This index measures how successful a country is at doing business and providing a good life for its people.
5 The latest index shows Switzerland at number one, followed by the USA and Singapore.

Other reports highlight how Asia-Pacific now leads in many sectors. For example, *Business Facilities* magazine reports that China, the USA and Brazil lead the world in investments in renewable energy, and the world's top locations for logistics are Hong Kong, Memphis and Shanghai. Top of the table for artificial intelligence and robotics – key industries of the future –
10 are Singapore, Shanghai and Dubai. Europe still dominates in the quality of life rankings, however, and Vienna, Zurich and Munich get the top three places.

Asia-Pacific benefits from a big talent pool of skilled graduates from top institutions such as the National University of Singapore and Tsinghua University in Beijing, among others. It also has a business-friendly culture and access to major sea routes, making it a great environment for
15 new businesses. The consultancy Deloitte looked at the fastest growing start-ups in Asia. The top two were Devsisters, a South Korean mobile game developer, and Hi-Target Digital Cloud, a Chinese manufacturer specialising in 3D laser applications.

Compass, a San Francisco-based research firm, recently ranked the top four global start-up locations in the world as: Singapore, Bangalore, Hong Kong and Kuala Lumpur. In the Compass
20 report, Professor Richard Wong from the University of Hong Kong said that start-ups are important in the process of innovation, and this process is moving from the USA and Europe to Asia-Pacific. He takes Hong Kong as an example. According to him, it has always been good at manufacturing, trading and services, but now it is starting to be good at innovation as well.

Unit 3 ❯

1 **Match the phrases (1–6) with their definitions (a–f).**

1	High Street shop	**a**	the number of products waiting to be sold in a shop
2	stock levels	**b**	a large building for storing products before they are sold
3	goods	**c**	a shop found on a main street of a town
4	warehouse	**d**	a store where manufacturers sell directly to the public
5	manufacturer	**e**	things that are made to be sold
6	outlet store	**f**	a company that makes a particular type of product

2 **First read the title of the article. Guess which sentence (a, b or c) summarises the article. Then read the article quickly to check your answer.**

a Customers buy goods online, receive them, but then decide they don't want them. The goods are returned, but often cannot be sold again at full price.

b Delivery companies like DHL, FedEx and UPS try to take goods to the customer's house. But the customers are often not at home, and the goods are returned to the warehouse.

c Because online shopping is growing so fast, the quality of products is going down. Many items have to be returned to the manufacturers because of quality control.

3 **Read the article carefully. According to the article, which of these things can happen to returned goods?**

They can be …

1 damaged by the delivery company that takes them back. ☐
2 inspected and cleaned if necessary. ☐
3 thrown away. ☐
4 given free to people who work for the manufacturer. ☐
5 sold again in cheap supermarkets. ☐
6 sold in street markets in poor countries. ☐
7 sold on eBay. ☐
8 sold again by some of the top 20 U.S. retailers. ☐

4 **Look at the phrases in bold in the article. Then choose the meaning (a or b) of each phrase.**

1 **a** The goods move from a warehouse by boat.
  b The goods move from a warehouse by any kind of transport.

2 **a** Eight percent of all bought things, measured by the number of items.
  b Eight percent of all bought things, measured by the amount of money that people spend.

3 **a** It costs so much money to process the returned items – manufacturers make no profit.
  b It costs a lot of money to process the returned items – this reduces the profit a lot.

4 **a** Optoro's technology shows the retailer where to sell the goods a second time in order to make the most profit.
  b Optoro's technology finds someone else in the same town who really wants the goods.

5 **a** Many retailers get 15–30 cents instead of 100 cents.
  b Many retailers get 115–130 cents instead of 100 cents.

5 Write the missing letters to make words from the article.

1 If a High Street shop does not look modern, we can say it is old-fa _ _ _ _ _ ed.

2 The way that the store is arranged and looks inside is its d _ _ _ gn.

3 If a returned product is packaged again, it is _ _-packaged.

4 If a product is sold at less than the normal price, we can say it is sold at a dis _ _ _ nt price.

5 To say 'less than 50 percent', we can say 'less than h _ _ f'.

6 A website where users give the content – like Optoro, Facebook or YouTube – is called a pl _ _ _ _ rm.

7 If goods are not wanted, we can say they are _ _ wanted.

8 To say something is two times the size, we can say it is d _ _ ble.

Online retailers face growing problem of returned goods

It's a well-known story: retail is moving online. Shopping districts in towns and cities are suffering as old-fashioned High Street shops close down. Costs on the High Street are just too high: staffing, rent, store design, transporting goods to the store, managing stock levels, etc. It's so much easier for customers to order online – [1]**the goods are shipped from a large**
5 **warehouse** straight to their home. But wait. There is something that is starting to cause real headaches for online retailers – the increasing number of returned goods.

How big is the problem? Last year, Americans returned $260 billion in unwanted goods, and that represents [2]**8 percent of all purchases**. But in specific areas the problem is much worse – for example, clothing returns can be up to 40 percent. People order three or four items of
10 clothing in different colours and sizes when they only plan to buy one. They try them at home, choose one, and return the rest.

[3]**Returns cut deeply into manufacturers' profits.** The items have to be checked, cleaned if necessary, and then re-packaged to sell again. The processing costs are so high that many goods are simply thrown away. Others are sold at a discount price in cheap supermarkets and outlet
15 stores, and some find their way onto Amazon or eBay as 'Like new' items. In general, less than half of returned goods bought online are re-sold online at the full price.

The problem of returned goods is giving new opportunities for start-up companies such as Washington, DC based Optoro. [4]**They provide a technology platform that finds the 'next best home'** when a product is returned to a warehouse or store. The unwanted goods are sent to
20 wherever offers the best resale price. Tobin Moore, CEO of Optoro, says '[5]**Many retailers are getting 15 cents to 30 cents on the dollar** for these returns because they're having such trouble economically processing them and getting them to the next best markets.' Moore says he can double or triple this figure. Optoro is used by sixteen of the top 20 U.S. retailers.

Unit 4 ➤

1 **Read the article quickly and choose the statement that sums up the main idea.**

1 Everyone should follow their dreams. If you have a passion for something, then in the end you will find a way to make your dreams come true.

2 'Follow Your Dreams' only happens in movies. In real life you wake up and your dream has gone. Dreaming just wastes your time.

3 It's better to get a regular job first and then see how realistic it is to follow your dreams.

2 **Read the article again and find words that match the definitions below.**

1 student who does a job for a short time to get experience (Para. 1) _____

2 no longer working because you are old (Para. 1) _____

3 working for yourself rather than a company (Para. 2) _____

4 protection from bad things that could happen to you (Para. 2) _____

5 detailed study of something in order to discover new facts (Para. 3) _____

6 one of a series of actions you take to reach your goal (Para. 3) _____

7 based on facts as they really are (Para. 5) _____

8 money that you pay to live in a house that belongs to someone else (Para. 5) _____

3 **Match 1–5 with a–e and 6–10 with f–j to make phrases used in the article.**

1 ask   **a** some money before you follow your dreams

2 suffer   **b** a question

3 make   **c** a lot of research

4 save   **d** a mid-life crisis

5 do   **e** a choice about which road to go down

6 enter   **f** with friends

7 spend   **g** your passion just as a hobby

8 go out   **h** a new market

9 make   **i** a small start

10 keep   **j** time on everyday things

4 **Decide if the two phrases have a similar (S) or different (D) meaning.**

1 follow your dreams / do what your heart tells you __

2 time to spare / time to waste __

3 it sounds nice / it seems like a nice idea __

4 need more experience / need to get more contacts __

5 do research / get more information __

6 understand the market / develop your ideas __

7 existing company / current workplace __

8 a passion / a part-time job __

9 a steady salary / regular payment for your job __

10 a 'nine-to-five' job / an exciting job full of new challenges __

5 **Correct the one incorrect word in each sentence to make phrases from the article.**

1 You might be a young intern working while you stutter at university.

2 In our lives we can make a chance: to go down the safe road or the risky road.

3 Maybe you need to save some money first, or you need more experiments.

4 You have to really underline the new market you are going to enter.

5 Look for small ways to drive your ideas before you take a big step.

6 Some people prefer to spell time on everyday things like going out with friends.

7 In the end the best clue may be to find a stable job with a steady salary.

8 You can keep your passion just as a hotel.

6 Complete the dialogues with *have* or *did*.

  1 **A:** Akari, _____ you leave your job and start as a yoga teacher? You were talking about it the last time we met.

    B: Yes, I _____ . It was difficult at first, but now I give lessons three times a week at a health centre.

  2 **A:** Riku, _____ you ever worked as a yoga teacher? You are so good at explaining all the different positions.

    B: Yes, I _____ actually. I did some yoga teaching last summer during the holidays.

Should you follow your dreams?

Should you follow your dreams? This is a question just about everyone asks at some stage in their life. You might be a young intern working while you study at university. Or a manager suffering a mid-life crisis. Or a retired person with lots of time to spare. At any point in our lives we can make a choice: to go down the safe, boring road or the risky,
5 exciting road.

'Follow your dreams' is certainly the message we get in movies and popular culture, and is often what our friends tell us. But let's think about why it might not be the best idea. For one thing, being a self-employed yoga teacher might sound nice, but it does not give much financial security – at least not in the beginning. Maybe you need to save some money first,
10 or you need more experience, or you simply need more contacts to open doors.

Jonathan Black gives career advice in the *Financial Times*. He says that you need to do a lot of research before you follow your dream. If your dream is to start a new business, you have to really understand the new market you are going to enter. He suggests that you look for small ways to develop your ideas before you take a big step. Perhaps you can do
15 something inside your existing company.

And what about those of us who don't have any big dreams? In her blog post 'The Problem with "Follow Your Dreams"', Melissa Kirk says that most people don't really have one particular passion. People might actually be happier spending time on everyday things like raising children, going out with friends or cleaning the house.

20 In the end, the best solution may be to find a stable job with a steady salary, and at the same time find a way to research your dreams and perhaps even make a small start. Then, if you find your dreams are not realistic, you still have your 'nine-to-five' job to pay the rent. You can keep your passion just as a hobby.

Unit 5 ⟩

1 Match the words (1–5) with their definitions (a–e).

  1 data   **a** money that a company receives

  2 revenues   **b** an amount of money that you borrow

  3 loan   **c** information that a computer or a human can use

  4 interest   **d** a measurement of how good someone or something is

  5 rating   **e** the extra money you must pay back (in addition to what you borrow)

2 Complete the paragraph using words 1–5 from Exercise 1.

> If you want to borrow money, for example to buy a car or get a mortgage, you go to a bank and ask for a [1]_____ . You then make monthly repayments to the bank until you pay back everything. Of course, the bank will also charge you [2]_____ , so you pay back more than you borrow. This extra money that the bank receives is an important part of their [3]_____ and helps them to be successful as a business. Does the bank lend to everyone? Of course not. It depends on your credit [4]_____ , which is a measurement of how good you have been with money in the past. To give a fair measurement, the bank will use all sorts of [5]_____ such as your salary, your payment history for past loans, how much money you owe at the moment, etc.

3 Read the article quickly and decide if these statements are *true* (T) or *false* (F).

  1 Facebook and Google use data from your internet activity to help advertisers give you personalised ads. But they don't collect every word you type – it would be too complicated as there are so many words. __

  2 At the moment, we get loans from banks. In the future, we might get loans in very different ways. __

  3 Most people don't worry about how their data is used. They are happy to get a free service and ads that are interesting to them. __

4 Find the underlined words in the article that match these definitions.

  1 a short description that gives the main details about a person _____

  2 a short phrase that is easy to remember and is used in advertising or politics _____

  3 the freedom to do things without other people knowing _____

  4 the person who gives you a loan _____

  5 the way a situation is developing or changing _____

  6 to believe that someone is good and honest _____

5 Match the sentence halves.

  1 Many successful companies have a business   **a** of risk using data.

  2 Google and Baidu have powerful search   **b** a negative.

  3 Companies can pay for data and then give you   **c** personalised ads.

  4 Different lenders might offer a different rate of   **d** model based on data.

  5 Artificial intelligence would calculate the level   **e** interest.

  6 Most people see personalised ads as a bonus, not   **f** engines.

6 In each sentence, fill one gap (a or b) with *will* and leave the other gap empty.

  1 If you [a]_____ search for 'Paris hotels' on Google, then for many days after you [b]_____ get ads for hotels in Paris when you use the internet.

  2 In the future, fintech [a]_____ use artificial intelligence and huge amounts of data – if the ideas in the article [b]_____ happen.

  3 If you [a]_____ ask me, no one really knows what [b]_____ happen in the future.

  4 How [a]_____ regular banks continue to make a profit if they [b]_____ make fewer loans?

It's the data, stupid.

The 1992 U.S. presidential campaign was won by candidate Bill Clinton, who had the <u>slogan</u> 'It's the economy, stupid.' These days, in modern business, 'It's the data, stupid.'

The most successful companies in the world have a business model based on data.
5   Facebook and WeChat, for example, give you a service that's impossible not to like
– the ability to connect and share with friends and family. The service is free, but
these companies know your personal <u>profile</u>, your interests and all the words in
your posts. Advertisers pay them for this data. Google and Baidu offer powerful
search engines, and it's hard to imagine life without them. Again, their services are
10 completely free, but the companies have very high revenues. Every word you type
into the search engine is recorded, and this means that companies can pay for that
data and then give you personalised ads at the top of your search results.

This <u>trend</u> to put data at the heart of business is going to grow and grow. Let's take
the example of finance, with 'fintech' (financial technology) one of the hottest new
15 industries. In the future, to get a loan to buy a new car, you might use fintech rather
than a regular bank. A fintech app could use data to find people all over the world
who can lend you money, perhaps at different rates of interest. How would the
<u>lender</u> <u>trust</u> you to repay? Easy. Artificial intelligence would calculate the level of
risk using data. This data would come from your bank of course, but might also
20 come from unusual places like your star rating on eBay, your career history on
LinkedIn, the kind of people you have as connections on social media, etc.

Data, about you, is one of the world's most precious resources, perhaps more
important than oil, diamonds or gold. And yes, <u>privacy</u> may be an issue, but users
of websites and apps are happy to exchange their personal data for the free service
25 they get. In fact, many see the personalised ads as a bonus, not a negative.

Unit 6 ⟩

1. **Match the soft skills 1–5 with the definitions a–e and the soft skills 6–10 with the definitions f–j.**

1	emotional intelligence	a	we look at things in a fresh, new way
2	creative thinking	b	we look at something complicated and understand it
3	analytical abilities	c	we keep positive and think that good things will happen
4	decision-making	d	we understand our feelings and the feelings of others
5	optimism	e	we look at the facts and then make the right choices about what to do
6	problem solving	f	we are confident of success and not afraid of difficult jobs
7	flexibility	g	we look at a difficult situation and know what to do
8	can-do attitude	h	we understand how people behave with each other
9	collaboration	i	we can easily change when a situation changes
10	interpersonal awareness	j	we can work together with other people to produce something

2. **Read the article quickly and choose the best summary.**

   a Teamwork is becoming less important in business. At job interviews, they will ask you about soft skills.

   b Soft skills are becoming more important in business. At job interviews, they will ask you about teamwork and other things that show your personal qualities.

   c Soft skills like teamwork or collaboration or interpersonal awareness are all the same and are not very important. At job interviews, try not to answer questions about soft skills.

3. **Find and underline each phrase in the article. Then look carefully at the context and decide if the meaning is a or b.**

   1 operational skills (Para. 1)

   a the knowledge and ability to do the basic, technical, day-to-day tasks in a job

   b the ability to operate complicated equipment in a factory

   2 face to face (Para. 2)

   a talking to another person close together and directly

   b sitting on the other side of the desk in the office

   3 conflict with another team member (Para. 3)

   a serious disagreement between you and one of your colleagues

   b poor communication between you and one of your colleagues

   4 the company's values (Para. 4)

   a the company's ability to make money

   b beliefs about what is important in the company and how people should behave

   5 your background and experience (Para. 5)

   a the education and training you received at school and at work

   b all the things you have done in your life that are important for the job

4. **Decide if these statements are *true* (T) or *false* (F).**

   1 Teamwork is about working with people near you.

   2 Soft skills are connected with personality.

   3 Many CVs contain examples of why candidates are good team players.

   4 In job interviews, you need to explain difficult situations to the interviewer.

   5 Theresa McHenry does not value soft skills.

   6 McHenry suggests that employees at Microsoft will not stay in the same positions.

5 Complete the sentences with the words in the box. Then check your answers in the article.

about	across	from	in	of	to	under	with

1 You might be working _____ different time zones.
2 Soft skills relate _____ your personality.
3 Soft skills include staying positive _____ pressure.
4 Soft skills are difficult to identify and test _____ a job interview.
5 This presents a problem to the interviewer on the other side _____ the desk.
6 _____ her point of view she needs some evidence.
7 She is likely to ask a job candidate to talk _____ some concrete examples.
8 Go to a job interview prepared _____ stories that show your personal qualities.

6 Decide which sentence (a or b) makes the most sense.

1 a These days, someone in business needs soft skills.
  b These days, everyone in business needs soft skills.
2 a In a job interview, someone might ask you to tell a story that shows your soft skills.
  b In a job interview, everyone will ask you to tell a story that shows your soft skills.
3 a Is emotional intelligence something you are born with?
  b Is emotional intelligence everything you are born with?
4 a In modern business, teamwork is something.
  b In modern business, teamwork is everything.
5 a Show interest in other cultures. Everyone comes from somewhere.
  b Show interest in other cultures. Someone comes from everywhere.

From teamwork to soft skills

The speed of change in modern business is fast. These days you will need other skills besides the operational skills related to the job itself.

So what are these other skills? Well, the first is definitely teamwork. You will be working with people on a variety of projects, from different departments, and from different cultures. You might be working across different time zones, and meeting your colleagues via the internet rather than face to face. So you will need things like emotional intelligence and communication. These qualities are often referred to as 'soft skills' because they relate to your personality. Other soft skills include creative thinking, analytical abilities, decision-making, staying positive under pressure, problem solving and flexibility.

One feature of soft skills is that they are very difficult to identify and test in a job interview. This presents a problem to the interviewer on the other side of the desk. For example, many of the CVs and résumés that she receives will include the phrase 'good team player', but from her point of view she needs some evidence. She is very likely to ask a job candidate to talk about some concrete examples. She might ask: 'Can you give me an example of when you solved a problem as part of a team?' Or perhaps: 'Can you give me an example of conflict with another team member? How did you handle it?' You will need to have stories ready to demonstrate your soft skills, not simply say that you have them.

Theresa McHenry, a director of Human Resources at Microsoft, puts soft skills in another context – whether a candidate's personality fits with the company's values. In a *Financial Times* article, she says: 'Everyone we hire is Microsoft first and the job second.' Although their jobs change, an employee might stay at Microsoft for years. She identifies the core Microsoft values as a can-do attitude, optimism, interpersonal awareness and collaboration.

The lesson is clear: go to a job interview prepared with stories that show your personal qualities in action, and don't just talk about your background and experience.

Unit 7 〉

1 **Match the words in bold with the correct definition (a or b).**

1 The key to long-term success in business is **innovation**.
   a new ideas, new methods, new technologies, new products
   b leaving a large, old-fashioned company to start a new company
2 Steve Jobs was well known for his strong views on **market research**.
   a designing a new product through research and development
   b collecting and analysing information about customers
3 People are interested in new **challenges**.
   a strange things that nobody can explain
   b things that need a lot of skill and energy to do, especially things you have never done before
4 Only large companies have the **resources** and time.
   a things you can use to reach a goal, such as money, people and equipment
   b long-term strategy and plans

2 **Read the article and choose the best summary.**

a Steve Jobs thought that innovation comes from small companies. Anne Marie Knott also thinks this.
b Steve Jobs thought that innovation comes from small companies. Anne Marie Knott thinks that innovation comes from market research.
c Steve Jobs thought that innovation comes from creative leaders. Anne Marie Knott thinks that innovation comes from R&D in large companies.

3 **Match the sentences halves. Then check your answers in the article.**

1	Rival companies were investing lots of money in	a	microwave oven.
2	Apple was the one to innovate and create a	b	places.
3	You need a culture where people are interested in	c	R&D.
4	Most start-ups try to innovate but don't survive in the	d	market-leading product.
5	Innovation can come from many different	e	market.
6	It took over 20 years to launch a successful	f	new challenges.

4 **Complete the sentences. Put the letters in the brackets in the correct order.**

1 Steve Jobs had strong views on market _____ . (rearsech)
2 You need people who are interested in new challenges and new _____ . (sotioluns)
3 Anne Marie Knott does not reject the _____ of R&D. (imtanporce)
4 Only large companies have the _____ and time to do R&D. (rercsoues)
5 By the time consumers see a 'new' product, it has probably already been under _____ for years. (deopmvelent)

5 **Complete each sentence with one of these words: *innovate, innovation, innovative*.**

1 The reality is that _____ can come from many different places.
2 People think that small companies are better at creating new ideas, but in fact, large companies can also be _____ .
3 In the technology sector, Apple is often the one to _____ and create market-leading products.

6 **Complete each sentence with one of these words/phrases: *can, can't, don't have to*.**

1 You _____ launch a high-technology product until it's been fully tested.
2 Different people have different opinions about market research, and you _____ agree with Steve Jobs completely.
3 New ideas in business _____ come from market research, R&D or the minds of creative leaders.

Where does innovation come from?

The key to long-term success in business is innovation. But where does innovation come from? There are several possible answers: market research, the R&D department, or the minds of creative leaders.

Steve Jobs was well known for his strong views on the first of these, market
5 research. He didn't think it worked, and used the quote (which many people say comes from Henry Ford): 'If I'd asked customers what they wanted, they would have said faster horses!' Jobs also didn't believe in R&D. When Apple invented the Mac, rival companies were investing lots of money in R&D, far more than Apple. But Apple was the one to innovate and create a market-leading product. Jobs
10 thought new ideas came from the minds of creative leaders – people like him – rather than R&D. As well as that, he thought there has to be a company culture where people get excited by new products, and where people are interested in new challenges and new solutions.

Anne Marie Knott, a Professor at the Olin Business School, does not reject the
15 importance of R&D. She wrote an article for *Harvard Business Review* called 'There's No Good Alternative to Investing in R&D'. In it, she says that many beliefs about innovation are not true – for example the belief that start-ups are more innovative. In fact, most start-ups try to innovate but don't survive in the market. She believes that large companies are more innovative, either because they have R&D
20 departments, or because creative people come from other large companies where they were not happy. She says that only large companies have the resources and time to create a market for the new product.

So it looks like innovation can come from many different places. And by the time consumers see a 'new' product, it's probably already been under development for
25 years. It took over 20 years to launch a successful microwave oven, for example.

Unit 8 ❯

1 Match the words/phrases (1–6) with their definitions (a–f).

1	fossil fuel	**a**	equipment that collects the sun's energy to make electricity
2	renewable	**b**	a large factory where an industrial process happens
3	solar panel	**c**	able to replace itself naturally or easily
4	turbine	**d**	a source of energy like oil or gas that was formed millions of years ago from dead plants
5	battery		
6	plant	**e**	a large machine that produces power by using wind to turn a wheel
		f	an object that provides electricity for something such as a smartphone or car

2 Read the article quickly. Match the figures in the box with the information.

> 7   45   50   85   318   930

1 global investment in fossil fuels last year ($bn)
2 global investment in renewable energy last year ($bn)
3 typical price of a barrel of oil between 2005 and 2014 ($)
4 China's share of total global investment in solar power (%)
5 number of green cars that the Chinese government wants by 2025 (million)
6 Asia's share of energy use in the world in the next 20 years (%)

3 Read the article again and decide if these statements are *true* (T) or *false* (F).

1 The world is rapidly changing to renewable energy like solar and wind.
2 The fall in the price of oil to $50 a barrel was good for green energy.
3 The most difficult part of solar energy is installing the solar panels in hot, dry deserts.
4 China is an expert in the study of batteries.
5 Many consumers do not like electric vehicles because they have to connect the car to an electricity supply every few days.
6 Tesla does not have battery farms outside of the USA.
7 Tesla is working with a Chinese company to build a huge battery plant in Qinghai province.
8 In the future, Asia might use little of the world's energy.

4 Look at the phrases in bold in the article. Then choose the meaning (a or b) of each phrase.

1 **a** not using as many fossil fuels as before
  b not being able to find enough fossil fuels
2 **a** Green energy is now more expensive in relation to oil.
  b Green energy is now cheaper in relation to oil.
3 **a** very easy
  b quite easy, compared to other things
4 **a** China is in front of another country, and is going faster and faster.
  b China is behind another country, but is going fast and will soon be at the same level.
5 **a** The amount of electricity and other forms of power that people want.
  b When there isn't enough electric power and so people ask the government for more.

5 Fill in the missing letters to make words from the article.

1 The fi_____es show that the world is slowing shifting from fossil fuels.
2 The price of oil fe_____ to around $50 a barrel.
3 China holds 45 percent of the total global invest_____ in solar power.
4 Electric vehicles are a major green business opp_____unity of the future.
5 The market for EVs will be limi_____ .
6 The f_____us of the world economy is slowly moving to the Asia-Pacific.

6 Sofia is giving some advice to her friend Miguel. Complete what she says using *should, shouldn't* and *could*.

1 Miguel, your car is so old. It keeps breaking down. You really _____ drive it anymore.

2 Miguel, you know you were talking about electric cars the other day? And you said they were too expensive? Well, how about asking your parents to help with the money? Or maybe you _____ get a loan from the bank?

3 Miguel, an electric car would be perfect for you. You only drive a short distance to work. I really think you _____ think about buying one.

China now the leading player in green energy

The International Energy Agency (IEA) has released a new energy report. The figures in it show that the world is [1]**slowly shifting from fossil fuels** such as oil, gas and coal, to renewables such as solar and wind. But the pace of change is slower than you might think. Last year, businesses invested $930bn in fossil fuels,
5 while investment in renewables was much less, at $318bn.

One reason why green energy is not growing so fast is the price of oil. From 2005 to 2014, oil was around $85 a barrel, but after that it fell to around $50 a barrel. Of course, this created problems for companies like ExxonMobil, Shell and Chevron. But it also created problems for [2]**green energy, which is now less competitive**.

10 Another issue for green technology is batteries. It [3]**is relatively easy** to place tens of thousands of solar panels in a hot desert area, or hundreds of wind turbines just off the coast. The problem is storing the energy that is produced in batteries. China has become a world leader in research into battery technology, and is a clear leader in green energy more generally. For example, China holds 45 percent of the total
15 global investment in solar power, according to the IEA report.

It is a similar story with electric vehicles (EVs), a major green business opportunity of the future. The car itself is not so difficult to build, but the market for EVs will always be limited if cars need recharging every few days. Tesla has giant EV battery farms in California and South Australia, but [4]**China is catching up**. BYD, China's
20 largest EV maker, has opened a huge battery plant in Qinghai province. As part of its long-term plans, the Chinese government is hoping for 7 million eco-friendly cars by 2025.

It is well known that the focus of the world economy is slowly moving to the Asia-Pacific and Indian Ocean regions. The IEA report confirms this – Asia could
25 represent half of the total global [5]**energy demand** within 20 years.

Unit 1 ❯

1 **1** merger
  2 expansion
  3 capacity
  4 fuel
  5 hub
  6 demand
  7 efficient
2 **1** 6.2 (Para. 1)
  2 fuel (Para. 1)
  3 Xiong'an (New Area) (Para. 2)
  4 $400 million (Para. 3)
  5 Chile's LAN and Brazil's TAM (Para. 3)
3 2
4 **1** expansion
  2 growth
  3 increase
  4 development
  5 strengthen
  6 connection
5 **1** to
  2 at
  3 in
  4 from
  5 of
  6 in
  7 for
  8 between
6 **1** higher
  2 more efficient
  3 lower
  4 largest

Unit 2 ❯

1 **1** b **2** e **3** c **4** f **5** d **6** a
2 **1** Switzerland
  2 China
  3 Hong Kong
  4 Singapore
  5 Vienna
  6 Singapore
3 **1** F – The report is about global competitiveness. **2** T **3** T
  4 F – Hong Kong has always been good at manufacturing, trading and services, but now it is starting to be good at innovation as well.
4 **1** b **2** e **3** a **4** d **5** f **6** c
5 **1** Different areas of business such as banking, logistics and retail are called industry sectors.
  2 A ranking is a position on a list to show how good something is compared to something else.
  3 A large group of skilled workers in a country or city can be called a talent pool.
  4 When there is a positive view of business in a country or region, we can say there is a business-friendly culture.
6 **1** c **2** a **3** c **4** b **5** b

Unit 3 ❯

1 **1** c **2** a **3** e **4** b **5** f **6** d
2 a
3 2, 3, 5, 7
4 **1** b **2** b **3** b **4** a **5** a
5 **1** old-fashioned
  2 design
  3 re-packaged
  4 discount
  5 half
  6 platform
  7 unwanted
  8 double

Unit 4 ❯

1 3
2 **1** intern
  2 retired
  3 self-employed
  4 security
  5 research
  6 step
  7 realistic
  8 rent
3 **1** b **2** d **3** e **4** a **5** c **6** h **7** j **8** f **9** i **10** g
4 **1** S **2** D **3** S **4** D **5** S **6** D **7** S **8** D **9** S **10** D
5 **1** ~~stutter~~ study
  2 ~~chance~~ choice
  3 ~~experiments~~ experience
  4 ~~underline~~ understand
  5 ~~drive~~ develop
  6 ~~spell~~ spend
  7 ~~clue~~ solution
  8 ~~hotel~~ hobby
6 **1** did, did
  2 have, have

Unit 5 ❯

1 **1** c **2** a **3** b **4** e **5** d
2 **1** loan
  2 interest
  3 revenues
  4 rating
  5 data
3 **1** F – Every word you type into the search engine is recorded.
  2 T
  3 T
4 **1** profile
  2 slogan
  3 privacy
  4 lender
  5 trend
  6 trust
5 **1** d **2** f **3** c **4** e **5** a **6** b
6 **1** a – b will
  2 a will b –
  3 a – b will
  4 a will b –

Unit 6 ❯

1 **1** d **2** a **3** b **4** e **5** c **6** g **7** i **8** f **9** j **10** h

2 b

3 **1** a **2** a **3** a **4** b **5** b

4 **1** F – Teamwork is about working with people in different places.
 2 T
 3 F – Many CVs don't contain examples/evidence of why candidates are good team players.
 4 T
 5 F – She identifies the core Microsoft values as a can-do attitude, optimism, interpersonal awareness and collaboration.
 6 T

5 **1** across
 2 to
 3 under
 4 in
 5 of
 6 From
 7 about
 8 with

6 **1** b **2** a **3** a **4** b **5** a

Unit 7 ❯

1 **1** a **2** b **3** b **4** a

2 c

3 **1** c **2** d **3** f **4** e **5** b **6** a

4 **1** research
 2 solutions
 3 importance
 4 resources
 5 development

5 **1** innovation
 2 innovative
 3 innovate

6 **1** can't
 2 don't have to
 3 can

Unit 8 ❯

1 **1** d **2** c **3** a **4** e **5** f **6** b

2 **1** 930 **2** 318 **3** 85 **4** 45 **5** 7 **6** 50

3 **1** F – The world is slowly shifting from fossil fuels.
 2 F – It also created problems for green energy, which is now less competitive. **3** F – It is relatively easy to place tens of thousands of solar panels in a hot desert area. **4** T **5** T
 6 F – Tesla has giant EV battery farms in California and South Australia. **7** F – BYD, China's largest EV maker, has opened a huge battery plant in Qinghai province. **8** F – Asia could represent half of the total global energy demand within 20 years.

4 **1** a **2** a **3** b **4** b **5** a

5 **1** figures
 2 fell
 3 investment
 4 opportunity
 5 limited
 6 focus

6 **1** shouldn't
 2 could
 3 should

1 〉 Letters

Lead-in Business letters usually have a more formal style than emails. The opening and closing of a letter changes when you know the name of the person you are writing to. Different countries may have different requirements when writing letters. This example shows a typical UK formal letter, with the name of the person you are writing to on the left and the sender's name and address on the right.

Model answer

Marek Dabrowski   Adams and Wright Ltd
Link Communications   201 Park Road
3 Booth Business Park   Lynwood
Limerick   Norfolk
V94 W983   NT1 7NP
Ireland   England

                                    5th September 20

Dear Mr Dabrowski,

Thank you for your recent order. As you are a regular client, we would like to give you some news about the company.

We are improving our delivery service. Customers can now receive their orders seven days a week. Goods will also be delivered in five days instead of eight days. We hope that these changes will help all our business customers.

Because of this new service, we need to increase our prices by 3 percent from 1st November. As you know, we have not raised our prices for three years. We are keeping the rise small so that our prices remain competitive.

Enclosed with this letter is the new price list. Please contact us if you have any questions.

We thank you for your business and look forward to supplying you in the future.

Yours sincerely,

Mia Green

Enclosed: price list

Functional language

Opening and closing a letter

	You know the name of the person you are writing to	You don't know the name of the person you are writing to
Opening	Dear Ms/Mrs/Miss/Mr Mills,	Dear Sir/Madam,
Closing	Yours sincerely, Kind regards,	Yours faithfully*, Kind regards,

Yours faithfully is not used in the USA. *Yours truly* or *Sincerely* would be used instead.

Getting started

Opening sentence	Thank you for your recent order.
Reason for writing	As you know, (the recent rise in fuel costs makes deliveries more expensive). We now need to (increase our prices). Thank you for your recent order. I am writing to (ask for details about your products).
Explanation	We are keeping the price rise small so that our prices remain competitive. The order was late because of a technical problem. We are improving our delivery service so customers can now receive their orders seven days a week.

Ending a letter

Referring to documents	Enclosed with this letter is (the new price list). We enclose (the application form) with this letter. Please find (the new brochure) enclosed.
Closing remarks	Please contact us if you have any questions. If you have any questions, please do not hesitate to contact us. We thank you for your business and look forward to supplying you in the future. We appreciate your business and hope you will understand our situation.

2 ❯ Online reviews

Lead-in Reviews can be important to businesses. You can find online review forms for products or services for travel, hotels, restaurants, etc. Some forms ask customers to rate their experience using numbers, stars or symbols. Other forms ask a series of short questions and writers can write their own reply, or sometimes they can choose from a list of responses. When leaving comments, it is a good idea to think about what was positive and negative about the experience. The responses on an online form are often short.

Model answers ## Short online reviews

> **How many stars do you give your hotel experience?**
> (5 stars = excellent, 1 star = bad)
> ★★★★☆
>
> **What did you experience when you arrived at the hotel?**
> Check-in was quick ✔
> Someone took my bags to the room ☐
> Staff were friendly ✔
> Receptionist gave me an information brochure ✔

Longer online review forms

How often do you stay at this hotel?	▼
I stay here once a month.	
What was the purpose of your visit?	▼
A business trip to a conference in the city centre.	
What did you like about the hotel?	▼
The location of the hotel is perfect for the city centre. The staff are always friendly and helpful. The rooms are large and clean.	
Was there anything you weren't happy with?	▼
There was an event at the hotel and it was very noisy. I ate in the hotel restaurant in the evening and the service was slow.	
Would you recommend us?	▼
I highly recommend the hotel because it's comfortable and in a great location. It's a great place to stay on business. However, I won't use the restaurant again.	

Functional language   Background

Saying how often you visit	I stay at the Merlin Hotel once a month. We usually eat in the restaurant at least once a week. We (ate) there on Monday with some clients. I visited last week with (some friends). We often bring our clients (to the Lodge). We had dinner there (two days ago). We sometimes have company lunches there.
Talking about purpose	It was a business trip to (a conference in the city centre). We were celebrating (a sales contract with clients). It was for (a company event).

Good and bad points

Talking about good points	The staff are always friendly and helpful. The rooms are (large and clean). The location of the (restaurant) is perfect. The (food) is always excellent. The view (from the hotel) is wonderful.
Talking about bad points	There was (an event at the hotel) and it was very noisy. (I ate in the hotel restaurant in the evening and) the service was slow. We waited too long for our food. It is too expensive. I won't use the restaurant again.
Recommending	We highly recommend it (because it's comfortable and in a great location). I'm afraid I cannot recommend (your restaurant).

3 ❯ Emails

Lead-in Emails can be informal (more like spoken English) or formal (like a business letter). The subject line of the email helps the reader to understand what the email is about. Emails usually use polite or friendly phrases to start and end the communication. When writing to people outside of the company, the first email may be more formal or longer. When an email conversation develops, the style may become more informal and similar to the style of internal emails.

Model answers

From: Anton Lewis, Events Manager

To: Rosa Santos, Jenson International Hotels

Subject: Conference arrangements

Dear Ms Santos,

I am writing to enquire about conference facilities at your venue. We are looking for a venue for a conference for our international sales team next July. We need to have a large room for the presentations and also 50 rooms for the delegates for two nights.

We would like breakfast, lunch and dinner and also tea and coffee during the conference. Could you confirm that the hotel can provide transport from the airport?

If possible, I'd like to see a plan of the hotel, and please could you send a brochure with details about the conference facilities?

I would like to arrange a visit to the hotel next Thursday. Are you available then?

Please contact me if you have any questions. I look forward to hearing from you.

Kind regards,

Anton Lewis

Dear Mr Lewis,

Thank you for your email and for your interest in our hotel.

I am delighted to confirm that we can meet next Thursday. Would you like to meet in reception at 2 p.m.? I can show you the hotel facilities, and we can discuss your conference needs.

Feel free to contact me if you have any questions. I very much look forward to meeting you next week.

Kind regards,

Rosa

Rosa Santos

Hotel Manager

Hi Rosa,

Many thanks for your email. This is to confirm that Thursday at 2 p.m. is fine.

I look forward to meeting you next week.

All the best,

Anton

Functional language

Starting an email

Formal	Informal
Dear Sir/Madam, Dear Ms/Mrs/Miss/Mr/Dr Bell, Dear Tonya,	Hi Miku, Hi Team, To all staff,

Asking for information

Reason for writing	I am / I'm writing to enquire about (the sales conference). I am / I'm asking for information about (your courses).
Asking for information	Could you tell me (when the project starts)? Please can/could you let me know (who to contact in HR)? Can/Could you confirm that (this information is correct)? I would like to know (how far it is to the hotel). We would also like more information about (conference rooms).
Giving information	We are looking for (a venue). We need to have (a large room for the meeting). We would like to book (four rooms).

Making requests

Saying what you want done	Kate, could you (check the dates)? Could Liam (meet the client at the airport)? If possible, I'd like (to see the plans). Would you (contact the team)? Please (send me a copy of the report).
Saying when you want the action completed	I'd be grateful if you could send me (the data) by (Friday). Do you think I could have (a reply) by (Monday)?

Making and confirming arrangements

Making arrangements	Are you free on (the 12th) for (a meeting)? Could we (have a conference call) to discuss (the project)? Can we meet on (Wednesday afternoon)? Are you available (next week)? Would you like to meet (on the 8th) to discuss (the presentation)?
Thanking someone for writing	Thank you for your email. Many thanks for your email.
Confirming that the arrangement is possible	This is to confirm that (Monday at 3 p.m. is fine for the meeting). I am delighted to confirm (that I can come to the training course).
Apologising because the arrangement is not possible	I'm sorry but I cannot/can't (go the meeting next week). Unfortunately, I am unable to attend (the conference). I can go to the (morning session), but I can't go to the (afternoon session) because (I have a meeting).

Ending an email

Inviting questions	Feel free to call me / contact me if you have any questions.	
Concluding	I am looking forward to hearing from you. I hope to hear from you soon. I look forward to our meeting on Tuesday. I very much look forward to meeting you (next month).	
Ending	**Formal**	**Informal**
	Kind regards, Regards,	Best wishes, All the best, Best,

4 ❯ Giving updates

Lead-in   It is common to give a written update about a project or task. Updates are often used in a range of internal communications such as emails, reports, intranet posts or company newsletters.

Model answer

Update on plans for new factory in India: location and changes

As you know, we are going to build a new factory in India. Last month in the staff meeting, we had presentations to discuss ideas for three possible locations and we also discussed staff working hours. We are now ready to update you on these developments.

Firstly, we are going to build a new factory in Noida. We will also open new offices in Gurgaon. The company is planning to employ more than 300 staff in Noida and 150 in Gurgaon.

Secondly, we want to introduce new working hours for all employees. Staff in IT, HR and Marketing will be able to work from home one day a week. We also plan to give other departments flexible hours to start and finish work from Monday to Friday.

We know that you will want to have more information about these plans. Therefore, we are holding a meeting next Wednesday to answer questions. We will explain how we are going to put these proposals into action.

This is an exciting time for the company. We are growing and changing, and we hope that this will help all our teams around the world.

Functional language

Requesting an update

Asking for an update	Could you let me know how (the project) is going? Can we have an update (on the tasks)? I would appreciate (some news about progress).

Giving an update

Purpose of the update	As you know, (we are looking at new locations). We are now ready to (open the new factory). The company is planning to (employ more staff). In this update, we will (give staff information about the location).
Giving details and explanations	Firstly, (we are going to buy new machines). Secondly, we are (going to) introduce (safety regulations). We also plan to (build new offices). (The board of directors) has decided to (close the city centre store). We are ready to propose a number of changes (as a result of our research). This will reduce (the cost of the products).
Next steps	We are therefore (holding a meeting next week). Therefore we (are having a team meeting to answer questions). We will explain how we are going to put these proposals into action.
Concluding in a positive way	This is an exciting time for our company. We hope this will help all our teams.

5 ❯ Short communications

Lead-in

- Short communications at work can be electronic emails, short emails or short notes.

- When we communicate with colleagues, we often use informal language.

- We use more formal expressions with senior staff or people from outside the company. This can be both in emails, texts and electronic messages.

- We sometimes use abbreviations to keep communications short or leave out some words so that the information can be read quickly.

- Emails usually use normal punctuation, but messages and notes sometimes miss out full stops, commas, etc.

Model answers

More informal

> On my way. Flight late. In taxi now.

> Approx. 15 mins. OK? Presentation ready to go.

> Thanks. Will do!

> Are you at the conference, Jamal?

> What's your ETA?

> No prob. FYI boss here. Good idea to message him?

More formal

> Apologies, my flight was late. I am on my way.

> Yes, I'll be with you in 10 minutes. The presentation is ready to go.

> Thanks for letting me know, Jamal. Will you be here in time for the presentation?

> Excellent. Message me when you arrive at reception.

Hi Jamal,

Well done with your presentation last week. The CEO would like a report on the sales conference. Can you arrange this by EOD? I am in Dubai until Wednesday and WFH on Thursday. Can we meet on Friday to discuss the next conference? We want you to give another presentation.

Regards,

Louisa

Messages for Jamal

- Louisa phoned. Has to cancel meeting Friday. New date TBA.

- CEO wants report by COB.

- BTW sales team are celebrating tonight. Want to join us for dinner?

Functional language Messages

Informal	
Use shortened forms	no prob (instead of *no problem*) approx. (instead of *approximately*) On my way. (instead of *I'm on my way.*)
Don't use pronouns	~~She~~ Has to cancel meeting on Friday.
Don't use articles	In ~~a~~ taxi now. ~~The~~ Sales team are celebrating tonight. ~~The~~ CEO wants report.
Don't use unnecessary words	Flight late. (instead of *My flight was late.*)

More formal	
Use full forms	No problem. I'm on my way.
Use pronouns	**My** flight was late.
Use articles	**The** presentation is ready to go. **The** CEO would like a report.
Use all words	I'll be with you in 10 minutes.

Abbreviations

Abbreviation	Meaning
ETA	estimated time of arrival
FYI	for your information
EOD	end of day
COB	close of business
WFH	working from home
BTW	by the way
TBA	to be arranged
TBC	to be confirmed
ASAP	as soon as possible

6 ❯ Presentations

Lead-in Some presentation slides are visual, using pictures or charts to illustrate information. Other slides contain key information that the speaker wants to communicate to the audience. When you prepare slides, it is useful to think about the language you want to use and the amount of information you put on each slide.

Model answers

Step 1
Communicate with customers.

Step 2
Ask questions and listen to feedback.

Step 3
Research new ideas.

Finding solutions

Making a difference

Changing the world of IT

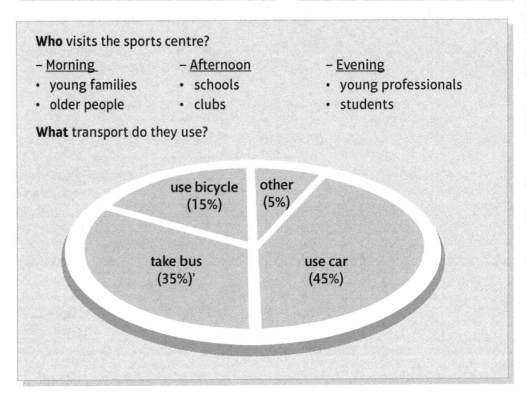

Who visits the sports centre?

– Morning
- young families
- older people

– Afternoon
- schools
- clubs

– Evening
- young professionals
- students

What transport do they use?

use bicycle (15%) other (5%) take bus (35%)' use car (45%)

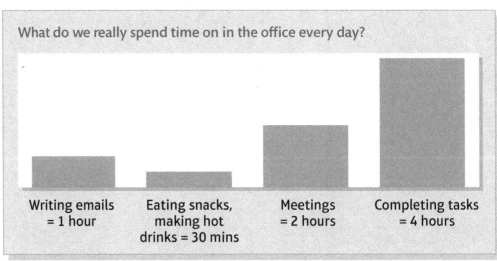

What do we really spend time on in the office every day?

Writing emails = 1 hour | Eating snacks, making hot drinks = 30 mins | Meetings = 2 hours | Completing tasks = 4 hours

Functional language

Preparing slides

When you are preparing slides for a presentation, it is a good idea to use a dictionary to check spelling. Use of colour, pictures, charts and diagrams can make the slides more interesting. However, think about the colours and pictures that you choose. Are they easy to read and understand? Here are some more tips when preparing slides.

Tips	Examples
Use similar grammar forms on each slide	**infinitives: communicate** with customers, **ask** questions **gerunds: finding** solutions, **making** a difference **nouns:** cars, businesses, emails
Drop articles	**definite (*the*):** make product (<u>not</u> *make the product*) **indefinite (*a/an*):** send email (<u>not</u> *send an email*)
Use bullet points	**use (•) for main lists:** • use car **use (▪) for secondary lists:** ▪ students
Use pictures and charts	• picture, photo • diagram, table or chart • symbols (e.g. ©)

Talking about slides

When you are presenting a slide, it is a good idea not to just read the words on the slide. Use the slide to help communicate your ideas. Here are some useful phrases for using slides in a presentation.

Introducing a slide	Here you can see (three steps for helping customer communication). If you look at this slide, you can see that (more people use cars than bicycles). This slide shows (that we are not always working when we are in the office).
Moving from slide to slide	This next slide shows (what we want the company to focus on). Moving on, let's look at (some details about our customers).

1 ❯ Presentation skills

Lead-in   Presentation styles can differ from country to country. Here are some questions to research before you prepare a presentation:

1 What information can you present in slides or pictures? What information is better spoken?
2 When you present data, how much detail do you need to give? Will the audience prefer exact and detailed facts and figures or approximate information?
3 Will people expect you to answer questions during the presentation or at the end?

Getting started

Welcoming your audience	Thank you for coming today. I'd like to thank everyone for being here.
Providing an outline of the talk	I'm here to talk about (our latest sales figures). The talk is in (three) main parts.
Telling the audience when they can ask questions	Feel free to ask questions (during) the presentation. I'll be happy to answer questions (at the end) of the presentation.

Structuring a presentation

Getting started	So, let's get started. I'd like to start off by talking about (the survey).
Focusing on a point	Let's look at (the figures) in more detail.
Moving from point to point	Now let's move on to (the sales for July). Next we'll look at (the results).
Signposting	First of all, Firstly, Secondly, Then, Finally,
Introducing a co-presenter	I'll hand you over to Alex (to look at the data). Now, Kim will (explain how we did the survey).
Summing up	To recap the main points, (we need to sell more products). So, just to sum up, (we will do more research). In summary, (this was a very successful year).
Finishing	That brings me to (the end of my presentation). Thank you for listening.

Presenting facts and figures

Referring to figures in visuals	As you can see, (sales increased in November). Have a look at (this chart), which shows (profits for last year).
Explaining data	To put that in context, that's (the best result for five years). To give you an idea of how much that is, it comes to (over a million).
Highlighting main points	The key takeaway here is that (our products are too expensive). This clearly means that (customers like the new design).
Giving approximate figures	**More than >** over (half) **Less than <** almost (a third), nearly (one in three), under (5 percent) **Approximately** roughly (3/4), around (40 percent), about (1/4)

Managing questions

Inviting questions	Does anyone have a question? Any questions? Are there any (further) questions?
Thanking	That's an interesting question, thanks. It's a good question, thanks. Thank you for your question.
Repeating and checking understanding	So the question was (why are we opening a new office). Claire asked (about the computers), right? So you want to know about (the costs).
Asking for clarification	Sorry, can you repeat your question, please? I'm sorry, I'm not sure what you mean. What do you mean exactly?
Making sure the question is answered	Does that help? I hope that answers your question.

2 ❯ Meeting skills

Lead-in

Meeting styles may differ from country to country. Here are some questions to research before you prepare for a meeting:

1 Will the meeting have a leader?
2 Is it likely to be formal or informal?
3 Is there an agenda or other documents that will be used in the meeting?
4 Will the meeting have someone to take notes?
5 Are you expected to comment on ideas during the meeting?

Opening a meeting

Welcoming people	Nice to see everyone. Thank you all for coming today.
Getting started	Let's start. I'd like to start (on time).
Stating purpose	One reason for the meeting is to (discuss the new computers). The main aim today is to (agree on the IT budget). The reason I want to (discuss this) is to (decide on where to move the sales team).
Allocating tasks	Could I have a volunteer to (take notes)? (Meg), can I ask you to be time-keeper?
Referring to the agenda	Does anyone want to add anything to the agenda? Let's look at (Item 3, the sales results). Sorry, can we just go back to (Item 1)? So, moving on to (Item 4).

Asking for and giving opinions

Asking for opinions	What do you think, Austin? Does anyone have any ideas?
Giving an opinion	I think it's a good idea to (open a new store in Milan). We can (talk to the New York office). I'm not sure about that.
Agreeing/ Disagreeing	I agree with Vincent. Sorry, I don't agree.

Responding to ideas		
Supporting an idea	What a good idea! I really like that idea. I think that's a great idea. That might not be such a bad idea. Let's do it!	
Building on an idea	While we are on the subject of (design), why don't we (decide on a new logo colour)? (And) doing that means we could also (arrange to meet the team in Singapore). If we do that, we can also (buy new desks for the office).	
Questioning an idea	(Of course) there is the question of (price). What can we do about that? I'm just wondering about the amount of (people at the event). How can we manage that? It's a good idea, but (do we need more time)?	

Closing a meeting

That's everything on the agenda. Thanks for coming to the meeting. Thanks, everyone. See you at the next meeting (on Friday).

3 **>** Telephone skills

Lead-in

Some ways of making a phone call may differ from country to country. Here are some questions to research before you make telephone calls:

1 Are calls usually short and factual or is some small talk expected?

2 Is it usual to speak to a receptionist first?

3 Is it usual to give explanations when an appointment changes? Do you just apologise or give details about why you need to change?

Starting a call

Starting a call	Hello, my name is Martin Becker. Can I speak to the Finance Manager, please? Hi, this is Luiza from Marketing.
Receiving a call	Hello, Bowbrick Engineering. Hi, Himari Tanaka speaking.
Saying why you are calling	Can we arrange a meeting to talk about the project? I'd like some information about your products.

Making arrangements

Asking for an appointment	I'm calling to arrange an appointment (to look at the new offices). Can we meet to discuss (the new brochure)?
Suggesting dates	I'm free on (Tuesday afternoon). How does (2 p.m.) suit you? How about (Friday)?
Saying a date is not possible	I'm busy all day (Monday). (Thursday)'s out for me, I'm afraid. Sorry, (Wednesday afternoon) isn't possible.
Agreeing on a date	Yes, (Thursday morning) is fine. See you on (Friday at 3 p.m.).

Changing arrangements

Explaining that you need to change	I'm calling about our meeting on the (28th). Do you mind if we fix another time to meet?
Apologising	I'm really sorry about this. I know it's a bit short notice. Sorry to bother you.
Talking about the change	Can we bring it forward? Do you want to postpone (the meeting)? Let me just check my schedule. I'll check my diary.
Suggesting new date	Is (Wednesday afternoon) possible for you? Which is better for you: (mornings) or (afternoons)?
Fixing a new date	So, just to confirm (we'll change the meeting to the 12th). We're all set for the (19th).
Thanking	Thanks for being so flexible. Thank you for your help.

Leaving a message

Taking a message	Can I take a message? Do you want to leave a message? Would you like to leave a message?
Responding	No, thanks. I'll call back later. Yes, please. That'd be great.
Leaving a message	Can you tell (her) that (Fabio Russo) called? Ask (him) to call me back (this afternoon), please. Tell (Mrs Deakin) that (Shelly) phoned about (the meeting).

Asking for and giving clarification

Asking for clarification	Sorry, I can't hear you. The line is bad. Can you speak up/louder, please? Could you repeat that, please? Did you say (4231 3218)?
Giving clarification	Yes, that's 4231 3218. Yes, that's right. I said the hotel is in (Lille) not (Lyon). No, it's (fifty) not (fifteen). Do you want me to spell that?

Ending a call

Thanks for calling. Thank you for your call. Good to speak to you, bye.

4 > Dealing with technical problems

Lead-in

Technical problems can occur at work while using a computer. When dealing with technical problems, consider the following:

1 Is the best way to report a problem by telephone, online or in person?

2 What information will the person need to help you?

3 What will help you explain a problem clearly? (For example, write notes and use a dictionary to help with technical vocabulary.)

Dealing with the IT department

Explaining a problem	I'm having a problem with (my computer). I can't connect (to the internet). I need to get (into my account). How do I (open the file)? I'm having trouble (opening a document).
Solving a problem	You need to (shut down the computer). Can you try (shutting it down)? Try (your name and password). I'll (come and) do it for you.
Checking the problem is solved	Does it work now? Do you need any more information? Is there anything else I can help with?
Responding to help	Yes, it works. It's fine now. No, there's still a problem. That didn't work.
Thanking	Thank you for your help.

Dealing with problems in online meetings

Explaining a problem	I'm afraid I can't hear you very well. The connection is bad. You keep cutting out. I can hear a lot of (background noise). There's (a bit of) an echo. The screen is blank.
Solving a problem	Have you switched on (your webcam)? If you can just check (your volume), please. Would you mind (hanging up) and I'll (call you back)? Could you move closer to the microphone? Would you mind using the (mute button)? Can you move (your phone) away from (the computer)?
Checking the problem is solved	Is it working? Is that better? Can you (hear/see me) now?

1.1.1

N = Narrator A1 = Alex A2 = Alessio A3 = Amira

N: In a global economy, many companies do business overseas. This means that workers often travel to see their colleagues or clients abroad. There are many reasons why people travel for work.

A1: I go abroad to complete projects which are set by my company. Those projects can include setting up certain systems, laptops, docking stations, etc.

A2: I need to travel for work because sometimes the projects I do are based somewhere outside London, where I live, so I've been travelling to France, to Italy, to Spain, to Romania.

A3: I need to travel because we work with big brands and multinationals, and they want to understand different people in the different markets and countries, so we travel across the world.

N: An important part of business travel is organising transportation. When people travel internationally, they often fly, though in some cases taking the train is an option.

A1: I travel for work once or twice a month, on a regular basis. I tend to fly short haul and I use two different airlines.

N: Alex makes the most of his travel time and keeps busy during the flight.

A1: When I'm flying for business I tend to get my laptop out and do some work during the flight, and half an hour before my plane lands I remove my laptop, put it back in my bag, and get ready for the landing.

N: On business trips, you may need to stay overnight. It's important to book accommodation that is suitable for your trip and has everything you need, so you can keep working during your stay.

A2: The accommodation where I like to stay when I travel for work is … is hotels, usually, but they need to be very close to the place where I need to go to work. What I expect at my location is wi-fi because I need to work most of the time when I'm back in my room. And, of course, parking, because usually I need to hire cars or a vehicle from the airport to the workplace.

N: When travelling for work, you may not know much about the local area and how to get around. Find out about transportation before you go. And when you get there, ask for help if you need it, or ask for directions.

A3: When I have to go from a business meeting to another meeting, I either use public transportation, because it's a really good way to mix with the locals, or I use a ridesharing app. I always worry about getting lost but it's part of the adventure. I carry an online map on my phone and, if I do get lost, I just ask people and they're really helpful.

N: Even if you've planned ahead, things can still go wrong. Your flight could be delayed or there might be a mistake with your hotel reservation. It's rare, however, to find a problem that cannot be solved.

A3: I remember once, I was at the airport lounge waiting for my flight, and I got really confused with timings; and then I get to the gate and it's written in huge red letters 'gate closed', and I start panicking. Thankfully, the staff were really helpful and they helped me through. And they rushed me to the plane through a back door, and I made my flight.

N: Like anybody who's done the same thing several times, regular business travellers have advice they can offer to others.

A2: My top travel tip when travelling for work is to be very efficient in organisation. Because this gives you time also to enjoy the place where you are going, after you've done your business.

1.3.1

J = Jasmine D = Driver G = Graham

J: Is it always this busy?

D: Not always. It depends. So, what are you doing in Dublin?

J: I am starting a new job on Monday. I'm a trainee at TGC. They're an HR consultancy firm. They advise companies on different aspects of their business – recruitment, company strategy, that kind of thing. They've invited all the new recruits to a welcome dinner. And it's happening … right about now.

G: Jasmine just sent me a text – she's stuck in traffic but she'll be here soon. In the meantime, welcome to TGC. Cheers!

1.3.2

O = Orla A = Azra S = Shaun J = Jasmine

O: Where do you come from?

A: I'm from Turkey. But … I've lived in Dublin for years.

O: Ah. You're basically a native now. What do you think about this restaurant?

A: It's … a nice place.

S: Ah, the traveller is here!

J: Sorry I'm late. The traffic was a nightmare.

S: Friday night traffic. Always terrible. It can be like a car park out there sometimes. It can take me hours to get home.

J: Really? So you live outside the city?

S: Not as bad as Los Angeles, though. I was at a conference there last year. The traffic was so bad I arrived late and missed my presentation. The boss was not happy. But that's nothing compared to my flight from Dublin to Bangkok a few years back. Did I ever tell you that story? They lost all my luggage. I tell you, I'm never flying with that airline again.

1.3.3

T = Thiago J = Jasmine Al = Alex Az = Azra

T: Hi. I'm Thiago.

J: Jasmine. Nice to meet you.

T: You too. How long was your trip?

J: About an hour.

T: Shaun says you're American. Where are you from?

J: That's right. I'm from Boston. I went to university there. Do you know it?

T: No, I've never been, but I'd like to.

J: Thiago, that's a Brazilian name, isn't it?

T: It is. My father's from Brazil, but I'm Italian. So … do you know Orla?

J: Yeah, I met her at the interview. She's really nice. Hey … What do you know about working at TGC?

T: Not much.

Al: So, I heard you come from Turkey. Whereabouts?

Az: Well, I was born in Istanbul, but my parents moved to London when I was five. We go back quite often to see family. Do you know Turkey?

Al: A little. I went there on holiday about three years ago. Which do you prefer, London or Istanbul?

Az: Hmmm. That's difficult! I love them both.

Al: No more difficult questions, I promise. We're supposed to be relaxing.

Az: No problem.

1.3.4

Let me give you some advice when making small talk. Number one: choose your topic carefully and don't be too negative. Don't talk about personal finances, politics or religion, or more personal topics. Be prepared to listen and remember to show interest in the other person and their opinions. Showing interest is simple. If you're sitting down, move your body forward a little, use eye contact and of course smile as you speak. Watch the other person's body language and if they start to look bored, change the subject. Most importantly, don't dominate the conversation.

Follow the AAA model that Azra used earlier in the video. AAA is a simple formula. Answer the speaker's question, add new information and then ask him or her another question. The conversation will run smoothly if you follow this model. Try it and see.

2.1.1

P = Presenter V = Vaiva Kalnikaitė

P: When a new company launches, or an established company opens, a new branch, there's a decision to be made about where to locate the business.

It's an important decision to get right, and there are a number of factors which could influence it. These might include access to skilled staff, good transport links and reasonable rents for factory or office space.

Dr Vaiva Kalnikaitė launched her company, Dovetailed, in 2010. It's a technology design studio and innovation lab.

V: We tend to work on projects that have human interaction so often it will be projects where we design software or, for example, an app, or it could also be a physical object – for example, we designed a 3D printer for printing food.

P: When Vaiva set up her company, she decided to locate it in Cambridge – a city famous for its university.

V: I was an intern in Cambridge with Microsoft and I really liked Cambridge because it's a very international city, it's a very vibrant city; it's full of really interesting companies from very small start-ups to well-established companies, and that's a really good reason to set up a business in that kind of environment.

P: Dovetailed is now a member of several business networks, which has clear benefits for the company.

V: Being part of these networks, we have access to local investment groups and we've been successful in getting some funding for some of our products.

P: Many companies based in Cambridge are attracted by the chance to connect with the university.

V: We were really interested in working with the university, so we talked to various departments to see if we can collaborate on something.

P: Today Dovetailed is part of a business programme at Cambridge University's Judge Business School and receives advice and support from the school.

V: We also work with, for example, engineering department and we have summer interns who come and work at Dovetailed. It's been really helpful to have an association to Cambridge University because it's given us, as a brand, global recognition.

P: For Dovetailed, locating the company in Cambridge has helped to attract talented staff, who want to work in a lively town.

V: Cambridge is a really nice place to live in, people can cycle everywhere, walk everywhere. My journey to work is three minutes by bike. There's lots of social things happening, lots of interesting cafés opening and it's very close to London.

P: Dovetailed has clients in London, so good transport links are important.

V: It's very important for us to be able to travel to London very quickly. It takes about 50 minutes by train or we can drive to London on a motorway. Again, it takes just over an hour.

P: So how does Vaiva feel about her decision to locate Dovetailed in Cambridge?

V: I'm very happy to have chosen Cambridge as a location to set up my business. I think it's an amazing place to live and work, and it's given us a lot of opportunity to grow.

2.3.1

S = Shaun A = Alex

S: Here it is. Your first assignment. Ready?

A: Yes, I …

S: Don't worry, you'll be fine. Alright. Here's the situation. We're meeting Nick from Zapna. They're a clothes manufacturing firm with a distribution centre in Poland. Their Assistant Manager is going on maternity leave and they need to find someone to cover. Now, Nick's a nice guy, but he talks too much and he can be unclear about what he wants. I can get impatient with him sometimes. Come on. Let's do this.

2.3.2

N = Nick S = Shaun A = Alex

N: So Marta's post will be vacant soon. And as her post is vacant, we need someone to fill it. We'll need someone for about a year, as that's how long she's away. She's on maternity leave. Did I tell you that? I should also add that we did talk about taking someone on for longer, maybe eighteen months, so they could …

S: Cover the handover period. Yeah. Great. Understood.

N: That's right. But … is a six-month handover really needed? It's expensive. And …
A: Sorry to interrupt … but I think a handover period is important. But how about two months instead of six?
N: That could work. Or three months, maybe. Shaun?
S: I agree with Alex. So, that's a fourteen-month contract. Can you just confirm that for us, Nick?
N: Yes, I suppose I … fifteen months. Just to be on the safe side.
S: Great. Fifteen months. Now, about the benefits package you're offering …
N: Well … And as you know, I'm really busy at the moment. Also, I'm not a logistics expert, so I don't always know which technical questions to ask. The last time I interviewed …
S: Let me just clarify once more. Alex is your dedicated HR Consultant. Anything you need, he can help you. No need to worry.
N: I really appreciate it. It's wonderful to have you with us, Alex. We've always had an excellent service from your firm. Are you enjoying your time there so far?
S: I'm dying for a coffee. Coffee break? Back here in fifteen minutes.
A: Great.
S: See? On and on. Drives me crazy.
A: I could ask the questions when we go back in.
S: Sure. Be my guest.

2.3.3
A = Alex   N = Nick   S = Shaun
A: So, Nick, what you're saying is you want someone with logistics experience?
N: Correct, but they also need a diploma in management.
A: Great. And can I just check, you're looking for someone with a good language level?
N: Exactly; fluent in English and Polish.
A: Does that mean you want to hire someone locally?
N: No, not necessarily, but they must be prepared to move.
A: And what would make this appeal to applicants?
N: Well, we're offering an excellent package.
S: Yes, you said that, but could you be more specific?
N: I mean there's a good bonus scheme and a subsidised staff canteen.
S: And there's an international airport not far from Poznań, right?
N: That's right, Poznań has its own airport.
S: And is there a relocation package?
N: What do you mean by a relocation package exactly?
S: Well, you know, help with moving costs …
A: I think what Shaun means is, the best person may not live locally. Are you happy to cover the cost for the right candidate to move to Poznań?
N: Possibly. What I mean is, it's a sensitive topic. We need to keep costs down.
S: Yes, of course. We understand.
A: And you're looking to interview a maximum of six people. Is that right?
N: Six is perfect.
A: So, I think that covers everything. We'll get to work and send you a list of candidates as soon as possible.
N: Great, thanks, Shaun.
S: Nick.
N: Thanks, Alex.
A: Nick.
S: Good work, Alex. Well done.
A: Thanks.

2.3.4
In professional situations, we sometimes meet people, like Nick, who are unclear about what they want. Checking and asking for clarification is a good way to guide the other person so you can understand exactly what they want.
But how do you do this in English? Saying 'What do you mean?' may not be enough to clarify the information you need. Instead, ask 'What do you mean by …?', or 'Could you be more specific?' Alex also rephrases questions to help Nick be more specific. And this works nicely. You can start by saying 'What I mean is …'. Closed questions will then encourage the other person to confirm their needs. Closed questions will force the other person to answer 'Yes' or 'No', or give a simple direct answer. Finally, repeating the other person's words and adding the expression 'Is that right?' is useful to ask if you are still unsure.
And if you are the speaker, notice the body language of the listener. Often, the listener's facial expression will tell you if he or she has understood. So, if necessary, offer to clarify. Use expressions like 'What I mean is …' or 'Let me clarify'.
Remember, conversation is two-way. It's not always your responsibility to understand!

3.1.1
CS = Colin Shenton   M = Man   W = Woman
P = Presenter   I = Interviewer   C = Customer
CS: We like to describe it as home.
M: You can help yourself to snacks along the way.
W: You really concentrate how much work you can fit in.
CS: Everything in Ziferblat is free, except for the time that you spend.
P: Ziferblat is a café and social space with an unusual business model. You check in and out at a hotel-style desk, stay as long as you want, use the wi-fi and eat and drink as much as you like. Your bill is calculated at 6p a minute, including VAT. The largest branch of this international retail chain is here in Manchester, in northern England.
CS: Ziferblat is a Russian word, it means 'clock face', uh it's the same in German, and it's simply because our pricing mechanism is completely unique. We charge six pence a minute. Start your stopwatch on your iPhone if you like, and work out to the penny what your bill's gonna be.
I: You must get some people who try to abuse the system, 'I've only got 20p in my pocket, I can dash in, wolf down coffee and cake and leave,' does that happen?
CS: It happens and it's absolutely fine. I'm not even sure I'd call it abuse, what we offer is no minimum, no minimum charge, so if somebody feels they want to come in and eat as much as humanly possible – that's absolutely fine.
I: You feel under time pressure because you know that each minute counts.
C: I don't personally worry too much about that, although I, I think it's mounted up a bit this morning.
W: You do think about it after a couple of hours here, but I think it's really good because you concentrate how much work you can fit in.
M: Such a nice creative atmosphere, and the wi-fi is really good, so for uploading things, that's perfect.
CS: I think our smallest spend was three minutes, which is 18p – somebody wanted to go to the loo. Our longest stay was 11 hours, which was a guy based on his laptop who's writing a book. We ask that people respect the space, but this has been a really positive experience in human nature.
P: The business makes a profit. This branch serves 12,000 customers each month.
I: You've got one of these in London, but you've got several in the north – in Manchester and Liverpool – and you're rolling out more. Why is it you're able to expand up here?
CS: One principle reason, which is rent. We could do it in London if we were charging 20 or 25 pence a minute, but that adds up pretty fast, £15 an hour starts to sound expensive.

3.3.1
A = Azra   T = Thiago
A: Thiago. Is everything OK?
T: It's just this report I'm doing. For Shaun. It's such a lot of extra work. And I'm nearly a week late with it. If I don't finish the report soon, Shaun is going to kill me!
A: Why don't you ask him for an extension?
T: Shaun? Are you joking? Last time I missed a deadline, he nearly put me on the next flight home to Milan! It's Shaun. You haven't seen me …
A: Shaun …

3.3.2
S = Shaun   T = Thiago
S: Ah, Thiago! There you are! Just the person I was looking for! Have you got a moment? Any progress with that report?
T: Er … well …
S: Right. Sounds like there's a problem.
T: I'm just really busy with two other projects, and …
S: Thiago, it's no good making excuses. Time management is part of the job.
T: I know, I know.
S: You're holding everyone up. The report is a week late, and I need it for tomorrow's meeting with the directors. So, what's the delay?
T: Figures. I, er, still need some figures from Accounts, you …
S: Why didn't you ask me to get the figures? Any time over the past seven days? Right, that's enough. I'm bringing in Jasmine.
T: Shaun, I just need a bit more time.
S: You've had time. I'm calling Jasmine now. And I want that report on my desk by 2 p.m. tomorrow. No excuses.
T: Jasmine's going to go crazy when she finds out that we have to do overtime tonight. I guess I'm Mr Popular around here …
S: Was I hard on him? A little. But he has to learn. He can't keep missing deadlines. Anyway, Jasmine should be able to help him out.

3.3.3
T = Thiago   S = Shaun
T: Shaun. Do you have a minute?
S: For you, Thiago? I've got two. Now. How are you doing with that report?
T: I'm still having some problems, I'm afraid.
S: Right. You realise I have a meeting with the directors tomorrow afternoon? I wanted it done by then.
T: I'm really sorry. I'm so busy with other projects at the moment. And Accounts didn't get back to me with the figures I need …
S: OK. Let me deal with Accounts. And I'll see if I can get one of the other trainees to share some of your workload. Just for a few days. Does that help?
T: Yes, it helps a lot.
S: Now, what else can we do to get this report finished? What if I bring in Jasmine to help you out?
T: No, no, I can manage.
S: Look, we don't have much time. Let's speed things up. How about asking Jasmine to help you with some of the figures?
T: Yes. OK.
S: Good. I'll give you three more days. But no more. Don't let me down. Of course, this doesn't help me with the directors' meeting tomorrow.
T: Why don't I just write an executive summary of the main points? You can give them that.
S: Alright, yes. Good idea.
I like Thiago's attitude. He definitely has potential. We just need to work out how to improve his time management. Easier said than done, maybe.
T: Result! I can't believe it. I got the extension I needed. Problem solved! Well, until the next one comes along …

3.3.4
When you're trying to solve problems at work, you have two basic options – focus on the problem or focus on the solution.
Now, focusing on the problem can be very effective when it's a simple technical problem. But workflow problems are usually people problems, and they're more complex. In Video A, Shaun made a big mistake. He dealt with a people problem as if it was a technical problem. He focused on what went wrong. He blamed Thiago for not completing the report, so it's no surprise there was an argument.

And when Shaun asked Thiago and Jasmine to do overtime, it was not the best solution.

In Video B, Shaun was much better. He focused on the solution from the start. Instead of asking what went wrong, he asked questions that focused on help: 'What can we do to get this report finished?' and 'What if I bring in Jasmine to help you out?' As a result, we saw Shaun and Thiago working together to complete the report. Shaun also offered to help Thiago get the figures he needed from the Accounts department. And Thiago offered to write a short summary for Shaun to give to the Board of Directors. It was a win–win situation.

4.1.1

P = Presenter S = Sharni L1 = Lauren L2 = Laurie

P: The way we work is changing fast and one clear example of this is our work patterns. This includes the hours people work, the type of contract employees have, and even the number of different jobs they work in. The traditional work pattern was based on permanent employees doing full-time jobs and fixed working hours. The typical office worker in the UK and North America worked from Monday to Friday and had a working day of nine o'clock to five o'clock. Indeed, people talk about 'nine-to-five jobs' to describe traditional office work. However, that is changing. Today's global economy needs more flexible work patterns, not nine-to-five jobs. We talked to some people about their working lives.

S: I'm Sharni, and I'm an Accountant. I work full-time flexible hours, so that means some days I start early and finish early, and some days I start later and finish later. And I'll take breaks depending on what I need to deliver for the day. Some days I work in the office and some days I work at home. I have my office set up at home, so I have everything I need to work as if I was in the office. I like working flexible hours – it gives me the ability to manage my career but also be there for my children. This type of working isn't for everybody. Some people will work better with a fixed schedule and set hours. The advantages for my employer for me to be a flexitime worker means that I'm a much happier employee. I can still maintain all aspects of my personal life and still pursue my career.

P: Some people don't have permanent jobs with one employer but work for employment agencies that find them temporary jobs in different companies.

L1: My name is Lauren. I'm a temporary worker and that basically means that I work for an agency that sends me on different assignments in different companies. I started temping during university, and I am still temping whilst I'm looking for a permanent role. The contracts that I'm assigned on last from around a couple of days to a few months, and this can include a range of different roles, such as clerical as well as reception work. The advantages of being a temp worker are ... it gives you insight into loads of different industries and it allows me to see what kind of permanent roles I'll be interested in. There are some disadvantages to working as a temporary worker and these include lack of job security, and it makes it difficult for career progression. Being adaptable is a very important skill in the job market, and ... erm, temp work definitely allows me to build upon that skill.

P: Freelance work for more than one company at the same time is also more common today.

L2: My name's Laurie. I'm a gig worker. And ... gig working means when you do lots of different types of jobs to earn a living. I work in the television industry, and a typical week for me might involve ... I might write a script, I might direct a film or I might do some camera work. Depending on how many projects I have, I may work 20 hours one week and 40 hours another week. One advantage of being a gig worker is that it allows a lot of variety in my working life. Another advantage is that it allows me to do things, in my free time, that I wouldn't ordinarily be able to do if I had a full-time job. One of the disadvantages to gig working is that there's not that much income security, so you don't always know where your next pay cheque is coming from.

P: It's clear that today there are many more work patterns than in the past. It's also clear that our working lives will continue to change in the future, and we will have to adapt to that.

4.3.1

O = Orla S = Shaun

O: Good meeting with Léana?

S: Great, thanks. She's already spoken to some of the other directors about my idea.

O: What do you call it again? Reverse coaching?

S: Yes. A lot of companies are doing it. I don't know if you've noticed ... but a few of the directors sometimes have problems with office technology. The thing is, we have all these people in junior positions working for us, who practically live their whole lives online. Social media, apps, you name it. So, the idea is they spend some time with the directors who need a bit of help using business apps, social media and so on. It's basically one-on-one coaching.

O: Perfect. What do they think?

S: Well, I'm meeting them later this afternoon. I guess we'll find out!

4.3.2

S = Shaun E = Ethan M = Michael ('Mike')
T = Thiago J = Jasmine

S: Ideally, you'd meet with the directors, say, once a week. What do you think? Sounds good? Great. So ...

E: Shaun? Erm, sorry to interrupt, but I thought we were here to discuss this.

S: We are. We're discussing how to do it right. So, Thiago. You're our tech guru. Do you want to work with Léana?

M: So ... we're doing this? You've already made the decision?

S: Well ... yes. Léana has approved it. Come on, it'll be fun! You get to work with the people running the company. It's great for your career!

T: Sorry, Shaun, but how do we find time for this? We're all really busy.

S: It's an hour a week. That's all.

J: Um, Shaun. We're not trained coaches. I'm not sure I'd be comfortable working with people like Léana and Graham.

E: Look, Shaun, let's not rush into anything. We don't have to take an immediate decision on this. Can we go away and think about it?

S: Think about what? These people pay your salaries. They need your help. It's that simple.

T: Will we get paid extra? I'm just asking ...

S: I'm disappointed, guys. Really disappointed. I have a great idea ... and this is how you react! Anyway. I've told Léana about it. It's going ahead. So, you can either like it or learn to like it. Right. Who's going to work with Graham?

4.3.3

S = Shaun T = Thiago J = Jasmine
M = Michael ('Mike') E = Ethan

S: Now, we already have the go-ahead from Léana. But I'd like to get your input before we finalise anything. So, what does everybody think? Thiago, you're our tech guru, what are your thoughts on this?

T: Will we have time for it?

S: OK, it's a fair point. We'll figure out a way to fit it into your schedules. Any other thoughts?

J: We're not trained coaches. Are we qualified to be doing this?

S: Hmm, I take your point. How about we arrange some kind of training for you? Just the basics. It shouldn't be too hard. Mike, you haven't said anything so far. I'd like to hear what you think.

M: Why don't we call it 'tech assistance' instead of coaching? It sounds more informal. More comfortable.

S: Mm, you may have a point. Jasmine, what do you think of Mike's idea?

J: I like it. 'Tech assistance' sounds fun.

S: It will be! Does anyone have anything else they'd like to add before we move on?

E: If we're going to be coaching the directors, maybe they could coach us, too? They could teach us a lot about the business.

J: That's a great idea. We're helping them, they're helping us.

S: OK. I'll mention it to Léana. Right, well, thanks for your input, everybody. Now we just have to decide which directors you're working with. Graham, anybody?

4.3.4

In business, it's important to make good decisions. But when those decisions affect other people, it's really important to make sure you involve them before going ahead.

In Video A, Shaun discovered that having a great idea is not enough. You need to persuade your team that it's a great idea, too. Often, the best way to do this is to ask for their input and let them see for themselves how good your idea really is.

Of course, involving others in your decisions can take a little longer. You took time to develop your idea. So your team needs time to think about it, too. And sometimes people don't have much input to give. But by showing them you value what they say, as Shaun did in Video B, you may find they can make your idea even better! In fact, we saw that Michael and Ethan were able to do this. More importantly, your idea will become the team's idea. And because it's now the team's idea, everyone on the team will want to make it work.

5.1.1

I'm here in Mumbai where queues like this outside banks have become a common sight. And that's the story across the country. Last week, the Indian government announced that 500- and 1,000-rupee notes would be completely abolished. So I want to find out how far I can get without a single penny in my wallet.

A lot of people who have suffered from this cash crunch are small businesses who have to buy their goods up front.

Now, businesses like this stall, something that you find on every street corner in a city like Mumbai. Paan is a stuffed betel leaf chewed by millions of Indians.

Thank you.

Great. So, he accepts credit cards, so I don't have to give cash. I've got away with it here. Mobile wallets, where you can load money onto an app, have been around for years and have been gaining in popularity, too. But since the currency announcement has come in, some payment gateways have been seeing a rise of up to 400 percent in customers.

OK, that's great. So he's accepting money via mobile wallets, but vegetables are an everyday item normally paid in cash. So are customers ready to go cashless?

By taking this step, the government is hoping to get more people and businesses into the financial system. And this will also help increase tax revenues. Cash? So there you have it. I managed to do most of the things without cash. But then I need cash for something that millions of Indians do every day – getting around town. And without everyone willing to turn to technology even in these difficult times, the Indian government's hopes of becoming a hundred percent cashless economy could still be far off.

5.3.1

S = Shaun O = Orla

S: Orla. On your way to the project meeting?

O: Yes.

S: It's the first time this team's worked together, isn't it? No pressure ...

O: Well, we're really just working out team roles today. The client pitch is not for another six weeks. The question is, do I just *tell* them what I'd like them to do or let them figure it out themselves? Part of me wants to let *them* decide. Part of me just wants to tell them ...

S: Well, there are some strong personalities in that team, so I wouldn't give them too much freedom. I'd just *tell* them if I were you.

O: I'll let you know how it goes ...

5.3.2

O = Orla J = Jasmine A1 = Azra A2 = Alex
T = Thiago S = Shaun

O: That's the project covered. Now, team roles. Alex, I'd like you to be pitch leader. You've got the most project management experience. Now, Azra, I thought lead presenter for you this time. We've talked about you wanting to develop your presentation skills. Jasmine, I'm going to ask you to be the learning designer.
J: Oh, erm …
O: Problem?
J: Well, no, it's just quite a lot of responsibility.
O: You're a Learning and Development Specialist, and you're a responsible person. You'll be fine. Finally, Thiago. Tech support. You're so good with technology.
A1: Actually, Orla, I'm really not comfortable presenting. Especially in front of a new client.
A2: I agree. Azra should be the pitch leader on this one, and I can take care of the presentation. And maybe Thiago could help me out. He needs something bigger than tech support.
T: Yeah, why do I always get tech support?
A1: And … well … maybe Jasmine also feels like I do. About her role.
J: I am worried. It's a big responsibility.
A2: Perhaps Thiago can help me present and do the slides.
T: Wait a minute. I'm doing the presentation and the slides?
O: Everyone! Please! Your first time together as a team and you're arguing about everything! Let's just think about this.
S: Sounded lively in there.
O: I don't think this is going to be easy.

5.3.3

O = Orla A1 = Azra A2 = Alex T = Thiago

O: OK, you all know each other quite well. So let's decide the team roles among ourselves. Is that OK with everyone? Alex. Azra. I was thinking you could head up the project together as pitch leader and lead presenter. How would you feel about that?
A1: Me as pitch leader?
O: If you don't mind.
A1: Actually, Orla, sorry, but I'd rather not be the lead presenter if that's OK with you. I'm really not comfortable with that role.
O: But … don't you want to develop your presentation skills?
A1: I do! But one step at a time. I'm quite good at communicating one on one – but presenting to a new client? I'm not sure I'm the best person.
A2: Perhaps Azra and I could swap roles.
O: Well, I did want you as pitch leader, Alex, but if you're both happy to exchange roles, then that's fine with me. Right, Jasmine, I'd like you to be the learning designer. Relax! You have the expertise, and I'll be here to help you out if you need it. Just look at it as a challenge. Now, Thiago, you're our tech expert, so how would you like to do the PowerPoint for us again?
T: I don't mind. But I'd prefer not to do that again if I have a choice.
A2: Actually, Orla, I think Thiago might do a good job as co-presenter with me. Didn't you win a public speaking competition at university or something?
T: I won two of them.
O: Nice idea, Alex, but who's going to do the PowerPoint? No offence, but it's not really your strong point, is it?
A2: Maybe Thiago and I could work together on both? Thiago's a lot better with technology than I am, but I can help him with some of the other stuff.
O: OK. Great. I think we've got the team roles covered. So, just to summarise …

5.3.4

It's a key question when building a team: do you simply tell people what you want them to do, or do you let them decide? After all, they know what they're best at, and what skills they still need to develop.
In Video A, we saw Orla taking the first approach. And immediately we saw a negative reaction from the team. When Orla gave Alex and Thiago roles she knew they were good at, she didn't consider if they might like to develop new skills. And with Azra and Jasmine, Orla went too far in the other direction. She gave them challenges they didn't feel prepared for.
But both of these problems were solved in Video B. This is because they negotiated their own team roles. Jasmine kept the role Orla suggested, but the others changed or shared roles. In this way, there was room for them to improve their skill set without challenging them too much.
When you're building a team, you want people to do things they're good at, and also excited about. You can trust each team member to know what these things are. And if you show that you trust them to be involved in the decisions about their roles, it gives them confidence, and builds their trust in you. This is the ideal scenario.

6.1.1

P = Presenter R = Roy White B = Brent Jennings
T = Team member Dr R = Dr Rick de Decker

P: Whether we play team sports in our free time, work on joint projects or are part of a team at work, most of us have to cooperate with others on a regular basis. But there is one context in which teamwork is especially important … and that's when danger is involved. At more than 1,000 metres high, Table Mountain towers over Cape Town in South Africa. Easy access from the city makes it very popular with tourists and hikers. But with over eighty rescues a year, it is more dangerous than people realise.
R: Table Mountain is not a simple mountain, it's not an easy mountain.
P: This is why the Table Mountain Rescue team is always ready. If someone has an accident on the mountain, it's the team's job to get them down. This hiker was on his way down from the mountain with a friend when he fell and hurt his leg. He can't walk, so the rescue team has to get him to safety. With the sun going down, the team has to work in the dark. They need to be very careful and very patient or they will put everyone at risk.
B: The main problem is that you don't ever get two people carrying a stretcher. You'll have maybe nine, ten people carrying a stretcher at any one point; and that whole group has got to make its way down safely.
P: By working together, the team has reached the bottom safely. The members of the Table Mountain rescue team have faced many difficult situations together, but it takes more than practice and experience to work well as a team.
B: You can't just expect rescue experience alone to give you what you need in a rescue team.
P: Lots of personal skills are necessary for a good team worker. But being a good communicator – knowing what to say, when to say it, and how to say it clearly – is one of the most important. And connected to that, of course, is the ability to listen to others.
T: Woah, woah, woah, slowly guys!
P: You also need to be reliable, so the rest of the team can trust you.
Dr R: If you get that level of trust with somebody who is on the ledge above you, then you've got a really good team going. But that takes some doing, it takes quite a lot of training to get to that level.
P: Even in experienced teams, people may disagree, so good team members need to know how to deal with arguments, stay calm and help everyone reach agreement – in other words, they need to be good at conflict management. If team members show each other respect, a solution can usually be found. When the work is finished, the team can relax, talk about what went well and get ready for the next rescue.

6.3.1

T = Thiago J = Jasmine

T: Coffee? Hell-o!
J: What? Oh, thanks. Sorry, I'm just thinking about this Miami thing.
T: You're going to Miami?

J: Hopefully, yeah. I put in a proposal for a talk at the Global HR Leadership Conference. Orla said I should give it a try. And … I don't believe it. That's an email from them. The conference organisers. Ah … this could be so great for my résumé. 'No'. They said 'no'.

6.3.2

T = Thiago J = Jasmine A = Azra

T: I'm sorry, Jasmine. That's too bad. But … look on the bright side.
J: What bright side?
T: Erm …
J: Exactly.
T: Come on, it's no big deal. It's just a conference, after all.
J: Thiago, it's the biggest HR conference in the world! And I should be speaking at it. Now I've got to tell Orla they rejected me.
T: Orla will understand. Come on. Cheer up! Look … some of us are going for a drink after work. Why don't you come along?
J: You know what? I don't really feel like hitting the pub right now.
T: Harry's Bar. At six. You know … if you change your mind. And, hey, Orla thinks you're great. We all do. Don't worry so much.
A: Jasmine! Thiago told me your news. You must be so disappointed!
J: Well. Life goes on.
A: Oh, poor you! I know exactly how you feel! Listen, if you need someone to talk to about it, just let me know, OK?
J: Thanks, Azra.

6.3.3

A = Alex J = Jasmine

A: Miami?
J: Thiago. He told you.
A: No secrets in this place. I'm sorry it didn't work out for you. I hope you're not too disappointed.
J: Thanks. Maybe Thiago was right. It's no big deal.
A: It sounds like you put a lot of work into it.
J: Yeah, well …
A: And I know how important it was to you. So I can understand how you feel. Did the organisers tell you why they didn't accept you? They can be very selective.
J: They said I had an interesting topic, but it didn't really fit this year's theme.
A: So. You had the right topic. You just picked the wrong year. It happens.
J: Looks like it. I didn't really think about the conference theme. Stupid of me.
A: You can always try again. You'll know next time. If it makes you feel any better, I had to apply to engineering school three times before I finally got in. My advice? Put it behind you and move on.
J: I guess I just wanted to impress Orla.
A: Orla likes you. Everyone does. But you haven't been here long. Don't try to run before you can walk. The question to ask yourself is: What can I learn from this?
J: Yeah, I see that now.
A: Look at it this way: you missed out on a trip to Miami, but now you'll be free to help me with the Ferguson pitch.
J: The Ferguson pitch?
A: Yeah. Shaun thinks you're ready to start presenting to clients face to face. So you'll be my co-presenter to start with. What do you think? More fun than talking to a roomful of strangers in Miami?

6.3.4

Business life can have its disappointments as well as its successes. When the presentation doesn't go well, or we don't get the promotion, what do we do? Well, we might turn to the colleague we trust the most for support and advice.
In Video A, Thiago's response to Jasmine's bad news was to avoid it. Then, he tried to change the subject by inviting her out for a drink with the group. He didn't seem to care very much.
Azra did the opposite. She showed too much

emotion, and it was annoying for Jasmine. In Video B, Alex got the balance right. He said he understood how Jasmine felt, but he didn't pretend to know exactly what she was feeling. He looked for positive things while accepting her disappointment. Most importantly, he was able to empathise – which means to share the experience of another person – and this can make the other person feel better.

7.1.1

P = Presenter S = Simon Lyons

P: Any company offering goods for sale is under constant pressure to improve existing products and to bring new products to market. But any product, whether it's a mobile phone, a new medicine or a washing machine, must go through a period of research and development – R&D – to make improvements to the design, ensure that it's safe, and that consumers will want to buy it. Simon Lyons runs a small design company, Version 22, in Loughborough, a town north of London. In 2016, the company launched a clever product called Nimble.

S: Nimble is a one-finger safety cutter. You put it on your finger tip; it's got a tiny blade at the tip, and you can use it to cut open boxes and parcels that come through the post, food packaging, product packaging.

P: Simon first had the idea when he was studying at university and entered a competition.

S: The brief was to look at these videos of elderly and disabled people describing problems they had at home, and to pick one of those problems and to design a solution. The one problem that kept coming up the most was people with arthritis in their hands, really struggling to open food packaging in the kitchen.

P: After he had the idea, Simon began the research and development process.

S: Starting the R&D process is quite simple – just a pen and paper. So, really rough sketches, coming up with as many different ideas as possible. I then try and make a very, very low-cost prototype. This was the first ever prototype I made of Nimble, which was made out of a finger of a kitchen glove cut off, some plastic from an A4 folder, and the tip of a knife blade.

P: Simon's design won the competition. The prize money allowed him to produce more advanced prototypes.

S: I started doing 3D-printed prototypes of lots of different designs before I got to a final design that I was happy with. One of the main design challenges I had with Nimble was designing it so it could be worn and used by as many people as possible, so having it as a one-size-fits-all design.

P: And how did Simon decide on the colour?

S: Yellow's a brilliant colour for people with visual impairments; and as Nimble's especially useful for people who are blind or partially sighted, yellow was the obvious choice then.

P: Once Simon was confident with the design, Nimble was ready for user-testing.

S: It was important to user-test Nimble to get as many perspectives on the product's usefulness, design and function as possible. I found users to test Nimble by attending a few trade shows, and this way I got about 150 people signed up. I sent out early prototypes of the product to these people, and they used them for about a month and gave me their feedback. Thankfully, the feedback we got from our testers was positive, which meant that we didn't have to make many changes to the design at all.

P: With the R&D stage successfully completed, Nimble was ready to be launched.

S: Nimble's been commercially available for about one and a half years, and it's been selling really well. We've shipped around 30,000 units to about 80 countries around the world so far.

P: So, what's the next product from Version 22?

S: So, the next product we've got coming out is something quite different. It's called Mobu, and it's a tiny little cable clip which will stop your earphones tangling in your pocket, and it works together with another product to keep your cables organised around your desk and around the house.

7.3.1

T = Thiago A = Azra

T: Whose training session are you in? I'm with Shaun.

A: Orla. I'm looking forward to hearing about this new expenses system.

T: Me, too. The current one is so complicated. And I hate having to keep my receipts when I'm travelling. It should be an app – something easy to use.

A: Exactly. Anyway, enjoy the training.

T: I just hope it's not too boring.

7.3.2

S = Shaun T = Thiago C = Caroline

S: What would your ideal expenses system look like?

T: An app?

S: You're in luck. Say hello to *Expenses 220*. A new app – really easy to use. No more Excel spreadsheets. No more paper receipts. Let me take you through the process. So, to create an expense report, you enter the expense item and date, choose the currency and enter the amount, take a photo of any receipts …

T: Are you following any of this?

S: Additional comments in the comment box, and then save it. So, you can go back to your claim as many times as you like … all you need to do is use the drop-down menu …

C: Sorry, Shaun. None of this is clear to me.

T: Yeah, I didn't follow everything either.

S: Come on, guys, it's not that difficult! OK … one more time. Use the drop-down menu to make changes – but make sure your settings are put to the relevant currency. Got it? Of course you have. Now, moving on to …

7.3.3

O = Orla A = Azra T = Thiago

O: OK, so you start by selecting 'Create an expense report'. Do you see that? Then, enter the expense item – like this: 'hotel bill'. After that, enter the date. Don't enter it manually, just select the 'calendar'; because it's the easiest thing to do. Any questions so far? The next step is to choose the type of expense – select this from the menu. You must do this because Accounts need the information for reporting reasons. So, in this case you're going to choose 'Business meal with client'. Right. Once you've done that, choose your currency, and enter the amount. The default setting is euros, so be careful if you need another currency. Then, save your claim and you're almost finished. The last step is to take a photo of your receipt and it'll be saved automatically with your electronic claim. When you have completed all the steps, press 'Submit', and you're done! Any questions?

A: When should we send in our claims?

O: By the end of the month. Oh, and also, the app will remember your data, and that will really save you time! Does everybody understand? Now, it's not perfect and there might be teething problems, but I think …

A: How did it go?

T: Don't ask. You?

A: Great. So I'm guessing you need a lesson from me on how this thing works?

T: I'll buy you a cappuccino! With chocolate!

A: It's a deal.

7.3.4

To explain a procedure clearly, follow these four steps.

Step 1: Speak clearly and make sure you sound interested, even if you're not, or you've already explained the same procedure a hundred times.

Step 2: Divide the stages of the procedure into small parts or pieces of information. It's a lot easier for someone to understand small pieces of information than the whole procedure all at once.

Step 3: Use words like 'first', 'second' and 'next' to order your explanation, just like Orla did. These will help the listener remember the different steps.

Step 4: Use examples where necessary and always

invite the other person to ask questions, to check they have understood or need more detail. There you go – a very simple and effective procedure.

8.1.1

P = Presenter M = Matías Alcalde
J = Juan Pablo Alvarez

P: Punta de Lobos in Chile is one of the best places to surf in South America. In the summer months, 5,000 visitors arrive every day at this popular surf and tourist destination. In recent years, developers have made plans for large construction projects along the cliffs. However, many in the community were not happy about this. The Punta de Lobos Foundation is an organisation created by local people to fight these plans. We spoke to Matías Alcalde, the Foundation's director about why they are against the building projects.

M: Uh, a lot of private projects, uh, real-estate projects – big ones – were wan–, wanted to be developed here, like where we're standing here, there will be uh, houses hanging on the cliffs, uh, four buildings, seven stories high like a surf resort, or not even a surf resort, but huge density of construction and people coming in here. We have a real threatening situation for such a special place like … like this one.

P: The Punta de Lobos Foundation works with other conservation groups, such as Save the Waves. Together, they want to stop private construction on the coast and to keep the cliffs open to the public. They also want to solve other problems caused by the large number of visitors.

M: It was a mess here, if you put a thousand or fifteen hundred cars here, uh, you … you can take an hour, hour and a half to just go a mile out back to the highway. And the second thing is that there were no bathrooms here.

P: The foundation is looking for solutions to these problems. They've already improved the traffic situation and installed eco-bathrooms for visitors. They've also put a fence along the cliff to protect it from visitors' feet. Some local businesses see conservation as important, too. This small hotel is by the beach at Punta de Lobos. Designed to have as little impact as possible on the area, it was built with local and recycled materials. I spoke to Juan Pablo Alvarez, the hotel manager.

J: It's only in the archi-, architecture, we don't want it to be uh, like a big hotel five-star resort, we have 12 rooms, we could have, like, 40, 50, but we wanted to offer something different, something special. This is a very sensitive and special place and spot for us, so we wanted to … to protect it.

P: Matías Alcalde sees Punta de Lobos as an important conservation project for the rest of Chile. It is not only about protecting one favourite surfing location in the country.

M: We're very eager that Punta de Lobos is successful, because it's the example in order to scale this project throughout Chile, uh, there's a need on conservation in Chile, we are a developing country, we're just getting started and we can learn from so many mistakes that, through Punta de Lobos, we can set the example for future developments along the coast.

8.3.1

S = Shaun T = Thiago D = Della

S: You're holding everyone up. The report is a week late, and I need it for tomorrow's meeting with the directors. So. What's the delay?

T: Figures. I, er, still need some figures from Accounts, you …

S: Why didn't you ask me to get the figures? Any time over the past seven days? Right, that's enough. I'm bringing in Jasmine.

T: I'm sorry, Jasmine. That's too bad. But … look on the bright side.
Della.

D: Yes?

T: You sent me a load of emails.

D: The reminder about your expenses claim, yes. I think I only sent two. The first, and a follow-up.

T: No, you sent at least three.
D: Ah. Yes. Three. Well, I was worried.
T: Well, it's quite stressful receiving all these emails. If I didn't respond, there's a reason.
D: Well, I'm sorry you feel that way, Thiago. This is our normal procedure. So …

8.3.2

O = Orla T = Thiago

O: Come in! Nervous? Don't worry. Let me explain the process. We'll start with the positive feedback, then we'll move on to some areas for improvement. Is that OK with you? So … you've been with us for six months. How do you feel it's gone so far?
T: I think I'm doing well. I don't think there have been any problems, but I'd be interested to hear what you think.
O: Well, in general, we're pleased with your progress.
T: OK. I'm glad to hear that.
O: You're enthusiastic and you work hard. You're great with technology – that's always a benefit. You're warm and in general you have good interpersonal skills. We saw how you tried to help Jasmine after the Miami conference issue – you were very supportive.
T: That's good to know, thanks.
O: And, of course, you have an excellent sense of humour. However, I have to point out some areas for development. It's important to give what we call 'corrective' feedback. To support you in your professional development.
T: Everyone can improve, right?
O: Exactly.

8.3.3

O = Orla T = Thiago

O: So, there are a couple of areas for improvement … like your time-management skills. Shaun mentioned that you were late finishing a report for him. And you've missed other deadlines. How do you feel about this aspect of your work?
T: I guess I am sometimes late.
O: You've been late a few times with your expenses claims, too. We think you could improve your admin skills more generally.
T: Yeah, OK, admin's not my strong point.
O: Well, OK, but the reason we're concerned is that it creates problems for other people. The company could miss a deadline with a client. So we really need you to respect all your deadlines from now on. And please remember to submit your expenses claims on time. Now we have the new app, there are no excuses.
T: Sure. Will do.
O: Now … about your relations with some of the older members of staff … Della in particular.
T: I get on well with Della.
O: Well, she thinks you're sometimes a little disrespectful.
T: Really? Are you sure she means me?
O: I think it's your tone of voice. So, it's not what you say, it's how you say it. You can sound a bit impolite, even aggressive at times. What do you think? Would that be a fair assessment?
T: Well, I try to respect everyone …
O: We're worried because the way you communicate could have a negative impact on the team and also on relations with our clients.
T: I never meant to upset anyone.

O: I can see that. But I would like you to pay more attention to this in the future.
T: Yes, yes, of course.
O: And we really love your enthusiasm. So, more of that, please. Do you have any questions about the feedback?
T: No, I don't think so. I appreciate your comments, thanks.
O: OK. So, in summary, we have agreed your goals.

8.3.4

In our professional lives, we all have to receive corrective feedback from time to time and some of us might also have to give corrective feedback. So here's some advice.

First of all, how to give corrective feedback. Here, you can follow a simple model. Prepare the person before giving the feedback and then ask for their agreement. Say something like, 'We need to discuss some areas for improvement. Is that OK with you?' As you give the feedback, give clarification or examples where possible. Then end by inviting the person to assess their own performance. Phrases such as 'Would that be a fair assessment?' encourage the person to remain positive about the feedback.

Secondly, receiving corrective feedback. One of the most difficult things is to stay positive and diplomatic if someone is giving you feedback. 'Your feedback is very useful, thanks.' is a good expression to use. Or when you want to apologise for negative behaviour, say, 'Yes, I accept that is sometimes a problem for me.'

Finally, I would always suggest you thank the person for their feedback. That way you end on a positive note.

1.01

A: Welcome, Alicia. Thanks so much for taking the time to talk with us on *World of Work* today.
B: It's my pleasure, Marek. Thanks so much for inviting me on the show. It's exciting!
A: I'd like to start by asking this: What does an Events Manager do?
B: I manage events …
A: Oh, right – OK, so the job title says it all: Events Manager.
B: Right. So what that means is that I help people plan events: parties, conferences, corporate hospitality events – that kind of thing.
A: What about weddings?
B: No – not at all. Weddings are *harder* than business lunches and are usually done by people who only plan weddings.
A: OK, so who are your clients?
B: I'd say about ninety percent of my work involves businesses – planning events for corporate clients. I sometimes do parties for individual people, but not very often.
A: OK. So when you plan an event, what do you do? Where do you start?
B: First, I have to find out what the client wants. That means finding out what type of event it is, and also when they want to have it. Because usually, an event is for some reason, like a grand opening, or welcoming new employees or something – so the timing is usually important.
A: OK, I see. And what about money?
B: Yes, of course. We have to talk about budget at the first meeting, because I have to think about the cost for every decision I make. I try to find the best location for each event. I can't choose the most expensive hotel in town for an event for someone with a small budget. For a cheap event, we choose the least expensive venue possible. So we have to choose a venue – a location – carefully.
A: Sure. And for you, are some venues better than others?
B: Definitely. Planning an event outdoors is always the biggest challenge.
A: Because …
B: Because of the weather. You can't control that!
A: Sure, of course. So after you've talked about schedule, budget and venue, what then?
B: They usually want me to think of something special – you know, to come up with an original idea.
A: Like …
B: Well, I did a tenth anniversary party for a software company, and we did a circus theme.
A: A circus theme?
B: Yeah – we had clowns, a guy who did magic – and the location was actually a big tent – like a circus tent – in a park. We had about five hundred people there – five hundred guests. It was amazing. Everyone had a great time.
A: Was the circus event more difficult than your usual events?
B: No, not really. We usually have some kind of entertainment, but we also have to arrange food, tables and chairs …
A: Wow.
B: I usually have to organise a sound system for the speeches and music …
A: So there are a lot of details.
B: It's all details!
A: Well, that's a good introduction to my next question.
B: OK.
A: What skills are necessary for an Events Manager?
B: Well, we've already talked about attention to detail.
A: What else?
B: Organisation – the ability to organise is super important.
A: Organising what?
B: Everything: Schedules, budgets, food orders, teams of people … . Getting the right staff for an event is really important – you need the right people.
A: Ah, yes, people. Do you need people skills?

B: For sure. You really need to get on with people – you need to manage people well, because the job is all about people – about making people happy. My top priority is client satisfaction.
A: And for you, are any of the skills more important – or less important?
B: Honestly, I don't think so. You need all of them. If you love people but you can't organise, then you can't do this job. If you pay attention to detail but can't manage a budget – forget it!
A: OK, well, that makes sense. This is really useful for our listeners, thanks Alicia. Please stay with us. We're going to take a short break. When we come back, we'll be asking Alicia about …

1.02 L = Laura J = Jakob

L: How are you doing, Jakob?
J: OK so far, thanks. I'm looking forward to meeting everyone.
L: Great. So, first, I'll explain the schedule for the day.
J: Sure.
L: So, we'll start with the induction briefing, where you learn about the company. And then you can meet the team. The health and safety training with the other interns is at 10.45. That gives us plenty of time.
J: How many other interns are there?
L: Five. They're mostly from abroad, so it's a really international group this year.
J: Right, OK.
L: And this afternoon you can set up your email account. Our IT technician, Sue, has created a username for you, and temporary login details are on your desk. Sue's really helpful. Just call her if you have any problems.

1.03 S = Sue J = Jakob

S: IT help desk. Sue speaking.
J: Hello, Sue. This is Jakob Davis. I'm …
S: … one of the new interns. Hi, Jakob. How can I help you?
J: I'm having problems with the IT.
S: Ah, what kind of problems?
J: I can't connect to the intranet. I don't know how to log on.
S: It should be quite simple. You need to use your login details.
J: I tried my username and password, but …
S: Can you try logging on again?
J: Er, just a minute … no, it's not working.
S: OK, no problem. Can I just check your username?
J: Intern82.
S: Are you sure? 82 or 32?
J: Er, it looks like 82.
S: Sorry, it's my writing, it's difficult to read. Try 'intern32'.
J: Ah, that works, thanks. The other thing … I need to get a company email address. How do I set up my email account?
S: I'll set that up for you. Can you just remind me of your family name?
J: Davis.
S: D-A-V-I-S?
J: That's right. And Jakob is J-A-K-O-B.
S: J-A-K-O-B, thanks. So your email address will be Jakob dot Davis at htm.com. Give me a few minutes and I'll call you back. What's your extension number?
J: Er … sorry, Sue, I'm having trouble finding my extension number. I was going to ask my colleague for help, but she's just gone into a meeting and …
S: That's OK. I can help you with that. Just a minute, er, – here we are, Jakob Davis – extension 5182.
J: 5-1-8-2 – got it.
S: I'll call you back in a few minutes to confirm your email address.

2.01

A: Is there enough space in this room for the meeting?
B: Yes, but I think there are too many chairs.
A: You're right! I'll move some next door.
B: And it's too hot in here, isn't it? Let's open the windows.

A: Oh no! There's too much noise from outside. I'll put the air conditioning on.
B: OK! I see there are not enough glasses. I'll get some more from the kitchen.
A: Is there enough time to make some photocopies?
B: Yes! We have lots of time. It's still too early for people to arrive.

2.02 J = Josh S = Samia

J: Hey, it's Josh, how are you?
S: Fine, thanks, Josh. How are you?
J: Good, thanks. Listen, did you get the agenda for this afternoon?
S: Yes. You didn't get it?
J: No.
S: I'll send it to you. And the minutes from the last meeting. Got them?
J: Thanks. Oh, no, Don's chairing again; that means it'll go on and on.
S: Yes, probably. So you're going to present the results of your market survey?
J: Which item is that? Oh, yes, four. It's quite interesting actually.
S: Really? And did you prepare anything for Item 3?
J: The financial report? No, that was an action point from the last meeting for Mike. Anyway, what's Item 5 all about? Micro-kitchen? What's that?
S: Dierdre wants to set up an office kitchen. I think it's quite a good idea.
J: I see you're organising the office party again this year, Samia!
S: Yes, that's me, Item 6 – it's the only item I'm interested in.
J: No surprises. What are you planning?
S: Ah, you'll have to wait and see.
J: Item 8 – Close – that's *my* favourite item … Do you think we'll leave on time, though, with Don in the chair?

2.03 Don = Don J = Josh E = Ellen S = Samia
H = Harry De = Deirdre

Don: Everyone ready?
J: Samia will be a little late. She's on another call.
Don: OK, but I'd like to start on time; it's a full agenda today. Can you tell her what we said, Josh?
J: Sure.
Don: Right, so let's start. Nice to see everyone and welcome back to Ellen.
E: Thanks, it's lovely to see everyone.
Don: So, one reason for meeting is to introduce you all to Harry. He started on Monday and he'll be helping us with our finances.
All: Hello, Harry. / How are you doing? / Nice to meet you.
Don: Does everyone have a copy of the agenda? Does anyone …
S: Hi, everyone. Sorry I'm late.
Don: Samia, hello. Take a seat. The main aim today is to catch up before the holidays. Does anyone want to add anything to the agenda?
All: Not really. / No. / I'm fine.
Don: We have AOB if anything comes up. Harry, can I ask you to be time-keeper?
H: OK.
Don: And could I have a volunteer to take the minutes? Josh, Ellen?
E: OK, sure. I can do that.
Don: Thanks for agreeing. I know it's a busy time. So, let's look at Item 1, Matters Arising from the last …
E: Sorry, can we just go back to Item 2? What was the decision? I didn't quite understand it …
Don: So, moving on to Item 5: this is Deirdre's point, I think. Harry, how are we doing for time?
H: We're on time for the moment.
Don: Great. Deirdre, over to you.
De: Thanks. I'd like to talk about the micro-kitchen we agreed on at the last meeting.
J: Did we?
De: Ah, yes.
S: … And *you* even agreed to help set it up.
J: Did I? Oh, OK, sorry.
De: Right. The reason I want to discuss this is to agree on a budget. I found some possible suppliers, but of course we need to get some quotes.

H: What did you include in the budget?
De: It seems contractors for micro-kitchens supply everything. I think a maximum of 500 pounds a month is reasonable. What do you all think?

3.01
1
A: We need something for dinner.
B: OK, I'll get some chicken on my way home this evening.
2
A: Where shall we get the presents for the family?
B: I just want to buy everything in one place. You know I hate going around different shops all day.
3
A: You know it'll be Noah's birthday soon. He's five on Thursday.
B: That's right! Let's get him some children's stories for his birthday.
4
A: Are you all right? You look a bit tired.
B: Yeah, I've got a terrible headache. I need to get something for it.
5
A: I should get something to wear for that job interview but I haven't got much money.
B: Try Zara or H&M. Their prices are reasonable.
6
A: Where did you say we're going again?
B: Bluewater. It says on the website that there are 330 stores and 40 cafés under one roof.
7
A: I love that fresh bread you bought in that new place. Let's go there again.
B: Yes, and they have a really nice selection of cakes as well.

3.02
Extract 1
A: Hello, Tony. Did you have a nice holiday?
B: Yes, we had a great time, thanks Sonia.
A: Where did you go? I can't remember if you told me.
B: Istanbul.
A: Ah, yes, that's right.
B: You see my wife went to a conference there last week. And I decided to go with her. Well, I didn't go to the conference. I spent the day visiting the city when Barbara was at work. Then we had dinner together in the evenings. She was working Monday to Friday but she wasn't working at the weekend. We went to the Grand Bazaar on Saturday.
A: Oh, the Grand Bazaar, I heard it's fabulous.
B: Yes, it is. Did you know it's one of the largest and oldest covered markets in the world?
A: Really?
B: Yeah, there are, I don't know, thousands of shops. I mean, we were browsing for hours but we weren't looking for anything specific and we didn't see half of it.
A: Did you buy anything in the end?
B: Yeah, a Turkish carpet. You know, the carpet seller served us tea when we sat down, and then we negotiated the price.
A: Sounds interesting. Did you get a bargain?
B: No, I don't think so, but we really liked the carpet and the experience was fun.
Extract 2
C: Hey! Did I tell you I went to that new shopping mall yesterday?
D: No, what's it like?
C: It's cool. One clothes store had magic mirrors.
D: Magic mirrors? What are those?
C: It's basically augmented reality. So I could try on different styles and colours without putting on clothes. It uses special computer software.
D: Like a video game.
C: Yeah! You know how I really don't enjoy shopping for clothes. The stores are always busy and there are long queues for the changing rooms. Then you spend hours trying on clothes. Then more long queues to pay the cashier. But with a magic mirror I can try different clothes and colours in less time, which makes shopping a bit easier.

D: So, what did you get?
C: Well, there were a couple of nice suits, but I didn't know which style or colour I liked best, so I didn't buy anything. But I have the store's app on my phone.
D: What's that for?
C: Well, when I left the store, they sent me a list of the clothes I tried on to my phone, and I can order online when I decide. Have a look and help me choose.
D: Ah, oh is that the time? What was I thinking? I was talking to Martin earlier and I agreed to help him with something. I'll see you later.
Extract 3
F: Hello, Rafa! Sorry! Did I interrupt you? Were you eating?
E: No, no, I was having a coffee.
F: So, how are you?
E: Very well, and you? How's it going in Shanghai?
F: Not bad, not bad.
E: How's your Chinese?
F: Don't ask! I didn't speak much Chinese when I arrived here a month ago and I don't speak any more today. It's fine in the office because everyone speaks English. But shopping is more of a problem.
E: What about ordering in restaurants?
F: Oh, that's easy. Lots of restaurants here in China have picture menus. They're great!
E: So you can see exactly what you're ordering?
F: That's right! Anyway, the other day I heard about these new automated convenience stores.
E: Automated? You mean with robots? Artificial intelligence?
F: No, not exactly, just self-service with no human staff. I was walking to the metro yesterday when I saw one. When I went in, I chose my food, paid and didn't interact with a single person.
E: How does it work?
F: First you give the company all your personal details. Then you can use your phone to enter the shop with a QR code and you scan the bar codes on products and pay with your phone, too. You also scan another QR code to leave the store.
E: Wow! But don't some people leave without paying?
F: I don't think so. There are security cameras and an alarm system. They're watching you and they have your personal details!
E: Ah! I see. So, it sounds like a good option for you.
F: Well, yes and no. There's not much fresh food, it's mostly snacks and instant noodles. I was looking for something healthy. And my soft drink was warm but I couldn't return it or complain to anyone. I'm not sure I like the future of shopping.

3.03
1 Did you have a nice holiday?
2 ...the carpet seller served us tea when we sat down ...
3 I could try on different styles and colours ...
4 when I left the store, they sent me a list ...
5 I didn't speak much Chinese when I arrived here ...
6 when I went in, I chose my food ...

3.04   T = Tony   S = Sonia
T: So, how was work when I was away last week?
S: We were very busy without you. We got another big order from Piotr.
T: Again? Did he pay us for the last order?
S: No, not the full amount. I wrote him an email about it when I received the new order. He rang me immediately and said he'll pay us this week.
T: That sounds good. And did you meet the new Marketing Manager when she started last week?
S: No, I didn't see her. She definitely didn't come to the office. In fact, I think she starts this week.
T: Yes, you're right! I thought it was last week.

3.05   C = Carl   I = Inés
C: Right, morning, everyone. Thanks for coming in. OK, let's get started. This is Inés from customer research ...
I: Hello, everyone.

C: Inés has joined us today to help me present the results of last month's customer service survey. As you know, improving customer service is one of our main objectives this year. Now, as you can see, this was a three-stage survey. So, first of all, I'd like to start off by talking about stage one, the customer satisfaction ratings. Secondly, I'll go on to talk about the in-store interviews. And then I'll hand you over to Inés to talk about stage three, the focus group results. Finally, there'll be time for questions at the end. OK? So, let's jump right in. Have a look at this. This is the customer feedback station we now have in all our megastores. Customers simply press the button that shows how satisfied they were with our service. Was it great, good, not good or bad? Then we process their feedback. Here's a full breakdown of the figures by region and store.

3.06
OK, now let's move on to the in-store interviews. First of all, why did we do them? Well, when we sent our researchers into the stores, they noticed that a lot of people weren't using the customer feedback stations at all. So, obviously, these people do not show up in our customer satisfaction figures. Fortunately, plenty of people *were* leaving positive feedback. But *why* were they positive? And how many other people were they telling about us? Again, we had no data for this. So we organised a team of interviewers to stop customers as they were coming out of the store, and this is what we found. First, the good news. Every customer who rated our service as 'great' told us they regularly recommend us to others – on average, *five* other people, which is very encouraging. But, now, the bad news. For every customer who rated our service as 'bad', and explained the reasons, eleven other unhappy customers were not leaving any feedback. They were just going home unhappy. And, frankly, that's a disaster! OK, let's look at the interview data in more detail.

3.07   C = Carl   I = Inés
C: So, just to recap on the main points so far. The in-store interviews now give us much more accurate figures for customer satisfaction. But they still don't tell us what we can do to improve our service. OK, that brings me to the end of *my* part of the presentation this morning. Inés, over to you.
I: Thanks, Carl. Well, now, let me try to answer Carl's question. As you know, last month we set up fifteen focus groups in different cities around the country. And one thing we did was ask them to text us ten adjectives to describe the ideal mobile phone Sales Adviser. Here's a diagram of the results. Now, to help them choose a mobile phone, we were expecting people to want a 'knowledgeable' and 'informative' Sales Adviser. But, as you can see, mostly what they wanted was someone 'helpful' and 'friendly'. And that's where some of our sales teams are failing.
So, just to sum up: Too many of our customers are currently leaving our stores unhappy with the service they received. This is not because our Sales Advisers don't have complete product knowledge. They do. It's because they simply don't have the people skills they need to give helpful and friendly service. And that's why I'm recommending that we now make people skills training a priority. OK, let's wrap it up there. Any questions? Yes, Hugo ...

4.01
1
I thought it was a good idea to go part-time at the hospital when my daughter was born, but it's hard work. It sounds nice to say I only work three days a week, but nurses work long hours and a nine-hour shift usually turns into 11 or 12 hours. That's more than most people who work in full-time jobs. And it isn't always possible to take my breaks if there is a lot of work to do.

2

I'm studying for my degree in tourism management and I work for an agency in my free time. Doing temporary jobs is a good way to earn money at weekends and in the holidays. It's the time when hotels need extra staff. If there's a big event or conference on in the city, I miss classes for a few days. But next week I'm starting as an intern with a big hotel chain so I'm leaving the agency work. I know the hotel is a good employer and I hope they'll offer me a permanent contract after my internship.

3

I'm a self-employed driver and I get my work from a taxi service app on my phone. I don't have a fixed schedule and I decide my own working hours. I can work as much or as little as I want and I'm paid for each job I do. But after a ten-hour shift, drivers have to take a six-hour break, by law. But my working day is typically five or six hours. I don't want to work more than that, you see, I retired last year, and this is just some extra money on top of my pension.

4.02

A: Have you ever bought a good business book?
B: No, I've never bought one but I've read a few from the library and I've seen some business experts on YouTube, like Daniel Kahneman. He's written a lot about how we make decisions and how we don't think as clearly as we believe we do.
A: Ah, yes! What was the title of that famous book of his?
B: *Thinking, Fast and Slow*. You know, he's a psychologist but he's won a Nobel Prize for Economics.
A: Really? That's interesting. I've never seen him talk. You know, I've started that book several times, but I've never finished it.

4.03 L = Lou   I = Ian

L: Hello, Ian?
I: Speaking
L: Hi, Ian, it's Lou.
I: Hi, Lou. What's up?
L: Listen, sorry to bother you. I'm calling about our meeting on Wednesday the 17th.
I: Uh-huh.
L: I'm afraid Sally can't make it.
I: Ah.
L: Yes, it's my fault. I forgot she's in Vienna all week. Do you mind if we fix another time to meet?
I: Sure. Let me just check my schedule.
L: Thanks. I appreciate it.
I: Do you want to postpone the meeting till the following week?
L: Actually, no. That's Berlin Expo week.
I: Oh, right, of course.
L: So, I was wondering if we could bring it forward. How about the week beginning the 8th?
I: Wait a minute, that's next week, isn't it?
L: Yeah, sorry. I know it's a bit short notice. That's why I'm calling.
I: Well, er, let's see. I'm free on Wednesday morning. That's the 10th. Any good?
L: Erm, could we make it the afternoon?
I: Mm, no good, I'm afraid. I've got a staff training session.
L: Well, … How about Thursday the 11th? After lunch?
I: I'm busy all day Thursday. Friday might be OK … How does the afternoon suit you?
L: Friday the 12th? No, Friday's out for me, I'm afraid. Oh, dear, I'm really sorry about this.
I: No problem. Look, let me see if I can move the training session and call you back.
L: Good idea.
I: OK, leave it with me. Talk to you later.
L: Thanks, Ian, bye.
I: Bye, now.

4.04 I = Ian   J = James

I: Hello, James. It's Ian.
J: Oh, hi, Ian. What can I do for you?
I: It's about our training session next Wednesday.
J: Ah, yes, …

I: Change of plan. We need to change the training to another day, I'm afraid. I've got an important meeting with Lou and Sally from head office and it's the only time we're all free.
J: Oh. Well, it's a bit last minute, but, OK, what day were you thinking?
I: Well, why don't we just move the training to the morning? I think that's the easiest.
J: Wednesday morning? Ah, I think I've scheduled the staff performance reviews for then … Sorry, I forgot to tell you … yeah. Performance reviews: Wednesday morning.
I: Well, move those to Friday!
J: Friday. All right. Which is better for you: morning or afternoon?
I: Erm, morning's better. Oh, wait a minute. I've got a meeting with the IT team on Friday morning. OK, that can wait. Let's postpone it till the afternoon!
J: Postpone … IT meeting … OK, so that's training on Wednesday the 10th in the morning.
I: Uh-huh.
J: Performance reviews on the Friday morning, the 12th.
I: Fine.
J: IT meeting in the afternoon. And that leaves you free on Wednesday afternoon for your meeting with the people from head office.
I: Brilliant! I knew there was a reason I made you my assistant. Thanks a lot, James.

4.05

L = Lou   I = Ian

L: Good afternoon, Lou Klein speaking.
I: Hi, Lou. It's Ian again.
L: Hi, there. Any luck changing your schedule?
I: Yes. We're all set for the 10th.
L: Fantastic. So, just to confirm – we're meeting in your office on Wednesday the 10th at, erm, how about 3 p.m.?
I: Sounds good.
L: That gives you time to set up for the presentation before we arrive. Oh, and I invited Tom Banks to join us. He works for Sally in research. So, there'll be four of us in all.
I: Fine. Hm, with four of us I'd better ask James to book a meeting room. And how about something to eat afterwards? There's a nice restaurant just near the office. I could book us a table if you like.
L: Perfect. Thanks a lot for being so flexible, Ian.
I: No problem. See you on Wednesday.

5.01 E = Ella   D = Dan   I1 = Interviewee 1
I2 = Interviewee 2   I3 = Interviewee 3
I4 = Interviewee 4   I5 = Interviewee 5
I5 = Interviewee 6

E: Hello, listeners, and welcome to *It all adds up!*, the programme that talks about money. I'm your host, Ella Leeson. Today we're going to start with more tips for saving money. Dan Parks went into the street to talk to people and get ideas for saving money on living expenses. Dan?
D: Thanks, Ella. I went to London's Oxford Street earlier this week and asked people how they spend less and save more. Here's what they said.
I1: Make your own food, so you don't spend money on lunch.. If you take your lunch to work, you will save hundreds a year.
I2: I don't have a car now – I sold it! You will save thousands – and become healthier – if you cycle to work instead of driving.
I3: Stop using your credit card. Pay it off. Only spend money you already have – don't borrow it.
I4: Save money every month for emergencies. Then, when you have a problem with your house, or you need a new car, the money will be ready.
I5: Don't buy a new car. If you buy a car that's just one year old instead of a new one, you will save a lot of money.
I6: Go to the cinema on a discount day. My local cinema is cheaper on Mondays. There are special prices online.
D: Smart people out there in Oxford Street, Ella.
E: You're right. Lots of great ideas for spending less and saving more.

D: Right – a little bit here, a little bit there. It all adds up!
E: It all adds up! So, Dan, what can consumers expect in the next few months?
D: Well, the first thing we're looking at is a possible small increase in interest rates.
E: But that's not official yet, is it?
D: No, the government hasn't confirmed it, but it looks very likely.
E: What will that mean for consumers?
D: If interest rates increase, borrowing will go down. People borrow more when loans are cheaper.
E: So if people are thinking of borrowing … ?
D: They should do it now, before interest rates go up.
E: OK. Anything else?
D: Housing costs will go up – people who own a home will pay a little more each month.
E: So, not great news.
D: No, but it is good news for people with savings. If banks raise the interest rate on savings, savers will earn more. That means it's a great time to start saving, or to increase saving.
E: It all adds up!
D: It all adds up, Ella!
E: Anything else?
D: Just one more thing before I go. International exchange rates. We're watching China closely, because its economy is really strong at the moment. Electronics imports here will be more expensive if China's currency becomes stronger.
E: OK, so if you're thinking of getting a new TV …
D: … now may be the time. We'll probably start to see prices go up in a couple of months.
E: Thanks, Dan. Some great tips!
D: Thank you, Ella.
E: That's it on money saving for this show, but now we're going to move on to …

5.02 L = Liz   M1 = Male 1   F1 = Female 1
M2 = Male 2   F2 = Female 2

L: Good morning! Could I just ask you to raise your hand if you have children in their late teens or early twenties? You're probably the ones with the largest debts. Hm, quite a lot of you. And that's not really surprising because, like me, you're the right age. Most of us in this room belong to what we call Generation X – the generation born somewhere between the mid-nineteen-sixties and the late seventies. Of course, the younger ones among us, born between the early eighties and the mid-nineties, are Generation Y, also known as the Millennials. You still have teenage kids to look forward to! And it's teenagers and young adults that I'm here to talk about today. Born between the mid-nineties and the early twenty-tens, we call them Generation Z. They are already about a quarter of the total population and they will soon be our biggest customers. Now, when I say Generation Z, what words and phrases can you think of to describe them? Anybody? Yeah … ?
M1: Live for today!
L: Uh-huh.
F1: Always online.
L: Right.
M2: Don't want to work!
F2: No idea about money!
L: Oh, dear. We're getting a bit negative, aren't we? Well, I think some of the research I'm going to share with you this morning may just surprise you.

5.03

Now, just a moment ago some of you suggested that Generation Z 'lives for today', 'doesn't want to work' and 'has no idea about money'. So let's see if that's true. Have a look at this chart, which shows the results of our survey of the financial habits of people aged sixteen to twenty-one. As you can see, roughly three-quarters of them are already earning their own money through some kind of full- or part-time employment. To put that in context, that's almost the same as the figure for Generation Y. So that shows Generation Z is certainly not afraid of work! You can also see that nearly two-thirds of them have their own savings account. In fact, around one in five has had one since the age of ten. But perhaps the most surprising thing is that over one in ten of them are already saving for retirement! A retirement which may be over fifty years away! Another interesting thing is that just under three out of every ten are strongly against any kind of debt – especially, college debt. Let's not forget that college debt is currently over one and a half trillion dollars in this country and has been a major financial problem for Generations X and Y. The key takeaway here is that Generation Z likes to save, but doesn't like to borrow. Obviously, that's good news for those of you running savings accounts. But maybe not such good news for those of you working in the loans department!

5.04

So, how do we market personal banking services to Generation Z? Well, you were right about one thing. Generation Zers *are* 'always online'. On average, they are currently spending over ten and a half hours a day working or playing with digital content. To give you an idea of just how much that is, multiply it by the total number of Generation Zers in the USA, and it comes to around a billion hours of online activity every day! That's enough time to watch every movie ever made – one thousand times! But here's the really surprising thing. Our studies show that more than half of Generation Z say they actually prefer face-to-face communication. That's over forty million people who want to talk to us in person! So, in summary, if we want to attract this new generation of customers, we need to make sure we connect with them on a personal level. And, in terms of selling banking services, this clearly means that we need to be doing a lot more than just social media marketing.

6.01 A = Anatol M = Michael E = Erin

A: Right, I'll get straight to the point. New graduate applications are almost 30 percent down this year. And, as a result, we're not recruiting the number of management trainees we need. Now, we have a good reputation. We pay well. And we offer excellent benefits. So what's happening?
M: It's a new generation, Anatol. Graduates today just don't want to work for big organisations like us anymore. Besides, most twenty-one-year-olds simply aren't interested in insurance as a career.
E: To be honest, it's also a question of the work culture. College-leavers these days prefer the workplace to be informal and ... well, *fun*!
A: *Fun?* We're an insurance company, Erin. What do you want? Music on the TV and pinball machines in reception?

6.02 A = Anatol M = Michael E = Erin

A: OK, so, let's get some ideas written up on the flipchart. 'How ... do... we ... attract ... new ... graduates?' How about attending more careers fairs?
M: No, that's a complete waste of time. Students can find out all they need to know about us online.
A: More talks at universities, then?
E: No, there's no point. Michael's right. Job-hunting's all online these days. Now, a video promotion on YouTube – that might be more effective.
M: We tried that before and it didn't work.
A: We're not doing very well, are we? Erm, let's look at what more we can offer as an employer. Erin, any ideas?
E: Well, most of the people I interview tell me they expect training.
M: Yeah, but we're already doing that.
E: *Real* training, Michael. Like sponsored diplomas, MBAs.
M: You want us to pay for *trainees* to do *MBAs*? We don't have the budget for that!
A: OK, look, there's far too much negativity in this meeting. I suggest we go away and think about this a bit more and meet again in a couple of days.

6.03 A = Anatol E = Erin M = Michael

A: So, Erin. Let's start with you.
E: OK, well, we all agree that our biggest problem is getting new graduates to think about insurance as a career. So I suggest we introduce twelve-month internships. Believe it or not, it's actually harder to get a paid internship these days than to get a job! I think we'll find it easier to recruit students *before* they graduate rather than after.
A: Mm. I really like that idea. And twelve months is long enough for them to learn something about our business.
E: Exactly. And while we're on the subject of learning the business, why don't we provide personal coaching as well? Teach them the professional skills they don't learn at university.
A: Good idea. Of course, there *is* the problem of cost. What can we do about that?
E: Couldn't we just spend more on student internships and less on graduate recruitment?
A: You know, that might not be such a bad idea. Now, Michael, you're looking at how we market ourselves to graduates. What have you got so far?
M: Yes, well, the first thing is: we need to go mobile with our advertising. Most students prefer to use their mobiles to look for work. So, this is the perfect way to reach them as soon as we have job opportunities.
E: What a good idea! And doing that means we could also make job offers a lot faster – direct to the applicant's phone. Did you know that at the moment, a quarter of the people we offer work to have already taken another job by the time we contact them?
A: Really? But that's terrible ...
E: OK, as we know, another difficulty we have is our size. So the question is: how do we make our large company feel like a small one? And I think the answer is to put our trainees into smaller project teams.
A: Actually, I think that's a great idea. And if we do that, perhaps we can also create a bit of friendly competition between teams. Might make things more ... *fun*. As you say, Erin, that seems to be important nowadays.
M: Mm, it's a nice idea, Erin. I'm just wondering about the amount of reorganisation it'll need. How can we manage that?
A: Mm, good point. Let's see what the board thinks.

7.01 S = Sam A = Andrea

S: ... So, on behalf of the team, I'd like to thank Andrea for such an informative presentation. Thank you very much, Andrea, it was really interesting – I learnt a lot.
A: No problem.
S: Now, we've got about fifteen minutes for questions, but before we go into the question and answer session, I just want to mention a few ground rules. Firstly, could you just give your name and division before you speak, so that we know who you are? Can you keep your questions brief, so everyone has the chance to speak? Also, please help your colleagues by speaking slowly and clearly ... and loudly enough. And lastly, don't forget to use the mute button when you're not speaking, to stop any background noise.
All: Yeah, no worries. / Sure, yeah, no problem. / Yeah.

7.02 S = Sam D = Donna P = Paul K = Karl L = Lena

S: Right, is everyone ready? Donna, have you switched on your webcam? I can't see you. Your screen is blank.
D: Sorry, my camera doesn't work properly. I'll switch it off anyway because it slows down my internet connection.
S: Oh, OK. That's fine.
P: Hello ... can, can I ask ... easily, and ... so that's a problem if ...
S: Paul, Paul? Paul, you keep cutting out.
P: Sorry, what ... say ... Sam? ... hear you ... well.
S: You keep cutting out, Paul.
P: OK, ju ... moment. Is that ... better now? ... I ... can hear, hear ... you.

S: We still can't hear you properly. The connection is bad. Would you mind hanging up and I'll call you back. Hi, Paul, are you there?
P: Yes. Can everyone hear me now?
All: Yes. / Loud and clear.
K: Karl here, HR. Sam, did everyone receive my notes from earlier?
L: Karl, I'm afraid we can't hear you very well, either. You're very quiet. Could you move closer to the microphone?
K: OK ... Is that better?
S: Not really. If you can just check your volume settings, please?
K: Sure. Any better?
S: Yes, but now there's a bit of an echo. Can you move your mobile phone away from your computer?
K: There we go, how about that?
S: Much better, thanks. I got your notes, by the way, so thanks for those. If we ... Sorry, is someone in a café? I can hear a lot of background noise.
L: Sorry, it's me: R&D. I'm not in the office today.
S: No worries. Would you mind using the mute button? I can almost smell the coffee.
L: Yeah, of course. Sorry, everyone.
S: That's better, thanks. Now, just one last request before we start. I know it's getting close to lunchtime for some of you. So if anyone is hungry, please feel free to eat your lunch as we speak, but just remember to use that mute button!

7.03

Good morning everyone, and thank you for coming. Firstly today, I'm going to answer the question you're all asking – why did we decide to make changes to the product packaging? Now, there are three main reasons for this.
One, we have received a lot of negative customer feedback about the packaging this year. Customers say it looks very old-fashioned and many have suggested they'd like it to be more colourful.
Two, as a result of the issues customers identified, we've seen falling sales over the last twelve months. And finally – three – we feel we should be using more eco-friendly packaging.
So, what are we going to do? Well, we've already decided to change the colour and to make use of recycled materials for the packaging. And we plan to do all this in just three months.
But, before we look at the details of the schedule, let's look more closely at the colours we're thinking of. Obviously we're keeping the yellow, but we are making it much brighter and we are thinking of adding one or two other colours, such as green or orange, which you can see here on this slide.
So, when exactly is all this going to happen? The first month, we're going to decide on the colours and the designers will produce the final design. We'll also choose the new material. In the second month, we will set up and start production. There'll be a press release, and we'll let everyone know about the launch date. And finally, in three months, we will launch our rebranded product line.

7.04

Today I'm going to talk about redesigning our best-selling product, the walking frame for people who need support when walking. Some people might ask: why change it if it's selling well? Well, everything can be improved so, firstly, I'll talk about the reasons for doing this. New developments in technology have made it possible to make a product which is much lighter and stronger than before. Secondly, new competitors are coming into the market and will begin to take some of our market share if we don't do as well as them.
Now, let's look at the most important parts of this new design. As I said before, the new design means that is much lighter and stronger. This makes it much easier for older people or weaker people to move about. They don't have to pick up a heavy object. Also, there's a new non-slip material on the bottom of the frame, which makes it much harder to push over than others on the market.

Finally, I want to look more closely at the sales forecast for next year. As you can see from this graph, we expect sales to increase rapidly once the new product is on sale. In the first quarter we are expecting sales of around £1.5 million, doubling to nearly 3 million by the end of the second quarter. The next-quarter sales may slow down a bit as they always do in summer, but we expect them to reach £4 million by the end of the year.

8.01 M = Matt K = Kyra

M: The time now is ten to eight and I'm sure many of our listeners sitting in traffic jams on their way to work will be interested in what my guest today has to say. Kyra Sharma, university lecturer and consultant in public transport, is here with me to talk about her new book, *Travel Chaos*. Kyra, welcome.
K: Thank you, Matt.
M: Kyra, you say in your book that people shouldn't drive in cities. So, why is the car the worst way to get around?
K: Well, a car feels convenient for the person driving, but it's not the most efficient use of space. In busy urban areas there isn't enough space for everyone to drive around. Cars cause massive congestion on city streets, which causes serious air pollution as well as noise problems.
M: You talk in your book about the impact of technology and the transport solutions it offers. For example, electric vehicles, driverless cars, car sharing and software apps to help us get around.
K: Yes, there's a lot of fantastic technology now: electric cars help us to reduce air pollution, satellite navigation helps us to find quicker routes, and software apps allow us to share cars with people doing similar journeys. It's great that technology is giving us more efficient ways to travel and power our vehicles, but these things aren't enough. Our city streets are too crowded for the number of cars we have these days. There is not enough space. We have to reduce traffic on the roads – driverless technology, satellite navigation and electric cars don't solve that problem.
M: Doesn't car sharing reduce car use?
K: If it's real ridesharing with several people sharing a car, not one person hiring a car, then yes, but it's much better to 'rideshare' on buses and trains.
M: So, what is the solution? How should governments plan urban mobility?
K: Well, they should simply spend more on public transport. I mean mass transit systems including urban trains, underground or metro, buses and trams. It's the most efficient way to get around in a big city. As I explain in the book, there are excellent examples in developed countries in Asia: for example, in Hong Kong, Korea and Singapore. Most European cities are now using cleaner energy in public transport, and finding ways to reduce the number of cars on the roads. For example, London has a congestion charge and other cities could use a similar method to reduce the number of cars in the centre. Major cities are now promoting walking as part of a healthier lifestyle, and cycling by having more cycle lanes and public bike-hire schemes. Our cities are growing very fast and we need solutions that improve the quality of life for the people living and working in them.
M: Kyra, thank you for coming to talk to us today. So, that was Kyra Sharma talking about her new book, *Travel Chaos*. Coming up next the latest travel news …

8.02 E = Elena S = Steve T = Ted K = Kiera
B = Ben

E: So it looks like we're running out of time and I do want to give you a chance to ask a few questions. If I can answer your questions, I will, but please understand I may have to get back to you on certain points. I hope that's OK. So, does anyone have a question? Yes, Steve.
S: Thanks. I had a question about the open space issue.
E: Sure. What did you want to say?

S: Personally, I don't mind working in an open-plan office, I've done it before. But I know it's not for everyone. Most of our communication with clients is by email, so noise really isn't a problem anymore. My question is about meetings.
E: What do you mean, exactly?
S: Well, I just want to know if there will be rooms provided to hold meetings?
E: I believe so. So, the question is about meeting rooms. Ted, can I pass this one to you?
T: Sure. In the new building there'll be five closed meeting rooms on each floor, as well as some open space for more informal one-to-one meetings. You can reserve the closed meeting rooms using an online booking system. It should work very well. I hope that answers your question, Steve?
S: Yes, it does, thanks.
E: Kiera, do you have a question?
K: Yeah. Can I ask about the timing? When does the move take place?
E: It's a good question, thanks. I didn't mention that, you're right. The final stage of the move is scheduled for the end of May. I'm not sure about the exact dates; it will depend on the team. But you'll be told a long time before you have to move. Does that answer your question?
K: Not quite. You said we'd have to move into temporary office space first.
E: That's right. Most of you will go straight to the new site, but some people will move temporarily to the Oxford Road office while they finish the building work. OK?
K: Yeah, thanks.
B: I have a question, Elena. Can I … ?
E: Yes, Ben, of course.
B: How do we get to and from the Oxford Road branch? It's quite a long way from here.
E: Thanks for your question. Yes, the company will put on a shuttle bus service between the two sites which should make it easier. I understand it takes around twenty minutes. Does that help?
B: Sure. And do you know who's actually moving over there?
E: So, Ben asked who's moving to Oxford Road, right?
B: Yes.
E: As I understand it, it's only the payroll and finance departments. Anyone who is moving has already been told about this.
B: So I guess I'm not on the list. That's good. I really didn't want to move twice!

8.03 E = Elena J = Jen T = Ted

E: OK. Are there any more questions? It looks like we've got time for one more.
J: Yes, I have a question.
E: OK, Jen, go ahead.
J: To be honest, Elena, I'm really not happy about this move and I definitely *not* happy about moving from my own office into an open-plan office. Unlike Steve, I can see *lots* of problems with that. Who decides who sits where, for example?
E: Sorry, you're asking how we allocate space. Is that right?
J: Yeah, because I don't see that working very well. I think the best places will all be reserved, anyway.
E: Well, … I'm not sure I can answer that, but thanks for the question. Ted, can I ask you to respond to this one?
T: Of course. So to answer your question, Jen, we're not talking about hot-desking, …
J: Oh, right, because that's what I'd heard.
T: No, not at all. Everyone will have their own desk. And these will be allocated fairly; no one will be allowed to reserve the 'best desk'. We're also introducing a clean-desk policy. So this means we need to keep the space as tidy as possible, but everyone will have storage space for their files; we hope that will help.
J: So, not only do I have to share my office with ten other people, but now I can't even choose my own desk. What if I don't like where I've been placed? Who can I speak to about that?

E: I'm sorry, I'm not sure what you mean.
J: Well, basically, I want to know who I can complain to …

BW1.01

A: Hi, Junko.
B: Hello, Sam.
A: We need to go over a couple of the details of your visit next month before we finalise the arrangements.
B: Sure, OK.
A: You want to arrive in Sydney on the second of June, right?
B: Yes, that's right. I'm flying from Osaka to Sydney on the second.
A: OK, good. And for the hotel, how many rooms do you need? Are you coming on your own?
B: Yes, that's right – it's just me this time. So I need a single room.
A: No problem. There's a great hotel downtown – it's next to our offices in the city centre. We'll book one room for two nights.
B: Great. Thanks.
A: Now, after we've had our meeting in Sydney and seen some of the venues here, we can visit one other city. We need to choose either Melbourne or Brisbane.
B: OK, well … what's the difference?
A: Well, Melbourne is bigger than Brisbane …
B: OK …
A: But for us, Brisbane is slightly better.
B: Why is that?
A: The venues we use in Brisbane are better than the ones we use in Melbourne. We use the two most popular live music venues – medium-sized live music venues. We have a great community there. Don't misunderstand me – our venues in Melbourne are good, but in Brisbane, they're the best.
B: OK, I see. So … are Brisbane audiences smaller?
A: Ah, well, that's a great question. Brisbane audiences may be a bit smaller, but they really love music. Honestly, for me, Brisbane is probably the best place to start.
B: That sounds fine, Sam. Let's go to Brisbane.
A: OK, great. Now, in Brisbane, you have a couple of choices of places to stay. I can recommend a hotel in the city centre very near one of our music venues, but it's a bit expensive. If you want a cheaper place – maybe a bit quieter – we can arrange a bed and breakfast. There's one we like in Spring Hill.
B: Oh, let's see – actually, maybe the quieter option? The B&B?
A: OK, that's fine. And finally, when are you returning to Japan?
B: Well, I want to depart on June fifth, but I'm not going back to Japan. I'm going to Singapore.
A: Oh, great. OK. I'll make a note of that.
B: Sure. Is there anything else?
A: I don't think so. We're really looking forward to seeing you!
B: Yes, me too.

BW1.02

1 Sam, there's a serious technical problem at Sydney airport. Our flight is going to land at Canberra, not Sydney! The problem may continue until tomorrow.
2 Hi Junko. I got your message. Yes, I saw it on the news. It's a computer problem. Don't worry! We can make new arrangements for Canberra. I'll send you another message soon!

BW2.01 E = Ewa M = Mark
Extract 1

E: Now, I've done an online search and spoken to some estate agents and I've made a selection of three places we can see on our trip to Berlin this week.
M: OK! Great! Good work!
E: So, take a look at the photo of this first office. It's empty at the moment so you have to imagine it with furniture. We'd need to buy office desks, chairs, and everything.

M: Yes, those old wooden floors, doors and window frames look lovely. Where is it?
E: It's in Prenzlauer Berg. It's a fashionable neighbourhood in northeast Berlin. It's in a beautiful old building and various creative and media start-ups are already using the building.
M: How big is it?
E: The space is 120 square metres, and that includes two meeting rooms, a kitchen and two toilets. Oh, and the agent says there's a nice park in front of the building; we could sit and relax in the lunch break. And lots of cafés, bars and restaurants are within walking distance.
M: What about transport links?
E: The location is close to public transport. Actually it's never really a problem in Berlin. All these offices I'm showing you are well connected and easy to reach from the main train station and airports.
M: Sounds good. And the rent?
E: That's 2,600 euros a month. There's a deposit to pay of 7,800 – that's three months' rent. Then there's a six-month minimum period to rent the place, with a three-month cancellation period.
M: Um! It's quite expensive. Maybe we don't need so much space. We could probably find something somewhere in the UK for that price …

Extract 2
E: Well, wait a minute … I've looked at properties in other parts of Berlin, too – what do you think of this one?
M: I love it. Nice big windows, the office looks very bright in the photo. And this one has furniture!
E: The place is a co-working space in an old factory building in Kreuzberg. That's a trendy neighbourhood in the south of the city.
M: How big is it?
E: In total it's 400 square metres on two floors. Freelancers pay to rent workstations and there's space for around 40 people. Lots of independent creative workers are based there.
M: Workstations?
E: It means desks. And there is a room we can book for free for private conferences and meetings. We also get high-speed internet, use of the printer and also a shared kitchen with free coffee and water.
M: And it would be easy to talk to people we might want to work with.
E: That's right!
M: What can you tell me about the neighbourhood?
E: Very multicultural with exciting arts events. Lots of graffiti on the walls and bohemian cafés, that sort of thing.
M: Sounds like a nice place to live, too. I could walk or cycle to work every day. And the rent?
E: It costs just 300 euros per workstation, per month.
J: So, as there are four of us, we could have a shared work space for just 1,200 euros a month, and we could rent more workstations as the team grows.
E: Yes, it's an option with lots of choices. There's no deposit to pay, a two-month minimum period to rent a workstation and just one month cancellation.

Extract 3
E: So … That brings me to the third option. Here's the photo. It's an 'office room'. Basically, that means a company is offering a separate room on the tenth floor of their company offices. It's in the heart of the city, the Mitte district – that means 'in the middle' and it's where all the main tourist sights are – the Brandenburg Gate, the Potsdamer Platz and lots of big companies.
M: Sounds like a prestigious location for the company address.
E: Yes! This one is in a big modern office building with lifts and views over Alexanderplatz. The office room is 25 square metres, so it's probably big enough for five or six people.
M: But there isn't a separate meeting room?
E: No, but I thought of that. They also have a 15-square-metre office room for rent on the same floor, so we could rent two rooms and use one as a meeting room. The rent includes furniture, internet, cleaning service and use of the company's shared kitchen and bathrooms.
M: So, how much is the rent?

E: For the big office room it's 1,200 euros a month and there's a 1,200-euro deposit to pay. There's a three-month minimum period only to rent the place and just one month cancellation.
M: So, the same price as the co-working office. And if we rent the two rooms?
E: That's another six hundred a month. So, for two rooms we're talking about 1,800 a month rent and 1,800 deposit.
M: Could we just rent the small office and the four of us work in there for a few months instead?
E: No way Mark! Don't be crazy!

BW2.02 **E = Ewa   M = Mark**
E: OK, so let's make a list of the pros and cons of each office and see if we have a clear winner.
M: OK, I'll start with the Mitte office. It's in a great location, prestigious address but the company there is in finance, so we have nothing in common with them. It'd be better to be in a place with other new creative companies I think.
E: True! Being around other start-ups makes more sense for us. I wouldn't rent a flat in that area either. It's too expensive. Though that's not a major problem because the public transport network is so good. I love the idea of working in the city centre.
M: What about the Prenzlauer Berg office? Great old building! It would certainly give us room to grow. Having a big office would be expensive now, but we could save money in the future if we didn't have to move again soon.
E: True! I liked the office, but it was a bit darker than I expected. That concerns me. I like a bright space to work in.
M: I guess we could buy some bright lights. There's no lift though and it's three flights of stairs up – not all our clients might like that.
E: And the co-working space in Kreuzberg? There were certainly a lot of fun people there and I loved the terrace. Great to have some outside space.
M: Yes, but I wonder how much work we'd get done. It would be easy to get distracted and spend all day chatting in that office!
E: And I'm worried about the lack of privacy. I mean, our projects are confidential. I don't think clients would feel happy about us being in a co-working space. And trying to book that one meeting room when we need it could be difficult.
M: Still, it is the cheapest option, and we'd make friends quickly in Berlin. We should decide soon. Rents are rising fast in the city. But do you really think Berlin is the place for us? I'm still not sure about this move abroad and I'm not sure what Paul, Yelena and the rest of the team are going to say about it ….
E: I'm sure they'll love the idea! Berlin is really multicultural. It has a real buzz about it.
M: I'm not sure. I think I'd miss London, you know. Oh … time to go or we'll miss our flight.

BW3.01
Extract 1
A: Just one last question. What kind of stores do you want to see in this area?
B: Well, I don't really go to stores much. I do most of my shopping online. But I think this area needs some more nightlife. There are places to go in the evening after work but some of them are really expensive and the others get really busy. We're a young group in my office and we like to socialise around here after work sometimes, but when you leave the office in the evening, it's hard to find somewhere to go in the local area.

Extract 2
A: I just want to ask you one final thing. What type of store does this neighbourhood need, in your opinion?
B: Well, I don't live around here, I work in an office over there but I like to go shopping in my lunch hour. You know, last week, I wanted to buy some personal care products, like shampoo and deodorant, but couldn't find anything I liked. I prefer to buy products that are 100 percent natural. It's something that I don't mind paying extra for if the quality is good. There are a few stores around here but there isn't much variety.

Extract 3
A: Thank you for your time. Can I ask you one final question? Is there any particular kind of store missing from this area?
B: Erm, well, I'm a big fan of small fashion boutiques and good-quality second-hand clothes. I go all over the city to find stores that I like. I prefer not to shop in big chain stores and shopping malls because I don't want to see the same shirt I'm wearing on someone else. I like to browse for original clothes, things that you can't buy anywhere else. And I like to mix and match styles, I don't want to just wear the fashions and colours that are popular right now.

BW4.01 **C = Clara Olsen   A = Álvaro Martínez**
C: So, at this point I'd like to talk about the work culture of Holsted Pharmaceuticals. There are four main areas I want to mention.
First of all, I want to talk about the working hours at Holsted. The usual working week is 37 hours from Monday to Friday. That's typical of Denmark in general. You aren't expected to work long hours.
As for the working day, the timetable at Holsted is quite flexible for most employees. Staff can decide their start times, finish times and lunch breaks depending on their individual needs.
We understand when employees need to collect children from school or have to leave early for personal reasons, like a dentist's appointment. It's completely acceptable to do that. Whenever possible we give employees the opportunity to adapt their working hours to their family's needs. Our company work culture is very relaxed but effective.
Secondly, I want to talk about how we organise work and the relationship between managers and staff. There is a tradition that employees have a lot of individual responsibility for how they organise their own time and work. It is not generally the manager who decides how employees do their work. It is very important that staff meet deadlines and do their job well, but exactly how employees organise their time or projects is their responsibility.
And a third important point to mention is that all employees in Holsted are encouraged to tell us their ideas and opinions. This is very important because a level of staff participation and openness helps us to make better decisions.
And finally, I should say a word about meetings. It's very important at Holsted to arrive on time to meetings. It shows you are professional and organised.
A: Sorry, sorry I'm late. I've just come from another meeting. So, what have I missed?

BW4.02 **C = Clara Olsen   M = Marina Beltrán   A = Álvaro Martínez**
C: So, Marina, can you tell us more about the research your department has done?
M: Yes, well, you can see from this bar graph: the working day is very long here in the Madrid office. On an average day only half of our employees leave work by six o'clock. At seven o'clock twenty percent of the staff are still here in the office and ten percent are still at their desks at eight in the evening.
C: That's incredible! When do they spend time with their families? What time do they have dinner?
M: Yes, these working hours are obviously a disaster for family life.
A: Well, it is fairly normal to do this in Spanish companies. And people have dinner late. We have a 'split' working day where we start at 8.30 and go for lunch about two o'clock. We have two hours for lunch so you get back to work at four.
It's a good time to be sociable with co-workers, or go home for lunch if you don't have to travel far, or have business lunches. A long lunch break means finishing work late. It's always been part of our work culture.
M: I agree with Álvaro. It is traditional but I think many employees would prefer a shorter lunch break and the opportunity to go home an hour earlier.

A: I don't think so. It's the way we do things. People like to have a good lunch, not have a sandwich at their desks like they do in other countries.

M: Perhaps, but a lot of our employees are probably tired because of the long working hours and they won't get so much work done late in the day. Long hours can also be a cause of accidents at work and sick leave.

C: Has that been a problem here?

M: I don't know about our company, but international studies show people do more work within shorter hours. I mean, just look at Germany.

C: Yes, that's true. Who has ever done their best work when they're very tired?

BW5.01

Welcome, everyone. We're really happy to see so many people here, so much interest in making our town a better place. The purpose of today's meeting is to discuss practical ideas and real solutions. We've had discussions with quite a few of you already, and there are five main ideas we'd like to discuss today. So I'll introduce the ideas, and then after that, we'll have about ten minutes to discuss each of them.

So, here we go. The first idea is to get more tourists here. We would hire an advertising agency and advertise nationally or internationally about our great town. Tourists would come and spend money here.

Two. Create a local currency. Towns and cities all over the world have done this. It doesn't replace our national currency – it's money you can spend in local businesses. This encourages people to shop here in town.

Three. A time bank. In a time bank, anyone can offer their skills – a doctor, a car mechanic, a cleaner. If you work for someone for two hours, then you get credit for it, and you can ask someone to work for you for two hours.

Four. An online exchange – probably on social media – for second-hand goods. There are a few marketplaces that people use online, but we could have our own, just for people in this area, and people could trade things for other things.

Five. Start a Saturday market for local goods in the town centre. This could be vegetables, things you make at home, possibly second-hand items. We could do this every Saturday, or maybe once a month.

So, those are the main ideas to discuss today. Now we'll take about ten minutes for each idea, and after that we'll vote and choose three that we think are the ones that are the best …

BW5.02

OK, so now we've counted the vote, and we've decided to consider the following three options more seriously. First, we'll look at creating a local currency. Second, we'll see about setting up a time bank. Finally, we'll consider the idea of a Saturday market in town. Thanks a lot, everyone. We'll contact you all by email before the next meeting.

BW5.03   E = Ellen   D = David

E: So, what do you think of the proposed projects?

D: They're interesting ideas.

E: Yeah. Will you vote?

D: Sure, yeah. But I haven't decided yet – I think they could all be useful. The local currency idea is definitely interesting. It would be good for local business.

E: Do you think? It seems kind of a strange idea to me – kind of weird – and I know other people who think it's strange, too. But maybe we're just old-fashioned.

D: You may have a point there!

E: I like the sound of the Saturday market. That's just a good, honest idea that everyone can understand. People will see it as a social event.

D: Yeah, maybe. But I think it's a bit boring compared to the other two. I mean – it's easy to sell old stuff, right? Why not just sell it online? Don't you think the time bank could be good? I mean, you're an accountant. If you join a time bank, people will definitely want your services.

E: Maybe that's what scares me! I have a job – I'm too busy for extra work.

D: I'm with you. I'm the same. I'm not sure I want to trade any of my skills. Sometimes it's easier just to pay people.

E: Yeah, definitely.

D: I think if we create a local currency, local businesses will definitely get a boost.

E: Maybe – but I'm not so sure.

D: Well, I think that one's going to get my vote.

BW6.01

I studied maths at university, but I didn't really think about what kind of job I could get. Everyone thinks if you study maths, then accounting is a natural job to do afterwards. So that's why I'm doing this now. But you know what? It isn't the numbers that I love – it's solving problems. When you study maths at university, you realise that actually, it's a very creative subject – almost like some kind of art, or poetry. And for me, accounting just isn't very creative. So I'm not that happy in my work, but I just don't know what I should do – what job I want to get. But something needs to change.

BW6.02

I love the work I do – I love design. But in my last job, I was part of a team. Now, in this company, I'm the designer – I work alone. One good thing is that I can concentrate – because everyone is busy doing their own job – no one bothers me … or talks to me. Natalya can't afford another designer. But to have good, creative ideas, I really need to talk with someone – share my ideas – see what other people think about my work. That's what was great about my last job. I'm not sure what we can do, though. The company isn't going to hire a new employee now.

BW6.03

It isn't easy running a small company. I'm very lucky to have João and Leila working for me. They work hard and they care a lot – but I know they aren't completely happy. The truth is, I'm not completely happy, either. I started this company because I wanted to make and sell amazing chairs, not because I wanted to be a full-time manager. Every day there are problems to solve with suppliers, emails to write, phone calls to make. I need help, but I can't afford to hire a new employee.

BW6.04

I had some great news today – we've made a big sale to a hotel group – two hundred and twenty chairs in the next year. That's wonderful, because it will give me enough money to hire someone part-time to help me manage the business. I really need someone to get things organised – someone who can deal creatively with the suppliers and schedules and all that.

BW7.01   S = Sofia   O = Oscar

S: That factory tour was really interesting, Oscar. Thanks.

O: You're welcome. I think we've got a great team here. And our customers are some of the biggest international companies. They must have quality.

S: I can see that you're giving them that. But what's your production time?

O: From our three production lines, we can do 3,000 pairs in twelve weeks. That's a high-quality shoe with nice details.

S: You mean twelve from order?

O: Yes, usually. Maybe a bit longer.

S: OK. Well, I think we can probably make some savings there – speed up production time and cut down on costs – you know, find ways to lower them – spend less in general.

O: Well, maybe. What do you suggest?

S: I think there are some new machines you might be interested in. More automation could increase your rate of production by maybe twenty or thirty percent.

O: I was afraid you were going to say that.

S: What?

O: More automation. We take pride in working with our hands. We really value our workers' skill. I'm not sure we're ready to make any big changes there.

S: OK, well, that gives us something to talk about!

BW7.02   S = Sofia   M = Mario   O = Oscar

S: Before we decide on your shoe designs, we need to know how you're going to make them.

M: Sure.

S: So if you're going for a more handmade style, production will be slower, and there will be less automation. I'm not sure I'd recommend it at this point. It may not be very cost-effective. I think more automation is the best thing to do. Oscar, do you agree with what I am saying?

O: Well, OK …. But these machines aren't cheap. If we don't improve the factory, we could probably take on a few more workers. And that will only cost us money if we really need to increase production.

S: Sure. I think we're probably talking about the highest quality footwear in that case. And to make it work financially, I'm pretty sure you're going to need to be able to deliver more shoes more quickly.

O: OK, I understand that. Mario – what are you thinking?

M: The designs I'm working on are definitely very high quality – with some really nice details that are finished by hand.

S: They sound great, Mario, but I think breaking into the market – you know, starting to sell a new product – may be harder with a really high-quality shoe …

M: Yeah, I understand that. But it's like this: Zapatos Trujillo S.A. have made other people's shoes for forty years, and we're good at it. Now we'd like to make some shoes that we are all really proud of – something we can take to the big trade shows, the big fashion footwear shows – you know, Paris, Berlin – and really show people what we can do. Those are the shoes we want to make.

S: OK, that's clear. So let's see how we can make it happen.

BW7.03   S = Sofia   J = John

S: Hi, John.

J: Sofia, hello. How's everything going in Mexico?

S: Good, mostly. Zapatos Trujillo S.A. are doing a lot of things right already, so I feel good about the company …

J: But something's bothering you.

S: Well, I really think automation is the answer here. If they want to increase their annual production, they really need to buy some machines.

J: But they want to keep making handmade shoes.

S: Right.

J: Well, from our own experience, we can offer plenty of success stories about automation, right? I mean, most shoe makers who finally try it agree afterwards that it's helped their business. So maybe you need to tell them about some of the other companies we've worked with.

S: Yeah, that's a good idea. I haven't tried that, but I will.

J: And give them some options. You can show them exactly what automation can do for their profit, but the final decision has to be theirs. In some cases, it really isn't about the money, and that's OK.

S: Yeah, you're right. OK, well, I'll get back to working out some of these numbers. Always good to talk to you!

J: Good luck Sofia. I'm around if you want to talk again.

BW8.01   P = Patricia   D = Davy   J = Joe

P: Now that we've measured our energy use and waste, we can use that to help us plan the GO project and decide what our priorities are.

D: Yes, it's very important to have this data. Obviously, I can see lighting is a big cost at the moment but the LED lights in the new building will help reduce costs there.

P: And the new motion sensors they're installing.

D: Motion sensors?

P: Yes, these can detect movement in certain areas and switch the lights on and off without anyone having to touch them. Places like the toilets, corridors, storerooms, the stairs and in the car park. But the new building will have them everywhere.

D: Good idea. That's the lighting cost reduced. What else can we do?

P: Well, as you can see from the pie chart in my report, the computer servers are costing us quite a lot of money. First of all there's the cost of the electricity to run the machines and second, there's the cost of cooling and ventilation to keep the server room at the right temperature. Are there any possible savings there?

D: What about 'cloud computing'? I mean, do we need servers in the office now? It's possible to use a cloud computing service.

P: Do we know what the options are? What are the security risks? And the costs of the service?

D: I understand there are fewer risks with cloud computing than having our own servers. I'll talk to the IT department, Patricia. We'll look into the options and the costs and tell you what we find out.

P: Thank you. Now what about waste, especially paper use? I know that paper itself is not very expensive for the company compared to other costs, but everyone is printing too much. The current printers are old, always break down and some employees complain they have to print documents three or four times because the print quality is so terrible.

J: They are terrible! When you think about the paper and toner we waste because of this, then it is clear they are not cost-effective. I think we need new multifunctional machines that print, photocopy and scan.

P: I agree! There'll be costs to upgrade, obviously, but we will save money, too. Joe, would you find out more about those for us? Get some prices and see how we could do this?

J: OK, Pat, I'll do that.

P: Right, so Davy, you'll find out more about cloud computing, Joe, you'll work on the printers and I want to look at a new recycling scheme to find out how we can recycle more of our waste. I mean, two kilos of waste per person per day is not good. I know we won't make big savings, but it is important for our image and our reputation as a green company to help protect the environment. Sorry. Hello! Really? OK, I'll come down. Sorry, we'll have to end there. There's a problem at reception.

D: OK, sure

J: No problem. See you later.

P4.08

1 I've never bought any good business books. But I have read a few.
2 I've read a few, too. I read some when I was a student.
3 I've heard of Daniel Kahneman. I think he's won a Nobel Prize.
4 Yes, he has. He's written a lot about how we make decisions.
5 Have you read this book? I started it once or twice, but I've never finished it.
6 I've just finished it. I liked it.

P6.02

/ɪ/	give	busy	city	issue	simple
/iː/	feel	believe	complete	metres	people
/aɪ/	price	climbing	high	hiker	reliable
/ɪə/	near	clearly	experienced	realise	zero

P6.07

1 Do you have everything you need?
2 Print out an extra copy.
3 I've looked everywhere for it.
4 A copy of the report and a pen or pencil.
5 I'm glad you're all here.
6 Just ask if you need help.

P7.02

1 I can't open my door with my key card.
2 You can use the check-in kiosk.
3 You can't go directly to the gate.
4 Can I check in without my ID?
5 This robot can't talk, can it?
6 Yes, it can!

P8.04

1 We could catch a bus or get a taxi.
2 We shouldn't wait here any longer.
3 Do you think I should walk more?
4 Yes, and you could, easily.
5 They should spend more on public transport.
6 Yes, they definitely should.

Pearson Education Limited
KAO Two
KAO Park
Hockham Way
Harlow, Essex
CM17 9SR
England
and Associated Companies throughout the world.

www.pearsonELT.com/businesspartner

Business Partner A2+ Teacher's Resource Book with MyEnglishLab
© Pearson Education Limited 2019

First published 2019
Second impression 2024

ISBN: 978-1-292-23717-6
Set in Burlingame Pro
Printed and bound by CPI Group (UK) Ltd, Croydon, CR0 4YY

We are grateful to the following for permission to reproduce copyright material:

Text
165, Financial Times Limited: Black, Jonathan, Do I build a steady career or follow my entrepreneurial dreams? Financial Times, Apr 1, 2018. © 2018, Financial Times Limited.